Handbook of Psychiatry and the Law

Ebrahim J. Kermani, M.D.
New York University
School of Medicine
New York, New York

YEAR BOOK MEDICAL PUBLISHERS, INC.
CHICAGO • LONDON • BOCA RATON

1   2   3   4   5   6   7   8   9   0   93   92   91   90   89

Kermani, Ebrahim J.
   Handbook of psychiatry and the law.

   Includes bibliographies and index.
   1. Forensic psychiatry—United States.   2. Psychiatrists—Legal status, laws, etc.—United States.
3. Child psychiatry—United States.   I. Title.
II. [DNLM: 1. Psychiatry—handbooks.   2. Psychiatry—
legislation.   WM 33.1 K39h]
KF8922.K47   1989   344.73'041   89-5664
ISBN 0-8151-5087-3   347.30441

CONTENTS

FOREWORD

It is difficult to write a foreword to this text which has accepted the challenge of dealing at length with the broad areas of encounter between psychiatry and the legal system. The topics selected range from relatively clear issues such as confidentiality to terribly opaque ones such as surrogate mothers. Even a casual review of the chapter headings will cause the reader to pause at the complexities inherent in the topics this volume bravely engages.

The author uses a method based on the chronologic presentation and explication of actual case law. In this sense, he uses the "data" of the legal profession so as to understand the issues as they have evolved historically. This approach is particularly useful for the student who can see how the attitudes of the courts have evolved and how they have shaped law over time. The method makes the book of greater value to both the beginner and experienced practitioner.

The author makes a very real effort to try to make the evolution of the legal and psychiatric conflicts appear reasonable, notwithstanding the tensions that exist between the legal and psychiatric communities that are not based on "reasonable" differences. There are conflicts that derive from differences in perceived role functions and in the world views that separate these professions and these make a peaceful reconciliation highly improbable.

One can see the biases of the legal profession enter the law in subtle ways. A patient who refuses to participate in a research study is presumed to have the competence to refuse. A patient who agrees to participate in that same study will have his "rights" protected. Apparently, the right to refuse is less in need of protection than the right to participate. This hierarchy is not based on a rational need to protect but represents the values and role functions of the legal profession. Clearly, there can be dangers associated with a research project, but equally clearly there can be benefits to the individual subject as well as to the class of people called patients. The imposition of personal values through the vehicle of the laws can masquerade as the protection—ofttimes selective protection—of rights.

Other examples of this tension can be found in the right to be treated and the right to refuse treatment. It is theoretically possible to hold a psychiatrist liable for withholding a treatment that the patient refused, if it is later ascertained by a court that the psychiatrist failed incorrectly to question the patient's competence to refuse. How much easier it is to reflect with judicial calm and in precise detail on problems long after the problems have occurred. It is unfortunate that clinical decisions cannot be made at the leisurely pace of a legal trial.

To the clinician one of the most confusing situations is that a patient may be committed by the court for involuntary treatment and then still have the right to refuse medication. It is as if just the experience of being in a mental hospital is inherently therapeutic. Can such a baseless fantasy be really accepted as the explanation? Or, in fact, are we dealing with a prejudice in which the legal profession does not trust the medical profession and wishes to be involved, as if courts reside on some higher moral plane? This is particularly painful to the practitioners of medicine who do not find the ethical standards of the legal profession to be so glorious as to warrant this self-aggrandizing role.

The courts like clarity, but clinical situations are frequently ambiguous. If a clinician believes a patient to be planning to injure another person, the clinician is reponsible to warn that person. This is a clear situation which poses little conflict for most clinicians. The ambiguousness is in the real situation in which there is some risk to another person but where the clinician feels correctly that he or she has a positive relationship with the patient and may be more effective in preventing harm if the patient's revelation is held as a confidence. Violating the confidence will almost certainly destroy the therapeutic relationship, particularly with a paranoid patient. The clinician must judge which action in fact will provide the greatest safety for the potential object of the attack. Can the clinician be infallible? Obviously not. Yet, if the court holds that the duty is to warn whenever there may be a danger, there is little doubt that clinicians will tend to err on the side of protecting themselves rather than their patients' welfare.

The author points out that the courts see electroshock therapy as a hazardous procedure and therefore feel compelled to protect the patient from these putative dangers. Unfortunately, the courts are in total error. The procedure is a safe one. Can we argue that the misperceptions of the court should, nevertheless, lead to regulation and law based on those misperceptions? Should we not argue that when a judge is wrong there must be a process for correcting the misapprehensions underlying the decision? Courts increasingly appear to be sensitive to data that support the decisions they choose to make. Social science data do not tend to be of the hardest sort and therefore lend themselves to judicial abuse.

In many ways, one must recognize that the lawyer and the clinician think differently and make different assumptions. The lawyer looks for preciseness and the clinician lives with ambiguity. The lawyer speaks of conditions such as "beyond a reasonable doubt" while a clinician speaks of behaviors as being present "with some frequency." These very different experiences and the underlying assumptions of the respective disciplines must lead to profound tensions. Finally, lawyers and clinicians fulfill different role functions. The lawyer is an advocate. The lawyer takes the position proposed by the client and argues it as forcefully and effectively as possible. The clinician operates more frequently in locus parentis. The clinician does what he or she believes to be in the patient's best interest. While there is an advocacy element there is an element of playing the role of the healer. Patients abandon some autonomy when they assume the sick role in order to receive the benefits of that role. The sick or patient role is totally different from the client role that the same person may have with an attorney. These conflicts between role models and disciplinary assumptions cannot be avoided. Nevertheless, a book of this sort has great value because it helps both the clinician and the legal practitioner to understand better the points where conflict must arise and to try to find more effective ways of helping the person in distress, no matter how we may disagree about the definition of helping or distress.

Robert Cancro, MD
Professor and Chairman
Department of Psychiatry
New York University School of Medicine

PREFACE

Just a few decades ago mental health professionals played at most a peripheral role in the judicial process. Today their input is often decisive, and it is pervasive as well, to the extent that nearly every aspect of the process is affected by psychiatric criteria. Of course, during these decades the mental health professions have come to play substantial roles in many facets of daily life such as school and work, whereas once psychiatry was applied only to the profoundly psychotic. Just as psychiatry has rapidly become a vital element in the legal process, the authority of the law over matters once reserved for psychiatrists, such as civil commitment, forced medication, and electroconvulsive therapy, has been greatly expanded. The interface of psychiatry and law today is a fact of life.

This book has been conceived and prepared with the broad goal of serving as a teaching tool. The specific objectives of the book are fourfold: (1) to provide an introduction to the topic of psychiatry and law for mental health professionals; (2) to provide a reference of relevant legal decisions for those interested in the topic; (3) to function as a handbook for those studying for a variety of specialty examinations; and (4) to acquaint mental health practitioners with the legal issues that they are likely to encounter in their practice.

The book's methodology is historical, presenting actual court rulings on each subject chronologically. These landmark cases are analyzed and discussed from the perspectives of psychiatry and law. Presenting the actual cases seemed the only valid technique to this writer, because rulings often depend on how the judges and finders of fact interpret the minutiae, a process which could not be accurately duplicated in a fictional account. In other words, broad principles derive from the details, so idiosyncrasy will always play a part in a system such as ours, which is responsive instead of dictatorial. To see just how that happens is as important as understanding the underlying philosophical framework. Thus, concepts such as "the duty to warn" and "competency to stand trial" are substantiated by actual cases described in narrative and followed by commentary from concerned specialists and the author.

Common medical, psychiatric, and legal vocabulary and Latin phrases have been used in order to preserve the academic value of the book for those scholars and researchers interested in the scholarly aspect of the issues. However, a glossary at the end should prevent these terminologies from being an obstacle to beginners in this field or to a general reader. The subject matter is summarized as follows.

SECTION I: GENERAL PSYCHIATRY

Psychiatry and Tort Law

Mental health professionals, like all other citizens, are expected to act prudently, and take precautions against creating risk or injury to other citizens. Once a professional such as a psychiatrist has agreed to provide services for a patient, a physician-patient relationship is established in which the psychiatrist or other caregiver has a duty to exercise knowledge, skill, and good judgment in taking care of his patients.

Psychiatrists have a duty to act nonnegligently. If their conduct falls below the level of professional standards, a lawsuit can be brought against them by their patients, and the triers of fact may find that they breached their duty.

The plaintiff-patient in a negligence suit must prove to the triers of fact that the alleged injury would not have occurred or rarely occurs in the absence of negligence, that the psychiatrist had exclusive control over the instrumentality that caused the injury, that the patient did not contribute to the injury, and finally that the psychiatrist and plaintiff-patient were the only ones with access to the actual occurrence.

Underlying these expectations and duties is the concept of tort, derived from the Latin *tortus*, or "twisted." In law, tort signifies a wrong; specifically a private or civil wrong or injury resulting from a breach of the legal duty originating in society's expectations of responsibility in interpersonal conduct.

Under this doctrine, a psychiatrist or other mental health professional may be found negligent in a variety of categories. The five major pillars of tort law in psychiatry that confront the practitioner are (1) confidentiality, (2) informed consent, (3) sexual encounters, (4) suicide, and (5) duty to warn and protect and prediction of dangerousness.

Confidentiality in a psychotherapeutic relationship is not only an ethical issue, but a legal one. Psychiatrists or other mental health professionals cannot publish their patients' life histories for self-serving purposes. The confidential relationship between therapist and patient creates a fiduciary duty from the therapist to the patient, and unauthorized release of said information breaches fiduciary duty, leading to lawsuits. The doctor-patient privilege is a legal concept designed to protect the patient, and only the patient can waive the privilege. In certain circumstances, however, courts may order psychiatrists to release and reveal specific information in the interest of justice. If psychiatrists refuse to do so, they can be held in contempt of court and sent to prison. The doctor-patient privilege remains in force after the patient's death. In cases of suspected fraud perpetrated by clinicians, the court is sensitive to the competing interests of confidentiality and justice, and requires disclosure of information limited to facts bearing on the possible fraud.

All persons, competent or incompetent, have the right to determine what shall be done with their own bodies. The law makes it clear that patients should receive adequate information from their physicians and after they comprehend it, they should voluntarily consent before any procedure is commenced. Patients have a right to know of all possible side effects, complications, and what may ensue after a certain procedure. If a patient is mentally incompetent to make a decision and give informed consent, the court might utilize substitute judgment, in which case the judge decides what the incompetent person would want if he or she were not incompetent. The judge, acknowledged to be a reasonable person, receives the necessary information and then gives consent with the presumption that that was what the patient, if competent, would have decided.

In emergency situations, the law permits the physician to start treatment without a patient's consent, abiding by the assumption that rational persons would want treatment.

Professionals have a duty to exercise reasonable care to safeguard their patients from suicide. This duty is more restrictive when a patient is voluntarily or involuntarily confined to a psychiatric ward, and specifically if the patient was admitted to the hospital because of suicidal tendencies. The court does not accept arguments that volitional or negligent acts by a patient contributed to the suicide. In suicide allegations, the court wants to learn whether the caretaker exercised reasonable care and precautions as measured by the degree of care, skill, and diligence customarily exercised by other psychiatrists or hospitals in the community.

Sexual encounters between therapists and their patients are not only unethical but grounds for malpractice as well. The court will try to find out whether the transference and the countertransference were mishandled. The court will determine therapists to be liable if they have acted in a seductive, suggestive manner. Also, the court has extended the scope of malpractice to situations where the therapist was sexually involved with the patient's spouse.

In landmark cases covering "duty to warn and protect," two trends emerged in court rulings. The first indicates that the confidential character of patient-psychotherapist communications must yield to the extent that disclosure is essential to avert danger to others, and communication privileges end where the public peril begins. The second trend indicates that the existence of a special relationship between psychotherapists and patients does not mean that the duties stemming from that relationship are owed to others at large. The author argues that the original Tarasoff doctrine is sound from both the perspective of public policy and psychotherapeutic practice, but that its extension, which has occurred in several other cases, is problematic for psychotherapists.

Alcoholism and Drug Addiction

This chapter discusses whether alcoholism and drug addiction are considered diseases in a medical context, or manifestations of abnormal personality. The relationship between these two conditions and psychiatric disorders is also explored.

According to law, alcoholism is a handicapping condition and therefore discrimination in the form of job termination due to alcoholism is illegal. Nevertheless alcoholics, even when intoxicated, are legally liable for their behavior and its effects. If they commit a crime they can be prosecuted as a competent person, and may not claim as a defense their alcoholic condition.

Drug addiction itself is not criminal behavior. As with alcoholics, however, drug addicts cannot escape legal responsibility for their actions, unless they can prove that the drugs have made physiologic changes in their brain, and even then they must meet the criteria of the insanity defense.

Right to Treatment and Right to Refuse Treatment

The legally recognized purpose of psychiatric hospitalization is to offer treatment to mentally ill persons. The law requires that states provide adequate care to institutionalized patients, and if the state fails in this, the Department of Justice has the obligation to compel the state to comply with its responsibilities. The patients have a right to receive such treatment as will help them recover or improve their mental condition. Furthermore, a state may not confine an individual to a mental hospital unless it offers some sort of treatment, training, or habilitation to help that individual improve or be cured of illness.

While patients have the right to receive treatment, they also have the right to refuse treatment in nonemergency situations. In such cases, patients must be given a judicial hearing and the state, which has the burden of proof, must show with clear and convincing evidence that the patients lack the capacity to make their own treatment decisions, that is, medicating mentally ill persons against their will is a judicial function and is not to be relegated to medical authorities.

The courts have found that psychiatric patients, like any other citizens, have a right to the protection of the due process clause of the Fourteenth Amendment and to be free from unjustified intrusions such as forced medications.

Intrusive Modalities

Electroconvulsive therapy (ECT) is a treatment of choice for severe depression. The complication rate is very minimal. Nevertheless, society and the legal establishment view ECT with skepticism. Legislatures and courts have greatly curtailed this form of treatment, seeing ECT as a form of hazardous and unusual treatment. Therefore, the courts have imposed various requirements to be fulfilled prior to the administration of ECT.

Seclusion and restraint is a form of treatment useful for assaultive, aggressive patients for the purpose of maintaining a patient's safety and the safety of others. It is not illegal to place a patient in restraint so long as the mental health professional has exercised sound judgment.

Psychosurgery is surgical intervention to sever fibers connecting one part of the brain to another or to destroy certain tissue in the brain in order to alter behavior. The number of these procedures has been declining. However, a few operations are still being performed on violent epileptic patients. The court is mainly interested in whether such patients are able to give true informed consent or not.

Hypnosis, although an unreliable procedure, may be used in order to enhance the memory of a witness, plaintiff, or defendant. However, the state should adopt certain procedural safeguards as prerequisites to admitting testimony containing hypnotically refreshed recollection.

Traumatic Neurosis

Experiencing trauma can trigger an affliction called "traumatic neurosis." Its many psychiatric symptoms range from impaired memory to depression. Organic problems can also arise from traumatic neurosis. There are two categories of legal claims based on traumatic neurosis: tort actions and workers' compensation.

Witnessing stressful events can cause psychological harm, and a witness may bring a lawsuit for liability against the responsible party. Being a victim of sexual harassment on the job is a trauma-producing phenomenon likely to cause traumatic neurosis.

Under the Workers' Compensation Act, compensation is awarded for the incapacity to work because of injuries arising from and during employment. Benefits are allowed only for the inability to work, and negligence is not an issue. Claimants must demonstrate, at the very least, that their employment contributed to if not caused their disability. Some courts accept purely mental stimuli as a causal basis if these can be connected specifically with employment. Others courts require that a physical injury be the catalyst for the neurosis. The prevailing view is that mental disability should be treated no differently from physical injury. Courts generally have not considered a claimant's preexisting mental condition as an essential criterion, focusing instead on whether or not the work contributed to the disability. The "preliminary link theory," which requires a presumption of compensability, has been adopted by some courts. If an emotional injury stems from stress and not trauma, to justify a compensation award it must arise from stressors of greater dimension than the quotidian tensions most work entails. Thus the countless stresses and strains experienced daily during employment do not constitute grounds for award of compensation.

Contractual and Testamentary Capacity

A person who executes a will must possess mental capacity at the time of execution for that will to be legally valid. The testator or testatrix must have a sound mind, understand the nature of his or her acts, and know the natural objects of his or her bounty and the extent of property. Such a person must be acting voluntarily, free of the undue influence of others.

Civil Commitment

Civil commitment is a last-resort option of involuntary placement in a mental institution for the purpose of treatment. State police powers and the doctrine of parens patriae are both vehicles for initiating commitment. Law enforcement agencies or family and friends of mentally ill persons can request their commitment, and patients should be apprised at all times of their rights. The court has ruled that patients must be examined by the psychiatrists signing papers in favor of their commitment. Patients are appointed counsel by the court to represent their point of view and articulate their wishes in a legal forum.

Clinical findings show that committed mental patients are less likely than voluntary ones to have prior hospitalization, and are no more likely to suffer psychosis. Furthermore, civil commitment has been used as a social policy tool to rid the public of violence-prone persons.

The standard of proof for civil commitment is clear and convincing evidence, and proof of incapacity must be thoroughly documented and properly presented.

Civil commitment has no specific duration, but procedures allow petitioners hearings to contest their hospitalization. Hospitalization is not to be seen as punishment for insanity defendants. For transferees from prisons to mental institutions, due process must be adhered to. The guidelines of due process established by law for all involuntary patients create an unfortunate adversary relationship between patient and psychiatrist.

Outpatient commitment is a new and controversial phenomenon. Criteria are more lenient, but the effectiveness of outpatient commitment is questionable. Finally, the issue of civil commitment of homeless persons is explored.

Competency to Stand Trial

The doctrine that a mentally ill person cannot be put on trial has an ancient history, but its modern form developed in the United States starting in 1960 when the US Supreme Court ruled that defendants must have the ability to understand the proceeding against them and be able to consult with and assist their attorneys. Lack of these abilities constitutes incompetency to stand trial.

In succeeding years the Supreme Court extended its first decision and ruled that indefinite commitment of criminal defendants solely on account of their lack of capacity to stand trial violates due process. The Supreme Court justices have warned both sides in the trial courts to be alert, before and during the course of the trial, to evidence suggesting possible incompetency of a defendant, and that they have the responsibility to report such evidence.

Clinicians have a complicated job in assessing competency. They must approach the task with clinical thinking, keeping in mind that their role is to provide factual clinical material for the courts. A variety of tests have been introduced to aid this process.

Judging the competency to stand trial of a defendant who is on medication or has what is called "synthetic sanity" has brought a new dilemma for mental health professionals. Many courts bar the trial of a defendant taking anti-psychotic drugs because the defendant's unmedicated demeanor is very important for the jury to see.

In spite of the extensiveness of the doctrine prohibiting the trial of incompetent persons, courts in areas far from the intellectual centers of the country may remain unaware of, feel unaffected by, or be uncertain of how to implement the doctrine, and defendants in those jurisdictions may therefore be denied its protections.

Insanity Defense

The history of the insanity defense goes back over 2000 years, with the state of insanity being compared to a child's innocence. Modern formulations of the insanity defense have sprung from the M'Naghten ruling in mid-nineteenth century England. Recent examples are the doctrine of criminal behavior as the result of mental illness, and the implementation of standards set forth in the American Law Institute tests.

The content of expert psychiatric testimony has been restricted to medical issues and how certain states can affect behavior, and psychiatric labels and broad speculation have been prohibited.

According to some studies, crime is more prevalent among mentally ill people, while other studies negate that finding or remain inconclusive. One study of death row inmates strongly suggests that the incidence of mental illness in criminals is much higher than generally thought, and that their mental illness often goes unrecognized.

It has been determined that defendants have a right to psychiatric assistance when their mental state at the time of the offense is an issue in a trial, and also to mitigate a capital sentence. In both cases the scope of this assistance has been defined.

The use of a new concept "guilty but mentally ill," as an alternative verdict has caused controversy. Almost no legal or medical professional groups have favored implementation of this verdict, which is supposedly another option, but more often becomes a compromise. Some states have abolished the insanity defense altogether, in the belief that individuals who act with a proven criminal state of mind are accountable for their acts regardless of motivation or mental condition.

The US Supreme Court has struggled with the insanity issue on several occasions, although the insanity defense is technically an issue of state law rather than the US Constitution. The Court decided that if a defendant keeps silent after receiving a Miranda warning, that silence may not be construed as evidence that he or she comprehended the warning. Spontaneous confession, even if attributable to mental illness, is not to be construed as a forced confession and may be used in a court of law, in the view of the Supreme Court.

The positions of professional organizations directly involved in the insanity defense issue are discussed. These groups include the American Psychiatric Association, the American Bar Association, the American Medical Association, and the American Civil Liberties Union.

A variety of issues affect the parameters, procedures, and utilization of the insanity defense, including posttraumatic stress disorder, heat of passion, pathologic gambling, and multiple personality. These issues along with relevant court rulings are covered.

Psychiatry in the Sentencing Process and the Death Penalty

The arguments for and against mental health professionals participating in death penalty proceedings are both compelling. Both appear in Supreme Court decisions addressing this issue and in the work of researchers studying it. One conclusion is that permitting the presentation of psychiatric testimony mitigating the death sentence necessitates allowing the presentation of exacerbating evidence as well, in which case the psychiatrist testifying for the prosecution does not violate the Hippocratic oath. Certain safeguards should be instituted for such testimony, however.

While mental health professionals joined others in the trend to abolish the death penalty in the early 1960s, actually a majority of these professionals believe it is an effective deterrent.

The ethics and ramifications of mental health professionals predicting the future dangerousness of capital defendants have sparked debate, and the way was cleared by the Supreme Court for these professionals to contribute in that regard. The Supreme Court asserted that although predicting future dangerousness is difficult, it should not therefore be avoided.

Defendants cannot be compelled to incriminate themselves in examinations by prosecution psychiatrists without the protections of the Miranda doctrine.

After continuing controversy, it is argued that mental health professionals may have a moral rationale for treating death row prisoners even if doing so makes the prisoners competent for execution.

SECTION II: CHILD AND ADOLESCENT PSYCHIATRY

The Rights of Children Under the U.S. Constitution

Children's rights under the Constitution have been consistently upheld, but with limitations. The degree of limitations usually depends on two factors: (1) the general political climate in the country, and (2) the specific issue. Minors under a defined state age are entitled to First Amendment rights which can be curtailed under given circumstances. The right to personal expression is guaranteed for everyone by the Constitution including school-age children. However, offensive, vulgar language can be punished by the school authorities if they deem it unsuitable. Discussion of controversial subjects in school can be silenced, and school authorities can act on behalf of parents to protect children from exposure to unsuitable material.

Minors retain a right to privacy when it involves very private affairs such as pregnancy and abortion. They need no parental permission or judiciary approval to obtain an abortion or contraceptives. However, they do not have the right to purchase pornographic reading matter.

The law is sensitive to children who need psychiatric treatment, but parental decision has a substantial role in providing that care and treatment. The parents may commit their child to an institution without a judicial hearing, and an objective party affiliated with the institution will review the case. When a conflict arises between the parents and the state regarding psychiatric treatment of the child, the parental authority supersedes that of the government.

In criminal proceedings children have the right to many aspects of due process of law. However, juveniles do not have the constitutional right to trial by jury, and the state can use preventive detention far more readily than it can for adult defendants to serve legitimate state interests. Corporal punishment in public school is not in violation of the Constitution, and it is not considered a violation of the Eighth Amendment.

The Rights of Handicapped Children

The Congress enacted several statutes in the 1970s which were intended to ensure that handicapped children receive an appropriate education. Recent cases have further defined, and in some instances expanded, the level of services required under the law.

The Education for All Handicapped Children Act (EAHCA) was designed to provide the funds necessary for states to implement programs and services for the handicapped in fulfillment of equal education. The possible need of handicapped children for psychological counseling (psychotherapy) in order for them to benefit from an educational program was recognized. Handicapped children may not be expelled from school for bad behavior if the behavior in any way resulted from their handicap.

Handicapped and retarded children are entitled to special protection under the Constitution, and city ordinance zoning laws cannot discriminate against them with housing restrictions. Critically ill infants have been the subject of regulations, but a lawsuit has recently limited the scope of the effect of the regulations. Children with acquired immunodeficiency syndrome (AIDS) have also been determined by the courts to be entitled to rights under statutes protecting the handicapped. Psychiatrists and mental health professionals who work with handicapped children are required to be aware of the developments in law and the promulgation of legislation, in order to give adequate and appropriate guidance to those who consult them.

Victimized Children

Millions of reports of child abuse are filed each year with governmental agencies. Mental health professionals have a special responsibility to report suspected abuse because they have a greater opportunity to observe potential cases. Failure to report suspected child abuse is a misdemeanor punishable by a fine and/or imprisonment. Psychiatrists are also vulnerable to negligence lawsuits for failure to report.

Risk factors for child sexual abuse have been clarified. Clinical manifestations of child sexual abuse are numerous and may continue into adulthood.

When allegations of sexual abuse arrive at the court of law, it is inevitable that the child will take the witness stand. This is likely to be traumatic for the child. Defendants have the constitutional right to cross-examine the witness, even when the witness is a child. They do not have the right to examine the records of protective agencies freely; however, a trial court may determine that some information in a file is material to the defense and release that information only.

The ability to tell a truth from a lie and know the importance of truth-telling, and not any specific age limit, are the criteria for a child's competency to be a witness. The child must have a memory sufficient to recollect events and the ability to communicate them. It is the task of the trial judge to decide whether or not a child is competent to testify, but mental health professionals can determine the credibility of a child as witness, and make recommendations to the court. Defendants have the right to be present during the trial, especially in all critical phases, and to exercise the Sixth Amendment right to cross-examine the child. However, during competency hearings, defendants may be excluded from the hearing since the matters under discussion are not directly related to their defense.

The practice of play therapy, in which children-victims demonstrate how they were abused by using anatomically correct dolls, has been limited by some courts and has caused controversy.

Child Custody

The doctrine of "the best interest of the child" is the principle by which the courts select the custodial parent. Often, courts impose the judges' personal moral values on the determination of which parent is the best choice for custody. Therefore, homosexuals have suffered denials of their fitness for custody based on their sexual orientation.

Courts can terminate the parental right if a parent is found to endanger the well-being of the child by abuse or neglect. But termination must be based on the standard of clear and convincing evidence. Mentally disabled parents cannot have their parental rights terminated solely because of their illness. Instead, it must be proved that their mental problems render them incapable of properly caring for their children, and that there is little hope for timely improvement of their condition.

Although the right of biological parents supersedes that of psychological parents, under certain circumstances the court will give custody to the latter if it is deemed in the child's best interest.

Joint custody is considered to facilitate communication between divorced parents, and help children thrive in spite of their situation. More than half of the states have laws providing for joint custody. A role for the mental health professionals in custody disputes is generally seen as inevitable to some degree, although therapeutic relationships should be kept as separate as possible from legal processes.

Finally, surrogate motherhood has caused controversy as well as social, legal, and psychological drama. The prevailing legal view is that surrogacy by itself is not against the law but that surrogacy contracts are unenforceable, and financial remuneration to the natural mother for allowing the adoption of the child by the infertile wife goes against the most fundamental ethics of this society.

The society that is seen through this psychiatric-legal lens is one in which philosophical values are actively employed as guides in resolving conflicts. Many of our most vexatious social ills are major elements in these conflicts. Mental health and legal professionals, more than almost any other groups, confront these problems daily and serve to eradicate them by aiding the mentally ill persons under their care to the best of their abilities. Considering the thicket of suffering in which the legal and mental health professions often function together, it is not surprising that their relationship itself sometimes needs healing. It is hoped that this book will facilitate mutual understanding between these two professions.

In the preparation of such a book, I am indebted to many; I should like to express my gratitude to many authors from whom I learned and borrowed. I would also like to acknowledge my appreciation to my editor, Cynthia Tokumitsu, who edited the text.

Ebrahim J. Kermani, MD

*Dedicated to my wife Bonnie and to
all those colleagues and scholars whose
work, research, and views I have utilized
throughout the pages of this book*

SECTION I
GENERAL PSYCHIATRY

1

Psychiatry and Tort Law

CONFIDENTIALITY

Hippocrates, the philosopher-physician of antiquity, suggested that physicians take the oath, "Whatsoever I shall see or hear in the course of my profession as well as outside my profession, in relation with men, if it should not be published abroad, I will never divulge, holding such things to be holy secrets." From that time on, the principle of confidentiality endured as the core of the patient-physician relationship.

Confidentiality is an essential ingredient in psychiatric treatment, according to the ethical principles promulgated by the American Psychiatric Association (APA). The private and sensitive nature of the information to which psychiatrists must be privy in order to treat patients requires that they be circumspect in the information they disclose to others about their patients. The welfare of the patient must be a continuous and primary consideration.

Psychiatrists may release confidential information only with the authorization of a patient or under appropriate legal compulsion. Even so, psychiatrists have a duty to protect patients by fully apprising them of the implications of waiving the privilege of privacy. Further, psychiatrists may disclose only that information relevant to a given situation. They should avoid offering speculation as fact. It is usually unnecessary and therefore unethical to offer sensitive information such as a patient's sexual orientation or fantasy material. When psychiatrists are ordered by the court to reveal the confidences entrusted to them by patients who divulged information in the belief that it would remain private, the psychiatrists can comply with the order, or may ethically claim the right to dissent within the framework of the law. When psychiatrists are in doubt as to the ethics of revealing certain information, the right of patients to confidence, and by extension, to unimpaired treatment, must receive priority. Psychiatrists should reserve the right to question the need for disclosure. If the court can demonstrate adequate justification for legal disclosure, psychiatrists may request the right to disclose only information that is relevant to the specific legal question at hand.[1]

Presenting a patient to a scientific gathering can be ethical if certain criteria are upheld, namely, that the individual's dignity and privacy are respected and his truly informed consent has been obtained. The confidentiality of the material presented at the gathering must be understood and accepted by the audience. Confidential material may be presented in scientific journals only for legitimate scientific purposes. It would be illegal and unethical for psychiatrists to publish material obtained during the course of psychotherapy in the self-serving form of fiction, even if they hide the identity of the patient.

An example of breach of confidentiality in the form of improper publication is found in *Jane Doe v Joan Roe and Peter Roe*.[2] The defendants, psychiatrist Roe and her psychologist husband, were sued for publishing the records of a patient. The plaintiff and her late husband were patients of Dr Roe for many years. Eight years after termination of treatment, the defendant-psychiatrist published a book that repeated verbatim the thoughts, feelings, emotions, fantasies, and biographies of the plaintiff and her late husband. After 200 copies of this book were sold the plaintiff brought a lawsuit for damages and an injunction to cease further distribution of the book. The defendant-psychiatrist, in her rebuff, claimed that while in therapy the patient had given her oral consent to publication.

The trial court found that the patient-plaintiff was entitled to the injunction and compensatory damages of $20,000. This finding rested on the contention that the oral consent given during treatment was totally ineffective. The court noticed also that physicians who enter into agreements with patients to provide medical attention impliedly covenant to keep in confidence all disclosures made by the patients concerning their physical or mental condition, especially in the psychiatric relationship. The court rejected the defendant's argument that her constitutional free speech right allowed her to publish the book. In the judge's view, there was no infringement of free speech because there was no prior restraint; the book had already been published, precluding censorship. In addition, the defendant-psychiatrist failed to demonstrate the scientific value of the publication.

Legal Doctrine of Confidentiality

The confidentiality at the heart of the relationship between physician and patient or therapist and client, imposes a duty on the physician or therapist not to disclose information concerning the patient that is obtained in the course of treatment. Release of information without the patient's consent constitutes an invasion of the patient's privacy. Moreover, disclosure violates the Hippocratic oath, constituting unprofessional conduct, which like other unprofessional conduct can be subject to hearings and eventually a lawsuit.

Patients should be entitled to disclose freely their symptoms, conditions, and complaints to their physician, therapist, or whomever they have entrusted themselves to as healer. Indeed, patients must feel assured that confidentiality will be upheld, or else they cannot freely disclose crucial material. To benefit from therapy, patients cannot fear that what they reveal will become public knowledge. Only in an unconstrained atmosphere can the goal of the therapeutic relationship be fulfilled.

When seeking therapy, a patient enters into a contractual relationship with the therapist. In the contract the therapist implicitly, if not expressly, agrees to keep confidential the personal information entrusted to him or her by the patient. This contract governs the broadest and most basic standards of medical conduct. It is such a fundamental element of our social structure that it need not be written out between a physician or therapist and each individual patient. The patient brings to the relationship a reasonable expectation of the contract being upheld. The physician adheres to this implied contract with the usual responsibility of the medical profession and the traditional confidentiality of patient communications.

The confidential relationship between the therapist and the patient creates a fiduciary duty from the therapist to the patient, and unauthorized release of information by the former breaches the fiduciary duty. In the view of the legal establishment, members of a profession, especially the medical profession, maintain this confidential or fiduciary capacity to their patients. They owe their patients more than just medical care for which payment is rendered; they have a duty to give total and comprehensive care, which includes aiding the patient in litigation, providing reports when necessary, and attending court when needed. Also included is a duty to refuse affirmative assistance to the patient's antagonist in litigation. Of course, physicians owe a duty to their conscience to speak the truth; however, they can choose the proper time to speak.[3]

When patients enter a therapeutic relationship, they must admit to their therapist the most important intimacies related to the health of their mind. Since lay persons cannot predict what the road to recovery will entail, they cannot sift through their life history and habits to determine what information is valuable to their mental health. Instead they need a guide. They must disclose all information in the consultations with their physician, even that which is embarrassing, disgraceful, or incriminating. The therapist-guide will then select the facts requiring further exploration. To promote full disclosure, the professional must extend the promise of secrecy. Even with such a promise, disclosure is often difficult and hesitant; without it, it is impossible. The candor which this promise elicits is necessary for the effective pursuit of mental health; there can be no reticence, no reservation, no reluctance when patients discuss their problems with their therapists or physicians. But the patient intends this disclosure to be private. If physicians or therapists reveal any confidence, surely this effects an invasion of the privacy of their patients. To reiterate, the preservation of the patient's privacy is not merely an abstract ethical duty on the physician's part; it is his or her legal duty as well.

The unauthorized revelation of medical secrets, or any other confidential communication given in the course of treatment, is tortuous conduct which may be the basis for an action for damages. Such unauthorized disclosure of intimate details of a patient's health may amount to unwarranted publicizing of the patient's private affairs with which the public has no legitimate concern, and can cause outrage, mental suffering, shame, or humiliation to a person of ordinary sensibilities. Patients may be allowed to recover damages for their suffering under the circumstances.

Any time physicians undertake treatment of a patient, they enter into the simple unwritten contract described earlier. Patients hope that they will be cured and physicians assume that they will be compensated. Patients rely on a warranty of silence from the physician-therapist; the promise of secrecy is as much an express warranty as is the advertisement of a commercial entrepreneur. Consequently, when physicians or therapists breach their duty of secrecy, they are in violation of part of their obligation under the contract.[4] They have betrayed their oath, they have broken the law of tort, and they are vulnerable to claims for damages.

Some Guidelines for Confidentiality

The APA provides guidelines for psychiatrists which state that psychiatrists should not discuss their patients with anyone who is not directly involved in the patients' care. Psychiatrists should limit the material that they enter into their patients' records to what is clearly necessary for the patients' care, and they should protect these records from being divulged to anyone without the patients' freely given and informed consent.

The APA recommends that special precautions be taken in certain situations. When evaluations are done for third parties such as courts, employers, workers' compensation boards, etc, the individual under evaluation must be informed of the need to make a report to the third party, and of the limitations of the patient-psychiatrist confidentiality. Psychiatrists also have a responsibility to the individual to limit the material contained in such a report to matters directly relevant to the purpose of the request, and to exclude any extraneous material that the individual has disclosed during the course of the evaluation. Further, psychiatrists must understand that patients, in many jurisdictions, have the right to inspect and/or obtain a copy of the medical records if they so request. Some states limit this access and permit psychiatrists to withhold from patients information that would have a negative impact on their health or well-being. However, the patient's record must be released to other physicians of the patient's choice.

Psychiatrists may possess copies of patients' medical records that have been obtained from other health care providers. Patient authorizations for psychiatrists to release information to other parties do not cover the release of these records unless they are specifically included in the release request, and their re-release is not otherwise prohibited. Psychiatrists should also remember that their ethical and legal responsibilities regarding confidentiality continue after the deaths of their patients. Privilege does not expire at a patient's death. It continues after death and may be claimed by the patient's next of kin or legal representative. This protection after death is based on the doctrine that privilege belongs to the patient and that even after death the patient must be free from embarrassment, and further that such embarrassment could extend to family members after the patient has died.[5] Release of privileged information to third parties after a patient's death must be done only after the issuance of an appropriate court order.

The APA has noted that physician-patient privilege is a legal concept designed to protect confidential medical information from disclosure in a judicial proceeding.[6] Such privilege is the property of the patient, not the physician, and may only be waived by the patient. This privilege covers almost all communications made by the patient during the treatment relationship, including the psychiatrist's observations, conclusions, and diagnoses. If made in the presence of a third party, privileged information loses special status.

When asked to testify in court or by deposition about privileged information, psychiatrists must decline to proceed unless the patient or the patient's legal representative executes a valid waiver, or unless the psychiatrist is compelled by the court to provide the information. Even when so authorized or compelled, if psychiatrists feel that the disclosure would be unethical or damaging to the patient, they should resist within the full limits of the law by using all available appeal procedures. If these fail, psychiatrists may, as a matter of conscience, still refuse to divulge the information requested, although they are then at risk of being held in contempt of court. It can be argued that the integrity of the patient-psychiatrist relationship and the integrity of the profession are protected by strenuous adherence to the principle of confidentiality. In effect, the value of the profession rests on that privilege being upheld. When in doubt, professional ethics require that psychiatrists give priority to the patient's right to confidentiality and to unimpaired treatment.

The APA takes a moderate-conservative stance regarding the outer limit of confidentiality.[6] In its guidelines, the APA falls short of recommending risking contempt charges for not divulging confidential information, and advises psychiatrists to leave interpretation of the scope and limitations of privilege to the courts and the legal system.

The Interest of Justice versus the Right of the Patient

According to the law, the right of psychiatrists to assert an absolute privilege concerning psychotherapeutic communications is not constitutionally guaranteed. If psychiatrists are compelled by the court to disclose relevant information that they obtained in a confidential communication, they should not assume that their constitutional right to privacy is being violated. Further, courts have articulated that if compelled disclosure derives from legitimate government interest, incidental infringement of psychotherapists' economic interests in the practice of their profession is not open to constitutional challenge.

There are differences between testimonial privilege and confidential communication. Testimonial privilege belongs strictly to the patient. It allows the patient to withhold from courtroom proceedings confidential communications made to the psychiatrist. Privilege is established by statutory law. There are circumstances when a patient cannot claim privilege of communication, for example, when the patient raises his mental or emotional condition as an element of his claim or defense in legal proceedings such as in the *Lifschutz* case discussed below. Other exceptions are court-ordered examinations, criminal proceedings, and involuntary civil commitments. Confidentiality originates as an ethical principle and usually is protected by common law in ordinary circumstances.

The issue of compelled release of confidential information is confronted in the landmark case *In re Lifschutz*.[7] The case opened when Dr Lifschutz, a California practitioner, disobeyed a court order to divulge confidential material that he obtained from his patient during the course of psychotherapy. Lifschutz was imprisoned after he was adjudged in contempt for refusing to obey the order of the superior court instructing him to answer questions and produce records relating to communications with his former patient. Lifschutz contended that the court order was invalid, unconstitutionally infringing on his personal constitutional right of privacy, his right to practice his profession effectively, and the constitutional privacy right of his patient. He also claimed that his right to equal protection of the law was violated since the law protects clergymen, who cannot be compelled by the court to reveal confidential communications under similar circumstances.

The instant proceeding arose from a suit instituted by Mr Housek, a teacher, against his student, Mr Arabian. Housek alleged that Arabian assaulted him and as a result he suffered severe mental and emotional distress. During the deposition process Housek stated, among other things, that he had received psychiatric treatment from Lifschutz over a 6-month period approximately 10 years earlier. Arabian subpoenaed Lifschutz's medical records. In the deposition process, Lifschutz appeared for the deposition but refused to produce any of his medical records and refused to answer whether or not Housek had consulted him or had been his patient. Housek, meanwhile, had neither expressly claimed a statutory or constitutional psychotherapist-patient privilege, nor expressly waived such a privilege.

In response to the psychiatrist's refusal to cooperate, defendant Arabian moved for an order of the superior court compelling the production of the subpoenaed records and the answers to questions on deposition. Lifschutz continued refusing to comply with the court order. The court eventually adjudged him in contempt and ordered him to be confined. On appeal, the Supreme Court of California met en banc. It recognized and acknowledged that an atmosphere of confidentiality is vitally important to the successful practice of psychotherapy. However, in balancing the need for confidentiality in the psychotherapeutic process with broad societal needs of access to information for the ascertainment of truth in litigation, the laws favor disclosure, concluding that a psychotherapist can be compelled to reveal relevant confidences of treatment when the patient tenders his mental or emotional condition as an issue in the litigation. Further, the California Supreme Court noted that no constitutional right expressly enables a psychotherapist to claim an absolute privilege concerning psychotherapeutic communications.

Confidentiality and Fraud

If there is a suspicion that a psychiatrist committed fraud against a third party, for instance, by overcharging Medicaid recipients, the psychiatrist may be compelled to disclose certain records. The psychiatrist bears the burden of proof that claimed services have indeed been rendered. In such instances, the court is not concerned with the medical necessity or quality of services, but in whether the psychiatrist has accurately represented the number of patients seen, the frequency of the patients' visits, and the length of time per visit or therapeutic session, and of course the name of the patient if a third party such as Medicaid must pay for the visit.

Advocates of absolute confidentiality argue that any relaxation in the standard of confidentiality, even in Medicaid cases, would needlessly undermine the guarantee of confidentiality created by the privilege. Because this guarantee is a fundamental prerequisite to successful psychiatric diagnosis and treatment, the effect would be to relegate psychiatric patients receiving third-party payment, such as Medicaid, to second-class psychiatric care.

If disclosure of records is absolutely necessary in fraud cases, then the dates, time, and length of therapy sessions plus the patient's name would suffice to prove that services were rendered. Therefore, no need exists to disclose the entire contents of the records, which would include the patient's personal emotional problems, when such disclosure would serve no practical purpose, and would likely cause harm to innocent patients.

The courts have been sensitive to the two competing interests in promoting fair and effective fraud investigations, concurrently ensuring that such investigations do not encroach on the crucial confidentiality interests of patients.[8]

In *Massachusetts v Kobrin*,[9] the Massachusetts appeals court held that psychiatric records reflecting a patient's thoughts, feelings, and impressions and containing the substance of the therapeutic dialogue are not subject to disclosure in a grand jury investigation. Dr Kobrin, a psychiatrist, was accused of fraud. He was required to submit portions of his records documenting, among other things, patient diagnoses, treatment plans and recommendations, and somatic therapies. The psychiatrist refused to submit complete medical records on the grounds of upholding the psychotherapist-patient privilege. The lower court found him in contempt of court. The appeals court, however, found that while both federal and state law require a Medicaid provider to keep such records, unlimited access to the patient's files is unnecessary to prosecute a fraud case. What is necessary and must be submitted are records of times of patients' appointments, patients' names, and fees charged.

INFORMED CONSENT

Seventy-five years ago, Justice Benjamin Cardozo proposed that "every human being of adult years and sound mind has a right to determine what shall be done with his own body; and a surgeon who performs an operation without his patient's consent commits [a battery] for which he is liable in damages."[10] Today, this doctrine still prevails in the courts of law.

In tort law, the phrase *informed consent* is used with respect to the requirement that patients be apprised of the nature and risks of a medical procedure by the physician. Physicians cannot validly claim exemption from liability for battery or from responsibility for other medical complications if they have not informed the patient of the possibility. If a patient has not given informed consent for a medical procedure, whether it be prescribing medication, psychotherapy, surgery, or any other procedure, the procedure is deemed to be unauthorized and the patient may be able to recover damages.

The concern of the law in informed consent is not the appropriateness of specific procedures or their effectiveness, but rather that information was properly provided to the patient, that the patient comprehended it, and that the patient voluntarily consented to the procedure. Each medical specialty makes unique demands on the principle of informed consent. In psychotherapy, the patient must be told of the difficulties and sacrifices of time and expense that a treatment course may involve.[11] Today, this means that a psychiatrist is expected to clarify to persons considering therapy the risk of pain involved in the therapeutic process, including transference and other elements of psychotherapy.

Information that a psychiatrist should provide to the patient includes the likelihood of any bodily harm, side effects, probability of success, and the alternative methods of treatment.

The Concept of the Reasonable Person
and the Right to Know

The law maintains an interest in whether all risks that a reasonable person should be aware of have been disclosed to a patient or not by a physician prior to commencing a procedure. Where lawsuits are in process, a jury must decide whether a reasonable, prudent person would have consented to the treatment had he or she been fully informed of the risks and alternatives.

The patient has a right to know of all possible side effects and complications of a procedure, and what may ensue after it. If the risk is minimal, even if only 1%, the right to be informed remains in force. This principle is amply demonstrated in *Canterbury v Spence*.[12]

> Plaintiff Jerry Canterbury consulted the defendant, Dr Spence, a neurosurgeon, for severe back pain. A myelogram revealed a "suspected" ruptured disc and a laminectomy was advised. The plaintiff, a 19-year-old, did not object to the proposed surgery, nor did he probe its exact nature. Spence told the plaintiff's mother that the operation was no more serious than any other operation. The mother signed a written consent allowing the doctor to go ahead with surgery. Spence had failed to tell her, however, that there was a 1% possibility of paralysis from a laminectomy. The day after his surgery, Canterbury fell while voiding unattended. As a result of the fall and a second operation, the plaintiff developed urinary incontinence, paralysis of the bowel, and a reliance on crutches for walking.
>
> The lawsuit against Spence was brought, among other things, for his failure to warn the patient of the possible complications, including the 1% chance of paralysis.

During the appeal experts were unable to determine unequivocally the cause of the paralysis, but the court ruled nonetheless that there was a recognized 1% risk of paralysis following laminectomy and that the physician's failure to reveal that small risk allowed a prima facie case based on a violation of the physician's duty to disclose. In addition, the court specifically rejected the view that a community standard defines the quantity or quality of information to be given to the patient. Rather, the court held that the patient's right of self-decision shapes the boundaries of the duty to reveal. The test for determining whether a particular risk must be revealed is its materiality to the patient's decision. All risks that a reasonable person should understand in order to make an informed decision must be included in a disclosure.

The appeals court continued that physicians are under an obligation to communicate specific information to patients and to alert patients to the abnormalities of their condition. They must warn patients of the risks of proposed therapy and the alternatives to the recommended treatment plan. Then the patients, and not the physicians, make the ultimate treatment decision, which they could not do without knowing their options; the decision becomes the responsibility of the patients. The doctor's duty to inform is comprehensive, and not based on a patient's request for information. The final standards for disclosure are set not by the medical profession for its own convenience, but by the law of reason, defining what an average patient would be entitled to know in a given situation. If the duty to inform is questioned in a legal forum and argued thoroughly, in the end a jury will decide whether a physician has fulfilled the duty of properly informing the patient.

Applicable standards for physicians' disclosure have been established by the courts. For example, in *Harnish v Children's Hospital*,[13] the Supreme Court of Massachusetts held that physicians have a duty to disclose in a reasonable manner all significant medical information that they possess or could reasonably be expected to possess that is material to a patient's decision to undergo a proposed procedure. In this case, the court defined "material" as the significance a reasonable person would attach to the disclosed risk or risks in deciding whether to submit to surgery or treatment.

If the potential complication from a procedure is too remote, and generally unknown to the medical community, then the physician cannot be held responsible. This was the determination in *Precourt v Frederick*. The Supreme Court of Massachusetts overturned a $1.4 million jury verdict against a Boston ophthalmologist found liable for failing to disclose the potential side effects of a drug he had prescribed. The court ruled that physicians have not violated their duty to disclose medical information unless it has been demonstrated that they knew or reasonably should have known that the probability of a particular risk occurring was more than negligible.

In this case as reported by Freishtat,[14] the plaintiff William Precourt filed suit with his wife, alleging that his physician had negligently prescribed prednisone, a steroid used to control inflammation. The plaintiff asserted that as a result of the drug treatment he developed severe damages to the bones of both hips. The plaintiff further alleged that the defendant, Dr Albert Frederick, knew, or reasonably should have known, that the use of prednisone presented a risk of the type of bone damage sustained by Precourt, and that he prescribed the drug without informing his patient of that risk. Precourt originally contacted Frederick for removal of a piece of metal which had lodged in the back of his eye. The physician removed the metal and prescribed prednisone. Initially the condition of the eye improved, but later it deteriorated. A second operation was unsuccessful. In subsequent years, the plaintiff developed problems with his hips and eventually, 4 years after the eye operation and taking prednisone, he was diagnosed as having aseptic necrosis.

Dr Frederick testified that he generally prescribed prednisone after surgery for 50% to 75% of his patients, and in his nearly 20 years of practice he had never seen any of his patients develop aseptic necrosis. However, through medical literature, conferences, and discussions with colleagues, Frederick acknowledged that he was aware of an association between the use of prednisone and aseptic necrosis. At the trial, the plaintiff called several expert witnesses who testified that aseptic necrosis was one of the major risks of prednisone use and that the development of side effects from the drug was directly related to the dosage and duration of the use of the drug. The jury found that Frederick was not negligent in prescribing the drug, but it did find negligence in Frederick's failure to inform his patient of the risks associated with its use, and awarded $1.4 million in damages to the patient. Frederick appealed.

After examining the facts, the Supreme Court of Massachusetts found no evidence in the record of the likelihood that a person would develop aseptic necrosis from taking prednisone, or that Frederick knew or should have known the likelihood to be other than negligible. Consequently, the plaintiff had failed to demonstrate that Frederick recognized or reasonably should have recognized that the undisclosed risk was material to his patient's decision.

The difference between the decisions rendered by the *Canterbury* court and the *Frederick* court is that in the former, the court presumed that the physician should have known about a 1% risk and informed the patient of that risk, whereas in the latter the court resolved that there was no reason to believe that the physician should have been aware of the existence of a minimal risk. For a physician to be negligent in not disclosing a risk, the risk must be of a type that a reasonable person would find material to his decision in selecting treatment.

In contrast to the situation facing the *Frederick* court, if physicians know that certain medical procedures carry possible complications, they must obtain a patient's written consent prior to commencing the procedure, and if they fail to obtain the written consent, the award to the patient could be very costly to the physicians and the malpractice insurers. For example, a North Carolina appeals court held that a hospital was required to ensure that the patient's informed consent to a vaginal delivery of a footling breech (feet first) baby be obtained prior to delivery.[15] In this case, the court awarded $2.425 million to the baby who was permanently injured during a breech delivery and $646,000 to the baby's parents for medical expenses. The court found that the hospital was negligent in its duty to obtain the parents' informed consent. While the physician and the nurses at the hospital knew that the baby was in a breech position, no one informed the mother or father about this fact or its significance and the possible complications if the physician performed a vaginal delivery instead of a cesarian section.

The application of the *Canterbury* and *Frederick* decisions to the practice of psychiatry is a tangled process. Explaining the remote side effects of psychotropic medications to patients may frighten patients off medication that may actually be the most effective and safe course for them to follow. In effect, psychiatrists must often choose between two unacceptable alternatives: ordering medication without prior informed consent, or giving priority to patients' rights while watching patients lose out on a healthy life because their illness prevents them from accepting medication initially. For example, if a psychiatrist describes the side effects of phenothiazine drugs, which are commonly used in treating schizophrenia, to a hypochondriacal, narcissistic, or paranoid schizophrenic patient, the patient may stop taking the medication, especially if he or she cannot reexperience the discomfort of the former untreated state. The patient's condition would deteriorate as a result, making a competent treatment decision even less likely.

The commonly accepted practice for psychiatrists is to start patients on medication first, and as soon as the psychosis subsides or their condition improves, the psychiatrist must explain to the patient what possible side effects and complications can result. This course of action is essentially a compromise, mildly diluting the right to be informed and to make an informed decision. On the other hand, many of the generally acknowledged benefits of psychotropic treatment would be wasted if some compromise were not made, because very often patients in acute psychosis resist and reject suggested treatment, especially patients in a paranoid mode. In such cases, psychiatrists consciously accept an extra risk in starting the patient on psychotropics, knowing that they cannot put their expertise, or for that matter, their compassion, to work without taking the first step.

The Concept of Voluntariness

When physicians disclose to patients the nature and probable consequences of a suggested treatment, the patient's acceptance of such recommendations should be entirely voluntary. Just what constitutes voluntariness, however, raises many tough issues. For instance, a physician's omission of information to the patient interferes with voluntariness. Withholding specific information can be interpreted as manipulating or forcing a patient to arrive at an opinion desired by the physician. Patients have a special vulnerability, for no matter how intelligent or well-informed patients are, their affliction will affect their perceptions. Physicians, on the other hand, have a special power: medical knowledge. This power can influence or confuse healthy people, let alone the more vulnerable patients. Physicians must not abuse their power by misrepresenting facts.

Each medical specialty has its weak spots in regard to maintaining proper disclosure to patients, areas where black-and-white answers—or questions— do not exist; areas eliciting strong emotions; areas where the potential difficulties are too esoteric for a layperson to grasp, no matter how clearly and respectfully explained. Often, pharmacotherapy and medication have proved to be psychiatry's Achilles' heel, so to speak, and some of the problems arising from this issue were discussed above. Psychiatric communities have become well-versed with *Clites v Iowa*,[16] a case that shows how administering a major tranquilizer without a patient's informed consent can bring a $760,000 award for a plaintiff in a malpractice lawsuit.

> Timothy Clites had been institutionalized because of mental retardation. His treatment plan included major tranquilizers to curb aggressive behavior. Clites developed tardive dyskinesia as a result of taking the tranquilizers, and

his father submitted a claim for damages to the Iowa State Appeal Board citing negligent use of the drug, physical restraints, and lack of informed consent. When the board failed to take action after 6 months, the father brought suit in state court. There was a trial, and the court awarded the plaintiffs $385,000 for future medical expenses and $375,000 for past and future pain and suffering.

The case was appealed on several grounds, but the court of appeals affirmed the lower court's decisions and held that some form of informed consent must be obtained prior to the administration of major tranquilizers. In this case, Clites's parents were never informed of the potential side effects of the short-term and prolonged use of major tranquilizers, nor was consent obtained to administer the drugs. The court ruled that evidence must clearly indicate that the patient understood his right to refuse treatment and then elected knowingly and voluntarily to waive that right and proceed with the treatment.

There was another way in which the physician in *Clites* betrayed the patient-doctor trust and his own professional ethics. The court found that the physician's administration of major tranquilizers had been designed as a convenience or expediency program rather than as a therapeutic program. This solution to the patient's behavioral difficulties certainly contradicted the primary, and legally accepted, healing and treating purpose of institutionalization.

Informed Consent and the Incompetent Patient

Advances in medical science have given physicians greater control over the timing and nature of death. Prior to the development of recent life-prolonging techniques, physicians perceived their duty as that of making every conceivable effort to prolong life. On the other hand, the eras past when that simple ethos prevailed did not offer the methods for postponing death regardless of the effects on the patient that today's physicians have at their disposal. These new techniques whereby life, at least a limited definition of life, can be sustained when all activities and functions intrinsic to the meaning of "living" have ended, engender grave questions for physicians regarding the once clear goal of acting in the best interest of one's patients.

If a patient is mentally incompetent to give consent for a lifesaving procedure, is a physician as a medical professional obligated to act as an agent of the state and protect the patient from further deterioration? Or is the physician's first obligation to uphold the unwritten constitutional right to privacy which exists in the penumbra of specific guarantees enumerated in the Bill of Rights?

Proper identification of state interests determines whether the circumstances are appropriate for the exercise of the privacy right. But in the course of investigating state interests in various medical contexts and under various formulations of the individual rights involved, courts have understandably reached differing views of the nature and scope of state interests.

Fundamentally, state interests are preservation of human life; and protecting a third party, particularly minor children, from the emotional and financial damage which may occur as a result of the decision made by an incompetent adult to refuse lifesaving or life-prolonging treatment.

The questions raised by legal experts as to what legal standards govern the decision whether to administer potentially life-protecting or life-prolonging treatment to an incompetent person encompass two distinct subissues. First, does a choice exist? That is, does the state have an unrelenting responsibility to order medical treatment in all circumstances involving the care of an incompetent person? Second, if a choice is deemed to exist under certain conditions, what considerations enter into the decision making process?

The principle of equality and respect for all individuals produces the conclusion that a choice does exist, according to Judge Liacos, who presided over the court in *Superintendent of Belchertown State School v Saikewicz*,[17] a case focusing on this issue which will be discussed in detail below. Judge Liacos believes that "we recognize a general right in all persons to refuse medical treatment in appropriate circumstances. The recognition of that right must extend to the case of an incompetent, as well as a competent, patient because the value of human dignity extends to both."

Under the doctrine of parens patriae, the state has the power to care for and protect incompetent persons. The existence of this power and the responsibility it contains has impelled the courts to order necessary medical treatment for incompetent persons facing an immediate and severe danger to their life. However, the "best interests" of an incompetent person are not served by imposing on such a person results not mandated for competent persons similarly situated. For the protection of an incompetent person, the law requires the state to recognize the dignity and worth of such a person and to afford that person the same panoply of rights and choices it gives competent persons. The trend lately has been for incompetent persons to retain the same rights under the law as competent persons. Thus the legal principle of equality in this context requires that in certain circumstances it may be appropriate for a court to consent to the withholding of treatment from an incompetent individual.

The landmark *Saikewicz* case illustrates the courts' consideration that a person has a strong interest in being free of nonconsensual invasion of his bodily integrity even if he is mentally incompetent. Belchertown State School, a facility of the Massachusetts Department of Mental Health, petitioned the court for the immediate appointment of a guardian ad litem, with authority to make the necessary decisions concerning the care and treatment of Saikewicz, who suffered from acute leukemia. Joseph Saikewicz was 67 years old with an IQ of 10 and a mental age of 2⅔ years. This mentally retarded person was in urgent need of medical treatment, yet his mental disability made him incapable of giving informed consent for such treatment.

The guardian ad litem was appointed, and he filed separate motions with the court indicating that Saikewicz's illness was an incurable one, and although chemotherapy was the medically acceptable course of treatment, it would cause Saikewicz significant adverse side effects and discomfort, and its life-saving benefits were limited. In the guardian's view, it was in the best interest of Saikewicz to be left alone and not be treated.

The court faced three issues for determination: (1) the nature of the right of any person, incompetent or competent, to decline potentially life-prolonging treatment; (2) the legal standards controlling the course of decisions as to whether potentially life-prolonging but not lifesaving treatment should be administered to a person who is incompetent to make the choice; and (3) the procedures that must be followed in arriving at that decision.

In order to make the final determinations, the Massachusetts court relied heavily on a well-publicized New Jersey Supreme Court case, also the subject of a mass-market movie, *In re Quinlan*.[18] The court compared the circumstances in the two cases in arriving at its decision.

To review *Quinlan*, Karen Ann Quinlan, aged 21 years, stopped breathing, for reasons not clearly identified, for at least two 15-minute periods on the night of April 15, 1975. As a result, this formerly healthy woman suffered severe brain damage to the extent that medical experts characterized her as being in a chronic persistent vegetative state. Although her brain was capable of a certain degree of primitive reflex-level functioning, she had no cognitive function or awareness of her surroundings. Karen Quinlan did not, however, exhibit any of the signs of "brain death" as identified by the Ad Hoc Committee of the Harvard Medical School, and was alive under controlling legal and medical standards. Nonetheless, it was the opinion of the experts and the conclusion of the court that there was no reasonable expectation that Karen Quinlan would ever be restored to cognitive or sapient life. Her breathing was assisted by a respirator, without which the experts believed she could not survive. It was for the purpose of getting authority to order the disconnection of the respirator that Quinlan's father petitioned the New Jersey court.

In a unanimous opinion, the Supreme Court of New Jersey held that the father, as guardian, with consultation and approval of the hospital's ethics committee, could exercise his daughter's right to privacy by authorizing removal of the artificial life support systems. The court thus recognized that the preservation of the personal right to privacy against bodily intrusions, not exercisable directly due to the incompetence of the right-holder, could still be exercised indirectly by one acting on behalf of the incompetent person.

The Massachusetts court in *Saikewicz* compared Karen Quinlan's situation with the one faced by Joseph Saikewicz, and found discrepancies. The court, after reviewing the historical perspective of the doctrine of the "substituted judgment" standard, held that the decision in such cases should be to follow what the incompetent person would want if he or she were competent. The court can accomplish this end by substituting itself as nearly as possible for the incompetent and acting on the same motives and considerations as

16

would have moved that person. In essence, such substitute judgment means that the court must create a hypothetical being, that is, the person the incompetent would be if he were not incompetent. In so doing, should the court conjure up an ideal, eminently reasonable "everyman," or should it attempt to formulate a character with the specifics of nationality, socioeconomic status, educational level, psychodynamic, etc, of the individual in question? Perhaps merging the two approaches provides the greatest fairness, for competent persons would combine their unique qualities with the generally held standards of the day in making their own decision.

Applying the doctrine of substitute judgment in psychiatric cases is similar to the process in the *Saikewicz* case. The decision to treat an incompetent patient, for his own good, is a judiciary decision in which the judge, as a presumed reasonable person, receives the necessary information and then gives consent with the presumption that that was how the patient would have decided if competent.

Emergency Situations

In emergency life-threatening situations when for a variety of reasons an individual is unable to give consent to a treatment or explicitly discuss the treatment, the physician may go ahead and start the treatment. The law assumes in emergencies that every rational person would want treatment.

The court usually sides with the physician in emergencies if the physician has treated the patient in good faith and there was no time for the doctor to obtain informed consent. *Fraiser v Department of Health and Human Resources*[19] provides an example of the legal course of such a situation. The appeals court affirmed a lower court's decision entering judgment against a patient who filed a malpractice suit. Allegedly, the treating physician misdiagnosed the patient and treated her with antipsychotic drugs without obtaining informed consent.

> Rosemary Fraiser, a 62-year-old mother of eight children, with a history of mental illness and hospitalizations dating back to 1973, brought the suit regarding medical treatment received as a result of three hospitalizations at a Louisiana state institution. She contended, among other things, that medications were given to her without her informed consent which led to the development of tardive dyskinesia. The trial court dismissed her claim. She appealed. The appeals court reviewed all allegations and concluded that because the plaintiff's psychiatric condition had been life-threatening, the question of informed consent was moot. Therefore, informed consent was not required in a life-threatening situation. Once a diagnosis of schizophrenia with life-threatening effects was made, the matter was settled. Regarding the tardive dyskinesia, the physician was deemed not negligent, since he followed the standard of reasonable psychiatric care, immediately discontinuing neuroleptic medication after tardive dyskinesia was developed. In extreme circumstances when legal niceties have to be dispensed with, therefore, physicians are given the benefit of the doubt and the implicit support of the legal system. Although still liable in all other

ways, such as professional competence, they are free to administer what they consider the most appropriate treatment at such moments if it corresponds to generally accepted practices in their field.

Problems of Informed Consent

Under the law a normal adult, in order to make a decision regarding treatment, first collects data, compares the data and deliberates on risks and benefits, then eventually makes a decision. This process requires a physician's assistance in all phases but the last. It would be ideal if comprehension and recollection were the exclusive factors employed in patient consent decisions. But in addition to these, many other factors including emotion, anxiety, distortion, and denial play pivotal roles in the patient's decision. Unconscious conflicts also can be determining factors in the decision.[20] It is especially difficult, therefore, for psychiatric patients to give informed consent. Informed consent means that a patient receives information from his physician and then uses that information to make a decision. There is an assumption that when patients are fully apprised of the benefits of the treatment and weigh them against the risks, or against other alternative treatments, they will understand the physician's reasoning in prescribing the treatment and consent. Or, they may refuse.[21]

Other studies present a more complex situation, however. One study has shown that disclosure of information was an important factor in only a small percentage of patient decisions, with other factors such as clinical psychopathology and personal attitudes influencing the decision to refuse or accept treatment by antipsychotic medication.[22]

Consenting to treatment may have little to do with comprehended information in nonpsychotic patients as well, regardless of illness. The conventional informed consent process appears to be of limited benefit in providing information that is measurably understood and used by patients.[23] This likelihood does not negate the value of the process, however, which still provides guidelines for physicians to function by, gives society a philosophical and practical framework whereby the responsibilities of each party in the treatment decision are delineated, and provides the legal system with standards and precedents to utilize when the process goes awry and requires legal intervention. Acutely psychotic patients, like nonpsychiatric patients, are able to read the informed consent information, and report that they do understand information about antipsychotic medication. Objective measures fail to confirm their confident self-reports, however. Many of these patients simply affirm understanding to mask their confusion while reading the information about the medication.[24]

Problems arising with informed consent for long-term maintenance pharmacotherapy and obtaining patient consent to neuroleptic treatment with the risk of tardive dyskinesia have raised questions about long-term recall and the competence of psychiatric patients as a special population. Jaffe,[25] in his study on 32 adult outpatients, 16 in psychiatric clinics and 16 in medical clinics, found that (1) there was a remarkable similarity in the degree of comprehension between psychiatric and medical outpatient groups, which suggests that psychiatric patients need not be considered any less competent than medical outpatients in assimilating necessary medication information; and (2) patients in both groups were knowledgeable about short-term side effects, usually as a consequence of personal experience with them. However, their knowledge was consistently inadequate regarding potential long-term side effects from their maintenance medication.

One key to comprehension is believed to be the severity of thought disorder. Further, investigators have shown that a relationship exists between psychosis and attention and information processing deficits, and, therefore, thought disturbances. It can be assumed, according to this study, that psychosis limits the capacity to comprehend.[26]

Refusal to consent to treatment is not related to the voluntary or involuntary status of the patients. Further, there is no significant relation between understanding and hypothetical consent to medication. The patients who understood the ramifications of a treatment were no more likely to consent to it. Apparently, the ability of the treating psychiatrist to persuade the patient and the effects of milieu and similar factors may play an important role. A study by Irwin et al[24] indicates that psychotic patients, particularly those with prominent thought disturbance, do not substantially understand information about antipsychotic medication. Irwin et al[24] and Mills et al[21] recommend that a meaningful informed consent may need to be delayed for the acutely disturbed patients until disorganization of thought can be treated with antipsychotic medication. Having the patient verbally assent to treatment, supplemented by proxy consent obtained from relatives, may be a more rational, effective, and humane procedure.[24]

An assumption is gaining precedence that current informed consent doctrine presumes a degree of recall and comprehension beyond the capabilities of most patients. The development of an appropriate doctor-patient relationship that reconciles the need for consent with patient limitations remains an important challenge for clinicians.[25]

SUICIDE

Suicide is the intentional taking of one's own life. Although the underlying factors that lead a person to perform this act may not necessarily be fully understood by that person, suicide is considered to be voluntary and intentional. In antiquity, the Jews, Greeks, and Romans viewed suicide as normal under various circumstances, including the avoidance of disgrace, dishonor, forced apostasy or slavery, preservation of chastity, expression of loyalty to a fallen leader, or grief for a deceased husband. Over time, society's attitude changed. In Athens it became the custom to chop off the hand of someone who attempted suicide, and in Rome and in early Christianity, honorable burial was denied to a person who committed suicide.

This change can be attributed to western civilization's growing emphasis on making human life the preeminent object of value, a change which is reflected in art and philosophy from antiquity through succeeding centuries. The ancient attitudes persisted through the medieval period, when Roman culture was the direct forerunner. By the fifteenth century, Greek and Roman culture was distant enough to have a Renaissance, but by then the Christian ethos, including rejection of suicide, had taken firm root, and the influence of the ancient cultures affected mainly aesthetics and science. The medieval English author, knight, and justice of the peace Geoffrey Chaucer, in *Canterbury Tales*,[27] presents a suicide, implementing not psychological motives but the spiritual motive of maintaining purity. Ironically, it is in the "Physician's Tale." In the story a maiden must submit to treachery and rape. Death is her only method of evasion, and she asks her father to slay her to preserve her honor. After he does so, the townspeople in the story and the author neither voice nor imply disapproval of the pair for their gruesome solution. Instead, they register implicit approval that the father and daughter chose the appropriate, albeit tragic, option under the circumstances. Chaucer's language in describing the death is austere and respectful. Shakespeare, living about 250 years after Chaucer, also writes about suicide, but he does so in dramatically psychological terms. *Romeo and Juliet*[28] is an example. Suicide for Shakespeare is a tragedy, and the tragedy always involves "multilevel" human misunderstandings. Rational motives for the suicide are drawn, but the real "story" lies in the psychological conflicts. Shakespeare's approach to suicide hardly differs from current attitudes.

By the eighteenth century, the revolutionary shift in perception aided by the Renaissance and Elightenment artists, philosophers, and scientists who explored anew all aspects of existence, had been absorbed and refined. In the 1700s, suicide was correlated to melancholia and society tolerated somewhat the final act of a suicidal person. By the 1800s, suicide was considered a symptom of insanity. In the nineteenth century, Durkheim attributed the cause of suicide to society and economic disintegration. In the twentieth century, suicide is seen as a deviation from a normal healthy mind.

No subject today in the field of mental health, according to Gralnick,[29] commands more attention than suicide. It is an irrevocable act. No matter what precautions are taken, the act is devastating to the deceased's survivors. Suicide arouses intense feelings of regret and guilt in survivors. Self-condemnatory feelings often overcome those who loved or were responsible for the self-destroyer.[29]

Dynamic and Clinical Aspects

The problem for the clinician is to identify accurately those individual patients at high risk for suicide and then to make a timely intervention. Suicide usually occurs in association with a variety of psychiatric disorders, mainly depression. The lifetime incidence of suicide among depressed patients is 15%. This annual rate is 3.5 to 4.5 times higher than that for other psychiatric diagnosis groups and 22 to 36 times higher than the rate for the general population. Clinicians are expected to predict with some certainty the risk of suicide and to initiate effective intervention.[30] Failing to identify people at risk for suicide can result in a liability suit. For instance, after a particularly disturbing group teen suicide in Bergen County, New Jersey, it was revealed that shortly before the tragedy one of the teens had sought help at a mental health clinic. The clinicians there apparently did not notice the extent of the boy's self-destructive drive, and his parents have brought suit against the clinic and clinician(s).

Freud and his followers conceptualized that an individual possesses two distinct instincts: libido or sexual instinct, and aggressive instinct. When a person turns his own aggressive drive against himself, depression and suicide may result. The psychoanalytic formulations of Freud and Karl Abraham regarding the phenomena of depression and suicide in relation to the aggressive instinct still remains the core of classic analytic theory. From this perspective, depression involves turning the original object-directed aggression against the incorporated loved object. Hostile and aggressive feelings toward others have either been denied, suppressed, or repressed, and as a result have been turned against the self.[31]

It has been observed that the feeling of hopelessness is a crucial psychological construct for understanding suicide. When depressed patients believe there is no solution to serious life problems, they view suicide as a way out of an intolerable situation. Hopelessness is a core characteristic of depression and serves as the link between depression and suicide. In a study on 207 patients hospitalized for suicidal ideation, after a follow-up period of 5 to 10 years, 14 patients committed suicide. Of all the data collected at the time of hospitalization, the feelings of hopelessness correlated to eventual suicide.[32]

It is expected that therapeutic intervention to rapidly reduce hopelessness will lower suicidal potential. One consideration in the evaluation of suicide is to discern whether the patient is delusional or not. A retrospective analysis has shown that a significant relation exists between delusions and suicide. A delusionary depressed patient is 5 times more likely to commit suicide than a nondelusional one.[33] Societal focus, particularly the media's publicizing of suicide stories, increases the likelihood of suicide.[34] The rise in suicide occurs only after the story appears, not before. Evidence is consistent with the hypothesis that publicized suicide stories trigger additional imitative suicides. This theory is demonstrated by the suicides of four American poets. Randall Jarrell and John Berryman, poets of high esteem, were closely associated professionally. Not long after Jarrell died by walking into traffic on a thruway near his home at night, Berryman committed suicide. More recently, Sylvia Plath became known for her poetic exploration of mental suffering and self-destruction. Her poems implied that the writing was saving her, but that was

Hopelessness
Delusionality

Recent/Publicized
Suicides
Imitation
Cause

Command
Hallucinations

not the case, and she committed suicide in young middle age. Shortly thereafter, Anne Sexton, a writer whose work had been frequently compared with
Plath's in style and substance, also perished by her own hand. It is almost
impossible to contemplate these four deaths without concluding that Berryman
and Plath influenced Jarrell and Sexton, respectively. Plath had studied with
a colleague of Jarrell and of Berryman, making the self-destruction seem
intergenerational among artists renowned for their exacting delineation of
anguish, hopelessness, and despair.

Alternatively, suicide of certain highly visible personalities or celebrities
may prompt a shift of attention to suicide in general, and it can trigger suicide
from grief instead of imitation. Of course, the opposing view is that such
stories only precipitate suicides that would have occurred soon anyway, in
the absence of the suicide story. To say "only," however, overlooks the fact
that some of those potential suicides might have been dissuaded from the act
in the interim. Media publicity of suicide and the impact it may have on other
people with suicidal tendencies became a focal issue in the Bergen County
group teen suicide mentioned earlier. Because of the sensational nature of the
suicide, media flocked to the scene in hordes and the suicide received almost
as much media attention as an international foreign policy scandal. In recognition of its own possibly damaging effects, the media publicized "crisis
centers" and "hotlines" for troubled people to call. As days passed, the media
shifted its attention from the original scene and began investigating its own
role in the debacle. Public debate arose over the presence of news media and
the effects of publicity on suicide-prone persons. The debate has died down
now, but it has not been resolved.

Some Facts about Suicide

The sample of facts about suicide given below shows that easy suppositions
can lead people astray in their perception of persons who take their own lives
or try to. Further, for physicians and mental health clinicians who have direct
or indirect responsibility over potentially suicidal individuals, familiarity with
as many facts as possible regarding suicide is advisable for the prevention
not just of suicide, but of liability suits for negligence or malpractice.

- Eight out of every ten eventual suicides give prior warning in clear
  terms to people who are close to them or to mental health professionals
  before making an attempt to terminate their life. The warnings can
  take many forms, from direct statement to fascination with death.
  Suicidal psychotic patients may register complaints of auditory hallucinations such as "Kill yourself . . . you are no good . . . ," etc.
- The depressed patients may complain that no one loves them, no one
  cares for them, and so on.
- Suicidal patients may not be suffering from serious mental disorders,

and the decision to kill themselves could arise suddenly and compulsively without any prior decision.

- Although suicide is not hereditary, there is evidence that suicide is more likely to occur in families where at least one member has already committed suicide.
- The passage of crises does not mean that the suicide risk is over. Suicides are known to increase dramatically after patients have terminated treatment, or their depressive condition has improved.
- There is a possibility that after the initial condition improves, patients may use their remaining energy for the purpose of committing suicide.[35]

The Doctrine of Liability

The doctrine of liability for failing to prevent suicide is based, as are other elements of psychiatry malpractice, on four elements: (1) a breach of a specific affirmative duty of care owed to the person committing suicide; (2) proof of the psychiatrist's relationship with the patient; (3) the psychiatrist's knowledge that the patient was likely to commit suicide; and (4) the psychiatrist's failure to take appropriate preventive measures. Consideration of those four factors plus how the suicide could have been prevented are matters decided by juries in specific lawsuits. In courts of law, the voluntary act of the deceased is irrelevant and does not break the chain of causation for the above four elements.[36]

In testimony on 32 suicide cases, Perr[37] noted that lack of adequate records was clearly responsible for one large settlement. Similarly, the lack of a hospital policy in dealing with suicidal patients was probably a major factor in another moderate settlement. In several cases, the issue of records was major, at trial or in settlement, even though the defense managed to win at the trial or obtained a modest settlement. Plaintiffs received monetary awards through settlement in at least six cases. Perr believes that suicide litigation represents a significant liability risk in the practice of psychiatry.

Psychiatrists and other mental health professionals have a duty to exercise reasonable care to safeguard their patients from suicide. The duty is more specific when a patient is voluntarily or involuntarily confined to a psychiatric ward. When a patient has been admitted to a hospital precisely because of suicidal tendencies, this duty attains its most substantial form. The management of the hospital is expected to exercise the same reasonable care to safeguard and protect the patient from self-inflicted injury or death, the duty being proportionate to the needs of the patient, that is, such care and attention as his known mental condition requires. Any departure from standard care will create liability for the hospital and the psychiatrist.

An example of how such liability was litigated is found in *Kent v Whitaker*,[38] in which a psychiatrist was found liable in the amount of $10,000 for the suicide of a patient who was admitted to a hospital for attempted suicide. Placed alone in a locked room, the patient subsequently strangled herself using plastic tubing. The court held that the psychiatrist had a duty to exercise reasonable care to safeguard the patient from suicide, which in this case meant constant supervision.

Similarly, in *Honey v Barnes Hospital*,[39] a hospital was found liable. A wrongful death action was brought by the parents of a man who committed suicide by jumping from a tenth floor window of a psychiatric intensive care ward. Since the man had been admitted to prevent suicide, the hospital failed to provide adequate locks for windows in the psychiatric ward, and since hospital employees knew that the decedent could open windows, the hospital failed to provide adequate supervision before the patient's death.

If psychiatrists notice suicidal tendencies in their patients, they have the duty to inform responsible hospital personnel so that close supervision of the patient will be provided. This is the subject of *North Miami General Hospital v Krakower*,[40] in which the deceased, Noah Krakower, was a man of known suicidal tendencies. He had been under the care of Dr Gilbert, a psychiatrist, for several years. Krakower was admitted to North Miami General Hospital under Gilbert's care for treatment. During a temporary release to get a haircut, Krakower attempted suicide and was seriously injured. He was returned to the hospital and because of the nature of his injuries, transferred to the orthopedic floor of the hospital. In the hospital record, Gilbert wrote: "suicidal precautions with 24-hour attendants." An attendant was secured by the hospital from a registry, but she was not informed of the patient's suicidal tendencies. The patient asked his attendant to carry his dessert to the refrigerator. While she was out, the patient jumped from the fire escape to his death. A court found the hospital and the psychiatrist negligent in failing to adequately inform the attendant of the patient's suicidal tendencies.

In a negligence malpractice suit for suicide, conduct on the part of the plaintiff that fails to meet the standard for self-protection constitutes contributory negligence. This is legally considered a contributing cause along with the negligence of the defendant in bringing about the patient's harm. In other words, the allocation of responsibility for damages incurred between plaintiffs and defendants is based on the relative negligence of each; the reduction of the damages recovered by negligent plaintiffs is in proportion to their contribution of negligence. In cases of suicide negligence, the court is not interested in learning whether patients contributed to their suicidal behavior through manipulative acts, suicidal gestures, or other similar things. In the view of the courts, patients known to harbor suicidal tendencies and whose judgment has been blunted by a mental disability should not have their conduct measured by standards applied to normal adults in normal situations. Where it is reasonably foreseeable that patients as a result of mental or emotional illness may attempt to injure themselves through suicidal behavior, those in charge of their care owe a duty to safeguard them from their self-damaging potential. This duty encompasses the foreseeable occurrence of self-inflicted injury regardless of whether it is the product of the patient's volitional or negligent act.

The issue of contributory negligence was presented to a New Jersey appeals court in *Cowan v Doering*,[41] and the appeals court affirmed a $600,000 judgment for a patient for injuries sustained when she jumped from the second floor while being treated at a hospital for an overdose. The appeals court found that the trial court correctly refused to submit the question of the patient's contributory negligence to the jury.

This plaintiff, with a history of two previous suicidal acts, took an overdose of sleeping pills. She was diagnosed as borderline personality. After she jumped out of the second-story window in a hospital, she brought a lawsuit against her psychiatrist claiming that the defendant psychiatrist failed to take precautionary steps to prevent her from attempting to commit suicide. The court sided with the patient and noticed that the patient had committed the very act that the defendants were under a duty to prevent. The evidence indicated that the strong sedative taken by the patient, combined with her mental illness, substantially clouded her judgment. Although the experts disputed the genuineness of the patient's attempted suicide, and whether her suicidal gestures were genuine or manipulative in nature, the court considered those questions as irrelevant and concluded that there is no contributory negligence in suicidal acts.

Patients thus can bring lawsuits against their psychiatrists after a suicide attempt, regardless of their motives. Lawsuits may be instituted to manipulate, or patients may simply regret the attempt and divert their anger against the psychiatrist. Patients are much more likely to win if they were released from a hospital setting and their suicide attempt followed their release.

> Bell attempted suicide shortly after he was discharged from a hospital, and brought an action, *Bell v New York City Health and Hospital Corporation*,[42] to recover for injuries sustained during the suicide attempt. Initially, Bell was admitted to the adult psychiatric unit of the defendant hospital pursuant to a court order obtained by his wife. He was released 1 week later on the recommendation of his treating psychiatrist, also a named defendant. A week after the release, Bell attempted suicide by dousing himself with gasoline and setting himself on fire. Bell had a long history of psychiatric disorders, including three prior suicide attempts. The psychiatrist who made the decision to discharge Bell apparently was not aware of his previous suicide attempts. During the course of his brief hospitalization, nurses noticed that Bell was delusional, and once, by order of another physician, he was placed in a straitjacket.

At the trial, the jury found that the decision to discharge the patient was a departure from proper medical practice and rendered a verdict in excess of half a million dollars for the plaintiff. On appeal, the appellate court sustained the jury's award of damages to the plaintiff, but noted that a psychiatrist cannot be held liable for an error in medical judgment. Claims of psychiatric malpractice involve conflicting public policy considerations. On the one hand, if each physician who released a confined patient was liable for every act the patient performed thereafter, practitioners would be understandably hesitant to strive toward the psychiatric objective of returning patients to society. On the other hand, there must be concern for the safety of the citizenry. Rules governing psychiatrists' liability are made to balance these competing interests. The court noted further that these policy considerations do not abrogate the psychiatrist's duty to base his decision to release the patient on a careful and competent examination. Psychiatrists are at fault if they fail to review prior medical records. The lack of familiarity with the nurse's note regarding the patient's delusion in the *Bell* case cost the defendant psychiatrist financially, professionally, and, no doubt, personally.

Mental Health Professionals Are Not Responsible for the Suicidal Acts of Their Patients

The first issue to clarify and reiterate when a psychiatrist's patient commits suicide is that the patient was being treated for an illness. When this illness ends in death, the tendency is to hold the physician and hospital responsible for failure to treat the patient successfully. If a physician performs negligently, and if the patient would not have been injured except for the physician's negligence, then indeed the latter is culpable.

However, for the case to have merit, it must be clear that the negligence was the probable cause of the injury. Hospitals are generally required to render only such care as the staff knew, or in the exercise of reasonable care should have known, the patient's condition required, which includes special precautions. This is measured by the degree of care, skill, and diligence customarily exercised by other hospitals in the community. The hospital's duty may extend to affording reasonable protection against self-inflicted injury if the patient is unable to look after his own safety.

A psychiatrist's liability is usually determined by the conformity test which means that a physician can be held liable and at fault if he or she departs from the standard of practice that prevails in a similar community. As long as physicians "conform" to local practice and the standards of their community, they are immune from fault.[43]

The court has an interest in whether a psychiatrist maintained adequate care for the patient or not. If the physician, using the standard measure of testing, concludes that a patient is not suicidal and then the patient kills himself, the physician is not responsible, as in *Brand v Grubin*.[44] In the *Brand* case, the psychiatrist maintained adequate care but allegedly failed to assess the patient's situation correctly and did not inform the patient's family. The psychiatrist was found not negligent and not liable for the decedent's death.

The issue the court must decide in order to determine whether a defendant was negligent or not is if the defendant, in this case a psychiatrist, utilized "the standard of care and skill of the average member of the medical profession practicing the specialty of psychiatry." In *Stepakoff v Kantar*,[45] a psychiatrist diagnosed the patient as a manic-depressive who was potentially suicidal. The psychiatrist wanted to go out of town one weekend, and arranged for another psychiatrist to cover for him. A day before his trip, the psychiatrist met with his patient on an emergency basis and then concluded in his note, left in the file: "There is a question of whether he will make it over the weekend." Before his trip, the psychiatrist spoke with the patient again by phone and the patient assured the psychiatrist that he did not plan to commit suicide. The psychiatrist left town. The next day the police found the patient in his garage, dead from carbon monoxide inhalation.

At the trial, two experts testified. One expert contended that the defendant's conduct did not conform to good medical practice, and that the defendant-psychiatrist should have involuntarily hospitalized the patient. The second expert concluded that the patient did not meet the requirements for involuntary hospitalization. The trial court directed a verdict for the psychiatrist on the issue of conscious suffering and a jury returned a verdict for the psychiatrist on the wrongful death claim.

The Massachusetts appeals court affirmed the dismissal of a wrongful death suit against the psychiatrist. Further, the appeals court also found that the trial court had acted properly in *refusing* to instruct the jury that "if the defendant knew or should have known that his patient presented a serious danger to himself, the defendant owed the patient a specific legal duty to safeguard him from that danger, or at least to use reasonable care to do so." Finally, the appeals court held that the widow could not recover on her claim for conscious suffering. The jury had found the defendant not negligent, and no claim for conscious suffering was warranted in the absence of a finding of negligence.

In *Stepakoff* and many other similar cases, it is clear that the courts of law are concerned with whether a professional exercised the "standard of care." The courts are not concerned with whether a psychiatrist or any other professional should possess advance knowledge of a future danger that may occur.

In any event, the suicide of a patient affects the psychiatrist significantly. The psychiatrist experiences feelings of anger, guilt, and loss of self-esteem, as well as intrusive thoughts about the suicide. Chemtob et al[46] in a national survey of 259 psychiatrists, found that 51% (n = 131) had had a patient who committed suicide. Of these, 65 reported a high stress level in the weeks following the patient's suicide. Almost all of those psychiatrists reported increased concern for and attention to the legal aspects of their practice.

SEXUAL ENCOUNTERS

Without exception, a psychiatrist engaging in sexual contact with a patient is behaving unethically. The APA states: "The necessary intensity of the therapeutic relationship may tend to activate sexual and other needs on the part of both patient and therapist, while weakening the objectivity necessary for control."[47]

While the vast majority of psychotherapists supports unhesitatingly this prohibition against sexual encounters between psychiatrists and their patients, studies show that about 7.5% are unwilling or unable to put that prohibition into practice.

Statistical Perspective

Sexual contact between therapists and their patients is not an uncommon phenomenon. Early surveys of psychiatrists and psychologists regarding therapist-patient sexual contact have shown that 5.5% to 10% of male respondents had engaged in sexual intercourse with their patients.[48,49]

In a nationwide survey of American psychiatrists, Gartrell et al revealed that 7.1% of the male respondents and 3.1% of the female respondents acknowledged having sexual contact with their own patients.[50] These investigators sent a 34-item questionnaire to 5574 psychiatrists, with answers being completed and returned by 1423 respondents (291 female and 1124 male). The highlight of this survey indicated that some of those offenders had (as the investigators put it) "multiple sexual contacts" with their patients. One even reported engaging in sex with 144 patients! Of the offenders, 56 (67%) had been sexually involved with one patient and 28 (33%) with more than one. The psychiatrist-patient sexual contact included genital contact 74% of the time; and in the remaining cases the contact consisted of kissing, fondling, and/or undressing. The sexual contact was undertaken for "love" or "pleasure" by 73% of the offenders. Intending to enhance the patient's self-esteem and/ or provide a restitutive emotional experience for the patient was the motivation for 19%. Overall, 25% of the offenders were pleased to have had this sexual contact, 35% had mixed feelings, and 40% regretted the experience. In the majority of cases the sexual contact took place after termination of treatment.

The same investigator found that most psychiatrists endorse an absolute prohibition against sexual contact with patients.[51] By large majorities, the respondents in a national survey affirmed their belief that such contacts are always inappropriate and usually harmful to patients.[52] These investigators have found that 90% of patients who had been sexually involved with a previous therapist suffered ill effects, as assessed by their subsequent therapists. Some had to be hospitalized, and in one case, a woman committed suicide.[53]

Exploitation of Women

In their ground-breaking book, *Human Sexual Inadequacy*, Masters and Johnson reported that a significant percentage of the women who came to their clinic for sex therapy had been sexually exploited by their previous therapists.[54] These included obstetricians, gynecologists, psychiatrists, psychologists, social workers, and pastoral counselors. Masters and Johnson have suggested that if a therapist becomes sexually involved with a patient, regardless of whether the seduction was initiated by the patient or by the therapist, the therapist should be sued for rape rather than malpractice; that is, the legal process should be criminal rather than civil. Stone[55,56] has noted that because of the usual absence of violence or threats of violence and the presumption that the woman had a choice, rape or criminal charges rarely can be brought against a psychotherapist. Those few criminal cases have involved some element of physical coercion or force rather than exclusively psychological coercion.

One of the most colorful cases in which a psychiatrist was sexually involved with a patient, *Roy v Hartogs*,[57] received worldwide publicity and further notoriety after the network television portrayal of the incident. Julie Roy, the plaintiff, testified that she had consulted Dr Renatus Hartogs, the defendant, because of her sexual problems. During the course of psychotherapy, she alleged, Hartogs had suggested that they have sexual relations as a part of her therapy. She claimed that as a result of his seduction, they had sexual relations over a 13-month period, and that during this time the defendant continued to treat the plaintiff. In voicing her grievance, the plaintiff argued that, because of her sexual relationship with her psychiatrist, her mental illness had been aggravated to the extent that twice she had to be confined to a mental hospital. In his defense, Hartogs asserted that the plaintiff was suffering from paranoid delusions with wishful thinking. Furthermore, he testified, he could not have had a sexual relationship with the plaintiff (nor in fact with anyone) because his testicles had been damaged and were atrophied!

The court found the psychiatrist guilty of the allegation in the complaint by the patient because the psychiatrist had had sexual relations with the patient as part of a prescribed treatment for the patient's sexual problems, and that such behavior was sufficient to make the cause of action rest on forcible sexual intercourse as an assault. The court stated further that the relationship between a psychiatrist and his patient is analogous to the guardian-ward relationship, that is, a guardian cannot claim that a ward is capable of consenting. The trial court awarded compensatory and punitive damages in the amount of $153,679.50. On appeal, the verdict was affirmed but damages were reduced to $25,000. Meanwhile, the insurance company denied liability to Hartogs on the grounds that the act of intercourse was not actually considered a treatment rendered under his policy. The court agreed with the insurance carrier, and the therapist again lost his case. Later, he lost his license to practice medicine.

The issue in the Hartogs case, as in many similar cases, was the problem of transference and countertransference, central features in any therapeutic relationship. Whether mishandling transference and countertransference actually results in sexual intercourse or not, a court can determine therapists to be liable if they act in a seductive or suggestive manner.

Mishandling of Transference

A defendant-psychiatrist was found responsible for unethical behavior in *Zipkin v. Freeman*,[58] a case frequently cited in the psychiatric-legal literature, because he mishandled transference. Margaret Zipkin consulted Dr Freeman, a psychiatrist practicing in Columbia, Missouri, for psychosomatic conditions. Freeman recommended psychotherapy which lasted 3 years. As a part of the treatment, Freeman invited his patient, the plaintiff, to social gatherings which included skating and pool parties, as well as taking trips with him out of state. Allegations further showed that the psychiatrist urged his patient to invest her money in his enterprises. On one occasion, during the course of psychotherapy, Freeman invited Mrs Zipkin into his home for "group swimming therapy" where a number of patients and their spouses were present, and some of those who attended, including Freeman, were nude. As her therapeutic sessions continued, Freeman reportedly informed the patient that he had reached the conclusion that she had "a desire to be a male; that she thought she had to compete with males in order to be anything and that she did not know what it was to be a woman."

Then, on Freeman's advice, Mrs Zipkin sought to divorce her husband in order "to get completely well." The divorce was denied. The psychiatrist then advised Mrs Zipkin to bring all her husband's new suits to his office for him to wear during psychotherapy sessions. This action, according to the psychiatrist's interpretation, would help the patient to discharge her hostility and anger. On another occasion, Freeman told Mrs Zipkin to go to her brother's office, as a part of the venting of her hostility, and search through the brother's desk for evidence of his cheating her. Mrs Zipkin accepted Freeman's advice and went through her brother's desk while the psychiatrist stood by and watched at the office door.

In his defense, Freeman argued that the issue at hand was not whether he had managed or mismanaged transference and countertransference. "The fact is that she came to him for treatment of headache and diarrhea by means of psychotherapy and was treated and cured."

The court found the psychiatrist guilty, and awarded $18,029.47 to Mrs Zipkin. In his closing remarks, the presiding judge added that the acts of Freeman had no reasonable connection with professional services.

Mishandling Transference to a Third Party

The foregoing cases involved psychiatrists who mishandled the transference phenomenon. However, the court has extended the breadth of malpractice liability to allow a patient to have a cause of action if the therapist engages in sexual contact with the patient's spouse (indirect transference). *Mazza v Huffaker*,[59] as reported by Simon,[60] demonstrates this principle.

> Dr Mazza, a dentist, received ongoing treatment for manic-depressive illness from Dr Huffaker beginning in 1975. Huffaker also took responsibility for the patient's wife, Jacqueline Mazza. Medication and psychotherapy were prescribed for Mazza. Allegations stated that during a session which was held on May 4, 1979, Mazza expressed serious concern in maintaining a healthy marital relationship with his wife and thought of his psychiatrist as his "best friend."
>
> On May 28, 1979, Mazza and his wife became separated. On July 6, 1979, Mazza unexpectedly went to his home to meet with his wife, and when he arrived at his residence, he found Huffaker's car parked near the house and saw his psychiatrist's clothes strewn around the family room. He entered the house and discovered his psychiatrist and his wife in bed together in the master bedroom. Mazza pulled out his gun and fired at Huffaker. The volley went over Huffaker's head. The two wrestled. Huffaker had his eyeballs badly bruised as Mazza was trying to gouge his eyes out. On July 10, 1979, Mazza was released from the hospital. He located Huffaker's car, slashed two tires, and stole Huffaker's briefcase and suitcase.

At the trial, the jury was instructed to find malpractice if any of the following were determined to be true: (1) that the defendant violated the standard of care; (2) that the defendant failed to recognize and guard against transference or countertransference phenomena in the treatment of Jacqueline Mazza; (3) that the defendant abandoned his patient (Dr Mazza); and (4) that the defendant continued treatment of Mazza after becoming emotionally and sexually involved with his wife.

The trial court found Huffaker liable for malpractice for having a sexual relationship with his patient's wife. The court awarded $102,000 in compensatory damages, $500,000 in punitive damages, and $50,670 for criminal conversation. Huffaker was allowed to recover $3,000 in personal injury and $85 in property damage. The North Carolina Court of Appeals, affirming the trial court's decision, recognized the psychiatrist's duty to maintain the patient's confidence and trust as essential for the efficacy of treatment in its rationale for ruling that Huffaker's conduct was negligent.

The trial court also created a unique third-party medical malpractice cause of action by permitting Mazza to recover on a malpractice claim for the treatment Huffaker provided Mrs Mazza. The appeals court found no error in the trial court's finding of malpractice for Huffaker's mishandling of transference phenomena toward Jacqueline Mazza. The interesting point is that in the Mazza case the jury was instructed to find malpractice for abuse of transference phenomena toward Mrs Mazza rather than Dr Mazza.

The case extends the scope of malpractice alleging mismanagement of transference phenomena by holding that a spouse will have a cause of action for malpractice under these circumstances. In the past, third-party actions by spouses in sexual misconduct cases have sought recovery through the negligent infliction of emotional distress, the intentional infliction of emotional distress, loss of consortium, alienation of affection, and criminal conversation, among other conventional negligence claims.

The Dynamics of Sexual Relationships with Patients

A sexually abusive therapist has a self-narcissistic disturbance. Such therapists have feelings of dominance and paternalism with grandiosity in relation to an idealizing patient with whom the therapist inexplicably seems to fall in love. Claman[61] believes that the therapists indeed fall in love, but with their own mirrored self-object, rather than with the patient as a separate and distinct person. The sexual contact that evolves is for the therapist a palpable manifestation of the reality of this encounter, the singularly concrete proof that the self-object is actual and not simply a fantasy or projection of his needs. According to this model, sexual intimacy with patients is a paradigm of self-object countertransferential acting out.[61]

Regardless of psychodynamic developments, the prohibition against sexual contact between patient and therapist is permanently established with the initial encounter and cannot be abrogated by termination. Relationships established after termination may be friendly, but they are not egalitarian, because the therapist must remain available so that the patient can reenter therapy at some future time if the need arises.

Some authors have compared prohibition against sexual contact with patients to the incest taboo.[62] This analogy accurately describes both the psychodynamics and the reality of the power relationship. Patients voluntarily submit themselves to an unequal relationship in which the therapist has the superior knowledge and power. Transference feelings related to the universal childhood experience of dependence on a parent are inevitably aroused. These feelings exaggerate the power imbalance in the therapeutic relationship and render all patients vulnerable to exploitation. The promise to abstain from abusing the position of power for personal gratification is central to the therapeutic contact; violations of this promise destroy the basic trust on which the therapeutic process is founded.[52] According to Herman, neither transference nor the real inequality in the power relationship ends with the termination of therapy.[52]

In spite of the instances when therapists do engage in sexual contact with their patients, the majority of therapists reject the idea of any sexual contact with their patient in any form or in any stage of treatment. This majority concurs that there must be an absolute prohibition against sexual contact with patients. A therapist who undertakes responsibility for treating a sexually abused patient may try to convince the patient that he or she should waive confidentiality and take steps against the former therapist. According to some psychiatrists, these actions may have therapeutically beneficial value for sexually abused patients. The real-world confrontation is considered a crucial therapeutic process to help such a patient master the trauma of the experience.[55,56]

DUTY TO WARN AND PROTECT, PREDICTION OF DANGEROUSNESS

Based on years of tradition originating with the Hippocratic oath, healing professionals including psychotherapists have regarded their patients' communications as absolutely privileged and confidential. With the *Tarasoff v Regents of the University of California* ruling,[63] courts throughout the United States have increasingly sought to place this tradition, with its assumptions of privilege and confidentiality, under judicial review. The result is a series of court decisions which to varying extents have limited psychotherapist-patient confidentiality in the interests of a presumably greater responsibility: the duty to warn another that his or her life is endangered by one's patient. This section reviews the "duty to warn" doctrine in light of the landmark 1976 *Tarasoff* decision.

The Tarasoff Decision

In *Tarasoff*, it was undisputed that on October 27, 1969, Prosenjit Poddar, an Indian national studying at the University of California at Berkeley, went to the apartment of another Berkeley student, Tatiana Tarasoff, and killed her. Mr Poddar had previously voluntarily undergone psychotherapy at the University of California (Cowell Memorial Hospital). During the course of his treatment he reported to his therapist, Dr Moore, that he intended to kill an unnamed girl who, on the basis of previous sessions, was readily identifiable by Moore as Tatiana Tarasoff. Moore, with the concurrence of two psychiatrists, concluded that Poddar should be placed under observation in a psychiatric hospital. Moore, first orally and then in writing, notified the Berkeley campus police, and Poddar was taken into police custody. The police, however, became satisfied that Poddar was rational and released him after securing his promise to stay away from Ms Tarasoff. Meanwhile, Dr Powelson, director of the Department of Psychiatry at Cowell Memorial, asked the police to return Moore's letter and directed that all copies of the letter and therapy notes that Moore had taken on Poddar be destroyed. Powelson ordered "no action" in regard to the initial order to place Prosenjit Poddar under mental observation.

The plaintiff's parents filed suit in California civil court, naming Dr Moore, the campus police, and the University of California as defendants. The following causes of action were alleged:

1. The defendants failed to detain a dangerous patient.
2. The therapist failed to comply with his *duty to warn* others regarding a dangerous patient.

3. Dr Powelson abandoned a dangerous patient by failing to hospitalize him.
4. The defendants' conduct constituted a breach of duty to safeguard their patient and the public.

The case was dismissed on the trial level, and this dismissal was affirmed on appeal. The California Supreme Court rejected the first, third, and fourth causes of action, but reversed the appeals court on the second cause of action, the negligent failure to warn and protect Tatiana Tarasoff.

Justice Tobriner, writing for the majority, reviewed the plaintiff's complaint and the defendants' answers with respect to the four allegations. He determined that the complaint was essentially based on two grounds: (1) the defendants' failure to warn Ms Tarasoff of the impending damage, and (2) their failure to bring about Poddar's confinement pursuant to the Lanterman-Petris-Short Act. The defendants in turn argued that they owed no duty of reasonable care to Ms Tarasoff and that in any event they had immunity from this lawsuit under the California Tort Claims Act of 1963 (Gov Code SEC 810ff). Justice Tobriner, writing for the majority, concluded:

> The defendants cannot escape liability merely because Tatiana herself was not their patient. When a therapist determines, or pursuant to the standard of his profession should determine, that his patient presents a serious danger of violence to another, he incurs an obligation to use reasonable care to protect the intended victim against such danger. The discharge of this duty may require the therapist to take one or more various steps, depending upon the nature of the case. Thus, it may call for him to warn the intended victim or others likely to apprise the victim of the danger, to notify the police or to take whatever other steps are reasonably necessary under the circumstances.

The court stated that the most important factor in establishing a duty to warn is *foreseeability*, that is, a defendant owes a duty of care to all persons who are foreseeably endangered by his patient's conduct. The court recognized that the common law has traditionally imposed liability only if the defendant bears some special relationship to the dangerous person or the potential victim and concluded that in this case, the therapist-patient relationship satisfied the essence of this requirement. The court based this decision on the case of *Johnson v State of California*,[64] in which a suit against the state was upheld because the state failed to warn foster parents of the dangerous tendencies of their wards, and the case of *Merchants National Bank and Trust Co of Fargo v United States*,[65] in which the Veterans Administration arranged for a person to work on a local farm but did not inform the farmer about the man's psychiatric history. In this case the VA was found liable for the wrongful death of the farmer's wife after she was killed by the employee. The liability was found in spite of the fact that there had been no "special relationship" between the VA and the farmer's wife.

The *Tarasoff* court rejected the APA's amicus curiae which argued that therapists are unable to reliably predict their patients' violent acts. Instead, the court leaned heavily on the Fleming and Maximov doctrine in concluding that by entering into a doctor-patient relationship a therapist becomes sufficiently involved so as to assume some responsibility for the safety of not only the patient but also of any third person whom the doctor knows to be threatened by the patient.[66] The court stated that the public policy protecting the confidential character of patient-psychotherapist communications must yield to the extent to which disclosure is essential to avert danger to others, concluding, "the protection privilege ends where the public peril begins."

The dissent in *Tarasoff*, Justices Mosk and Clark, separately argued that psychiatrists do not possess a crystal ball previewing the future actions of their patients. They pointed out that a diagnosis of mental illness is not tantamount to a prediction of a patient's dangerousness. The dissent was further persuaded by the view that confidentiality is essential for effective treatment and that the imposition of a duty on doctors to disclose patient threats to potential victims would greatly impair treatment. The dissent's reading of previous court cases, the related literature, and amici briefs led them to conclude that the essence of successful psychotherapy is the patient's achievement of trust in the external world and, ultimately, in the self. This trust is itself modeled on and conditioned by a trusting relationship with the therapist which is established during treatment. If this trusting relationship cannot develop because of the potential for collusive communications between the psychiatrist and others, treatment will be thwarted.

Since the *Tarasoff* decision, the California state legislature has enacted into law a statute which has come to be known as the Tarasoff Bill. The bill fails to acknowledge whether or not a "duty to warn" exists but states that if such a duty does exist, then it arises only when a patient communicates to a therapist "a serious threat of physical violence against a reasonably identifiable victim or victims."[67] This statute limits recovery on the basis of a presumed duty to warn of situations which adhere very closely to the facts of *Tarasoff* itself. Other states have interpreted *Tarasoff* in much broader terms.

No Duty to Warn

In *Tarasoff* the defendants were held liable for failing to protect a specific individual from harm that might result from their patient's actions. The potential victim, Tatiana Tarasoff, was clearly identifiable by the therapist. What about a case, however, in which a threat is made and harm is imminent, but the potential victim cannot be identified? Courts throughout the nation have wrestled with this question and have arrived at different, sometimes contradictory, conclusions. A brief review and analysis of these rulings will help mental health professionals understand the safeguards which may be needed in any psychotherapeutic relationship.

A celebrated and dramatic illustration of how some courts have placed clear limits on the *Tarasoff* doctrine is found in *Brady et al v Hopper*,[68] heard in the US District Court in Colorado. James Scott Brady, the former press secretary to President Reagan, and others brought a multimillion dollar lawsuit against Dr John J. Hopper, the psychiatrist who had treated the would-be presidential assassin, John W. Hinckley, Jr. As a result of Hinckley's attempt on President Reagan's life in Washington, the plaintiffs in this case had sustained serious and debilitating injuries.

The plaintiffs alleged that Hinckley's father, John W. Hinckley, Sr, had sought to place his son in psychiatric treatment as a result of the latter's dangerous behavior (which included a drug overdose suicide attempt) and other emotional disturbances. The allegations further stated that Hopper had failed to discover through psychiatric interviews that his patient had serious emotional problems and could be dangerous. An autobiographical sketch that Hinckley wrote at Dr Hopper's behest on or about October 30, 1980 revealed that Hinckley suffered from anxiety attacks, that he felt his mind was on the "breaking point," that he was obsessed with actress Jodie Foster, and that he intended to study at Yale to be near Ms Foster. In addition, it made clear that he was preoccupied with the movie *Taxi Driver,* a film about a political assassination in which Ms Foster played a teenage prostitute. Hopper assumed that Hinckley had relatively minor problems and prescribed diazepam (Valium) and biofeedback as a course of treatment. In addition, he advised Hinckley's parents to encourage their son to be more independent in his financial and living situation.

Sometime in March of 1981 Hinckley left his parents' home and traveled from Denver, Colorado to Washington, DC. He arrived in Washington on March 29, 1981. The next morning he wrote a letter to Jodie Foster indicating that he would shoot President Reagan "as an historic act" to win her attention. Shortly afterward, Hinckley went to a Washington hotel with a loaded 22 caliber handgun and the following day, March 31, he shot President Reagan. In the course of the shooting, he shot and injured the plaintiffs.

According to the plaintiffs, the course of treatment prescribed by Hopper was not acceptable by the standards of the psychiatric profession. Hinckley was suffering from a psychiatric disorder in the schizophrenic spectrum, and had Hopper conducted a proper examination he would have learned that Hinckley had identified himself with the character Travis Bickle, the protagonist in *Taxi Driver*, who was a potential political assassin. Allegedly, Hopper knew or should have known that Hinckley posed a danger to himself and others and was capable of attempting a political assassination. The plaintiffs alleged that Hopper was negligent in his failure to warn law enforcement officials that Hinckley was a danger to himself and others. In addition, the plaintiffs alleged that Hopper had a duty to warn Hinckley's parents of the potentially dangerous situation of their child.

The defendant argued that if any duty existed under *Tarasoff* it was to President Reagan himself, such duty being obviated by the fact that the president had adequate secret service protection. In addition, the defendant argued that a duty to control the conduct of another for the protection of a third person is activated only if (1) a special relationship exists between the person supposedly in control and the person causing the injury, and (2) such relationship is attended by the *right* and the *ability* to control the conduct of the individual causing the harm. Hopper, it was argued, had no such right or ability. Finally, because Hinckley made no specific threats of harm directed against a reasonably identifiable person, no duty to control could exist.

The defendant concluded that weighing the risk, foreseeability, and likelihood that a voluntary outpatient with no history of violence would commit a violent act, balanced against the social utility of outpatient psychotherapy, the magnitude of imposing on psychotherapists a duty to control outpatients, and the consequences of imposing such a duty, led to the conclusion that no duty should be imposed on the defendant in this case. The defendant's request for a dismissal of the case was granted by the court.

The court in *Brady* refused to extend the Tarasoff doctrine to a setting in which there is no identifiable potential victim. In his opinion, presiding Justice Moore wrote: "The existence of a special relationship does not necessarily mean that the duties created by that relationship are owed to the world at large." The court concluded that "the plaintiffs' injuries were not foreseeable, therefore the plaintiffs fall outside of the scope of the defendant's duty." At the core of the *Brady* decision was the fact that no relationship existed between the defendant and the plaintiffs. One can only speculate how Brady would have been decided if Jodie Foster or John Hinckley's parents had brought suit against Hopper. The importance of *Brady* lies in the simple fact that the court refused to extend a psychotherapist's duty to warn persons unidentified by the patient or unidentifiable to the psychotherapist prior to the injurious act.

A number of courts have, along the lines of *Brady*, restricted the scope of the Tarasoff doctrine. In fact, throughout the nation a majority of lawsuits brought under the duty to warn doctrine have been rejected by the courts for a variety of reasons.[69]

In *Thompson v County of Alameda*,[70] James F., a delinquent child with a history of violent behavior, was released from the custody of Alameda County to his mother. Prior to his release, James F. had indicated that, if freed, he would kill a young child in his neighborhood. James, however, did not identify which child he would kill. After his release he did kill a 5-year-old girl in the neighborhood in which he and his mother lived. The parents of the victim brought suit against the county, alleging that it had acted recklessly in releasing a juvenile delinquent to the home of his mother despite knowledge that the delinquent boy had violent propensities toward young children. The plaintiffs also alleged that the county failed to advise or warn local police and the parents of young children near the residence of James F. The plaintiffs made explicit reference to the *Tarasoff* decision in their request for indemnification.

The court in *Thompson* rejected the plaintiff's allegations, stating that there is "no affirmative duty to warn of the release of an inmate with a violent history who has made non-specific threats of harm directed at non-specific victims." In contrasting this case with *Tarasoff*, the court concluded that "for policy reasons the duty to warn depends on and arises from the existence of a prior threat to a specific identifiable victim."

This policy was underlined in another California case, *People v Murtishaw*,[71] in which Justice Tobriner, who wrote the majority opinion in *Tarasoff*, commented once more that only if a victim is identifiable does a psychotherapist owe a duty to exercise reasonable care to avert the potential danger. In *Mavroudis v Superior Court of the County of San Mateo*,[72] the court again cautioned against construing the *Tarasoff* decision too broadly. In *Mavroudis*, the parents of a youth brought suit after having been attacked by their son who had undergone treatment for a psychiatric disorder. Here, the court placed weight on the privacy of the doctor-patient relationship and commented that if the patient does not pose an imminent threat to an identifiable victim, then disclosures about the patient are not required. In *Leedy v Hartnett*,[73] a Pennsylvania court echoed the sentiments of the California decisions, stating that the liability of psychotherapists must be kept within workable limits and that those charged with the care of potentially dangerous people must be able to know exactly when they are required to give warnings. The duty does not apply to the public at large.

In the author's view, mental health professionals and the institutions they serve can accept and even welcome the *Tarasoff* decision and subsequent decisions limiting the duty to warn to identifiable victims. These cases require psychotherapists neither to forecast the future nor to surrender vital aspects of their therapeutic endeavor. Inconsistency seems to be the current trend regarding this issue, however, and the influence of the original Tarasoff doctrine is waning. Cases maintaining the Tarasoff standard will be examined in this subsection, and cases extending it in the next.

In *Hinkelman v Borgess Medical Center*,[74] the Michigan appeals court affirmed the dismissal of a wrongful death action against a psychiatric hospital for allegedly failing to warn a third party of the danger presented by a voluntary patient. The patient signed out of the hospital his first day, but readmitted himself the next day. He was given antipsychotic medication and a social worker reported that he was unstable, violent, and resistant to authority. The patient surreptitiously left the hospital. Three weeks later, he shot his girlfriend and then himself.

A lawsuit was brought by the victim's family. The court found that there was no special relationship between the hospital and the patient to support imposing a duty to protect the victim. First, the patient was not in the hospital for any appreciable length of time. Second, the hospital was not afforded sufficient time to evaluate and treat the patient. Third, the hospital was not an agent of a psychiatrist who had a physician-patient relationship with the patient. Fourth, the victim was aware of the danger posed by the patient since she previously was attacked by him. The court found also that the hospital did not have a legal duty to keep the patient hospitalized. The patient was allowed to terminate his hospitalization, and the hospital did not possess the ability to control the patient's conduct.

In another case similar to *Hinkelman*, a South Carolina appeals court affirmed the dismissal of a wrongful death action brought against the Department of Mental Health.[75] In this case, a patient voluntarily admitted himself to a state psychiatric facility where he was treated and released. Three months later he shot and killed a man living next to him in a trailer park, after asking the neighbor to keep quiet because he had a headache.

The court found no reason to assert the patient's physician's duty to warn third persons that the patient was dangerous. There was no identifiable threat to the victim since he had not moved into the trailer park until after the patient was discharged, and there was no indication that the victim knew the patient prior to his discharge. The court also rejected the argument that expert scientific testimony was not needed to find the defendants negligent. As the court expressed it, the proper treatment of a mental patient and the standard of care required in discharge decisions were not matters of common knowledge to most laymen.

The *Hinkelman* and *Sharpe* decisions retain *Tarasoff*'s sensible limits for therapist and institutional liability. However, a much more distressing set of rulings imposing stricter liability on therapists for the acts of their violent patients have appeared in several jurisdictions. These decisions, we believe, threaten the practice of psychotherapy in ways that the earliest commentators on *Tarasoff* feared.

Duty to Warn

Lipari v Sears[76] represents a landmark extension of the Tarasoff doctrine to include all potential victims of a psychiatric patient, even when the patient is not perceived to be dangerous by his therapist and even where the patient's potential victims are unknown to the treating therapist and even to the patient himself. The facts of *Lipari* can be summarized as follows.

> Ulysses Cribbs was under psychiatric care at the day treatment center of the Omaha, Nebraska, Veterans Administration Hospital. The psychiatric records at the VA hospital indicated that Mr Cribbs exhibited no signs of dangerousness and that he had never threatened anyone. In September 1977, while he was still in treatment, he purchased a shotgun at Sears, Roebuck & Co. He did not report to anyone at the VA, however, that he had the gun. Three weeks after purchasing the shotgun he terminated his treatment at the VA against medical advice and 6 weeks later he fired the gun into a crowded nightclub, blinding a woman and killing her husband. The woman sued Sears, alleging that it was negligent in selling a shotgun to a mentally ill individual. Sears in turn filed an action against the VA hospital and Cribbs's therapists, arguing that the VA should reimburse Sears for part or all of any potential liability. Sears alleged that the hospital should have determined that Cribbs was dangerous and

therefore ought to be involuntarily committed. The plaintiff, meanwhile, also filed a similar suit against the VA.

The court allowed the suit, contending that under Nebraska law the relationship between psychotherapists and their patients gives rise to an affirmative duty for the benefit of third persons. This duty requires that therapists initiate whatever precautions are necessary to protect potential victims from their patients. "This duty arises only when in accordance with the standards of his profession, the therapist knows or *should know* that the patient's dangerous propensities present an unreasonable risk of harm to others." The *Lipari* court rejected the *Tarasoff* limitation that the duty to a third person should be limited to identifiable persons. The court essentially imposed a duty on therapists to *predict dangerousness in general terms* and to protect society at large from all "dangerous" individuals whom they have occasion to treat.

In *Petersen v Washington*,[77] a defendant was held liable for injuries resulting from a car crash to a party who was unknown to either patient or therapist. *Petersen* illustrates the extent to which courts can impose a duty to protect the public at large from the acts of mentally ill persons. In this case, a convict, Larry Knox, with a long history of drug abuse and antisocial behavior, drove his car past a red light and collided with another vehicle containing the plaintiff, Mrs Cynthia Petersen. Knox had been on probation after a conviction for burglary and two of the conditions of his probation were abstinence from controlled substances and participation in mental health counseling.

On April 16, 1979, some time before the collision, Knox, while intoxicated with "angel dust" (phencyclidine hydrochloride, PCP) cut off one of his own testicles with a knife. After emergency medical care he was sent to a state psychiatric facility where he was treated, temporarily committed, and eventually discharged. His treatment team had concluded that Knox's condition was in remission and that no further hospitalization was indicated. A few days after his discharge, he again became intoxicated with PCP, resulting in his reckless driving and the injury to Mrs Petersen.

Mrs Petersen sued the state of Washington and ten hospital staff members. She alleged that their treatment of Knox was negligent and his discharge improper, and that these derelictions were the proximate cause of her injuries. She additionally alleged that the state was negligent in failing to seek additional hospital or penal confinement of Knox due to his violation of probation.

A jury returned a verdict for the plaintiff. The state of Washington appealed on three grounds: (1) that the state owed no duty toward the plaintiff; (2) that the actions of the hospital were not the proximate cause of the plaintiff's injuries; and (3) that the state was immune from lawsuits of this kind. The higher court affirmed the verdict in favor of the plaintiff, using both *Lipari v Sears* and *Tarasoff*. It concluded that the treating physicians were under a positive duty to protect anyone who might foreseeably be endangered by Knox's drug-related mental problems.

It should be noted that the duty imposed by the *Lipari* and *Petersen* courts is very different from the "duty to warn and protect" imposed in *Tarasoff*. In *Tarasoff*, the court did not require therapists to make a scientific determination of the dangerousness of each of their patients, but rather to assess the seriousness of a specific threat to a specific individual. Thus, while the *Lipari* court required therapists to do precisely what the APA has said they cannot do, that is, predict dangerousness, the *Tarasoff* court imposed a much more limited duty: to warn potential victims and/or law enforcement authorities about a specific threat on a specific individual's life. The limitations of this duty are made clear, as discussed above, by the Tarasoff bill passed by the California state legislature. The duty under *Tarasoff* is different from that imposed in *Lipari* and *Petersen*, from both scientific and legal perspectives. Scientifically, the *Tarasoff* court is hardly asking the therapist to make a scientific judgment. Rather, the *Tarasoff* doctrine can best be construed as common sense, simply requiring a therapist to report a specific threat which he believes is serious. Legally, while *Lipari* and similar decisions require therapists to take action simply because of a patient's status ("dangerous"), which is not after all a crime, *Tarasoff* imposes a duty to report, in a limited instance, a specific action (threatening an individual's life) which in many jurisdictions is a crime.

Reid, in his analysis of the *Lipari* decision, argued that *on the facts* the case against the therapist in *Lipari* was totally without merit.[78] Nevertheless, because this and most similar cases, including *Tarasoff*, were settled out of court, we can never know for certain how a jury would have decided these issues. In *Lipari*, the defendant's attorney did not want to risk placing a blind widow with six children before a jury and thus Sears and the VA settled the case for more than $200,000. According to Reid, the practice of psychiatry is undermined when courts allow suits such as *Lipari* to proceed.

New Jersey, like Nebraska, has extended the duty to warn doctrine in a manner creating enormous limitations on the therapist-patient relationship. In *McIntosh v Milano*,[79] a young woman was killed by a man who had been in therapy with a psychiatrist for a period of 2 years. In the therapeutic sessions the patient had expressed intense feelings of jealousy regarding his girlfriend, the eventual victim, and her new boyfriend. In addition, he confided to his psychiatrist that on one occasion he had fired a BB gun at an automobile allegedly belonging to his ex-girlfriend. A review of the therapeutic records and the testimony revealed no indication that the patient either was dangerous or had threatened anyone. The plaintiffs, the victim's parents, argued in court that the defendant-psychiatrist should have known of the danger that his patient posed to their daughter and that he should have warned her or the authorities of this danger. The court agreed with the plaintiffs and asserted that psychiatrists have a duty to take reasonable steps to protect an intended or potential victim of a patient if it is, or should have been, determined that the patient may present a danger to that person or, more broadly, to the entire community.

The *McIntosh* court went beyond *Tarasoff* not only in its extension of the psychotherapist's duty to include the "welfare of the community," but in its conclusion that the duty to warn exists in instances where therapists "should have known" that their patients are dangerous. Unlike *Tarasoff*, where the main question was whether the therapist should violate confidentiality to *report a threat*, the issue in *McIntosh*, as with *Petersen*, becomes the therapist's duty to *predict and warn* about impending violence. It is almost as if the court reasoned that a lawsuit could be brought against a scientist who failed to predict, but allegedly should have predicted, an imminent earthquake. All the arguments supporting the impossibility of accurately predicting violence, although they did not synchronize with the facts in *Tarasoff*, are very much of the essence in *McIntosh*. Therapists who felt obliged to warn under the *McIntosh* doctrine could hardly treat emotionally disturbed or intensely angry patients without having to invoke the duty to warn, lest it later be determined that they should have predicted a violent act!

The *McIntosh* court compared the obligation of a physician to report certain medical conditions, such as venereal diseases, tuberculosis, and gunshot wounds, with its requirement that therapists warn about future violence. The comparison is imprecise because the physicians' obligation is to report the disease after it has developed, not to report behavior where it is possible or likely to effect transmission. The *McIntosh* court implies that there is a clear, definable condition called "being violent," and would place on the psychiatric profession a duty which our courts have consistently refused to place on themselves, that of labeling and effectively detaining individuals who have a certain "status" but who have neither committed nor even threatened to commit a specific crime. Such a "duty" not only rests on inadequate scientific understanding but threatens to undermine fundamental civil liberties as well.

Good Faith Test

Moves have been made to limit therapists' liability to narrowly defined situations in which the threat of harm to identifiable victims is present. For example, in *Currie v US*,[80] the federal court in North Carolina upheld the general idea of a duty to warn, but strictly limited that duty by employing a good faith test for determining liability.

Leonard Avery, a Vietnam veteran and employee of International Business Machines, had been in treatment at the VA medical center since April of 1981 for "rage attacks," which had caused him to miss work and even to discharge a gun. He was diagnosed as suffering from posttraumatic stress disorder, and was treated by a combination of group therapy, individual therapy, and medication. In October of 1981, Avery requested an emergency meeting with his therapist because of increasing agitation toward his former wife and anyone who would try to take away his "property." Avery agreed to a voluntary hospitalization after a telephone conversation with his attorney and his ex-wife. He calmed down and requested discharge, which was granted on the day after admission. Avery continued to have increasingly serious problems at work, but his absences were excused by IBM since he was attending the weekly group sessions at the VA hospital. Avery's therapist maintained close contact with the IBM medical department.

Avery's behavior appeared to deteriorate, his attendance at the group sessions dropped, and eventually he got into more conflicts with his employer. At one point he threatened to blow up the IBM medical facility. The IBM staff contacted the VA center, and the VA physicians advised them to take the threats seriously and contact the appropriate law enforcement officials. Soon thereafter, a VA psychiatrist contacted Avery, who agreed to admit himself voluntarily but then never followed through. As a result, IBM fired Avery. When his psychiatrist refused to write another excuse, Avery responded, "It is too late. You will read about it in the paper." The psychiatrist immediately warned IBM of the threat, but after discussing the possibility of initiating commitment with two VA staff psychiatrists, the therapist concurred with them that commitment was legally inappropriate.

When Avery failed to appear at the next group meeting, the VA psychiatric staff again discussed options. They concluded that Avery had threatened his therapists, who had notified IBM, the local police, and the FBI. But these officials had agreed that no police action could be taken. The staff also concluded that Avery was dangerous but not mentally ill within their interpretation of the statutes. Later the same day Avery went to IBM armed with a semiautomatic assault rifle and launched a full-scale attack, causing the death of Ralph Glenn. Avery was found to be sane by the trial court and was convicted of murder. The plaintiff, Ralph Glenn's wife, brought suit in federal court against the VA for negligence in not initiating commitment. The defense moved for summary judgment and dismissal of the suit.

The court found that the therapist had an affirmative duty to warn foreseeable third parties and rejected the defendant's distinction that the ultimate victim in the case had not been readily identifiable. The court also rejected the defendant's argument that there had been no duty to commit. This decision agreed with the federal court decision in *Lipari*, that to rule otherwise would allow a therapist to act in careless disregard of members of the public. The court noted also, however, that the judiciary system is not particularly qualified to review commitment decisions involving mental health and dangerousness. Such decisions require quick action; thus "after the fact, litigation is a most imperfect device to evaluate those decisions."

Further utilizing what is termed a "psychotherapist judgment" rule, the court would not allow liability to be imposed on therapists for simple errors in judgment, examining instead the good faith, independence, and thoroughness of decisions not to commit. The court then determined that the defendants had exercised reasonable professional judgment by repeatedly urging Avery to admit himself for treatment, by holding a series of staff conferences about Avery's threats, by warning IBM, and by notifying all appropriate law enforcement officers. The fact that they had been threatened along with IBM and had assumed significant personal risk by deciding not to initiate commitment demonstrates good faith. Thus, since the defendants had met their duty under the professional judgment rule, no material issue remained for the jury. The court granted defendant's motion for summary judgment. Law commentator R. D. Miller[81] has noted that the *Currie* court used the same rationale that the US Supreme Court used in *Parham v J.L. and J.R.*,[82] which advocated deference to professional judgment in clinical issues.

Punishment of Therapists

It seems that the courts have used the "duty to warn" concept to punish therapists in some instances for other's negligence or to compensate a particularly sympathetic victim or victim's family. In *Davis v Lhim*,[83] a patient was discharged from a state hospital in Michigan and 2 months later shot and killed his mother. The patient did not have a history of violence, but the expert witness for the plaintiff characterized him as "violence prone." The only concrete evidence for the plaintiff's case was a note written 2 years earlier in an emergency room indicating that the patient had threatened his mother. The court bent and distorted the Tarasoff doctrine to find that if the psychiatrist-defendant had only read the 2-year-old records he would have determined that the mother was an identifiable victim. The court found the psychiatrist negligent for failing to read the previous record.

In *Jablonski v US*,[84] a psychiatrist was again punished for failing to read a previous hospital record. In this case a patient, Mr Jablonski, killed his common-law wife, Mrs Kimball. Prior to the murder, Jablonski had been evaluated in an emergency room of a VA hospital in California, and the police did report to the psychiatrist on call that the patient was dangerous and had a history of crime. The psychiatrist on call did not commit the patient but suggested to Mrs Kimball that she keep away from him. Several days later, Mrs Kimball went to Jablonski's apartment and he killed her.

The district court judge found the hospital and the psychiatrist negligent for (1) failing to take the police recommendations into consideration; (2) failing to acquire past medical records; and (3) failing to *adequately* warn Mrs Kimball. The Ninth Circuit court affirmed liability on each of the three grounds.[85]

Not only can a third party bring a lawsuit against a psychiatrist, but sometimes the patient who committed the murder may hold his psychiatrist liable for emotional injury, as illustrated in *Swofford v Cooper*.[86] The patient, Swofford, with a long history of psychiatric illness, was committed to a state hospital because of homicidal ideation and threats to kill his family. After 11 months of hospitalization and treatment, the psychiatrist approved a therapeutic pass for the patient. The patient went home and fatally stabbed his father.

Three malpractice suits were brought against the psychiatrist: (1) the patient's mother alleged malpractice for the wrongful death of her husband; (2) she also sued on behalf of her deceased husband's estate for his pain and suffering prior to his death and for her own pain and suffering; and (3) the patient brought suit for his own pain and emotional suffering arising from his murder of his father and for expenses incurred in the criminal matters stemming from the stabbing. The patient further alleged that the psychiatrist was negligent in providing him with a therapeutic pass.

The psychiatrist argued that she was not liable because the stabbing was unforeseeable. The court sided with the patient, however, ruling that the issue was not whether the psychiatrist should have been able to anticipate the exact consequences, but that she should have foreseen that some kind of injury would result from her act or commission, (ie, approving the pass). Further, the court of appeals found that the patient could not be held as contributorily negligent, since the patient was psychotic when he stabbed his father. He was declared incompetent to stand trial. This ruling contains the unmistakable inference that the court virtually rewarded the patient for guilt originating in his slaying of his father, and punished the psychiatrist. In effect, the psychiatrist was in the wrong place at the wrong time. The description of exactly what constituted the negligence is so vague that determining its reasonableness is impossible. But it is conveniently malleable for use by a broad range of plaintiffs. If the psychodynamic arising from a patient's guilt for a reprehensible act ends in the patient's psychiatrist being liable for every party's suffering because the psychiatrist did not foresee or prevent the patient's acts, any psychiatrist is fair game. This standard of liability is "one size fits all." The number of such lawsuits will skyrocket. Furthermore, the effects on society of releasing from responsibility both criminals and those who have known and observed them for years, will, to say the least, be unfortunate.

Duty to Protect Property

There almost seems no limit to how far the Tarasoff doctrine will be stretched, and where the responsibility of therapists toward potential victims will end. According to some, a therapist has a duty to protect property as well as protect against personal injury. *Peck v Counseling Service of Addison County, Inc*[87] is an example. In this case, the plaintiffs' son set fire to their barn while the son was an outpatient receiving treatment from the defendant counseling service. While under therapy, the son confided to his therapist that he was angry with his father and wanted to get back at him by burning his barn. The therapist elicited a promise from the son that he would not burn down the barn, and believing the son would keep his promise, did not warn anyone of the threats. The son did not keep his promise and destroyed the barn by burning it to the ground.

The plaintiffs sued the counseling service for damages citing negligence in failing to take reasonable steps to protect the plaintiffs and claiming professional malpractice. The trial court dismissed the case because it found that there was no duty on the part of the defendants to take action to protect plaintiffs under Vermont law.

The case was appealed to the Vermont Supreme Court. This highest court in Vermont quoted from *Tarasoff* and concluded that whether or not there is actual control over an outpatient in a mental health clinic setting similar to that exercised over institutionalized patients, the relationship between a clinical therapist and his patient is sufficient to create a duty to exercise reasonable care to protect a potential victim of another's conduct. The high court rejected the argument that this duty should not be imposed on therapists because they have no advantage over anyone else in predicting future violent behavior. The court said that while this fact may be persuasive in some instances, it "does not justify barring recovery in all situations." Further, the high court noted that the plaintiffs' psychiatric experts testified that given the patient's history of impulsive, assaultive behavior, epilepsy, the possibility of a brain disorder, and alcohol abuse, the failure to reveal the patient's threats was inconsistent with the standards of the mental health profession. Moreover, the therapist did not have the patient's most recent medical history at the time of the threat, nor did the counseling service have a method of cross-referencing with outside physicians who were treating one of their patients. Even the defendant's own expert admitted that a therapist cannot make a reasonable determination of a patient's propensity for carrying out a threat without a complete medical history. Finally, the physician-patient privilege does not excuse the therapist's behavior because the privilege is not sacrosanct and can properly be waived in the interest of public policy under appropriate circumstances such as threat to an identified victim. Since a lethal threat existed for any human being in the vicinity of the conflagration, even though no death or injury in fact resulted, it was negligent not to have warned the parents.

Commentators have noticed that the *Peck* court has divided the new precedent into three elements, all of which carry possible consequences for providers of mental health care. First, the decision imposes the *Tarasoff* duty on all mental health professionals. Second, it demonstrates a legal scenario that in effect permits a single standard of care to be applied for all mental health professionals. Third, it creates liability for property damage as well as for personal injury.[88]

Analytic View

Since *Tarasoff*, courts in various states have responded to the duty to warn concept in one of two ways: either by holding close to the original Tarasoff doctrine and limiting its range of applicability (as in *Brady* and similar cases) or by broadening it to include unidentifiable potential victims of patients who have neither intimated nor threatened a violent act (as in *Lipari*). The author believes that while the original Tarasoff doctrine is sound both from the perspective of public policy and the perspective of psychotherapeutic practice (and that it does not violate the Hippocratic oath), the extensions found in cases such as *Lipari*, *Petersen*, and *McIntosh* as well as *Davis* and *Jablonski* are very problematic when viewed from either point of view.

From the perspective of clinical practice the objections to the duty to warn concept fall into three basic categories. Each of these objections helps to demonstrate that the very enterprise of psychotherapy is threatened by the duty to warn doctrine. While none of these objections is effective against the original Tarasoff doctrine, they are each sound when placed against the facts and implications of the *Lipari*-type cases.

The first objection is that mental health professionals have no reliable means for predicting that a given individual will perform a dangerous or violent act. Since psychotherapists cannot predict dangerousness with any degree of certainty, a duty to warn about dangerousness would place therapists in the position of having to report numerous "false-positives" to ensure that they would not miss reporting anyone who would ultimately commit a violent act. For many therapists this would mean reporting a significant number or even a majority of patients in their practice. In effect, this would turn psychotherapists from confidential consultants into law enforcement agents. Anyone electing to undergo psychotherapy would be submitting to an indirect form of police surveillance. This objection is applicable to *Lipari* and similar cases but not to *Tarasoff* and *Brady*. As indicated, the duty to warn concept in *Tarasoff* does not involve a crystal ball assessment of the future but rather an evaluation of what a patient has already said. While the potential for false-positives still exists (an individual could make a direct threat that is not really serious), the range of false-positives is far smaller and the consequences of reporting them far less grave. In fact, patients who make idle threats on other peoples' lives probably should suffer serious consequences, and therapists who occasionally report these threats to the police do not do their patients a disservice.

A second objection to the duty to warn, noted, for example, by the dissent in *Tarasoff*, is that the success of psychotherapy is based on the trust that evolves between patient and therapist and that this trust is itself predicated upon strict confidentiality between patient and therapist. While trust is an essential component of psychotherapeutic treatment, and such trust would be impaired by the abundance of collusive communications required under *Lipari*, the requirements of *Tarasoff* do not impair this trust, but can actually serve to enhance it. The trust that patients have for their therapists should involve not only a belief that the therapist will not breach their confidence, but also faith that the therapist cares enough about them to take measures to prevent them from causing themselves serious harm. Therapists must strike a balance between a commitment to foster patients' independence and a commitment to foster their responsibility and health. The issue arises whenever a patient threatens suicide. There is every reason for it to apply when a patient threatens murder as well. Certainly, incalculable harm can come to any person who commits murder. Therapists who report a threat of murder, far from showing their patient that they cannot be trusted, are presenting a very different message, a message that they care enough about their patient to set limits on the patient's self-destructive behavior and demand that the patient act responsibly toward the rights, and particularly the *lives*, of others.

A third objection to the duty to warn is that such a duty, if it became generally known or known to particular patients, would serve as a disincentive to patients discussing important psychotherapeutic material, specifically material involving their violent fantasies toward others. This disincentive, it is argued, would not only adversely affect the treatment of many potentially violent patients, but would actually also work against their potential victims who might otherwise have been protected as a result of patients' psychotherapeutic disclosures and working through of violent fantasies and intentions. The potential victims would be protected by the patients' having attained enough mental health not to inflict violence on others. At this point it is an open empirical question whether the duty to warn has or will have a chilling effect on potentially violent patients' self-disclosures in therapy. What seems quite clear, however, is that under the *Lipari* doctrine such an effect would be far greater, for patients would fear that not only their specifically communicated intentions but all of their interactions with their therapists could serve as grounds for a breach of confidentiality.

Individuals with violent or murderous intentions who subject themselves to therapy do so because of an ambivalence about the intentions themselves. Most often they have fantasies that their therapist will somehow prevent them from any act they feel they may commit. In telling patients that their confidentiality is assured unless there is an immediate threat to human life, our experience has generally been a positive one. Most patients, even those who have a history of violence, accept the limitation, many stating that they would assume and expect this to be the case. For those who balk at treatment under such conditions, a thorough discussion about the nature of the therapeutic relationship and the mutual responsibilities it entails frequently ensues. Indeed, such discussions have, in our experience, led to fruitful explorations concerning the patients' ambivalence about violence at a relatively early stage in the treatment.

The Tarasoff doctrine in its more restricted form does not mean that the reporting of a patient's dangerous intentions is an easy task. There are borderline situations that can arise under this "strict interpretation." To take one example, a patient who was manic in remission, but actively alcoholic, repeated that he was furious at his manager in the bank where he worked and that "sooner or later" he would shoot everyone in the bank. He repeated these threats on two occasions in psychotherapy sessions. Motivated by the Tarasoff doctrine but not completely sure that it applied to this case (was the threat really serious and really specific?) the psychiatrist called the bank manager and advised him not to aggravate this employee. The bank manager, who was aware of the patient's alcoholism but had no knowledge of the patient's manic disorder, took what he later called "appropriate action" in terminating the patient's employment. The psychiatrist reported his conversation with the bank manager to the patient who was infuriated and blamed the therapist for the loss of his job. Ultimately, the patient's feelings were worked through and he came to the realization that the psychiatrist's actions probably averted disaster.

This case illuminates several of the difficulties involved in applying the Tarasoff interpretation of duty. On the one hand it can be questioned whether the psychiatrist's warning in this case was sufficient, while on the other hand it could be argued that any warning under these circumstances constituted an unwarranted breach and that the therapist should be held liable for the patient's damages (loss of job) had the latter chosen to file suit. It is of note that in a New York case in which the patient sued his physician for breach of confidentiality, *McDonald v Clinger*,[89] the appellate court concluded that disclosure of confidential material about a patient will be justified if that patient poses a danger to others.

Beck has observed that most therapists do not distinguish potential from actual liability and they are not aware that liability is rarely found.[90] Many therapists are uncertain about the distinction between a duty to assess violence according to standards of reasonable care, and a duty to predict violence accurately, which they cannot do. According to Beck, liability should be limited to cases in which either the clinician fails to make a reasonable assessment or, having elicited a threat to a named victim, fails to act responsibly to protect the potential victim. Because an assessment of a patient's potential for violence requires professional judgment, malpractice rather than simple negligence is the appropriate standard for determining liability.

Psychotherapists can best function under a three-tiered conception of disclosure concerning potentially violent patients. The first tier would consist of all disclosures that are based on the therapist's judgment without a basis in the patient's word or deed. Such disclosures should be regarded as unnecessary and unjustified, and psychotherapists who make them would be liable for resulting damages incurred by their patients. The second tier would consist of disclosures that are at most partly prompted by a patient's threats, but where it is not clear that the threats are serious or specific enough to meet the strict standard of the Tarasoff doctrine. Such disclosures would be justified but not necessary and psychotherapists who made them or failed to make them would be liable to no one. The final tier would consist of disclosures that are serious and specific and thus clearly meet the Tarasoff criteria. Here a psychotherapist would be liable to no one for making the disclosure but liable to a potential victim for failing to do so. Such a system would leave the doubtful cases to the psychotherapist's discretion while clearly mandating behavior in clear-cut situations. Such a window of discretion makes sense both clinically and legally in a context where fine distinctions and judgments are hard to make and where genuine uncertainty exists. However, until such time as courts in the various states agree upon the duty to warn concept, therapists must take cognizance of decisions within the jurisdictions in which they practice and gauge their behavior accordingly.

REFERENCES

1. American Psychiatric Association: *The Principles of Medical Ethics with Annotations Especially Applicable to Psychiatry.* Washington DC, American Psychiatric Association, 1985.
2. *Jane Doe v Joan Roe and Peter Roe* 1977; 400 NY Supp2d 668.
3. *Alexander v Knight* 1962; 197 Pa Super 79, 177 A2d 142.
4. *Horne v Patton* 1974; 287 So2d 824.
5. *Eagles v Liberty Weekly* 1930; 244 NYS 430.
6. American Psychiatric Association: Official actions, guidelines on confidentiality. *Am J Psychiatry* 1987;144:1522–1526.
7. *In re Lifschutz* 1970; 467 P2d 557.
8. Taranto RG: *Commonwealth v Kobrin*: Massachusetts Psychiatric Society amicus brief *Newsletter Am Acad Psychiatry Law* 1985;10:11–12.
9. *Massachusetts v Kobrin* 1985; 479 NE2d 674.
10. *Schloendorff v Society of New York Hospital* 1914; 211 NY 125, 105 NE 92.
11. Freud S: On beginning the treatment, in *Standard Edition of the Complete Psychological Works of Sigmund Freud.* London, Hogarth Press, 1958.
12. *Canterbury v Spence* 1972; 464 D2d 722.
13. *Harnish v Children's Hospital* 1982; 387 Mass 152.
14. Freishtat HW: Informed consent: how little is too little? *J Clin Psychopharmacol* 1986;6:110–111.
15. *Campbell v Pitt County Hospital* 1987; 352 SE2d 902 (NC Ct App).
16. *Clites v Iowa* 1982; 322 NW2d 917 (Iowa Ct App).
17. *Superintendent of Belchertown State School v Saikewicz* 1977; 370 NE2d 417.
18. *In re Quinlan* 1976; 70 NJ 10, 355 A2d 647.
19. *Fraiser v Dept of Health and Human Resources* 1986; 500 So2d 858 (La Ct App).
20. Zeichner B: The role of unconscious conflict in informed consent. *Bull Am Acad Psychiatry Law* 1985;13:283–290.
21. Mills MJ, et al: Informed consent: psychotic patients and research. *Bull Am Acad Psychiatry Law* 1980;8:119–132.
22. Marder SR, et al: A comparison of patients who refuse and consent to neuroleptic treatment. *Am J Psychiatry* 1983;140:470–472.
23. Leonard SR, et al: Genetic counseling, a consumer's view. *N Engl J Med* 1979;287:433–439.
24. Irwin M, et al: Psychotic patients' understanding of informed consent. *Am J Psychiatry* 1985;142:1351–1354.
25. Jaffe R: Problems of long term informed consent. *Bull Am Acad Psychiatry Law* 1986;14:163–169.
26. Braff DL et al: Very short term memory dsyfunction in schizophrenia. *Arch Gen Psychiatry* 1977;34:25–30.
27. Chaucer G: *The Canterbury Tales.*
28. Shakespeare W: *Romeo and Juliet.* New York, The New American Library, 1963.
29. Gralnick A: Is suicide a cause of death? *Am J Soc Psychiatry* 1985;5:24–28.
30. Fawcett J, et al: Clinical predictors of suicide in patients with major affective disorders: a controlled prospective study. *Am J Psychiatry* 1987;144:35–40.

50

31. Freud S: Mourning and melancholia, in *Collected Papers*. London, Hogarth Press, 1950, vol 4.
32. Beck AT, et al: Hopelessness and eventual suicide: a 10-year prospective study of patients hospitalized with suicidal ideation. *Am J Psychiatry* 1985;142:559–563.
33. Roose SP, et al: Depression, delusions and suicide. *Am J Psychiatry* 1983; 140:1159–1162.
34. Phillips DP: The effect of mass media violence on suicide and homicide. *Newsletter Am Acad Psychiatry Law* 1986;11:29–31.
35. Resnik HL: Suicide, in Kaplan HI, Freedman AM, Sadock BJ (eds): *Comprehensive Textbook of Psychiatry*, ed 3. Baltimore, Williams & Wilkins, 1980, pp 2085–2098.
36. Drukteinis AM: Psychiatric perspectives on civil liability for suicide. *Bull Am Acad Psychiatry Law* 1985;13:71–83.
37. Perr IN: Suicide litigation and risk management: a review of 32 cases. *Bull Am Acad Psychiatry Law* 1985;13:209–219.
38. *Kent v Whitaker* 1961; 58 Wash2d 569, 364 P2d 556.
39. *Honey v Barnes Hospital* 1986; 708 SW2d 686 (Mo App).
40. *North Miami General Hospital v Krakower* 1981; 93 So2d 57 (Fla App).
41. *Cowan v Doering* 1987; 522 A2d 444 (NJ Super Ct App Div).
42. *Bell v New York City Health and Hospitals Corporation* 1982; 456 NYS2d 787 (NY App Div).
43. Smith J: *Psychiatric Malpractice*. Federal Publications, 1983.
44. *Brand v Grubin* 1974; 329A (2d) B2 Super Court of NJ.
45. *Stepakoff v Kantar* 1985; 473 NE2d 1131 (Mass Sup Jud Ct).
46. Chemtob CM: Patients' suicides: frequency and impact on psychiatrists. *Am J Psychiatry* 1988;145:224–228.
47. American Psychiatric Association: *The Principles of Medical Ethics, with Annotations Especially Applicable to Psychiatry*. Washington, DC, American Psychiatric Press, 1985.
48. Kardener SH, Fuller M, Mensh IN: A survey of physicians' attitudes and practices regarding erotic and nonerotic contact with patients. *Am J Psychiatry* 1973; 130:1077–1081.
49. Holroy J C, Brodsky AM: Psychologists attitudes and practices regarding erotic and nonerotic physical contact with patients. *Am Psychol* 1977;32:843–849.
50. Gartrell N, et al: Psychiatrist-patient sexual contact: results of a national survey, I: prevalence. *Am J Psychiatry* 1986;143:1126–1131.
51. Gartrell N, et al: Reporting practices of psychiatrists who knew of sexual misconduct by colleagues. *A J Orthopsychiatry* 1987;57:287–295.
52. Herman JL, et al: Psychiatrist-patient sexual contact: results of a national survey, II: psychiatrists' attitudes. *Am J Psychiatry* 1987;144:164–167.
53. Bouhoutsos J, et al: Sexual intimacy between psychotherapists and patients. *Prof Psychol* 1983;14:185–196.
54. Masters WH, Johnson VG: *Human Sexual Inadequacy*. Boston, Little, Brown, 1970.
55. Stone AA: Sexual misconduct by psychiatrists: the ethical and clinical dilemma of confidentiality. *Am J Psychiatry* 1983;140:196–197.
56. Stone AA: *Law, Psychiatry and Morality*. Washington, DC, American Psychiatric Press, 1984.
57. *Roy v Hartogs* 1975; 366 NYS 297, 300–301.
58. *Zipkin v Freeman* 1969; 436 SW2d 793.
59. *Mazza v Huffaker* 1983; 300 SE2d 833 (NC).
60. Simon R: *Mazza v Huffaker. Newsletter Am Acad Psychiatry Law* 1985;10:14–16.

61. Claman JM: Mirror hunger in the psychodynamics of sexually abusing therapists. *A J Psychoanal* 1987;47:35–40.
62. Searles HF: Oedipal love in the countertransference. *Int J Psychoanal* 1959; 40:180–190.
63. *Tarasoff v Regents of the University of California* 1976; 131 Cal Rptr 14.
64. *Johnson v State of California* 1968; 69 Cal 2d.
65. *Merchants National Bank & Trust Co of Fargo v United States* 1967; (DND) 272 FSupp 409.
66. *Fleming, Maximov.* The patient or his victim: the therapist's dilemma. *Cal Law Rev* 1974; 62:1025–1030.
67. Felthaus AR: Legislative update. *Newsletter Am Acad Psychiatry Law* 1985;10-3:20–21.
68. *Brady v Hopper* Civil Action 83-JM-451 District Ct, Colo.
69. Metzner JL: *Brady v Hopper*: the special relationship between foreseeability and liability. *Newsletter Am Acad Psychiatry Law* 1983; 8:34–36.
70. *Thompson v County of Alameda* 1980; 167 Cal Rptr 70.
71. *People v Murtishaw* 1981; 175 Cal Rptr 738.
72. *Mavroudis v Superior Court of the County of San Mateo* 1980; 161 Cal Rptr 724.
73. *Leedy v Hartnett* 1981; 510 FSupp 1125 (MD Pa).
74. *Hinkelman v Borgess Medical Center* 1987; 430 NW2d 547 (Mich Ct App).
75. *Sharpe v South Carolina Department of Mental Health* 1987; 354 SE2d 778 (SC Ct App).
76. *Lipari v Sears, Roebuck & Co* 1980 (July 17); 77-0-458 (D Neb).
77. *Petersen v Washington* 1983; 671 P2d 230.
78. Reid WH: Duty expanded to foresee dangerous behavior to non-specific victims. *Newsletter Am Acad Psychiatry Law* 1980; 5:17–18.
79. *McIntosh v Milano* 1979; 403 A2d 500 (NJ App).
80. *Currie v US* 1986; 644 FSupp 1074 (MD NC).
81. Miller RD: Currie v US: Tarasoff comes south. *Ment Phys Disability Law Reporter* 1986; 10:577.
82. *Parham v J.L. and J.R.* 1979; 99 SCt 2493.
83. *Davis v Lhim* 1983 (March 21); No. 59284 (Mich Ct App).
84. *Jablonski v US* 1983; 712 F2d 391 (9th Cir).
85. Mills MJ: The Tarasoff duties expand: Jablonski and Hedlund. *Newsletter Am Acad Psychiatry Law* 1984; 9:8–11.
86. *Swofford v Cooper* 1987; 360 SE2d 624 (Ga Ct App).
87. *Peck v Counseling Service of Addison County, Inc.* 1985; No. 83–062 (Vt Sup Ct).
88. Stone AA: Vermont adopts Tarasoff: a real barn-burner. *Am J Psychiatry* 1986; 143:352–355.
89. *McDonald v Clinger* 1981; 466 NYS2d 801 (AD).
90. Beck JC: The psychotherapist's duty to protect third parties from harm. *Ment Phys Disability Law Reporter* 1987;11:141–148.

2

Alcoholism and Drug Addiction

ALCOHOLISM

Alcoholism is perceived as a disease by many people today. Yet the confusion attending the meaning of "disease" as applied to alcoholism is rarely grappled with by those outside the medical and mental health professions. Is alcoholism a medical dysfunction, or a personality disorder? Does alcoholism have a physiologic origin with psychological side effects; or a psychic origin with physiologic side effects?

In the broadest and most fundamental sense, disease is a condition that departs from health. It is a destructive process effecting deterioration of an organ or organism via specific determinants. As both condition and process, then, alcoholism can be considered a disease in this comprehensive sense.

Statistical evidence supports the common observation that alcoholism is hereditary. Studies performed on twins, and on children who were separated from alcoholic parents and raised by nonalcoholic adoptive parents, have proved that genetic factors are a culprit in alcoholism's spread. By inhabiting the body's biochemical system, alcoholism produces pathologic tissue abnormalities.[1,2] While there is no doubt that alcoholism can run in families, however, its exact physiologic or biochemical origins have yet to be determined unequivocally. This unique mixture of the certainty of the genetic link, with the uncertainty of the physical source, leaves alcoholism in a state of limbo, defying definitive categorization.

Goodwin has compared alcoholism with lead poisoning.[2] Chronic lead intoxication is characterized by symptoms following a predictable course, with predictable complications. The best, and only satisfactory, treatment is abstinence from lead. Likewise, the symptoms of alcoholism follow a predictable course with predictable complications, and cease only with abstinence. The similarities between these two conditions arise only after the conditions have taken hold, however. Lead will have a toxic affect on any healthy person ingesting it, whereas alcohol will catalyze alcoholism only when a physical or mental predisposition exists in a person.

The complex social and legal questions arising from the disease issue of alcoholism complicate its medical aspects as well. The question of responsibility is most urgent. For example, victims of illnesses such as diabetes are obviously not responsible for being so afflicted. Their affliction may be interpreted as an act of God or a product of environment, but surely not as "their fault." They are classic victims of forces beyond their control. Even if they had a degree of control theoretically, it would be neutralized by practical ignorance of causes. A person who ingests lead does so unaware of the consequences.

Alcoholics, on the other hand, are aware that they cannot stop drinking once they start. This seeming helplessness contains an opportunity to control the disease, however—not by controlling the number of drinks, but by opting not to have one in the first place. Almost certainly alcoholics will be unable to stop drinking once they begin, and while this fact might elude them at their first episode, eventually it will be obvious. While this behavior fits into the "impulse control disorder" category, it fails to meet the criteria for the narrower medical concept of disease. This provides an interesting contradiction of interpretations: while many people in both the mental health professions and general population view alcoholism as a medical disease with psychological ramifications, the medical community perceives it, generally speaking, as a psychological phenomenon with physical ramifications.

Three distinct patterns of alcoholism have been described by the *Diagnostic and Statistical Manual of Mental Disorders* of the American Psychiatric Association (DSM-III-R).[3] The first is regular daily intake of large amounts of alcohol; the second is regular heavy drinking limited to specific occasions such as weekends or parties; and the third is long periods of sobriety broken by binges of daily heavy drinking which can last for weeks or months. The latter two patterns make the alcoholism harder to detect, since they mirror heavy nonalcoholic drinking, and there is less public awareness that they are forms of alcoholism. When people think of "alcoholism," they usually automatically imagine a daily heavy drinker. Therefore, the other patterns have an impact on alcoholics who are claiming disability for the affliction, in that their alcoholism is less likely to be common knowledge.

Alcoholism engenders accompanying symptoms and mental processes. Alcoholic persons utilize the defense mechanisms of denial, rationalization, and projection to minimize the seriousness of their problem to themselves and others. Bayog[4] has suggested that the relationship between alcoholism and psychopathology should be approached from the perspective that alcoholism itself is a traumatic experience capable of causing psychopathology.

Persistent denial coupled with impulsive, self-destructive behavior is an example of the type of complication produced by the trauma of alcoholism.

Usually alcoholism starts gradually, without the patient realizing that his or her behavior and feelings constitute the early symptoms of the disease. Patients find that their drinking is out of control, meaning that they cannot stop by force of will, and they will begin to feel guilty, bewildered, and frightened. Inability to regulate drinking leads to repeated, unpredictable episodes of drunkenness that in turn produce physical damage, impairment in interpersonal relationships, and damage to personal integrity, self-esteem, and status.

ALCOHOLISM, DRUG ADDICTION, AND SOCIOPATHIC BEHAVIOR

Alcoholism exists at a higher rate among the criminal population than among the general population in both sexes. One percent of the general female population suffers from alcoholism. This statistic grows to 50% when applied to the criminal female population. In the male criminal population, the 50% alcoholic rate also holds. Noteworthy regarding the women criminals, though, is the lack of association between recidivism and alcohol abuse, which contrasts the findings for male criminals.

Some investigators have distinguished between the sociopathic and nonsociopathic alcoholic. Sociopathic alcoholics have chronic deviant behavior with early onset of juvenile delinquency prior to the initiation of excessive alcohol intake. Therefore, alcohol abuse appears only to complicate an already deviant behavior pattern. In the nonsociopathic alcoholic, serious deviance does not precede alcohol abuse. The deviant behavior committed by the nonsociopathic alcoholic is less severe, begins at a later age, and is often committed in direct relationship to alcohol intake.[5]

Alcoholics with sociopathic personalities tend to be younger, have an earlier onset of pathologic drinking, and a higher prevalence of drug dependence. Furthermore, there is a higher incidence of alcoholism in their families. Adoption data have indicated that they are more likely to transmit alcoholism to their offspring and that their liability to develop alcoholism is less influenced by environmental factors.[6] Sociopathic alcoholics have a more rapid progression into problem drinking, more impaired control, and more psychological problems than alcoholics without sociopathic tendencies.

Lewis et al[7] have studied and analyzed the differences between depressed male alcoholics with and without antisocial personality (sociopathic). They found that from psychological and clinical points of view, the two groups were similar. Also, their ages, incomes, occupational levels, and depressive symptomatology were comparable. The antisocial personality subjects, however, did have more early childhood familial disruption and they were more likely to have a family history of antisocial personality (ASP) and drug use disorders. The differences between the two groups, those with and those without sociopathic personality, were reflected mainly in their alcohol symptomatology. Those with ASP had an earlier onset of heavy drinking and more alcoholic symptoms than those without ASP. The data of Lewis et al support the idea that individuals with more deviant behavior begin pathologic drinking earlier.

Criminal behavior and addiction appear to be correlated. In a group of 60 male patients from a London drug clinic, criminality, not addiction, has proved to be the dominant deviant behavior. This determination followed the reexamination of their conviction and addiction status. By the end of this 10-year follow-up study, 97% of the patients had received a court conviction.[8] Substantiating criminality as the primary deviance is the fact that 48% of the group had already been convicted of crimes before their first illicit drug use. During the 10-year follow-up period, 83% were convicted. Since almost half of the subjects had convictions prior to initial drug use, with the convictions nearly doubling after drug use, the premise that drug dependency is an expression of social deviancy is validated.

ALCOHOLISM, DRUG ADDICTION, AND PSYCHIATRIC DISORDERS

Substantial numbers of alcoholic patients meet diagnostic criteria for one or more additional syndromes as defined by DSM-III-R.[9] The studies were designed to determine the DSM-III-R axis I and axis II disorders in groups of alcoholics (230 men and 90 women), the relative age of onset of alcohol abuse or dependence, and whether the presence of coexisting disorders altered the course of the alcohol abuse or dependence.[10]

Depression is the most prevalent, and the most serious, psychiatric disorder coexisting with alcoholism, major studies show. But a high incidence of other coexisting disorders, especially in males, creates potential obstacles for the victims of alcohol dependence. For men, antisocial personality was by far the most pervasive coexisting disorder (49%), followed by substance abuse (45%) and major depression (32%). Women experienced depression as the most common additional disorder (52%), with phobia (44%), substance abuse (38%), and antisocial personality (20%) following close behind. Although two thirds of the women and one half of the men reported their first major depressions as occurring prior to the onset of alcohol abuse or dependence, diagnosis of serious depression or phobia did not suggest that these conditions exacerbated alcohol abuse, according to this study. One fourth of the sample were "pure alcoholics," free of additional psychiatric disorders.[10]

Different studies yield different results, however. In one study of 185 men and 186 women, alcoholics were found to suffer from multifarious symptoms and syndromes.[11] Among those symptoms, phobia and anxiety states both preceded and facilitated the development of alcoholism.[12,13] The presence of depression as a common denominator among drug addicts[14] indicates the possibility that drug abuse is a form of self-medication used to eliminate the symptoms of depression. These symptoms may include mood disorders, sleep and appetite disturbances, low self-esteem, and feelings of helplessness and despair. According to various surveys, such manifestations of depression occur in 30% to 60% of drug abusers.[15] At first, the depression is nondrug-related. Its apparently high rate of incidence in substance abusers, however, may support the foregoing hypothesis that they undertake self-medication to alleviate the depression's painful symptoms. Whereas a non-depressive drug experimenter will turn away from drugs after the initial excitement subsides, the depressed individual has discovered a means to counteract the depression symptoms, and will become an abuser. This vicious cycle proceeds as the deviance of addiction reinforces the depression while seeming to soothe its manifestations.

Many people mistakenly perceive alcoholism and drug addiction to be basically identical diseases or conditions, varying only in the substances abused. Similarities between the two do indeed exist: abstinence as monitored by Alcoholics Anonymous or Narcotics Anonymous is often legally accepted treatment; many fundamental symptoms are the same, namely the inability to stop consuming the intoxicant once started, the willingness to obtain the intoxicant at any and all costs, the vise of denial and deception. To look only at these resemblances would easily induce one to consider alcoholism and addiction the same. If this were true, it would contradict the foregoing finding of drug addiction as social deviance. The obtaining of drugs, however, must precede the using of them. Even if persons passively receive an illegal substance, they are in possession of choice. They know that the substance they hold and will ingest is illegal, and probably understand that it is addictive. Alcoholics, on the other hand, can be considered innocent when they first drink. Moderate drinking is a socially acceptable pastime that is quite safe for the majority, and alcoholics can reasonably assume that they will be in that majority, and not in the minority unable to tolerate alcohol. Alcoholics must "learn by experience" of their affliction. So alcoholics and drug addicts start from very different situations on their dark journeys.

A comparison of the natures of the abused substances further illustrates the difference between alcoholism and addiction. Alcohol is taken by most of the population over many years as a social pastime, without resulting in alcoholism. Drugs, though, are commonly known to catalyze addiction in the majority of people who use them with any frequency. There need be no predisposition making frequent drug-takers more vulnerable; rather, any person can become addicted. Addiction is the normal physiologic response to regular moderate doses of various drugs, while alcoholism is not the normal response to regular moderate alcohol intake. A physiologic or psychological irregularity is usually responsible for the inability to tolerate alcohol—although not for the refusal to modify behavior accordingly, as will be seen in a later section.

RIGHTS OF ALCOHOLICS

Alcoholism is interpreted under the law as a handicapping condition, and alcoholics therefore have the protection of the Rehabilitation Act of 1973. Government workers receive even more mandated support in this regard through the Comprehensive Alcohol Abuse and Alcoholism Prevention, Treatment, and Rehabilitation Act of 1970. This act requires agencies to maintain alcohol treatment programs for their employees and prohibits the denial of opportunities on the basis of prior alcohol abuse or alcoholism. Federal employers are required by law to take an active, collaborative role in assisting alcoholic employees to overcome their handicap before firing them for performance deficiencies caused by their drinking.

The rights of alcoholic government employees were bolstered by the District of Columbia federal court in the landmark case, *Whitlock v Donovan*,[16] summarized below. That decision was extended later beyond government employees to the general work force. The court in *Whitlock* specified that affirmative action must be undertaken, even to the degree of program modifications, unless the employer could demonstrate that such an undertaking would cause it undue hardship.

George Whitlock had an alcoholic seizure on the job at the US Department of Labor and was rushed to a hospital. He had worked there for 2 years when his alcoholism history began. Sometime after the emergency hospitalization he enrolled in an alcohol program and did well for a while. Then Mr Whitlock's absenteeism increased. By the following year his many absences seriously interfered with his responsibilities at the Labor Department and he was officially warned. During the next year, Mr Whitlock's condition worsened. His employer threatened him with suspension, demanding that he choose between suspension and treatment at a local clinic. Whitlock chose the treatment, but then failed to keep his appointments. When his alcoholism relapsed yet again, administrative procedure was set in motion to remove him, and eventually he was fired. Mr Whitlock filed a lawsuit against the Department of Labor, alleging that the government discriminated against him because of his handicap of alcoholism.

The court held: "It is plain that the Department of Labor treated George Whitlock with compassion and tolerance . . . however, it is also apparent that the Department fell short of the statutory mandate for accommodating handicapped employees." The decision continues: "To begin with, the agency did not comply with the 'firm choice' requirement that obligated the plaintiff to accept treatment or face disciplinary action." Thus the court set the tone for rigorous compliance by government employers with the regulations protecting the rights of their alcoholic employees as handicapped. The court stated further that an agency need not always offer leave without pay if another specific arrangement is available to the alcoholic employee. The agency must, however, consider such options for treatment and pursue them unless doing so would impose severe hardship upon the agency. "Once an employee has shown evidence that his handicap can be accommodated, the burden of persuasion is on the agency to show that it cannot accommodate the employee."

Whitlock could reapply for his job, the court ordered, and was to be given a fitness-for-duty examination at the department's expense. In the event that he was found fit for employment, the department was obligated to rehire him. If he was found unfit, the department must allow him to apply for disability retirement, retroactive to the date on which he applied for re-employment.

Although alcoholism is considered a handicapping condition, it is a unique category of handicap in which the victim retains personal responsibility and therefore may not be entitled to the full benefits allowed other physically and mentally handicapped persons. In an effort to resolve the issue of the degree of legal responsibility an alcoholic should be expected to maintain, the US Supreme Court heard two cases, *Traynor v Turnage* and *McKelvey v Turnage*.[17] These cases centered on alcoholic rights and the problems of alcoholics.

The primary issue facing the Court was whether the characterization of primary alcoholism as "willful misconduct" for the purpose of denying a veteran GI bill benefits is within the framework of the law or not. After hearing testimony, the highest court refrained from deciding on the medical aspects of alcoholism, specifically on whether or not alcoholism is a disease.

Petitioners in these cases were honorably discharged veterans who did not exhaust their GI Bill of Rights educational assistance benefits within 10 years following their military service as required by law. Under the law (38 USC SEC 1662 [A][1]), veterans may obtain an extension of the delimiting period if they can show they were prevented from using their benefits earlier because of a physical or mental disorder that did not result from their own willful misconduct. Petitioners Traynor and McKelvey sought to continue receiving benefits after the expiration of the 10-year period on the ground that they were disabled by alcoholism during much of that period. The Veterans Administration found that its regulation defined primary alcoholism (that which is unrelated to an underlying psychiatric disorder) as "willful misconduct" and therefore petitioners were not entitled to the requested extensions. The case passed through the lower federal court and arrived at the US Supreme Court for a definitive ruling.

In making its determination, the Supreme Court justices noted that the term "willful misconduct" has been used frequently in other veterans' benefits statutes, such as the statute denying veterans compensation for service-connected disabilities that are the result of the veteran's own willful misconduct.

The VA had long construed the term willful misconduct for the purpose of these statutes as encompassing primary alcoholism.

In addition, the highest court assumed that Congress must have been aware of the VA interpretation of willful misconduct at the time that it enacted SECTION 1662(A)(1), and that Congress intended this term to hold the same meaning within that statute as it did in other statutes concerning veterans' benefits.

In the view of the majority of the justices, it was clear that legislation precluded an extension of time to a veteran who had failed to pursue his education because of primary alcoholism. If Congress had intended instead that primary alcoholism not be deemed willful misconduct for the purpose of SECTION 1662(A)(1), as it had been deemed for the purposes of other veterans' benefits statutes, Congress most certainly would have said so. Further, Congress did extend prohibition against discrimination on the basis of handicap to any program or activity conducted by any executive agency (Public Law 95-602), yet did not affirmatively evince any intent to repeal or amend the willful misconduct provision; nor did Congress anywhere in language or legislative history expressly disavow its determination that primary alcoholism is not the sort of disability warranting an exemption from the time constraints of SECTION 1662(A)(1).

The majority noted, in sum, that even among the many who consider alcoholism a "disease" to which its victims are genetically predisposed, the consumption of alcohol is not regarded as wholly involuntary, and therefore primary alcoholism, unrelated to medical illness, can be characterized as a willful misconduct and this characterization does not contradict the prevailing law.

In arriving at this decision, four justices formed the majority, three dissented, and two did not participate. The dissenting justices recommended that both cases, *Traynor* and *McKelvey*, be remanded to the VA for individualized determinations, based on sound medical judgments of whether these men are otherwise qualified to receive veterans' educational benefits beyond the 10-year period.

This recommendation was based on their recognition that individuals suffering from a wide range of disabilities, including heart and lung disease and diabetes, usually bear some responsibility for their conditions. The conduct that can lead to this array of disabilities, particularly dietary and smoking habits, is certainly no less voluntary than the consumption of alcohol. Nevertheless, the VA has expressed an unwillingness to extend the definition of willful misconduct to all voluntary conduct having some relation to the development of a disability. For example, smoking has not been considered misconduct although it is a causative factor in the incidence of cancer and heart disease. It is unreasonable and illogical to apply one set of rules to alcohol consumption and a different set of rules to other factors contributing to disability.

ALCOHOLISM, DRUG ADDICTION, AND CRIMINAL RESPONSIBILITY

In *Robinson v California*,[18] the Supreme Court reviewed drug addiction from a constitutional rights perspective for the first time, and decided that no state statute could make an illness into a criminal offense because doing so would violate the Eighth and Fourteenth Amendments.

In this case, the constitutionality of a California statute making addiction to narcotics a criminal offense was challenged. Appellant Robinson was convicted by a jury in the Municipal Court of Los Angeles of using narcotics by injection with a hypodermic needle. At the appeal, the highest court in the state upheld the lower court's decision and the constitutionality of the statute.

The US Supreme Court, however, decided otherwise:

> It is unlikely that any state at this moment in history would attempt to make it a criminal offense for a person to be mentally ill, or a leper, or to be afflicted with a venereal disease. A state might determine that the general health and welfare require that the victims of these and other human afflictions be dealt with by compulsory treatment, involving quarantine, confinement, or sequesteration. But, in the light of contemporary human knowledge, a law which made a criminal offense of such a disease would doubtless be universally thought to be an infliction of cruel and unusual punishment in violation of the Eighth and Fourteenth Amendments.[18]

This "medicalization" of drug addiction aroused dissent, as well, from the minority of Supreme Court justices siding with California. California's treatment program for addicts, they noted, appeared more than adequate. Therefore "a volitional narcotic addiction poses a threat of serious crime similar to the threat inherent in the purchase or possession of narcotics," and California should therefore retain the power to deter the violation by punishment.

In spite of the above ruling, drug addicts may not claim freedom from responsibility due to their addiction as a means of escaping punishment if they are found guilty of committing a crime.

Alcoholics met harsher standards from the courts than did drug addicts. Their affliction was not considered an illness, and therefore alcoholics were deemed fully liable for any act committed or law broken while intoxicated. *Powell v Texas*[19] paved the way to convict criminals for laws broken not of their own volition but rather as a result of their habits, including the "habit" (as opposed to "illness") of drinking.

Chronic alcoholism was not a viable defense to the charge of being intoxicated in a public place, ruled the Texas county court judge in *Powell*. Leroy Powell was arrested for public intoxication, a crime that is stipulated in the Texas penal code. The trial judge, sitting without a jury, included in his findings-of-fact that indeed Powell was a chronic alcoholic and suffered from alcoholism, but ruled against allowing that condition to serve as a defense. He found the appellant guilty and fined him $90. Having exhausted all avenues of appeal in Texas, Powell turned to the US Supreme Court.

For the first time the Supreme Court confronted the medical profession's lack of consensus regarding the idea of alcoholism as a disease. The court, referring to the writings of Jellinek, mentioned that "alcoholism" has too many definitions and "disease" practically none.

The justices expressed in their opinions also, however, their uneasiness with using the criminal process to address the public aspects of problem drinking. This approach could not be defended as rational in an enlightened society. Yet, there was nothing in the Constitution directing that penal sanctions be designed to achieve therapeutic or rehabilitative results. The moral stance that our society has traditionally taken toward public intoxication is exemplified in its classification as criminal behavior and the use of punishment as a deterrence. This could lead alcoholics to conceal their drinking problem and thereby intensify related destructive behavior. Criminal sanctions may reinforce an idealized behavior standard without effecting the desired rehabilitation.

When comparing the *Powell* and *Robinson* cases, the Court observed that Texas had not sought to furnish a "mere status" as California had in *Robinson*. Texas also did not try to regulate the appellant's behavior in the privacy of his own home. Rather, it had imposed on the appellant a criminal sanction for public behavior which placed the health and safety of the general population as well as his own in possible jeopardy, and offended the moral and aesthetic sensibilities of a large segment of the community.

The court noted further that the behavior of an alcoholic who is intoxicated meets the criteria of mens rea. Criminal penalties may be imposed only if the accused has committed a specific act or engaged in specific behavior that society has a valid interest in preventing, or perhaps in historical common law terms, has committed an actus reus. If Leroy Powell cannot be convicted of public intoxication, the court added, then how can a state convict an individual for murder, if that individual, while exhibiting normal behavior in all other respects, suffers from a "compulsion" to kill which is an "exceedingly strong influence" but "not completely overpowering?" That argument could be extended ad absurdum. The courts do not consider drug addiction a mental illness, and therefore a defendant may not claim addiction as the basis for an insanity defense.

This prevailing opinion is illustrated in the landmark case *United States v Lyons*.[20] Former Louisiana sheriff Robert Lyons was indicted on 12 counts of knowingly and intentionally securing controlled substances by misrepresentation, fraud, deception, and subterfuge in violation of the federal criminal code. Lyons presented evidence of addiction arising from prescriptions of narcotics by physicians after surgery to ease pain. It was stressed that the addiction resulted from this original involuntary experience with narcotics and not from illegally seeking them out. The defense called expert witnesses who testified that the drug addiction affected his brain psychologically and physiologically, thus altering his personality completely. The district court rejected the above argument and excluded all evidence related to the defendant's drug addiction. Then a three-judge panel of the court of appeals reversed the lower court's ruling. The court of appeals held that the jury was the entity responsible for deciding whether involuntary drug addiction could be defined as a mental disease or defect. At the government's request, the appeals court agreed to rehear the case en banc before the full complement of 13 judges. Twelve to one, the court of appeals decided that addiction to narcotics, whether acquired voluntarily or involuntarily, without other psychologic or physiological complications, failed to merit classification as a mental disease or defect for substantiation of the insanity defense.

According to the court's view, first, the use of drugs involved an element of reasoned choice; second, considering that Congress has made possession and sale of narcotics a criminal offense, it would be anomalous to immunize drug addicts from other criminal sanctions; and third, the definition of "mental disease or defect" relies on legal and moral judgment, not medical opinion. The court agreed that evidence of drug-induced or drug-aggravated psychosis, or physical damage to the central nervous system, would be admissable to prove the presence of mental illness under an insanity defense. But it refused to accept evidence of drug addiction to show underlying pathologic abnormality.

The same court, in a seven to six vote, abolished the volitional prong of the American Law Institute (ALI) insanity test. It asserted that the prong does not comport with current medical and scientific knowledge. Further, an individual has little ability to assess self-control and there is a great risk of fabrication. Last, there is considerable overlap between the volitional prong and the cognitive prong, so that most defendants who failed the former would almost certainly fail the latter, rendering the volitional prong superfluous.

To preclude any unfairness to Lyons himself, the court vacated the district court's opinion excluding all evidence of drug addiction offered in support of his insanity defense. The case was remanded for a new trial in accordance with the Fifth Circuit's new insanity standard in which Lyons would be allowed to tender evidence that he was so physiologically damaged by his drug addiction that he was unable to appreciate the wrongfulness of his conduct.

Sometimes courts might reduce a sentence if the defense attorney and expert psychiatrist persuade them that a drug-addicted defendant can be rehabilitated, as in *Arizona v Rossi*.[21] Rossi was convicted of burglary, attempted murder, and murder. An Arizona court sentenced him to death. However, on appeal, the Arizona Supreme Court was convinced that the defendant had shown by a preponderance of the evidence that his cocaine addiction significantly impaired his capacity to conform his conduct to the requirement of the law. He could not demonstrate that his addiction impaired his capacity to appreciate the wrongfulness of his conduct. The defendant had attempted to cover up the acts he committed on the day of the crimes, and he was able to vividly recall details of the crimes. Nevertheless, the Arizona Supreme Court remanded the death sentence to the trial court to consider the impact of the defendant's cocaine addiction and potential for rehabilitation as mitigating factors. A neuropsychiatrist testified on retrial that the defendant was mainlining cocaine at or near the time of the crimes, and that his life was dominated and controlled by drugs and he would not have committed the crimes had he not been a cocaine addict.

The court found the neuropsychiatrist's testimony persuasive. Other experts also testified that, in general, chemical dependency fosters an insatiable and life-controlling craving for drugs which overwhelms the user's ability to control his physical behavior. All the experts agreed that Rossi could be rehabilitated in spite of his cocaine addiction. In response to this testimony, the trial court reduced Rossi's sentence.

In *Whitlock v Donovan*,[16] the case establishing alcoholism as a handicap, we have seen what can only be described as tremendous generosity toward people considered victims. The courts, and by logical extension this society, attempt to remove as much of the burden as possible from such victimization. Whitlock, basically, was relieved of his responsibility to perform his job because of his handicap, as long as he agreed to undergo treatment. In *Powell v Texas*,[19] on the other hand, an alcoholic is held completely responsible for his criminal behavior, in spite of the fact that the behavior clearly resulted from his alcoholic condition. The "compulsion to drink" relieved Powell of liability no more than a "compulsion to murder" would relieve a murderer. An alcoholic is not responsible for work, but is responsible for crimes. These extreme responses raise the question of whether this society can accept the fundamental inconclusiveness inherent in the dilemma of alcoholism.

The inability to accept a coherent working definition of alcoholism continues through the more recent *Traynor* and *McKelvey* cases, in which the US Supreme Court held that alcoholism was both disability and willful misconduct. The wisdom of the statutes designating alcoholism as willful misconduct was not questioned. Perhaps if a more consistent approach to alcoholism were developed, for instance, holding alcoholics liable for all their actions while at the same time providing an atmosphere free of the insinuation of shamefulness, there would finally be a reduction in the suffering of alcoholics, the suffering of those directly and indirectly victimized by their actions, and in the time and expense of court proceedings for crimes perpetrated as a result of alcoholism.

REFERENCES

1. Goodwin DW: Alcoholism and heredity: A review and hypothesis. *Arch Gen Psychiatry* 1979;36:57–61.
2. Goodwin DW: On defining alcoholism and taking stands. *J Clin Psychiatry* 1982;43:394–395.
3. American Psychiatric Association: *Diagnostic and Statistical Manual of Mental Disorders*, ed 3, revised. Washington, DC, American Psychiatric Press, 1987.

64

4. Bayog MB: Alcoholism as a case of psychopathology. *Hosp Community Psychiatry* 1988;39:352–354.
5. Shuckit MA: Alcoholism and sociopathy—Diagnostic confusion. *QJ Stud Alcohol* 1973;34:157–164.
6. Cloninger CR, et al: Inheritance of alcohol abuse: Cross-fostering analysis of adopted men. *Arch Gen Psychiatry* 1981;38:861–868.
7. Lewis CE, et al: The antisocial and nonantisocial alcoholic: Clinical distinctions in men with major unipolar depression. *Alcoholism Clin Exp Res* 1987;11:176–182.
8. Gordon AM: Drugs and delinquency: A ten year follow up of drug clinic patients. *Br J Psychiatry* 1983;142:169–173.
9. Powell BJ, et al: Prevalence of additional psychiatric syndromes among male alcoholics. *J Clin Psychiatry* 1982;43:404–407.
10. Hesselbrock MN, et al: Psychopathology in hospitalized alcoholics. *Arch Gen Psychiatry* 1985;42:1050–1055.
11. Bernadt MW, et al: Psychiatric disorders, drinking and alcoholism. *Br J Psychiatry* 1986;148:393–400.
12. Smail P, et al: Alcohol dependence and phobic anxiety states. I: A prevalence study. *Br J Psychiatry* 1984;144:53–57.
13. Stockwell T: Alcohol dependence and phobic anxiety states. II: A retrospective study. *Br J Psychiatry* 1984;144:58–63.X.
14. Rounsaville BJ, et al: Diagnosis and symptoms of depression in opiate addicts: Course and relationship to treatment outcome. *Arch Gen Psychiatry* 1982;39:191–196.
15. Mirin SM, et al: *Affective Illness in Substance Abusers in Substance Abuse and Psychopathology*, in *The Monograph Series of the American Psychiatric Press*. Washington, DC, American Psychiatric Press, 1984.
16. *Whitlock v Donovan* 1985; 9 MPDLR 34.
17. *Traynor v Turnage* US Sup Ct No. 86-622, and *McKelvey v Turnage* US Sup Ct No. 86-737, decided Apr 20, 1988. *United States Law Week* 1988; 56 LW 4319–4328.
18. *Robinson v California* 1962; 370 US 660.
19. *Powell v Texas* 1968; 392 US 514.
20. *United States v Lyons* 1984; 731 F2d 243.
21. *Arizona v Rossi* 1987; 741 P2d 1223 (Ariz Sup Ct).

3

Right to Treatment and Right to Refuse Treatment

RIGHT TO TREATMENT

The purpose of psychiatric hospitalization is treatment of mentally ill persons. Custody care is not the purpose of psychiatric hospitalization. A right to treatment is recognized by law and has been enforced by courts in many states. In addition, the Congress has reinforced the right to treatment by affording a judicial remedy for its violation. The states have an obligation to hire adequate staff members, meet a standard ratio for mental health professionals to patients, provide a professionally designed program to all institutionalized patients in need of such services, and deliver adequate medical care.[1-3] If a state fails to provide adequate medical or psychiatric care, the Department of Justice has the option of filing suit and charging the state for failure to comply with its legal responsibilities in that regard. Such a Justice Department lawsuit is usually based on the Civil Rights of Institutionalized Persons Act (CRIPA) which stipulates protection of residents in psychiatric institutions.[4]

The right of psychiatric patients to treatment while under hospitalization received close attention and judicial clarification in *Rouse v Cameron*.[5] The case has enduring historical significance in two regards: as a turning point in the understanding of psychiatric hospitalization, and as a clarification of specific rights deemed constitutionally defensible.

In *Rouse*, Charles Rouse was charged with carrying a dangerous weapon, a misdemeanor for which the maximum punishment was imprisonment for 1 year. Instead, Rouse was confined in St Elizabeth's Hospital, Washington, DC, under a finding of not guilty by reason of insanity. After 4 years of

66

hospitalization, Rouse claimed that he had not received adequate treatment from the time he had been committed.

The court ruled that the purpose of involuntary hospitalization is treatment, not punishment. Presided over by Justice Bazelon, the court specified:

> Indefinite commitment without treatment may be so inhumane as to be cruel and unusual punishment . . . such action is in violation of the statutory requirement for proper 'medical and psychiatric care and treatment' as stipulated in the 1964 Hospitalization of the Mentally Ill Act. If opportunity for treatment has been exhausted or is otherwise inappropriate, conditional or unconditional release may be in order.[5]

Criminal defendants who were found not guilty by reason of insanity obviously constitute the majority of beneficiaries of the *Rouse* decision. As will be shown, however, the courts extended the right to treatment to those patients who were involuntarily committed through civil procedures. In *Wyatt v Stickney*,[6] the concept of the right to treatment of mentally ill patients in mental hospitals is refined. This case began when a reduction in the Alabama cigarette tax forced the state to fire 99 employees at Bryce Hospital. Two classes of plaintiffs joined in the complaint, one represented by Ricky Wyatt and the other by five of the recently terminated employees. The defendants were Stickney, the executive officer of the Alabama State Mental Health Board, and other state officials.

The complaints alleged that the defendants had effected the staff reductions purely for budgetary reasons and that the reductions had been undertaken without notice or hearing, which violated the employees' rights under the due process clause; and that as a result of the discharges, the Bryce patients would be denied adequate treatment. The focus of the litigation shifted from the effects of the terminations to questions related to the overall adequacy of the treatment afforded at the Alabama state hospitals. The issue before the court was whether patients involuntarily committed through noncriminal procedures and lacking the constitutional protections that are afforded defendants in criminal procedures have a constitutional right to receive the individual treatment that will give each patient an opportunity to be cured or to improve his or her conditions.

The court ruled that civilly committed mental patients do have a constitutional right to such individual treatment as will help them to be cured or to improve their mental condition. On the other hand, the court also determined that the "need to care" for mentally ill patients and the need to relieve their families, friends, or guardians of the burdens of providing such care failed to supply constitutional justification for civil commitment.

The Supreme Court of the United States has addressed the rights and needs of mentally ill patients and the rights of institutionalized persons, and become involved in these complex and often controversial issues. One clear determination, occurring in *O'Connor v Donaldson*,[7] is that the state cannot confine persons to mental hospitals unless it offers some sort of treatment, training, or habilitation to help those persons improve or be cured of their illness.

Kenneth Donaldson was a patient in Chatahoochee State Hospital in Florida. Initially, he was committed on a petition filed by his father alleging that the son suffered from paranoid delusional thought. Donaldson remained in the hospital for 15 years. In the course of his hospitalization, he claimed to be a Christian Scientist and refused to receive electroshock therapy or medication as well as any and all commonly accepted psychiatric treatment. Donaldson made numerous attempts in state and federal courts to obtain release, all fruitless. Dr O'Connor, the psychiatrist responsible for Donaldson's case, rebutted Donaldson's attempt for release and interpreted Donaldson's various legal attempts as symptoms of paranoia litigation acts. The allegations include, among other things, that O'Connor exercised his discretionary power under the state law, and limited Donaldson's ground privileges in reaction to Donaldson's litigation efforts, confining him to a ward for the criminally insane, and stopping Donaldson's "occupational therapy." The evidence also indicated that O'Connor interfered with plans for Donaldson's release to various caretakers who offered to help.

Finally, Donaldson contacted Dr Morton Birnbaum, a physician and lawyer who was an advocate of the right to treatment for mentally ill patients. Although Birnbaum and Donaldson had differing views, they were able to compromise for a common cause: Donaldson believed in the "right to be left alone" and did not want any treatment as he believed he was not mentally ill. Dr Birnbaum advocated paternalism and wanted to improve the quality of treatment in state hospitals. Birnbaum and Donaldson petitioned the court in a class action law suit in which the court was asked to release Donaldson and the other patients in his section of the hospital because they were not receiving treatment. Second, Birnbaum argued that there was a constitutional right to treatment and he asked the court to order massive improvements in the section of the hospital from which Donaldson and the others were to be released.[8]

O'Connor's defense was that he had acted in good faith, since state law, which he considered valid, had authorized indefinite custodial confinement of the "sick" even if they were not treated and their release would not create a risk for themselves or of others. O'Connor insisted therefore that he was immune from any liability for monetary damages. The jury had awarded Donaldson with compensatory and punitive damages against O'Connor and a codefendant. The court of appeals affirmed the judgment. Finally, the case was brought to the US Supreme Court.

The specific issue before the Court was whether a public official has the responsibility to act to preserve the constitutional rights of an individual in spite of existing statutory authority permitting him to deny the individual these rights. The Supreme Court delivered a unanimous opinion. In the view of this Court, a state cannot constitutionally confine, without greater justification, a nondangerous individual who is capable of surviving safely in freedom alone or with the aid of willing and responsible family members or friends. Since the jury found, on ample evidence, that O'Connor as an agent of the state knowingly did so confine Donaldson, it properly concluded that O'Connor violated Donaldson's constitutional right to freedom.

The opinion of the Supreme Court in *Donaldson* illustrates that this is not simply a case of a person seeking release because he has been confined without anyone's obtaining a judicial confirmation that such confinement was warranted. Further, it was not alleged that Donaldson was singled out for discriminatory treatment by the staff of Florida State Hospital or that patients at that institution were denied privileges generally available to other persons under commitment in Florida. Thus, the question of whether different criteria for commitment justified differences in conditions of confinement is not involved in this litigation. Finally, there was no evidence whatsoever that Donaldson was abused or mistreated at Florida State Hospital, or that the failure to provide him with treatment aggravated his condition.

The Supreme Court, it has been noted, restricted itself to the question of the confinement of the nondangerous mentally ill and avoided focusing on the right-to-treatment aspect of the issue. The Court simply held that the district court did not err in instructing the jury that where nondangerous patients are involuntarily civilly committed to a state mental hospital, the only constitutionally permissible purpose of confinement is to provide treatment and that such patients have a constitutional right to the treatment that will help them to be cured or to improve their mental condition.[8]

The right to treatment was extended approximately 7 years after the Donaldson case by another landmark Supreme Court decision, *Romeo v Youngberg*.[9] This case also elucidated the nature of that right.

> Nicholas Romeo, a 33-year old, profoundly retarded person with a mental capacity of an 18-month old child, was uncommunicative and lacked basic self-care skills. Up to the age of 26, Romeo lived at home, but after his father died his mother complained that she was unable to care for him or control his violent outbursts. Therefore he was hospitalized in Penhurst State School and Hospital in Pennsylvania in 1974. During the course of his hospitalization, Romeo received numerous serious injuries, some self-inflicted, and because of his aggressiveness he had to be restrained under a physician's order. Romeo's mother brought suit against Pennsylvania state officials and the staff of Penhurst in the US district court in 1976. After an 8-day trial in 1978, a verdict was entered finding that the defendants had violated Romeo's constitutional right under the Eighth Amendment, to be free from cruel and unusual punishment.
>
> The Third Circuit Court of Appeals reversed and remanded the matter for a new trial. This court held that the Eighth Amendment was not an appropriate source for determining the rights of the involuntarily committed. Rather, the Fourteenth Amendment and the liberty interest protected by that amendment provided the proper constitutional basis for defining these rights. In applying the Fourteenth Amendment, the court found that the involuntarily committed retain liberty interests in freedom of movement and in personal security. These were determined to be fundamental liberties that could not be constrained except by an overriding, nonpunitive, state interest. The court found further that the involuntarily committed have a liberty interest in habilitation designed to "treat" their mental retardation.

The case arrived at the US Supreme Court, which recognized and established the following rights for Romeo and those similarly situated: (1) the right to safety in the institution; (2) the right to be free from unnecessary bodily restraints; (3) the right of habilitation or training for mental retardation. The Court agreed that persons such as Romeo had a right to minimally adequate training, but stated that the question of what constituted "adequate training" depended entirely on what constitutionally protected interests exist for any given individual. This implies the need for case-by-case deliberations to determine what the rights are in each unique circumstance, and precludes the use of a general definition which could be applied across the board. The Court rejected the Third Circuit court's contention that interests in safety could be compromised only after the state showed a compelling necessity for so doing. Instead, the Court held that as long as some professional judgment had been exercised, constitutional requirements would be satisfied. Professional liability would exist therefore "only when the decision made by the professional is such a substantial departure from accepted professional judgment, practice or standards as to demonstrate that the person responsible actually did not base the decision on such a judgment."

Commentary on *Romeo v Youngberg* has generally found in the case a clear expression of the right to treatment and habilitation.[10] While the clarification of what that treatment should consist of was avoided by the courts, the medical establishment retained discretion as to the patient's right to safety, with professionalism being presumed. This was a victory for psychiatrists and other mental health professionals, who would have found the Third Circuit court's restrictions and state intervention time-consuming, expensive, and an interference in their ability to heal effectively.

Although it is not stated by the Supreme Court that a mentally ill patient has a clear-cut right to treatment, the language of the Court's opinions unmistakably conveys that a mentally ill person cannot be kept in an institution without receiving proper treatment.

RIGHT TO REFUSE TREATMENT

The right to refuse treatment and especially the right to refuse psychotropic medication has received much more publicity than the right to treatment. Throughout the development of the common law there is overwhelming evidence that no right has existed longer, sunk deeper roots, or become more cherished than an individual's right to be free from unwanted and unwarranted personal bodily contact.

This common law protection against assault and battery has been reflected in the doctrine of informed consent, which means "voluntary, knowing, and competent" and is determined to apply equally to the forced ingestion of drugs. Forced medication is a form of unauthorized bodily intrusion, according to the courts, and as such is a violation of the equal protection guarantees of both state and federal constitutions. A growing body of federal and state case law recognizes at least a qualified constitutional right to refuse intrusive mental health treatment, including psychotropic medication.

The focus of controversy is actually quite broad: constitutional law implicitly recognizes that people have a strong interest in remaining free from nonconsensual invasion of their bodily integrity. Further, the right to privacy found in the penumbra of specific guarantees of the Bill of Rights encompasses the right of a patient to preserve his or her privacy against unwanted infringements of bodily integrity in appropriate circumstances. Finally, the constitutional right to privacy is an expression of the sanctity of individual free choice and self-determination; and there exists a general right in and for all persons, competent or incompetent, to refuse medical treatment in appropriate circumstances.

Protection of these personal liberties has its origins in the Constitution. The Fourteenth Amendment limits the state's power to deprive any person of life, liberty, or property without due process of law. The Eighth Amendment prohibits cruel and unusual punishment. The First Amendment protects freedom of speech and free expression of thought. Forced psychiatric medication can violate any or all of those fundamental rights.

The nature of psychotropic drugs has instigated a novel application of the First Amendment. The drugs utilized in forced medication can effectively create new thoughts or personalities, and compel individuals to relinquish their original beliefs which would presumably be interpreted by the medicators as delusional. The courts therefore have held that involuntary administration of drugs that affect mental processes could amount to a usurpation of individual rights under the First Amendment. Forced administration of the medication contradicts the First Amendment free speech and free expression prerogatives.

CURTAILMENT OF THE PSYCHIATRIST'S AUTHORITY

The discretion of psychiatrists to treat their patients when patient consent is withheld was limited by the court in *Rogers v Okin*.[11] This case was commenced on April 27, 1979, when several patients under the fabricated name of "Rogers" from the May and Austin Units of Boston State Hospital filed a civil rights action seeking to enjoin certain seclusion and medication practices at the hospital and to recover compensation and punitive damages from those responsible for such practices.

On April 30, 1975, the court issued a temporary restraining order prohibiting nonemergency seclusion and medication of voluntary or involuntary patients without their informed consent, or that of a guardian in the case of an incompetent. On May 8, 1975, the parties agreed to an extension of the temporary restraining order until a hearing on preliminary or permanent relief was concluded. Such a hearing commenced in the fall of 1975 and continued for six trial days. Procedural and technical uncertainties lingered until December 1977, when a trial on the merits began. In August of 1979, the trial ended. Within this 5-year period, 72 trial days were devoted to the testimony of more than 50 witnesses, most of whom were psychiatrists, psychologists, and other mental health professionals. The plaintiffs alleged that forcing them to take medications had denied them their constitutionally guaranteed right to refuse treatment. The plaintiffs urged the court to recognize this right but they did not maintain that such a right was absolute. They acknowledged that in emergencies the right must yield to the state's interest in medicating.

The defendants proffered a three-pronged defense to plaintiffs' allegations. First, they maintained that committed mental patients are per se incompetent to decide whether or not they should receive treatment. Second, they denied that any patient was forcibly medicated except under circumstances amounting to a psychiatric emergency. Third, they asserted that committed mental patients, whether voluntary or involuntary, have no constitutional right to refuse treatment in any situation—emergency or nonemergency.

The court's ruling was threefold:

1. Committed mental patients are presumed competent to manage their affairs, dispose of property, carry on a licensed profession, and to vote. That presumption of competency prevails unless and until there has been an adjudication of incompetency by a court following notices and hearings. So, generally, committed patients are competent to make treatment decisions.

2. In emergency situations, a committed mental patient may be forcibly medicated if a failure to do so would result in a substantial likelihood of physical harm to that patient, to any other patient, or to staff members of the institution.

3. Further, the court discussed the *Rogers* case in light of the Constitution and found that the issue at hand was not the validity of psychotropic drugs as a reasonable course of medical treatment. Rather, at stake was the more fundamental question of whether the state may impose once again on the privacy of a person, already deprived of freedom through commitment, by forcibly injecting mind-altering drugs into his or her system in a nonemergency situation.

On appeal, the First Circuit court affirmed in part and reversed in part. It agreed that mental patients have a constitutionally protected interest in deciding for themselves whether to undergo treatment with antipsychotic drugs. It also accepted the trial court's conclusion that Massachusetts law presumes involuntarily committed persons to be competent to assert this interest on their own behalf.

Contradictory conclusions were reached by the court of appeals, however, regarding the circumstances under which state interests might override the liberty interests of the patient. The court of appeals found that the state has two interests that must be weighed against the liberty interests asserted by patients: a police power interest in maintaining order within the institution and in preventing violence, and also a parens patriae interest in alleviating the suffering of mental illness and in providing effective treatment. Under a state's police powers, the court held, medication may be forcibly administered only on a determination that the need to prevent violence in a particular situation outweighs the possibility of harm to the medicated individual, and that reasonable alternatives to the administration of antipsychotics have been ruled out. Criticizing the district court for imposing what is regarded as a profoundly rigid standard, the court of appeals held that a hospital's professional staff must have substantial discretion in deciding when an impending emergency requires involuntary medication.

The court of appeals broadened the state's parens patriae powers somewhat, yet maintained certain limitations. For instance, while confirming that the parens patriae interest will justify involuntary medication only when necessary to prevent further deterioration in the patient's mental health, it stopped short of permitting involuntary medication to improve the condition. The semantic ingeniousness of using the essential difference between "prevent further deterioration" and "improve the condition" to guide the forcible administration of medication demonstrates just how delicate a situation this issue is considered by the courts. The court of appeals reversed the district court's conclusion that a guardian must be appointed to make nonemergency treatment decisions on behalf of incompetent patients. However, the court held that even for incompetent patients, the state's parens patriae interest would justify prescription only of such treatment as would be accepted voluntarily by the individual, were he or she competent. Finally, the court of appeals held that the patient's liberty interest in avoiding undesired drug treatment must be protected procedurally by a judicial determination of incompetency.

The judgment of the court of appeals involved constitutional issues and on that basis the US Supreme Court granted certiorari in *Mills v Rogers*,[12] then later declined to rule on the case and remanded it for further proceedings to the court of appeals to be decided in the wake of *Roe III*.[13]

Richard Roe III was an incompetent noncommitted mentally ill patient. His father applied for and received temporary and then permanent guardianship. Richard, the patient, became involved in assault and robbery. Along with guardianship, the lower court allowed the guardian authority to consent to involuntary treatment with antipsychotic medication. The case was appealed to the Supreme Court of Massachusetts. The two crucial issues facing the court were whether authorizing the guardian to consent to administration of antipsychotic medication usurped the patient's constitutional rights or not; and whether or not, if an incompetent refuses antipsychotic drugs, those charged with his protection must seek judicial permission to substitute judgment and render a decision on the patient's behalf.

The Massachusetts Supreme Court held that it was indeed an error to authorize the guardian to consent to administration of antipsychotic medication, and that those charged with the protection of an incompetent must indeed seek judicial determination of substituted judgment. The rationale behind this ruling is that the court must figure what the incompetent patient would decide if he were competent, and in doing so, the court should weigh the following factors: (1) the extent of impairment of the patient's mental faculties; (2) whether the patient is in the custody of a state institution; (3) the prognosis without the proposed treatment; (4) the prognosis with the proposed treatment; (5) the complexity, risk, and novelty of the proposed treatment; (6) the possible side effects; (7) the patient's level of understanding and possible reaction; (8) the urgency of the decision; (9) the consent of the patient, spouse, or guardian; (10) the good faith of those who are participating in the decision; (11) the clarity of professional opinion as to what is good medical practice; (12) the interests of third persons; and (13) the administrative requirements of any institution involved.

PROBLEMS OF MEDICATION REFUSAL

The issue of treatment refusal has ramifications beyond patients' rights and well-being. Institutions and relationships function by the authority of psychiatrists and other clinicians. Deference to the informed judgment of these professionals could be weakened if they are unable to act on their judgments and assessments. The web of relationships existing among mental health professionals, administrators, and patients has evolved naturally over a long period, not by proclamation from above. Mental health law observers have noticed that one of the fears psychiatrists entertained when the right to refuse antipsychotic medication was first raised was that an epidemic of refusals would sweep psychiatric facilities. This would certainly undermine their treatment efforts, and invite skepticism about mental hospital practices.

Several researchers have studied the characteristics of those patients who refuse treatment. In Marder's research,[14] a group of involuntary patients responded to a hypothetical question, with 15 saying they would refuse medication if permitted to, and 16 willing to accept the medication. The 15 patients refusing scored significantly higher on measures of conceptual disorganization, hostility, uncooperativeness, excitement, and unusual thought content. There were no differences in the degree of hallucinations or suspicion.[14]

Another study found that medication refusers fell into two categories: situational refusers, a diverse group of patients who on occasion refused medication for a short period of time (always less than 24 hours) and for a wide variety of reasons (57% of the sample); and stereotypic refusers, a group of chronically ill patients with paranoid traits who habitually responded to a variety of stresses with brief medication refusal (22% of the sample).[15]

Insight is provided by a look at the general attributes of medication refusers. According to the investigations of Appelbaum[15] and Keisling,[16] the more problematic, long-term refusers tended to be young, better-educated, more acute, with a higher level of functioning prior to the onset of illness. In other words, they are people more used to weighing their prerogatives and thinking for themselves, and could be seen as reluctant to renounce their self-determination. On one hand, it can be said that they fail to rationally assess the situation if they refuse medication that would certainly help them. On the other hand, however, they can be seen as clinging to their autonomy.

Appelbaum and Gutheil reviewed the reasons offered by the 23 refusers responsible for 72 episodes in their samples.[17-19] Among the subjects, 10 attributed their decision to side effects, with four considered to have a reasonable basis for their complaint; nine refused on delusional grounds; eight offered reasons related to concern with bodily privacy; seven gave angry or irrelevant reasons; three stood on their legal rights, and nine offered no reason at all.

COURTS GIVE LIMITED AUTHORITY TO PSYCHIATRISTS

While *Rogers v Okin* and *Mills v Rogers* were in progress, the Third Circuit Court of Appeals arrived at a different conclusion in *Rennie v Klein*.[20] John Rennie, a 40-year-old divorced man, showed symptoms of mental illness in 1971 which grew more serious in 1973 when his twin brother was killed. Shortly thereafter, he was admitted for the first time to the Ancora State Hospital in New Jersey. He was depressed and suicidal, and was diagnosed as paranoid schizophrenic. At various times during his stays, Rennie refused to accept medication. In his 12th admission in August of 1976, after an involuntary commitment proceeding, Rennie instituted a law suit charging the hospital with violating his constitutional rights. Later, he moved to amend his complaint to include class action allegations. The issue before the court of appeals was twofold: whether compulsory medication of involuntarily committed mental patients violated a liberty interest protected by the Fourteenth Amendment; and if such an interest exists, what procedures must the state follow to protect it?

The Third Circuit Court of Appeals held that patients involuntarily committed to state hospitals retain a constitutional right to refuse antipsychotic medication that may have disabling side effects. The state has a right to override the patient's refusal right when the patient is a danger to himself or others, but in nonemergency situations the state must first provide procedural due process. The court also concluded that there is a constitutionally significant difference between simple involuntary confinement and commitment combined with the enforced administration of antipsychotic drugs that may produce tardive dyskinesia. Thus, the right to be free from unjustified intrusions on personal security rises to the level of a liberty interest warranting the protection of the due process clause of the Fourteenth Amendment.

The court found the procedures outlined in the *New Jersey Administrative Bulletin* (78-3) to be constitutionally adequate to protect patients' rights. The *Administrative Bulletin* says that involuntary patients may have medication imposed on them if without it they are incapable of participating in any treatment plan that will give them a realistic opportunity to improve their condition, or if it will shorten the required commitment time, or if there is a significant possibility that the patients will harm themselves or others before their condition improves. Physicians are first required to explain to the patient the reason for taking medication. If the patient refuses medication, the proposed regimen is discussed with the treatment team. If the patient still refuses and no emergency exists, the medical director or his designee must approve the involuntary treatment and review the need weekly. According to the court these procedures satisfied the due process requirements and there was no need therefore to create an adversary atmosphere in the courtroom between the psychiatrist and his patients.

The decision in *Rennie*, unlike that of *Rogers*, does not require a substitute judgment by judiciary process. It leaves the judgment to professionals and internal due process rather than to judges or juries. The *Rennie* ruling is in accord with the US Supreme Court decision in *Romeo v Youngberg*, which states that a treatment decision made by a professional is presumed to be valid unless it is such a "substantial departure from accepted professional judgment, practice or standard as to demonstrate that the person responsible actually did not base that decision on such a judgment."

Appelbaum[15] has described five legal variations on the right to refuse treatment. *Variation A*: the patient is committed, regardless of patient's consent or refusal, and medication is administered; *variation B*: a committed patient refuses, but if an independent clinician's review of the appropriateness of the medication convinces the patient that it is appropriate, then the medication will be administered to the patient; *variation C*: the independent clinicial reviewer must decide, in addition to the appropriateness of medication, the status of the patient's competency and if the patient is found to be incompetent and the medication appropriate, then the medication may be administered; *variation D*: a patient is committed only if he or she is incompetent, in which case the medication may be administered even if the patient refuses; *variation E*: the judiciary system must review (1) the appropriateness of medication, (2) the patient's competency, and (3) the patient's best interests, or substituted judgment. If the court finds that the medication is appropriate, that the patient is incompetent, and the treatment is in the patient's best interest or that the patient would have accepted it if competent, then the judge may order treatment against the patient's wishes.

Refusal is not uncommon, Appelbaum has noted, but the refusing patient almost always seems to receive the treatment in the end. For example, in Massachusetts, a state using *variation E*, for more than 90% of the refusing patients brought before the court, the judge ordered medication. In Oregon, where an independent psychiatrist provides review, 95% of the refusals were turned aside.

CONTINUING PROBLEMS

New York as well as several other states have joined Massachusetts and New Jersey in extending the right of mentally ill patients to refuse psychotropic medication in nonemergency situations. In the cases of *Rivers v Katz*[21] and *Grassi v Crish*,[22] the highest court of the state of New York, the Court of Appeals, held that the due process clause of the New York state constitution affords involuntarily committed psychiatric patients a fundamental right to refuse psychotropic medication. The court based its holding on a series of prior landmark decisions establishing the doctrine that a patient's right to determine the course of his medical treatment is to be considered paramount to what otherwise might be the physician's obligation to provide medical care. Also, that the right of a competent adult to refuse medical treatment must be honored even though the recommended treatment may be beneficial or ultimately necessary to preserve the patient's life.

The New York Court of Appeals reviewed pertinent psychiatric literature and concluded that psychiatric illness is often circumscribed in its effects on mental functioning, leaving many capacities unimpaired, and that consequently psychiatrically ill persons may indeed retain the capacity to function in a competent manner with respect to decisions concerning their own bodies and the medical treatments they are to receive.

The court made an important distinction between the state's right of parens patriae and the state's right of police power. It held that while the state may indeed have a compelling interest under parens patriae to determine and provide care to citizens who are unable to decide and care for themselves, the decision to act on this interest is a judicial function and is not to be relegated to government or medical authorities. On the other hand, the state's interest in exercising police power to promote public safety can, at times, be exercised temporarily without judicial review. In emergency situations where the patient is an imminent danger to himself or others in the immediate vicinity, the state can justifiably give antipsychotic medication by force, with the medication continuing only so long as the emergency situation persists.

In nonemergency situations the court ruled that before medication can be forcibly administered, the patient must be provided with a judicial hearing at which he is represented by counsel. The state then has the burden of proof and must show with clear and convincing evidence that the patient lacks the capacity to make his own treatment decisions. In conclusion, the New York Court of Appeals held that in nonemergency cases, due process requires a judicial decision with respect to competency to refuse antipsychotic medication.[21]

Some courts have viewed the right to refuse medication as nonabsolute.

As an example, an appeals court in Indiana ruled that although an involuntarily committed mental patient had an independent liberty interest in not being forcibly medicated with antipsychotic drugs, based on the professional judgment of the treating physician, there was clear and convincing evidence that the medication was necessary.[23] In this case, M.P., an adult male with a history of delusions, suicidal attempts, and psychiatric hospitalization, was committed to the hospital. The patient was never adjudicated incompetent or found to be dangerous. A lower court had concluded that the patient's commitment to the state hospital should be continued and that the state should be allowed to forcibly medicate him with antipsychotic drugs. On appeal, the appellant challenged both parts of that order. The appeals court found and supported the need for hospitalization and the patient's inability to make rational choices concerning his treatment, including his need for medication. The appeals court referred to the Supreme Court's decision in *Youngberg v Romeo*,[24] and agreed that involuntarily committed mental patients have liberty interests protected by the Constitution in avoiding the unwanted administration of antipsychotic drugs. However, the court did not view the right to refuse as absolute. It could be restricted in order to further a substantial government interest if it met both procedural and substantive due process concerns.

In the view of that court and many others, the professional judgment standard must be applied in assessments of the patient's qualified constitutional right to refuse psychotropic medication, that is, involuntary administration of psychotropics is not intrusive per se as long as there has been no departure from professional standards. Over the years, the right to refuse treatment has taken two distinct forms. Massachusetts, Colorado, New York, and some other states share the premise that medicating a patient is a judiciary decision rather than a medical decision. Others states, including New Jersey and Minnesota, perceive the psychiatrist to function much as a guardian ad litem, or special investigator for the courts, as well as representing a kind of second opinion.

At the time the decision was handed down stating that psychiatric patients have the right to refuse medication, clinicians voiced concerns that such a procedurally cumbersome approach would lead to long delays before treatment could be instituted, resulting in prolonged suffering of their patients and needless prolongation of hospital stays.[15] This valid concern is balanced by the possibility that such procedures will place greater scrutiny on the medication of mental patients. While an occasional patient may be spared inappropriate medication, however, many more will suffer needlessly because of the delays such procedures would create.

A study by Veliz and James[25] shows that the *Rogers* procedures for the administration of antipsychotic medication are extremely time-consuming. They require an enormous investment in professional time for each case. Psychiatrists, in addition, feel that the hearing process adversely affected the relationship between the patient and the physician. In the same study, Veliz and James found that the majority of the 800 anticipated hearings would have involved patients who were accepting medication but who presented a question as to their competence to make treatment decisions. Since these patients had not been adjudicated incompetent, and since it was simply physically impossible to file 800 petitions, most of these patients were medicated. During the delay of up to 7 months between the time a physician files a petition and the time the case is heard, there is no legal authority for a physician to medicate a patient who may be incompetent to consent to treatment with antipsychotic medication, regardless of whether the patient agrees to take the medication. Veliz and James further noted that during the first year of implementation of the *Rogers* decision, in a Massachusetts facility for the criminally insane, from 98 cases submitted to the probate court for medication refusal hearings, only 39 patients (40%) were heard by the court during this time. Thirty patients (31%) for whom petitions were filed were discharged before a hearing was scheduled, and 29 cases (30%) were carried over into the next year. The court found that 35 (90%) of the 39 patients whose cases were heard lacked competence to make treatment decisions. Hearings occurred 2 to 7 months after petitions were signed by the treating physician.[25] In the other study,[26] in a civil state hospital it was found that only 4% of treatment refusals were upheld by the courts. The judges in a very small percentage of these cases agreed with the patient and overruled the hospital staff. So after the courts finally decide on each case, the consistency with which they uphold the doctor's medication recommendation is striking. An unfortunate result of the "right to refuse" seems to be an exorbitant court expense.

Today, a number of states have extended the right of mentally ill patients to refuse psychotropic medication in nonemergency situations. The essence of judiciary reasoning is that there is a crucial distinction between the state's right of parens patriae and the state's right of police power.

In nonemergency situations, before medication can be forcibly administered, patients must be provided with a judicial hearing at which they are represented by counsel. The state then has the burden of proof and must show with clear and convincing evidence that the patients lack the capacity to make their own treatment decisions.

There is always some ambiguity and in a certain respect it is impossible for a psychiatrist to implement and enforce the court order. The ambiguity regards terms such as "emergency situation," "imminent danger," and "persistence of danger." For how long can antipsychotic drugs be forcibly administered without judicial review? Does an emergency situation persist if in the treating physician's view the patient would be dangerous if the antipsychotic medication were discontinued, or does it terminate with the initial remission of psychiatric symptoms that follows the first injection of neuroleptic drugs?

The author agrees that the hospital psychiatrist must be given the power to administer forced medication in emergency situations, but the scope of this power must be more clearly defined. This would both strengthen patient rights and support the physician's responsibility to weigh many often contradictory factors in the final decision of whether or not to forcefully medicate. From both legal and clinical perspectives, a specific time frame for the exercise of such police powers without prior court approval would resolve much of the ambiguity inherent in the notion of an emergency.

Also, there is a question concerning the procedures that are to be utilized to force incompetent patients to abide by a court's parens patriae ruling. For clinical reasons, it is often impossible or unwise to inject or force-feed medication to patients. Lithium, for example, cannot be injected. In addition, there are clear medical risks in accosting physically ill or elderly patients. A patient who does not see any benefit in continued medication will be able, in many instances, simply to refuse further treatment in spite of the court's ruling. Legal sanctions would be completely ineffective with such patients. In essence, ordering grossly psychotic patients to take their medications would be tantamount to ordering them to relinquish their hallucinations and delusions. There is of course always the possibility that the court might side with the patient and refuse to grant his physicians the right to medicate him against his will. In such situations, the patient occupies the hospital bed for weeks and weeks, untreated, but too sick to be discharged, as the following case illustrates.

> Mrs Doe was brought to a psychiatric hospital by police after being found wandering aimlessly in the middle of traffic. Psychiatric examination revealed that the patient was acutely psychotic and delusional with a long history of previous psychiatric hospitalizations. The patient was admitted to the psychiatric ward on an emergency basis and was subsequently found to meet the criteria for schizophrenia according to DSM-III-R (see ref. 3, Chap.2). One of her delusions was that poison had been placed in her food and medication. She therefore refused to eat or to take the antipsychotic medication that she had been prescribed. The patient and her attorney strongly objected to tube feeding. An emergency court order was sought. The judge ordered tube feeding but did not allow the insertion of any medication in her tubes. Three weeks later the treating psychiatrist requested another court hearing. During this hearing the treating psychiatrist went through one hour of direct examination (by the hospital attorney) and cross-examination (by the patient's attorney) regarding the benefits and risks of neuroleptic drugs.
>
> At the end of the hearing the judge reserved his decision and a week later signed an order that the patient can be treated against her will with neuroleptic medication for a period of 90 days. The order did not specify whether long-acting, depot neuroleptics could be used. The patient refused to obey the court order. After a rather chaotic series of events, which by no means enhanced the patient's relationship with her physicians, the patient was medicated by injection of fluphenazine decaonate, a long-acting neuroleptic medication. Fortunately in this case, the patient improved to the point where she eventually accepted medication by mouth.

In this case a hospital bed was occupied by an untreated psychotic patient for over a month before a court ruling could be obtained. While this case (one of the first to be decided under the new ruling) ultimately ended happily, it is easy to imagine other situations in which psychotic patients in need of treatment would remain in this hospital unmedicated, and effectively untreated, for an indefinite period. A "catch-22" situation exists: during the often long waiting period, physicians cannot medicate patients without permission, but cannot effectively treat patients without medicating them. The physicians are thus forced to compromise either their legal or their medical responsibility.

In circumstances, then, where the court had refused to grant permission for forced medication of a psychotic patient or where a medical staff believes it is difficult or unwise to request or implement a court's parens patriae ruling, discharge from the hospital appears to be the only realistic option. Of course such disposition forces psychiatrists to face yet another dilemma: the potential consequences of releasing a psychiatrically disturbed person back into society.

The solution to this dilemma may be to have the psychiatrist inform the court in a de novo proceeding that the patient has continued to refuse medication and that the hospital staff is technically incapable of forcing such treatment, and without such treatment continued hospitalization is neither useful nor warranted. The author believes that under such circumstances the court should have the burden of making the final decision regarding the patient's release. There are, for example, many patients who refuse treatment, who may be dangerous someday but who are not imminently so, and it is time that the courts rather than physicians take official responsibility for determining their fate.

REFERENCES

1. *US v Colorado* 1986; No. 86-F 1470.
2. *US v Connecticut* 1986; No. 86-252.
3. *US v Michigan* 1986; No. 86-CU-73321.
4. *US v Oregon* 1986; No. 86-961-LE.
5. *Rouse v Cameron* 1966; 373 F2d 451.
6. *Wyatt v Stickney* 1974; 344 F Supp 373.
7. *O'Connor v Donaldson* 1975; 42 US 563.
8. Stone AA: *Law, Psychiatry and Morality*. Washington, DC, American Psychiatric Press, 1984.
9. *Romeo v Youngberg* 1980; 644 2d 147 Third Circuit.
10. Hickman F: Right to treatment revisited. *Newsletter Am Acad Psychiatry Law* 1982;7:33–36.
11. *Rogers v Okin* 1979; 478 FSupp 1342.
12. *Mills v Rogers* 1982; US Sup Court No. 80-1417.
13. *In the Matter of the Guardianship of Richard Roe III* 1981; 421 NE 2d 40.
14. Marder SR, et al: A comparison of patients who refuse and consent to neuroleptic treatment. *Am J Psychiatry* 1983;140:470–472.
15. Appelbaum PJ: The right to refuse treatment with antipsychotic medications: retrospect and prospect. *Am J Psychiatry* 1988;145:413–419.
16. Keisling R: Characteristics and outcome of patients who refuse medication. *Hosp Community Psychiatry* 1983;34:847–848.

17. Appelbaum PS, Gutheil TG: Drug refusal: a study of psychiatric inpatients. *Am J Psychiatry* 1980;137:340–346.
18. Appelbaum PS, Gutheil TG: "Rotting with their rights on": constitutional theory and clinical reality in drug refusal by psychiatric in-patients. *Bull Am Acad Psychiatry Law* 1979;7:308–327.
19. Appelbaum PS, Gutheil TG: The Boston State Hospital case . . . right to rot. *Am J Psychiatry* 1980;137:720–723.
20. *Rennie v Klein* 1981; 693 F2d 836.
21. *Rivers v Katz* 1986; No. 191 NY Ct App.
22. *Grassi v Crish* 1986; No. 191 NY Ct App.
23. *In re Mental Commitment of M.P.* 1986; 500 NE 2d 216, Ind Ct App.
24. *Youngberg v Romeo* 1982; 102 SCt 2452.
25. Veliz J, James WS: Medicine court: *Rogers* in practice. *Am J Psychiatry* 1987; 144:62–67.
26. Koge SK, Gutheil TG, et al: The right to refuse treatment under *Rogers v Commissioner*: preliminary empirical findings and comparisons. *Bull Am Acad Psychiatry Law* 1987;15:163–169.

4

Intrusive Modalities

ELECTROCONVULSIVE THERAPY

Electroconvulsive therapy (ECT) was introduced in the treatment of mental illness by two Italian physicians, Cerletti and Bini, in 1938. These physicians observed in the slaughterhouse that electric shock caused unconsciousness in livestock, making them unresistant to slaughter during the unconscious phase.[1]

The terms *electroshock* and *convulsion* are disturbing to most people. The idea of passing electricity through the brain sounds frightening, and people automatically associate electricity applied to the human body with danger and pain. It is not surprising therefore to see an "anti-ECT" sentiment pervasive in the political and judicial arenas.[2] Nevertheless, ECT is a valid treatment for severe mental illness. It involves a brief application of electric stimulus which produces a general seizure. Studies show that ECT is an effective treatment in severe major depression, in acute mania, and in certain schizophrenic syndromes, in comparison to medication. Some studies have shown that ECT is a superior treatment for short-term management of severe depression.

To maximize the benefits of ECT and minimize the risks, it is essential that the patient's illness be correctly diagnosed, and that the risks and adverse effects be weighed against the risks of alternative treatments. The risks and adverse effects in ECT can be divided into two categories: (1) medical complications, which can be substantially reduced by the use of appropriately trained staff, the best equipment, and the best methods of administration; and (2) side effects, such as spotty but persistent memory loss and transient posttreatment confusion. The mortality rate is reported to be from 2.9 deaths per 10,000 patients to 4.5 deaths per 100,000 treatments.

A host of potential physical complications loom, yet the complication rate is a mere 1% per 1300 to 1400 treatments. Before this percentage is judged as large or small, one must weigh it against the physical complications of other treatments, and of no treatment at all. The ECT complications include laryngospasm, circulatory insufficiency, tooth damage, vertebral compression fractures, status epilepticus, peripheral nerve palsy, skin burns, and prolonged apnea. During the few minutes following the stimulus, profound and potentially dangerous systemic changes occur, such as transit hypotension, bradycardia, or sinus tachycardia and hypertension. The effect of ECT on the central nervous system is seizure. After awakening, the patient experiences confusion, transient memory loss, and headache.

The time it takes to recover clear consciousness, which may be from minutes to several hours, varies depending on individual differences in response, the spacing and number of treatments given, and the age of the patient. Deficits in memory function persist after the termination of a normal course of ECT. The ability to learn and retain new information is adversely affected for a time following the administration of ECT. However, after several weeks these abilities return to normal.[3]

Consent for ECT

When the physician has determined that clinical indications justify the administration of ECT, the law requires and medical ethics demand that the patient's freedom to accept or refuse the treatment be fully honored. The physician must make clear to the patient the nature of the options available and the fact that the patient is entitled to choose among those options.

Commentators have questioned whether a severely depressed patient can validly consent to a course of ECT or, on the other hand, validly deny consent.[4] The same authors believe that the requirement of informed consent is a firm part of the ethical practice of medicine, and two separate problems make these questions appropriate and urgent where ECT is concerned.

One of the problems is that ECT is usually prescribed for patients who are seriously depressed and whose ability to objectively weigh options and use the necessary judgment might therefore be open to doubt. The second problem concerns the therapy itself: ECT has been held by some to be an intrusive physical technique with inherently unacceptable risks and hence beyond the range of an option for rational choice. These difficulties challenge the validity of informed consent to ECT. On a more practical level they throw open to question the current practices of employing ECT on the basis of patient consent. Culver et al,[4] in their study of a group of ECT candidates, concluded that in cases in which patients may die without ECT, physicians will not err morally by not respecting patients' informed decisions about such treatment.

The American Psychiatric Association Task Force has considered and discussed the nature of the consent dilemma as a four-part paradigm: (1) the competent patient who consents to treatment; (2) the competent patient who refuses treatment; (3) the incompetent patient who does not object to treatment; and (4) the incompetent patient who refuses treatment.[5] The American Psychiatric Association recommends that the competent patient who consents to treatment should receive it, and that the competent patient who refuses ECT should not receive it.

In cases of incompetency, what will be done is a matter to be settled by following statutes and court decrees according to state laws. The consent form should include information regarding the nature and seriousness of the disorder, the probable course with and without ECT, a description of the ECT procedure, the risks and side effects of ECT, the possibility of alternative treatment, the reasons why ECT has been recommended, a statement of the patient's (or the guardian's) right to refuse or to revoke consent once it is given, the time limits of a single consent, the fact that a new consent must be given for any additional treatment series, and the cost of treatment.

Judicial and Statutory Regulation

The political upheaval that the United States underwent in the 1960s, which exposed the systematic oppression of racial minorities by the country's established social institutions, had tremendous impact on the institutions and systems of the mental health field.[6] One of the offshoots of that revolution was the patients' rights movement, and ECT became one symbol of the plight of patients allegedly at the mercy of the mental health establishment. While the historical transformations of the era brought about some needed reforms, thoughtful questioning of status quo treatments, and refreshing dialogue on the meaning of mental health and insanity, it also had the unfortunate effect of sometimes casting the mental health establishment in the role of "the oppressor," and of instigating an adversarial relationship between psychiatrists and their patients.

As this era was coming to a close, a film appeared which seemed to sum up the fears about numerous aspects of mental health treatment, including commitment to institutions and ECT. This popular film, *One Flew Over the Cuckoo's Nest,* which was based on a novel, portrays not the reality of mental institutions and ECT, but rather the common misperception of them. To avoid jail, the protagonist gets himself committed as criminally insane, expecting a lark. Instead, he finds himself trapped in a Kafkaesque institution with sadistic, power-craving doctors and nurses intent on humiliating and depersonalizing patients. The protagonist does not escape, however, but selflessly returns to "help" the other patients. Of course, he is destroyed by the system, the brutality climaxing in bouts of forced high-dosage ECT and then psychosurgery. It can be surmised that the immense success of the book and movie originated not in their clarifying "the real truth" about the system, but rather in their confirming the popular "horror story" myth which to this day still burdens and unfairly distorts the image of mental health institutions. It is this mentality that sees psychiatric patients as "at the mercy" of the mental health establishment. While this movie was the creation of a respected director inspired by a genuine literary work, it sensationalized a serious issue. The message it conveyed aroused public debate about mental health practices, but the debate sprung from initial misunderstandings and was characterized by near hysteria. The public, which swung from disinterest about mental hospital procedures, to intense and lurid curiosity, and then eventually back to the original disinterest, is responsible for electing the legislators who author laws governing the use of certain procedures, including ECT. And these legislators, in the interest of getting re-elected, are quick to respond to surges of public passion.

In the general anti-ECT atmosphere that prevailed at the time, lawsuits were filed against hospitals, and legislatures were urged to severely restrict the conditions under which ECT could be performed. Legislatures responded and many statutes restricting the use of ECT were passed.[6] California, a state leading in the regulation of ECT, requires that psychiatrists or neurologists other than the patient's attending or treating physician examine all voluntary patients for the capacity to give informed consent to ECT. Further, California law provides that no patient may be judged incapable of refusal solely because of a diagnosis of mental illness or defect. In addition, any person who gives informed consent may revoke that consent at any time and the physician may not give more than a specified number of treatments, nor may treatments continue for more than 30 days. An involuntarily hospitalized patient deemed by a court to be incapable of giving informed consent may claim regained competency to consent or refuse at any time during the 30 days.

California's prejudice against ECT was concentrated most strongly in Berkeley. In November of 1982, Berkeley voters approved and subsequently the city council approved an initiative that made it a misdemeanor punishable by up to 6 months in jail and a fine of $500, or both, for administering ECT within the city limits. The Berkeley ban against ECT was struck down by the California courts. The appeals court found that the ordinance was preempted by state law, and constituted an unwarranted local infringement on a matter of exclusive statewide concern. Berkeley's outright ban was viewed by the court as being in conflict with the state's statutory schemes governing ECT, the right to services that would promote a person's potential to function independently, and the right to free choice.[7] It appears that the courts and legislatures disagree about who should decide when ECT is appropriate and what principles should guide the decision maker. Due process concerns favor some independent regulation of physician decision making, particularly in cases involving involuntarily hospitalized patients.

Impact was felt on a national scale regarding ECT use from the landmark case *Wyatt v Hardin*,[8] a continuation of *Wyatt v Stickney*.[9] The court set forth minimal constitutional standards for the treatment of mentally ill persons in Alabama state hospitals. These standards included mental patients' right not to be subjected to unusual or hazardous treatment procedures such as ECT "without their express and informed consent." The *Wyatt* court provided 14 rules to govern the administration of ECT to all patients, competent or incompetent, consenting or refusing. This court based its restrictions on the right to "constitutional and humane treatment." To oversee the upholding of this right, the court created an extraordinary treatment committee composed of a psychiatrist, a neurologist, a lawyer, and two other members nominated by the Hospital Required Human Rights Committee. The court permitted no one under the age of 18 to receive ECT and competent consenting adults could not be given ECT without the extraordinary treatment committee's approval. The committee's decision to administer ECT was also subject to court review if the patient or a member of the patient's family desired it. In spite of the court's decision in *Wyatt,* most other courts have tended to shy away from such extensive regulation as they are reluctant to practice medicine. Guaranteeing due process of law is one thing, but deciding what constitutes appropriate treatment under specific situations is another issue, and for another profession to grapple with.[6]

From the perspective of the judiciary, the most important issue is whether a willing patient is truly capable of giving informed consent or not. The judges are interested in understanding whether a specific treatment such as ECT is really essential, or perhaps even a matter of lifesaving. In *San Diego Department of Social Services v Waltz,*[10] the California appeals court reversed a lower court's finding that a mental patient had lacked the capacity to give or refuse consent to ECT.

> John Waltz had a long history of mental illness. Because of a kidney ailment, he could not take psychotropic medication and as a result his psychosis became more severe and he had to be hospitalized. In June of 1984, a petition was filed to determine Waltz's capability of consenting to ECT. Twice, a lower court found that he was unable to give consent and appointed a temporary conservator with the power to order ECT for him. Two ECT treatments were administered. In August of that year another petition was filed; again the court found that Waltz could not give consent and that the conservator should consent in his stead. On appeal, the higher court stated that the issue in such cases was not whether treatment is needed or whether it is the least restrictive alternative; such determinations are purely medical. The patient's ability to give informed consent was the only issue of concern. The court then found Waltz competent and capable of deciding for himself and rejected the physician's view that ECT was a matter of lifesaving for Waltz.

Manufacturers of ECT equipment are not immune from lawsuits, if a patient commences a claim of personal injury. In a lawsuit which appears to be the first of its kind, a patient filed a $100 million action against the manufacturers of an ECT machine, alleging that ECT caused her permanent injuries.[11] According to the allegation, the female patient suffered from amnesia as a result of ECT, "which impaired her ability to commit newly acquired information to memory and has impaired her cognitive functions and has resulted in permanent impairment of plaintiff's mental functioning, and other injuries." She alleged that the manufacturers of the ECT equipment were *strictly liable* in tort because they sold equipment that was "improperly and unsafely labeled, and failed to include proper, reasonable and adequate warnings of the damages inherent in the use of the devices." Also, the manufacturers had issued express and implied warranties that the equipment was safe and was fit for its intended uses. In the view of the plaintiff in this case, if the equipment was safe then why had she lost her memory! The plaintiff also sued the treating physician and the hospital for malpractice for prescribing and advising ECT when it was contraindicated and because they had not disclosed the risks thereof.

It appears that ECT is the treatment of choice for those depressed patients who do not respond to conventional treatment. Society and the judiciary system view this treatment as a deviation from accepted norms, however, and therefore the person giving the ECT is an easy target for lawsuits. Also, in court hearings, the judge or jurists may recall disturbing scenes from the movie *One Flew Over the Cuckoo's Nest* or other similarly inaccurate portrayals of ECT, which would be unfavorable to the defendant psychiatrists.

SECLUSION AND RESTRAINT

Among those conversant with the realities of psychiatric institutions, it is common knowledge that assaults on the hospital staff by patients are not uncommon. In a survey where questionnaires were sent to 115 psychiatrists, researchers found that 42% reported that they had been assaulted by some of their patients.[12] The nature of these assaults ranged from a mere slap across the face to serious injuries. Another study found that 24% of therapists, including psychiatrists, psychologists, and social workers, were assaulted in a single calendar year. While 24% of the psychiatrists were physically attacked, 19% were attacked more than once.[13]

Convit et al[14] contrasted a sample of 87 psychiatric inpatients known to have been assaultive while in the hospital with a matched group of nonviolent patients, to identify the personal risk factors that distinguished the two groups. Data were collected using a personal history interview, a neurologic examination, and an electroencephalogram. The four risk factors identified—neurologic abnormality, history of violent crime, history of violent suicide attempts, and deviant family environment in childhood—were used to develop a statistical model predicting which subjects in a sample of newly admitted patients would become assaultive during the first 3 months after admission. The predicted classification of patients was found to be significantly related to subsequent assaultive behavior.

Violent psychiatric patients can be divided into two broad but distinct types: those with a long history of violent behavior and those who became assaultive only after the onset of psychiatric illness. Patients in the first group, which can be characterized by the term "violent-depressive personality," have a long history of antisocial behavior in the form of assaultive, homicidal, and destructive acts, and a corresponding record of repeated imprisonment for violation of the law. These patients exhibit feelings of hopelessness, poor self-esteem, and severe depression. Self-mutilation and suicidal ideation and attempts are very common, as is homicidal behavior. The second group appears to become assaultive only after the onset of psychiatric illness. These patients, in contrast to those in the first group, do not reveal any history of sustained violence or psychopathic behavior. Often they give no warning signals. These patients tend to overestimate their own power and physical strength and, unlike those with a violent-depressive personality, are neither chronically homicidal nor suicidal.[15]

In light of the above, which does not take into account the incidence of violence toward other patients and self-violence, seclusion and restraint is a common practice in management of aggressive, violent, or assaultive patients in psychiatric settings. Regardless of the cause of violence, seclusion and restraint has been considered as a treatment modality by many investigators.[16,17] Somehow or other, mental health professionals must maintain order in the ward and restrain those patients who become violent.

The incidence of seclusion and restraint varies most directly according to two factors: the composition of the patient population and the treatment philosophy of the unit. Specific variables relevant to the incidence of seclusion include hospital setting and patient population (public or private), type of care (acute and chronic), and patient status (voluntary or involuntary). The philosophy of the unit toward the use of medication and medication-free observation for diagnosis or research relates directly to the incidence of seclusion. The lowest incidence of seclusion, 1.9%, was reported in a study of a chronic state hospital, and the highest incidence of seclusion, 66%, was found on a National Institutes of Mental Health (NIMH) research unit for schizophrenia where a treatment philosophy of medication-free maintenance was part of a research strategy and patients were managed almost exclusively through interpersonal therapies.[18]

The duration of seclusion is a complex variable which differs widely between studies. In some studies, it correlates with age, sex, and psychosis at the time of seclusion; in others, it appears more directly related to philosophy of care. Seclusion times range from a low mean of 1.29 hours to a high mean of 19.7 hours in a crisis intervention unit.[18] A prospective study finds the mean duration of seclusion episodes to be 10.8 hours, with a median of 2.8 hours and a range of ten minutes to 120 hours. Some very general patterns emerged: patients under age 35 spent more total time in seclusion than did older patients; patients who were psychotic spent more time in seclusion than nonpsychotic controls; and men had longer individual seclusion episodes than women. The same study found no relationship, however, between the patient's diagnosis, the precipitative factors, the number of prior episodes, and the duration of seclusion.[18]

Data from a survey of seclusion and restraint practices in New York state hospitals were analyzed by Carpenter et al[19] to determine if the practices differed by hospital location. The study included 19 hospitals: five in New York City, four in New York City's suburbs, three in large towns, and seven in small towns. Overall, New York City and large town hospitals had the highest rates of seclusion and restraint, but analysis by age group showed that New York City had the lowest rate for patients under age 35, who constituted the majority of patients being secluded or restrained, and large towns had the highest rate. Compared with suburban and small town hospitals, the New York City and large town hospitals used seclusion more often than restraint and had a higher ward census and a lower staff-to-patient ratio. In all groups, males and blacks were overrepresented compared with the hospital population. Carpenter et al concluded that the seclusion-restraint rate probably does not accurately reflect the actual incidence of violent behavior by mental patients in New York City hospitals.[19]

Although seclusion and restraint has been an accepted practice among mental health professionals, it has come under legal scrutiny in recent years. *Rogers v Okin*[20] is an example. The court made a distinction between restraint and treatment in this instance. Restraint may only be used in cases of emergency such as the occurrence, or a serious threat, of extreme violence, personal injury, or attempted suicide. Seclusion is a form of restraint, while medication, forced or voluntary, is treatment. The court continued that a patient, while secluded, cannot be forcibly medicated. The ruling implies that if a patient is given one form of emergency treatment, such as restraint, he cannot be given another, such as medication, simultaneously. It is further implied in the ruling that the necessity of selecting one treatment will encourage physicians to choose more carefully, as though, without the restriction, they would overstep professional discretion and simply heap treatments on patients to subdue them.

The issue of restraint has been brought to the attention of the US Supreme Court in *Youngberg v Romeo*.[21] Here, the Supreme Court gives clinicians flexibility in using restraint for control of violent patients. Nicholas Romeo, a profoundly retarded individual, was initially hospitalized at the age of 26 because his mother, with whom he had been residing, claimed she could no longer care for him or control his violent outbursts. While living at Penhurst State School and Hospital in Pennsylvania, he suffered numerous serious injuries, some self-inflicted, and because of his aggressiveness he was restrained under a physician's orders. Several years later his mother brought suit against Pennsylvania state officials and the Penhurst staff in the US district court. The verdict stated that the defendants had violated Romeo's constitutional right under the Eighth Amendment to be free from cruel and unusual punishment. The court of appeals reversed the decision, declaring that the Eighth Amendment was an improper source for the determination of involuntarily institutionalized patients' rights. It further declared, however, that the Fourteenth Amendment determined the liberty interests of committed patients, and that freedom of movement was a fundamental liberty which could be limited only by an overriding, nonpunitive state interest.

Finally, the Supreme Court received the case, and among the rights it upheld for patients such as Romeo were the right to safety in the institution and the right to be free from unnecessary bodily restraints. Most important, the Supreme Court differed from the Third Circuit court regarding the safety issue. The Third Circuit court had determined that interests in safety could be compromised only after the state could show a compelling necessity for so doing, and the Supreme Court held that as long as some professional judgment had been exercised, constitutional requirements would be satisfied. A gross departure from commonly accepted professional judgment, practice, or standards was the only basis for liability. Thus, in recognizing that Romeo's condition and propensity for violence precluded an absolute freedom from restraint since such freedom could cause harm to others, the Supreme Court returned some of the discretionary power to the physicians and psychiatrists who were actually in the decision making position during moments of crisis.

In conclusion, the highest court in the land accepted that restraining a patient for the purpose of safety is not illegal and that the professional judgment ordering the restraint could be presumed valid.

PSYCHOSURGERY

Since Egas Moniz and Almeida Lima performed psychosurgery on mentally ill patients more than half a century ago, psychosurgery has always been a highly emotional subject in social, psychiatric, and legal contexts. Loud protests have been raised against the use of psychosurgery in our modern society, and as a result the number of psychosurgical operations has dropped to only a few per year.

Psychosurgery is a surgical intervention to sever fibers connecting one part of the brain to another; or to remove, destroy, or stimulate brain tissue with the intent of modifying or altering disturbances of behavior, thought content, or mood for which no organic pathologic cause can be determined.[22] The sites of the lesions are the prefrontal area (prefrontal lobotomy), and different parts of the limbic system. The assumed benefits of performing psychosurgery are all derived from the interruption of the interconnection pathways between areas involved in the regulation of the emotions. Although there is no specific indication in psychiatry for psychosurgery, the assumption has been that it would be beneficial for a variety of psychiatric disorders, specifically sexual psychopathy and episodic aggressive and violent behavior.

Legal scholars have argued that, because mental patients have a mental incapacity, those who submit themselves to psychosurgery cannot give a truly informed consent and therefore all psychosurgeries could be considered illegal. A classic example is the landmark case involving Lewis Smith, *Kaimowitz v Department of Mental Health*.[23] Smith was committed to a state hospital in 1965 as a criminal sexual psychopath. He was charged with the rape and murder of a student nurse. In 1972 he was transferred to the Lafayette Clinic in Michigan as a suitable research subject for a study of treatment for uncontrollable aggression. Twenty-four such "psychopaths" in the mental health system were going to be used to compare the effects of psychosurgery on the amygdaloid portion of the limbic system. Smith signed an informed consent form for the experiment. He also obtained consent forms from his parents. A three-member review committee approved the program and the consents.

The news media learned of this experimental procedure. An outside attorney, Kaimowitz, filed a petition alleging that Smith and others similarly situated in the Lafayette Clinic were being illegally detained and that surgery must be avoided. Meanwhile, amici curiae were filed by humanistic organizations on behalf of the petitioner.

The court held that involuntarily detained mental patients must be so situated as to be able to exercise the free power of choice without any element of force, fraud, deceit, duress, overreaching, or other ulterior form of restraint or coercion. They must have sufficient knowledge and comprehension of the subject matter to enable them to make a truly informed decision. That decision must be a completely voluntary one on their part. To be legally adequate, a subject's informed consent must be competent, knowing, and freely given. After enumerating these circumstances, the court concluded that knowing consent is impossible, because the facts surrounding experimental brain surgery are profoundly uncertain. It is impossible for involuntarily detained patients to be free from coercion when their very release from the institution may depend on their cooperation with the institution and their giving consent to experimental surgery.

The psychosurgery procedure has been criticized on medical-ethical grounds as well. After all, the brain operation is presumably done on healthy tissue rather than on pathologic tissue, which departs from standard medical practice. Further, adverse changes in the patient's personality and the lack of scientific data to validate the indication for psychosurgery are areas of concern to ethicists.

Psychosurgery procedures have been declining sharply in recent years. A few operations per year are performed, mainly on violent epileptic patients who are not responsive to conventional treatment. No landmark case besides *Kaimowitz* has been brought up in a court of law. The few cases that were brought involved the issue of informed consent, and the court ruled in favor of the physician.[22]

In considering genuine knowing and informed consent to be impossible when the choice is psychosurgery, the court in *Kaimowitz* seems to mirror a general reluctance to employ techniques of such drastic and permanent consequences. The court's reluctance implies that it, too, cannot render completely objective decisions on the issue. How then can the mentally ill people who are the potential subjects?

HYPNOSIS

There is no single, generally accepted theory of hypnosis, nor is there consensus about a definition. Hypnosis requires at least the superficial cooperation of the subject, the development of rapport, and the subject's focused attention. Typically, some form of induction procedure is carried out that is believed to be effective in bringing about a hypnotic state, after which the subject grows increasingly responsive to the explicit and implicit suggestions of the hypnotist (or someone designated by the hypnotist). During this process, the subject is invited to suspend critical judgment and to accept rather than to question the suggestions given.[24]

Hypnosis has traditionally been regarded as a set of procedures that promote alterations in perception and/or memory of the subject who is exposed to these procedures. It has also historically been considered as both a state of heightened suggestibility and a form of hysteria and dissociation. Conventionally, when a clinician speaks of utilizing hypnosis, this can refer to the use of hypnotic inductions, the use of trance development and deepening procedures, and/or the use of hypnotic techniques quite independent of hypnotic trance. Each of these terms can be and is used interchangeably, although they refer to different facets of the hypnotic process.[25]

Freud recognized that the deep or buried memories which surface during hypnosis are not necessarily historically accurate, but rather a combination of fantasies, desires, and fears as well as true recollections of actual occurrences at different periods of time. This contradicts the common misperception that hypnotically induced recollections are always the real truth, removed from consciousness because of their troubling implications.

When hypnosis is used to refresh recollection, one of the following things occurs: (1) the hypnosis produces recollections that are not substantially different from nonhypnotic recollections; (2) it yields recollections that are less accurate than nonhypnotic memory; or, most frequently, (3) it results in more information being reported, but the recollections contain both accurate and inaccurate details. When the third condition results, the subject is less likely to be able to discriminate between accurate and inaccurate recollections.

Recollections obtained during hypnosis not only fail to be more accurate but actually appear to be generally less reliable than nonhypnotic recall. Furthermore, whereas in nonhypnotic memory reports there is usually a positive relationship between the accuracy of recollections and the confidence that the subject places in those recollections, both the hypnotic procedure and the subject's hypnotizability may serve to distort this relationship. The scientific literature indicates that hypnosis can increase inaccurate responses to leading questions without a change in confidence, or it can increase the subjects' confidence in their memories without affecting accuracy, or it can increase errors while also falsely increasing confidence.[24]

Hypnosis and the Judiciary System

Prior to the US Supreme Court's ruling on the admissibility of hypnosis in trial, which will be discussed later, different jurisdictions held different views. Some courts held that hypnotically enhanced testimony was inadmissible, regardless of the procedures employed.[26,27] Other jurisdictions adopted rigorous procedural safeguards as prerequisites to the admission of hypnotically refreshed recollections.[28] Finally, there are jurisdictions that admit testimony obtained through the use of hypnosis because the procedure merely affects credibility.[29]

The Supreme Court struggled with the issue of admissibility of hypnotically refreshed recollection and struck down Arkansas limitations on the use of hypnosis in trial.[30]

Petitioner Vickie Lorene Rock was charged with manslaughter in the death of her husband, Frank Rock, on July 2, 1983. A dispute had been simmering about Frank's wish to move from the couple's small apartment adjacent to Vickie's beauty parlor, to a trailer she owned outside town. One night a fight erupted when Frank refused to let the petitioner eat some pizza and prevented her from leaving the apartment to get something else to eat. When the police arrived on the scene, they found Frank on the floor with a bullet wound in his chest. Petitioner urged the officers to help her husband and cried to a sergeant who took her in charge, "Please save him" and "Don't let him die." The police removed her from the building because she was distraught and interfered with their investigation by repeated attempts to use the telephone to call her husband's parents. According to the testimony of one of the investigating officers, petitioner told him that when she stood up to leave the room, her husband had grabbed her by the throat and choked her and threw her against the wall, and at that time she walked over, picked up the weapon, and pointed it toward the floor. He hit her again, and she shot him.

Another officer reported a slightly different version of the events: Vickie stated that she had told her husband she was going to go outside. He refused to let her leave and grabbed her by the throat and began choking her. They struggled for a moment and she grabbed a gun. She told him to leave her alone, and he hit her, at which time the gun went off. In this account, she stated that it was an accident, and that she hadn't meant to shoot him. She insisted that she had to go to the hospital and talk to him.

Because the petitioner could not remember the precise details of the shooting, her attorney suggested that she submit to hypnosis in order to refresh her memory. The petitioner was hypnotized twice by Dr Betty Back, a licensed neuropsychologist with training in the field of hypnosis. Back interviewed the petitioner for an hour prior to the first hypnosis session, taking notes on the petitioner's general history and her recollections of the shooting. Both hypnosis sessions were tape-recorded. No new information was related by the petitioner during either of the sessions, but after the hypnosis she was able to remember that at the time of the incident she had had her thumb on the hammer of the gun and had not held her finger on the trigger. She also recalled that the gun had discharged when her husband grabbed her arm during the scuffle. As a result of the details that petitioner was able to remember about the shooting, the counsel arranged for a gun expert to examine the handgun. This inspection of the gun revealed that the gun was defective and prone to fire, if hit or dropped, without the trigger being pulled.

The prosecution filed a motion to exclude petitioner's testimony. The trial judge agreed with the prosecutor and held that no hypnotically refreshed testimony would be admitted, ordering the petitioner to limit testimony to "matters remembered and stated to the examiner prior to being placed under hypnosis." The jury convicted Rock on manslaughter charges and she was sentenced to 10 years imprisonment and a $10,000 fine.

Eventually the case arrived before the US Supreme Court. At issue was whether a criminal defendant's right to testify may be restricted by a state rule excluding posthypnosis testimony. In a five-to-four decision, the majority of the Supreme Court justices decided that the Arkansas per se rule excluding all hypnotically refreshed testimony infringes impermissibly on the criminal defendant's right to testify on his or her own behalf.

Despite any unreliability that hypnosis may introduce into testimony, the procedure has been credited as instrumental in obtaining particular types of information. Moreover, hypnotically refreshed testimony is subject to verification by corroborating evidence and other traditional means of assessing accuracy, and inaccuracies can be reduced by procedural safeguards such as the use of tape or video recording. The state's legitimate interest in barring unreliable evidence does not justify a per se exclusion simply because the evidence may be reliable in an individual case. In the *Rock* case, the expert's corroboration of the petitioner's hypnotically enhanced memories and the trial judge's conclusion that the tape recordings indicated that the hypnotist did not suggest responses with leading questions are circumstances that the trial court should have considered in determining admissibility, vacated and remanded. It seems that the Supreme Court has accepted the rules of those jurisdictions that adopt rigorous procedural safeguards as prerequisites to the admissibility of hypnotically refreshed recollections, such as in *State v Hurd*. Those procedures require that:

1. The hypnotic session be carried out away from the police station, and out of the presence of the police.
2. The session be conducted by a licensed psychologist or psychiatrist independent of and not responsible to the prosecutor, investigator, or defense.
3. Any information given to the hypnotist by law enforcement personnel prior to hypnotic sessions must be in written form so that the extent of the influence on the hypnotist may be subsequently determined.
4. The hypnotist should also obtain from the subject a detailed description of the facts as the subject remembers them, before a hypnotic induction is attempted.

5. All contacts between the hypnotist and the subject should be recorded so that a permanent record (video tape if possible) is available for study to establish that the witness' report during hypnosis has not been contaminated by leading suggestions made by the hypnotist.
6. Only the hypnotist and the subject should be present during each phase of the hypnosis session, including prehypnotic testing and the posthypnotic interview.[31]

Those justices dissenting have observed that a hypnotized person becomes subject to suggestion, is likely to confabulate, and experiences artificially increased confidence in both true and false memories following hypnosis. No known set of procedures can ensure against the inherently unreliable nature of such testimony. Further, the dissenters have noted that, overall, an individual's right to present evidence is always subject to reasonable restrictions, and must often give way to countervailing considerations.

Similarly, compulsory process clause decisions make clear that the right to present relevant testimony may in appropriate cases yield to accommodate other legitimate interests in the criminal trial process. The Constitution does not in any way relieve a defendant from compliance with these procedures for the presentation of evidence, which are designed to assure both fairness and reliability in the ascertainment of guilt. Part of this process is the exclusion of testimony whose trustworthiness is inherently suspect. The dissenters have concluded further that an understanding of the scientific aspect of hypnosis is still in its infancy and that the Constitution does not warrant that the Supreme Court mandate its own view of how the courts should handle the issue of hypnosis.

In many ways, hypnosis as an intrusive modality raises issues quite different from the three modalities discussed earlier. The concern for a patient's actual physical and mental well-being is not as urgent an issue as it is with seclusion and restraint, psychosurgery, or ECT. There is no question of administering hypnosis against a patient's consent: it is impossible. Indeed, the issue seems almost benign compared to the prior three; certainly it does not arouse the same emotional response.

It is erroneous, however, to consider the dilemma of hypnosis-enhanced testimony as "merely" a procedural question. When public safety depends in part on the conviction of criminals which in turn is based on evidence and testimony that a jury can depend on "beyond any reasonable doubt," the ramifications immediately become clear. If such testimony is to be admitted in court, all parties should be made aware of its uncertain nature. It would be a disservice to defendants, as well, to permit them to mistakenly believe a version of events simply because it was related during or after hypnosis, whether or not that false version paved the way for a nonguilty verdict.

Following the Supreme Court's decision on a defendant's posthypnotic testimony, state courts began to establish rules for witnesses' posthypnotic criteria. Colorado apparently is the first state to incorporate the *Rock v Arkansas* decision, using it to decide *Colorado v Romero*.[32] The Colorado Supreme Court found that neither automatic exclusion nor inclusion of posthypnotic testimony of witnesses in criminal trials would be proper. Instead, the court established procedures to assess the admissibility of such testimony in specific instances.

In *Romero*, the defendant was charged with felony murder and conspiracy to commit second-degree sexual assault. The Colorado Supreme Court noted in assessing the scientific and legal utility of hypnosis that the testimony was accurate because hypnosis produced accurate memory. The court ruled that the proponent of testimony from a previously hypnotized witness should bear the burden of establishing the reliability of such testimony whenever a challenge is made to its admissibility. In determining admissibility, the court stated, a preponderance of evidence is the suitable standard. The trial court, in making its rulings, should consider the totality of the circumstances, including factors such as the level of the hypnotist's training; the hypnotist's independence from the parties and law enforcement officers; the record, if any, of the hypnotist's knowledge of the case prior to hypnosis; the existence of a written or recorded account of the witness's knowledge before undergoing hypnosis; the existence of recordings of all contacts between the hypnotist and the subject; the presence during the session of persons other than the hypnotist and the subject; the appropriateness of the induction and memory retrieval technique used; and the evidence to corroborate the hypnotically enhanced memory.

The justices noted specifically that the Colorado courts were constrained by the US Supreme Court's decision in *Rock v Arkansas*, which required the lower court to make an individualized inquiry into the reliability of a witness's posthypnotic testimony. Even though the *Rock* decision dealt with the testimony of a defendant, the court concluded that it had broader implications for all witnesses.

REFERENCES

1. Kalinowsky LJ, Hippius H: *Pharmacological, Convulsive and Other Somatic Treatment in Psychiatry*. New York, Grune & Stratton, 1969.
2. Greenblatt M: Electroconvulsive therapy, a problem in social psychiatry. *Am J Soc Psychiatry* 1984;4:3–5.
3. National Institutes of Health: *Electroconvulsive Therapy*. Bethesda, Maryland, 1985.
4. Culver CM, et al: ECT and special problems of informed consent. *Am J Psychiatry* 1980;137:586–591.
5. American Psychiatric Association Task Force Report 14: *Electroconvulsive Therapy*. Washington, DC, American Psychiatric Press, 1984.
6. Winslade WJ, et al: Medical, judicial and statutory regulation of ECT in the United States. *Am J Psychiatry* 1984;141:1349–1355.

7. *Northern California Psychiatric Society v City of Berkeley* 1986; No. A26125, Cal Ct App 1st District (Feb).
8. *Wyatt v Hardin* 1979; Civil Action 3195-N, MD Ala.
9. *Wyatt v Stickney* 1971; 325 FSupp 781, MD Ala.
10. *San Diego Department of Social Services v Waltz* 1986; 225 Cal Rptr 664, Cal Ct App.
11. *Andre v Somatics Inc.* 1987; No. 9220, NY Sup Ct NY Cty.
12. Madden DJ, et al: Assaults on psychiatrists by patients. *Am J Psychiatry* 1976;133:422–425.
13. Whitman RM, et al: Assault on the therapist. *Am J Psychiatry* 1976;133:426–431.
14. Convit A, et al: Predicting assaultiveness in psychiatric inpatients: a pilot study. *Hosp Community Psychiatry* 1988;39:429–434.
15. Kermani EJ: Violent psychiatrict patients: a study. *Am J Psychother* 1981;35:215–225.
16. Gutheil TG: Observations on the theoretical bases for seclusion of the psychiatric inpatient. *Am J Psychiatry* 1978;135:325–328.
17. Binder RL: The use of seclusion on an inpatient crisis intervention unit. *Hosp Community Psychiatry* 1979;30:266–269.
18. Soloff PH, et al: Seclusion and restraint: a review and update. *Hosp Community Psychiatry* 1985;36:652–697.
19. Carpenter, MD et al: Variation in seclusion and restraint practices by hospital location. *Hosp Community Psychiatry* 1988;39:418–423.
20. *Rogers v Okin* 1979; 478 FSupp 1342.
21. *Youngberg v Romeo* 1982; 102 S Ct 2452.
22. Donnelly J: Psychosurgery in Kaplan HI, Freedman AM, Sadock BJ (eds): *Comprehensive Textbook of Psychiatry,* ed 3. Baltimore, Williams & Wilkins, 1986, vol 3, pp 2342–2347.
23. *Kaimowitz v Department of Mental Health for the State of Michigan* 1973; No. 73-19434.
24. American Medical Association: Scientific status of refreshing recollection by the use of hypnosis. *JAMA* 1985; 253:1918–1923.
25. Braun BG, Horevitz RP: Hypnosis and psychotherapy. *Psychiatr Ann* 1986;16:81–86.
26. *People v Shirley* 1982; Cal Rptr 243, cert denied 454 US 860.
27. *People v Hughes* 1983; 59 NY3d 523, 453 NE 2d 484, 466 NYS 2d 255.
28. *State v Hurd* 1981; 86 NJ 525 A2d 86.
29. *State v Williams* 1983; 662 SW 2d 277 Mo App.
30. *Rock v Arkansas* 1987; No. 86-130 (June).
31. Tuite PA, et al: Hypnosis and eyewitness testimony. *Psychiatr Ann* 1986;16:91–95.
32. *Colorado v Romero* 1987; No. 85SC382, 85SA389 (Colo Sup Ct) (Nov 9). *Ment Phy Disability Law Reporter* 1988;12:135–136.

5

Traumatic Neurosis

An emotional disorder is often triggered when a person experiences a sudden stressful psychogenic event or a physical injury. This corresponding mental affliction can be designated "traumatic neurosis." In psychiatric literature, traumatic neurosis takes a variety of guises including war neurosis, compensation neurosis, personal injury neurosis, and the modern term "posttraumatic stress disorder." The stressor in this syndrome is something that would evoke significant symptoms of distress in most people. The trauma may be solitary, such as rape or assault, or it may be communal, for instance, military combat. Stressors in this category include natural disasters such as floods, accidental disasters such as auto collisions, and deliberate man-made disasters such as bombings.

Psychiatric symptoms produced by the traumatic event vary. Commonly, the individual has recurrent painful, intrusive recollections of the event, or nightmares. Some victims complain of impaired memory or difficulty in concentrating and completing tasks. Activities or situations that arouse recollections of the traumatic event are often avoided, and trauma symptoms frequently intensify when the individual is exposed to circumstances resembling or symbolizing the original trauma. A person's general functioning may become disrupted, in both occupational and recreational realms; indeed every aspect of a person's life can be affected. Symptoms of depression and anxiety are quite common in the victims of traumatic neurosis, to the degree that normal functioning can be effectively paralyzed. Symptoms may appear immediately or soon after the trauma, but sometimes a latency period lasting months follows the event.[1]

Alcoholism, drug abuse, phobic disorder, antisocial personality, and major depression are found, either alone or variously combined, in a majority

98

of patients with posttraumatic stress disorder. In addition, persons with a past history of affective-related illness may be more likely to develop posttraumatic stress disorder.[2]

Sometimes persistent auditory hallucinations accompany posttraumatic stress disorder (traumatic neurosis) in the absence of any gross impairment in reality testing or other psychotic symptoms. The hallucinations are typically depressive and could drive the patient to suicide.[3]

Traumatic neurosis can give rise to a series of organic problems as well as psychological problems. These include functional and structural defects in the cranial sensory system consequent to high-intensity stimulation. Cortical, neuronal, and synaptic changes occur in posttraumatic stress disorder as a result of excessive and prolonged sensitizing stimulation leading to depression. The constant symptoms of the disorder are caused by changes in the agonistic neuronal system that impair cortical control of hindbrain structures affecting aggressive expression and the sleep-dream cycle.[4]

Freud recognized that traumatic neurosis could be handled positively and negatively. The positive, constructive approach attempts to bring the trauma into an experiential mode again by remembering, repeating, and fixating. These mental activities are analogous to the reexperience symptom whereby the victim relives the traumatic events. The negative, aggravating approach thwarts the reexperiencing of the forgotten event, and is thus a defensive reaction of avoidance, inhibition, and phobia.[5]

Legal claims for traumatic neurosis fall into two basic categories: (1) tort actions, in which an individual makes a claim for personal (emotional) injury occurring through the fault of another person. The fault may be intentional, such as sexual harassment by a male boss toward his female employee; or it could arise through negligence, for instance, witnessing the death of a close relative in an auto accident. According to prevailing law, in either case the victim can bring a lawsuit and can make claims for indemnity for emotional damages that were incurred through the alleged fault of someone else. (2) workers' compensation, whereby some work-related problem, for instance, an industrial accident or excessive stress, induces traumatic neurosis. In these disability claims, the fault, or negligence, is not an issue, for once it is determined that a worker has suffered an emotional disability from job-related trauma, he or she is entitled to compensation for treatment and loss of earnings, but is not entitled to indemnity for emotional damages under the tort law.

The industrial revolution of the late nineteenth century gave rise to the concept of workers' compensation neurosis. Injured persons felt victimized by industries and employers, and harnessed their collective power to utilize the resources of the legal system. Claims and lawsuits mounted. Eventually laws were passed placing the cost of occupationally induced disability on the employer without regard to who was responsible for the fault or negligence, removing workers' claims from the arena of litigation. In balance, no longer could employees sue their employer for negligence damages, and the employer was liable only for the actual cost of the disability. As the law now stands, financial compensation for lost work time is the worker's right, and the burden to disprove entitlement is shouldered by the employer's disability carrier.[6]

The cynical belief still persists that patients with traumatic neurosis will carry their symptoms as long as the possibility of monetary compensation looms. A study by Burstein[7] indicates otherwise, however. Burstein compared two groups of patients with posttraumatic stress disorder (traumatic neurosis). In one group, a motor vehicle accident catalyzed the disorder, and in the other a sudden loss had precipitated it. Those in the motor vehicle accident faced the possibility of monetary compensation, whereas the sufferers of loss saw no such chance to recover financially. Both groups reacted similarly to the factors studied, and monetary compensation was shown not to be the motivating source of symptoms.

WITNESSING STRESSFUL EVENTS AND BEING AN OBJECT OF HARASSMENT

Sometimes an observer suffers psychological harm after witnessing a disturbing occurrence. As early as the nineteenth century, the courts have taken note of that fact, albeit with little sympathy at times, with one court commenting that "mental pain or anxiety, the law cannot value, and does not pretend to redress, when the unlawful act causes that alone."[8]

The psychological cost of witnessing disturbing events is illustrated by Malmquist[9] in a report of a good samaritan couple who invited a neighbor to spend a night at their house. The next day they discovered that the neighbor had committed suicide in their kitchen by cutting his throat. They brought suit against the estate of the deceased, claiming that finding his blood strewn about their house caused them emotional distress. Cases such as this have been instrumental in the creation of a standard in tort liability whereby "nervous shocks" induced negligently or deliberately by a third person can be grounds for a lawsuit, regardless of whether the emotionally injured person was in a "danger zone" or not.

Dillon v Legg[10] is a leading case in this area, setting precedent for subsequent cases with similar circumstances. In *Dillon,* a mother was in close proximity to her daughter when the daughter was killed by the defendant's negligence in an automobile crash. The mother brought a lawsuit alleging that she suffered from "emotional shock" as she witnessed the accident. The court agreed, and in effect proposed guidelines for juries to follow in deciding liability in future cases. These guidelines include: (1) whether the third party was located near the scene of the accident in contrast to a distance away; (2) whether the shock resulted from a direct emotional impact on the third party from the sensory and contemporaneous observation of the accident, in contrast to learning of it later or from others; (3) whether the victim and the third party were closely related, in contrast to the absence of a relationship or a distant one. In its ruling the court rejected the outmoded notion that the witness must be fearful for his own safety, and thereby substantiated purely psychological phenomena.

Being sexually harassed on the job can create as much psychological stress as witnessing traumatic incidents. With this stressor, the victim is forced to be a party to the trauma. Sexual harassment occurs when a person in a powerful position exploits that position to impose sexual demands or pressures on an unwilling and less powerful person.[11] In most such cases, the exploiter is a male; the exploited, female.

A common pattern for sexual harassment is for sexual favors to be demanded in exchange for job opportunities, with the threat of retaliation if the woman refuses. Undoubtedly, women placed in this situation experience abnormal stress; they may feel insecure, fearful, and eventually suffer from anxiety and depression. The sense of powerlessness is heightened since frequently the victim has, or feels she has, nowhere to turn to make a grievance and receive justice within the company. The issue is still too controversial, and too prevalent, for open discussion within many companies.

Other forms of sexual harassment are constant touching, sexual remarks and slurs, and propositions. While direct threat is absent, a muted threat does hover in the sense that the victim knows she cannot comfortably denounce such behavior without calling her own character into question. Persistent subjection to these forms of harassment can cause women to suffer from isolation, avoidance feelings, lack of trust, and other stress symptoms.

If a victim feels she has suffered a personal injury constituting traumatic neurosis as a result of sexual harassment, she may bring a tort action. Or, if she has found that harassment has affected her so profoundly that she is unable to work, she may claim entitlement to workers' compensation. Tort actions claiming sexual harassment can take the form of battery, assault, and intentional infliction of emotional distress.[12]

Unlike other situations where a person brings suit for traumatic neurosis, the sexually harassed woman remains in a predicament. While her claim may be upheld and compensation awarded, this victim often continues to be victimized. She can be alienated because she "rocks the boat," or "drags someone's name through the mud," if her tormentor is a respected member of the company and community, known as a "family man" to whom many owe allegiance. Since he is usually powerful, people may see him as the victim and her as the aggressor harassing him with a lawsuit! On the other hand, the victim who brings a lawsuit is often the recipient of vague anger, with people complaining that because of her, they now cannot enjoy normal flirtation, cannot fraternally toss an arm around a shoulder, etc, because they are afraid of their behavior being misconstrued as sexual harassment. If a prospective employer learns that a woman brought such a suit against her former superior, he may be reluctant to hire her. If he does not fear such a suit against himself, he may wonder why she "really" was not promoted. Of course, he cannot phone for an objective and accurate reference. Knowledge of these unpleasant ramifications of using one's legal prerogatives to redress sexual harassment can exacerbate the victims's feeling of powerlessness, and therefore the overall symptoms of traumatic neurosis.

WORKERS' COMPENSATION

Emotional disabilities are compensable under the Workers' Compensation Act regardless of whether the source of the disability is a direct physical injury or a mental shock.[13] Under this act, compensation is awarded for the incapacity to work due to injuries arising from and during employment. However, benefits are to compensate strictly for the inability to work, and not for the injury, a crucial distinction between this form of financial recovery and negligence.

In *Carter v General Motors*,[14] an early case placing emotional injury in the realm of workers' compensation, the plaintiff Carter developed a psychosis and believed that it stemmed from emotional pressure encountered in daily work as a machine operator on assembly line production. He filed for workers' compensation. Although the psychosis condition of the plaintiff was confirmed, evidence and testimony were presented indicating that he had a latent mental disturbance involving a personality disorder and a predisposition to schizophrenia. In addition, expert testimony was offered that at the time of the hearing the plaintiff no longer showed the symptoms of psychosis. Although he could be employed again, physicians recommended that he not be because his predisposition to mental illness was activated when doing production work. The Workers' Compensation Board granted compensation for initial incapacitation and for continuance of compensation. General Motors appealed.

At this juncture, the issue before the court was whether psychosis resulting from the emotional pressure of daily work justifies workers' compensation. The court was convinced that a causal link did exist between the job and the mental illness, and that although the mental condition did not originate through physical injury to the claimant, for example, by head trauma, or by his observance of a fellow worker's injury, as expressly provided for in the act, he should be treated no differently from a worker incapacitated by physical injury, provided a causal connection is evident. Emotional disability, like physical disability, the court found, should be compensated.

Workers' compensation has covered the common manifestation of neurosis called conversion disorder, also known as hysterical neurosis. The essential feature of conversion reaction is a disturbance or change in physical functioning suggesting that the physical disorder is actually an expression of a psychological conflict or need. The disturbance eludes voluntary control, and after appropriate investigation cannot be explained by any physical or patholophysiologic mechanism. Symptoms of this disorder include paralysis, aphonia, seizures, coordination disturbances, akinesia, blindness, paresthesia, and other neurologic complaints. Individuals who develop conversion disorder may achieve the primary psychological aim of keeping an internal conflict or need hidden from awareness, or a secondary aim of avoiding a particular activity that is traumatic to them. Conversion disorder usually occurs in a setting of extreme psychological stress and appears suddenly.[1]

The courts view conversion disorder as an involuntary, undesired affliction that entitles the sufferer to workers' compensation. This view was clarified in *Brown & Root Construction Company v Duckworth*.[15] The claimant, Brown, alleged that his supervisor assured him of a promotion. After the claimant was told by his supervisor to forget about the promotion, Brown developed headaches, lost consciousness, and had to be hospitalized for nine days. Brown later applied for workers' compensation and was rejected by the employer. Next Brown went to court. At the hearing the employer argued that anxiety over promotions was merely a part of the job and unrelated to injury at the job. The Mississippi Supreme Court rejected the employer's argument and contended that the employer deliberately created heightened expectations of advancement in the claimant and triggered a reaction by doing something that the claimant reasonably perceived as a betrayal.

Promising a promotion and then not giving that promotion, in the court's view, is equal to harassment and the victim is entitled to some compensation. In *Brown,* the promotion was virtually assured by the employer, to the extent that the plaintiff was acting reasonably in expecting it and proceeding with his life and work in accordance with that expectation. He might have done otherwise if he had not received the assurance. In effect, such a promise influences many or all of the "life decisions" people would make in its wake, and to rescind it can undermine their stability, especially if they have organized their future around it. However, the *Brown* ruling rests on the promise being specific and substantial. It does not extend to likelihood of promotion, possibility of promotion, or qualified promise of promotion.

If employees develop anxiety related to the job they are entitled to compensation. Similar to the *Brown* case, in *Cooper v Workers' Compensation Appeals Board*[16] the California Court of Appeals held that a claimant sustained a psychiatric injury in the form of conversion reaction after being exposed to asbestos. Cooper alleged that he had been exposed to asbestos at work and the physician testified that Cooper suffered from conversion hysteria that was caused not by exposure to asbestos but by the fear of being exposed to asbestos. Additionally, Cooper's having been misdiagnosed as "asbestosis" probably worsened the anxiety. The court found that if it were not for the asbestos at the job site, Cooper would not have developed the fear of exposure to asbestos and asbestos-related disease that precipitated his conversion reaction. As with other job-related disabilities, therefore, the claimant was entitled to compensation. Entitlement to workers' compensation does not end with the death of the worker, and the immediate family may be entitled to compensation if work pressure has caused the employee's emotional distress, depression, or suicide. For example, in an action brought by a widow for workers' compensation death benefits following her husband's suicide, the Minnesota Supreme Court held that the employee's death was compensable because his work-related injury had caused or been a contributing cause of his suicide.

The deceased had sustained a disabling back injury on the job 9 years before the attempted suicide, underwent surgery twice, and experienced great pain, mental suffering, and depression. During the entire period between the accident and the suicide he was under the care of a psychiatrist. An expert for the claimant testified that the claimant's husband was a paranoid schizophrenic and unable to cope with his psychological problems before his accident, but whose physical disability made his psychological problems more acute. An expert psychiatrist for the insurance carrier agreed that the employee's injury and resulting disability were substantial contributing factors to the suicide, but refused to identify the injury as the single event that caused the suicide, emphasizing instead that the injury was only one of several stressful events in the employee's life. Since both psychiatrists agreed that the husband's injury and its consequences were substantial contributing causes to the suicide, the employee's death was compensable.[17]

In *Meils* and similar cases, the court does not consider the preexisting mental condition, such as paranoid schizophrenia, as an essential criterion. The court, in *Meils,* was concerned with whether a particular back injury brought the employee to the verge of suicide. Was it, as the saying goes, "the straw that broke the camel's back"? A preexisting condition may be quite severe and still be basically irrelevant to the determination by a court regarding worker's compensation. The court in a sense narrows its focus to events that transpired during work, and then rules on their impact exclusively.

The Oregon Court of Appeals held that a claimant's preexisting psychological condition was aggravated when he suffered an injury on the job. He injured his right knee and jaw while driving a truck, and was diagnosed as having depression secondary to the accident, with suicidal tendencies, and was unable to work for psychiatric reasons. The claimant also suffered from a preexisting psychological condition stemming from physical abuse as a child, high stress in Vietnam, and drug addiction. The court found that his preexisting psychological condition, which had been asymptomatic at the time of the accident, worsened as a result of his physical injury.[18]

If individuals have a prior psychological problem and develop a new psychological disorder because of their job, they would be entitled to compensation under the compensation act. The new problem need not necessarily arise from physical injury or pressure on the job. For example, a New York appeals court affirmed a lower court's decision awarding benefits for a "psychiatric injury" to a man who noticed distressful news in his personnel file. Testimony from the claimant's psychiatrist demonstrated that the psychiatric problem was directly attributable to the fact that the claimant saw his personnel file. Its contents included a newspaper clipping referring to his conviction for attempted armed robbery. The court did not care whether the item was true or not, or that the claimant had previous marital difficulties, anxiety, and depression, or that he had been off work for 2 months prior to viewing his file. The court was interested in whether seeing that particular newspaper clipping created a new psychiatric disorder, and found that it did, and therefore the claimant was entitled to workers' compensation.

Some courts use a "preliminary link theory" in compensation determination. This theory contends that the courts should discern whether, based on the evidence, there is a presumption of compensability that the employment contributed to the injury. That an employee assumes or perceives his employment as the source of his injury is not sufficient under this theory. The three-segment link between employment and the employee's injury and his or her resulting disability must be proved.

Based on this theory, the Alaska Supreme Court reversed and remanded a Workers' Compensation Board ruling that a claimant with a mental disability allegedly due to nontraumatic gradual work-related stress needed to show that her stress was greater than the stress other employees experienced.[19] The claimant Fox, a clerk, filed a workers' compensation complaint alleging a nervous breakdown due to employment-related pressure. She testified that she was not told what was expected of her, had been treated unequally, was denied requests to take vacation, was transferred without her knowledge, that her supervisor talked behind her back, etc. Before denying her claim, the compensation board cited a psychologist's report indicating that other factors unrelated to her employment had caused Fox's distress. Overall, the board found that claimant Fox could not demonstrate that she suffered greater stress in her job than did other employees.

The state supreme court rejected the board's findings. In this court's view, the requirement that the claimant show she suffered more than others was contrary to the fundamental principles of the Workers' Compensation Act, which should be read liberally, with the employer taking the employee "as he finds him." The court also rejected the claimant's argument that the "honest perception" test be adopted to substantiate a disability, since such a test is fundamentally inconsistent with the statutory requirement than an injury arise out of employment. Such a perception would originate, instead, in the individual.

This approach fails to take into account the fact that objective, environmental realities such as employment may or may not contribute to a disability. Further, it ignores the issue of whether an employee's subjective reaction to work stress actually contributed to the injury. In the preliminary link theory, claimants must present evidence only that the employment contributed to their injury. By adopting this theory, the courts have followed the general drift of workers' compensation rulings in looking solely at the employment and giving no weight to a variety of peripheral factors.

Contrasting this trend, a few states disallow workers' compensation for mental injuries resulting solely from mental stimuli. Some courts are insensitive to emotional injury and disability if it does not arise directly from physical causes. This is what happened to the claimant Tracy Followill in *Followill v Emerson Electric Company*.[20] Followill became disabled after arriving at the scene of a plant accident and seeing that his friend and coworker had been killed by having his head crushed in a die cast press. Although Followill sustained no physical injury, witnessing the horrifying scene led to constant nightmares and insomnia, hospitalization, and personality change. Psychiatric experts expressed the opinion that the claimant was 50% to 60% permanently disabled and might suffer from the consequences of posttraumatic stress disorder such as flashbacks and hallucinations while on the job. The claimant was denied compensation by an administrative law judge. However, a state court overturned that ruling and agreed with the psychiatrist, awarding $32,000 compensation.

On appeal, the Kansas Supreme Court examined prior court decisions interpreting key provisions of the workers' compensation statute, and concluded that only "traumatic neurosis" following physical injury and proved to be directly linked to such injury is compensable under the Workers' Compensation Act. The court therefore denied rewards to Followill since his mental disease originated with his response to a work-related traumatic experience and not with a work-related physical injury. The letter but not the spirit of the Workers' Compensation Act seems to have been upheld in this court's restrictive reading of it.

As has been shown, however, not all courts are so insensitive to emotional injury, or so narrow in their recognition of its sources. Some courts do hold that any disease, physical or emotional, originating in the course of employment is encompassed by the state workers' compensation statute. This was the case in *McGarrah v State Accident Insurance Fund*.[21] Henry McGarrah was employed as a deputy sheriff until he had to leave his position because of a mental disorder. He was convinced that his captain was conducting a personal vendetta against him, evidenced by such adverse decisions as moving him to a less desirable position, rejecting his promotion request, and reprimanding him in public. Eventually the deputy, McGarrah, suffered from depression and filed for workers' compensation alleging that his disorder appeared during the course of his employment. A psychiatrist testified that McGarrah suffered from anxiety and depression related directly to his job. The Workers' Compensation Board, nevertheless, did not award benefits and the case finally was heard in the court of appeals which reversed the board's decision. The Oregon Supreme Court noted that cases from different jurisdictions followed a basic principle in which a worker who is disabled by work-related mental stress should receive treatment identical to a worker disabled by a work-related physical injury.

Some courts have held that a claim would be compensable if the claimant's mental disorder were caused by circumstances to which an employee is not ordinarily subjected or exposed except during a period of regular actual employment. A claimant would be required to prove only that the stress arose from and during the course of the employment and that the employment-related stress suffered by the claimant was the major contributing cause of the claimant's mental disorder.[22]

The main doctrine supporting the workers' compensation system is that an employee's inability to work arises from impairments, which in turn arise from conditions somehow relating to his or her employment. If a mental disorder does not stem from trauma, to justify a compensation award it must arise from a situation of greater dimensions than the day-to-day emotional strain and tension that an individual ordinarily faces. Therefore, the workers' compensation doctrine precludes recourse for the countless emotional strains and difficulties that almost all employees encounter daily.

The cause of emotional injury, according to prevailing law, must be based on objective criteria, not simply a subjective perception by the person that an employment-related event caused stress or disease. The event must have actually occurred on the job and cannot be imaginary. While the disease need not be caused or aggravated solely by work conditions, evidence must be presented that compared to nonemployment exposure, work conditions are the major contributing causes of the claimant's disease or disorder.

Workers' compensation laws are effectively a compromise. For its willingness to compensate any work-related injury regardless of fault, the company gains release from the threat of costly negligence suits. Conversely, the employees, in their agreement to forego potential immense negligence awards based on injury, gain the opportunity to receive compensation for any job-related disability, again regardless of fault. Sometimes an injury to an employee can be traced directly to a company's negligence, and sometimes to the employee's own negligence, but in reality a good percentage of disabilities are caused by the whims of fortune, by life's vicissitudes, by mere chance. The workers' compensation system seeks to provide a remedy whereby the bonds of society and the social contract are maintained when a member of society is unable to keep pace because of a work-related injury. It is assumed that people who work thereby meet part of their social obligation, and thus earn this protection.

REFERENCES

1. American Psychiatric Association: *Diagnostic and Statistical Manual of Mental Disorders,* ed 3, revised Washington, DC, American Psychiatric Press, 1987 [DSM III-R].
2. Rundell, Ant, et al: Posttraumatic stress disorder's relationship to depressive illness. *Am J Psychiatry* 1986;143:267–288.
3. Mueser KT: Auditory hallucinations in combat-related chronic posttraumatic stress disorder. *Am J Psychiatry* 1987;144:299–302.

4. Kolb LC: A neuropsychological hypothesis explaining posttraumatic stress disorders. *Am J Psychiatry* 1987;144:989–995.
5. Eth S: Freud and traumatic neurosis. *Am J Psychiatry* 1986;143:1057.
6. Modlin HC: Compensation neurosis. *Bull Am Acad Psychiatry Law* 1986;14:263–271.
7. Burstein A: Can monetary compensation influence the course of a disorder? *Am J Psychiatry* 1986;143:112.
8. *Lynch v Knight* 1861; 11 Eng Rep 854.
9. Malquist CP: Children who witness violence: tortious aspects. *Bull Am Acad Psychiatry Law* 1985;13:221–231.
10. *Dillon v Legg* 1968; 68 Cal2d 729.
11. Sexual Harassment Claims of Abusive Work Environment Under Title VII. *Harvard Law Review* 1984;97:1449–1467.
12. Bursten B: Psychiatric injury in women's workplaces. *Bull Am Acad Psychiatry Law* 1986;14:245–251.
13. Compensation Laws 1948 and Compensation Laws Supp 1956, Section 411.1 et seq.
14. *Carter v General Motors* 1961; 106 NW2d 105.
15. *Brown & Root Construction Company v Duckworth* 1985; 475 So2d 813 (Miss Sup Ct).
16. *Cooper v Workmen's Compensation Appeal Board* 1985; 218 Cal Rptr 783.
17. *Meils ex rel Meils v Northwestern Bell Telephone Company* 1984;355 NW2d 710 (Minn Sup Ct).
18. *Chatfield v Saif Corp* 1984; 688 P2d 434 (Or Ct App).
19. *Fox v Alascom, Inc* 1986; 718 P2d 977 (Alaska Sup Ct).
20. *Followill v Emerson Electric Company* 1984; No. 55 753 (Kan Sup Ct).
21. *McGarrah v State Accident Insurance Fund Corp* 1983; No. 79-05440 (Or Sup Ct).
22. *Leary v Pacific Northwest Bell* 1982; 653 P2d 1293.

6

Contractual and Testamentary Capacity

The concept of contractual capacity has a history as old as the insanity defense. Judeo-Christian and Islamic law prohibited minors, feeble-minded persons and "lunatics" from engaging themselves in contracts. Roman and English law have also specified that "insane" persons cannot contract to do business, because they cannot understand the nature of contractual commitment.

In the nineteenth century, the US Supreme Court noted that "the fundamental idea of a contract is that it requires the assent of two minds. But a lunatic or a person *non compos mentis* has nothing which the law recognizes as a mind, and it would seem, therefore, upon principle, that he cannot make a contract which may have any efficacy as such."[1] For the validity of a contractual document to be upheld in a modern court, it must be established that the minds of the persons executing the instrument were not "weak" or "unbalanced" when the instruments were executed, and that each party could understand the purpose and effect of what they were doing in entering a contract.

Persons who have been adjudicated incompetent to manage their estate will have their affairs vested in the care of a guardian, and the power of the incompetent to contract is entirely withdrawn. Contracts made by incompetent persons shall be considered void.[2]

VOIDING A CONTRACT DUE TO MENTAL ILLNESS

Being ignorant of legal terms, rights, and procedures when one executes a contract is vastly different from failing to understand a contract because one is afflicted with mental illness. The former type of misunderstanding is an insufficient basis for voiding the contract. The latter noncomprehension, in some cases, will require that a contract be declared void.

An example of what can happen when an unbalanced person enters into a contract is provided in *Apfelblat v National Bank Wyandotte Taylor*.[3] The plaintiff, Apfelblat, executed two promissory notes to purchase two cars. Later, he was involuntarily committed and released. Since the notes were unpaid and due in lump sums, the plaintiff made interest payments and executed new notes to cover the accrued debts of the old notes. The plaintiff brought an action to dismiss the notes because of his lack of capacity at the time the original notes were executed. On appeal, the court noted that contracts made by mentally incompetent persons prior to a formal adjudication of incompetency were not void, but rather voidable. They could be rescinded by taking affirmative action; otherwise they would remain valid. Even voidable contracts could be ratified by actions, express or implied, that showed that the person had knowledge of material facts related to the initial contract. The plaintiff in this case did not argue that he had not understood the conditions of the renewal notes but rather that he had been ignorant of his legal rights at the time he executed the renewal notes.

Courts have ruled that the mental capacity of a contract executor or executrix must be taken into consideration by the parties involved at the time of the contract signing. If an executor or executrix of a contract does not have the mental capacity to proceed with the action, he or she cannot sell property or give a receipt, and the sale or the contract to sell must be annulled.[4]

If the court finds that individuals are incapable effectively to look after their affairs, specifically their financial situation, then the court might appoint a conservator. The conservator's task is to look after the affairs of the conservatee and to make sure that the conservatee does not engage himself in undesirable transactions. The conservator's task is also to give input and approve of all matters relating to the disposition of property and other transactions. The appointment of a conservator does not mean that the conservatee is incompetent and completely incapable. The sole purpose of a conservatorship is to afford the protections akin to those provided by a guardianship without the stigma of incompetency.[5]

TESTAMENTARY CAPACITY

When persons execute a will, they must possess mental capacity at the time of execution for that will to be legally valid. Mental capacity is termed "testamentary capacity" in this specific situation. Testators must possess "sound mind" and must comprehend the nature and extent of their property. They also should be familiar with the persons who are the natural objects of their bounty, and the dispositive effect of the act of executing the will.

The validity of a will and the testamentary capacity of a testator become an issue when the will is challenged by beneficiaries or potential beneficiaries.

Courts often hear evidence focusing on the mental state of the testator as it existed before and after execution of the will. The list of medical and psychiatric disorders that provide a basis for someone to challenge a will, or indeed actually impair a person's testamentary capacity, is substantial.[6] Any disorder that alters the moods or brain functions of a testator increases the vulnerability of that person's will to challenge.

SOUND MIND VERSUS UNSOUND MIND

The very first sentence of most standard wills starts "I, John Doe, being of sound mind . . . " This demonstrates the importance of the testator's "sound mind" to the will-making process and the enduring validity of their last will and testament. The courts' main concern in this issue is whether testators had a "sound mind" or "unsound mind" at the time they signed a will. Testimony of experts as well as those who are acquainted with the testator can be heard in order to help judges arrive at a decision. The question before a court, specifically, is if a deceased, at the time of signing a will, knew his next of kin, the nature and extent of his assets, and the size of the bequests.

An example of how a court interprets the meaning of "sound mind" is found in *In re Estate of Kern*.[7] When Kern died, she left $300 to each of her sisters and brothers and the remainder of her vast property to two lawyers and a couple. Another attorney who had prepared the will video-taped the signing portion of a meeting in which Kern was able to name some of her nieces and nephews and describe her property, personal effects, and various bank accounts. After her death, Kern's niece challenged the will. Witnesses such as Kern's housekeeper, nurse, and physician testified that the deceased was oriented and alert and never became confused until shortly before her death. The court found that evidence of sound mind at the time of execution was "overwhelming" and the will valid.

Mental instability due to mental illness, short-term memory lapses, and inability to make rational decisions, in the view of the courts, are signs of "unsound mind" and therefore the existence of those signs in a testator at the time of will execution makes a will invalid. A court may also need to determine whether a will has been based on an "insane delusion." Insane delusion, a term that courts usually use in lieu of psychotic delusion, differs from a mistaken belief. For example, a Michigan appeals court held that a testator's will was not made based on an "insane delusion" in *In re Estate of Sarras*.[8] Sarras had never married, had no siblings, and both his parents had predeceased him. When he left all his property to his friend, his cousin contested the will. A jury found that while Sarras had possessed testamentary capacity, the will was a result of his "insane delusion" that his family did not give him enough attention. Family members testified that he had a number of manic-depressive attacks requiring several hospitalizations, and that he had experienced a manic depressive episode when he executed his will.

The appeals court reversed this decision, concluding that Sarras' belief that his family was not providing enough attention was "most probably the result of a mistaken belief such as would not rise to the level of an insane delusion and it was not in fact a belief without any foundation or reason." Facts demonstrated that he was not invited to family functions, that family members had stopped performing his household chores, and that he was discouraged from visiting relatives.

UNDERSTANDING THE NATURE OF ONE'S ACTS

A testator or testatrix should appreciate the legal and binding nature of a last will and testament, and when executing the document should know exactly what he or she is signing. A testator must understand the personal, legal, social, and financial ramifications of this testamentary act. To produce a valid will, the testator must execute the will with a sound mind free of confusion from drugs, alcohol, or other substances.

If a will is challenged, the burden of proving lack of testamentary capacity rests with the party alleging such deficiency. The standard of proof is clear and convincing evidence.[9] For example, the Arkansas Supreme Court held that an 88-year-old woman did not have the testamentary capacity to make a will during her final stay in the hospital, based on testimony that at the time she signed the will, she was heavily sedated, upset, and confused, and kept asking, "Have I signed something I shouldn't?"[10] To enforce the validity of a will made by a person in such a condition is as unfair to her as to those left out because of her deteriorated situation. To ensure that people understand the act of producing a will when they become a testator or testatrix protects them from disposing of their assets in a way they would regret in happier circumstances.

NATURAL OBJECTS OF BOUNTY

When a testator or testatrix leaves family members out of a will, the law questions whether the testator was aware that he indeed had blood relatives and consciously did not include them in the will. Ignorance of the existence of blood relatives at the time of execution of a will constitutes a basis for challenge to the will's validity.

A testator in *Farner v Farner*[11] left all his assets to his nephew and deprived all other relatives of his bounty. Those relatives left out of the will challenged it, claiming that the testator was not aware of their existence. As evidence they presented an outpatient treatment card from a veterans' hospital with an illegible date, which they claimed showed that the testator needed treatment on the day after he executed the will. The court was not convinced in this case, holding that the evidence showed only that the testator may have had some medical problem on that day.

While a challenge to a will on this basis can be commenced with scant evidence, courts will generally hold the challenge only upon viewing conclusive evidence, as *Farner* demonstrates. Motives including resentment, anger and even avarice are often the catalyst for such legal action, and justices must wend their way through a thicket of emotions to uncover the facts.

THE NATURE AND EXTENT OF PROPERTY

If one's memory is hampered by mental dementia or other factors at the time of executing a will, the will can be declared invalid. Thus, the courts want to know whether a testator was aware of the size and extent of his property when he signed a will.

In *In Re Will of Slade*,[12] a New York appeals court held that a 91-year-old testatrix lacked testamentary capacity when she executed her will, based on evidence that she was suffering from degenerative dementia at the time. There was also evidence that the testatrix had been unable to transact any business and had not known what investments she owned. The year before the will was drafted, a conservator had been appointed based on the testatrix's apparent inability to care for herself: her house was littered with money and she had not paid taxes or utility bills. Furthermore, she believed that her total assets amounted to $10,000, when actually her estate was valued at $650,000. The testatrix's misconstrual of the extent of her own assets is central to the proof of lack of testamentary capacity in this instance.

UNDUE INFLUENCE

When someone unfairly influences a testator or testatrix as he or she drafts and signs a will, the will can be invalidated. A fine line exists between acceptable, normal influence and "undue influence." If a testator is in possession of clear mental faculties and influenced by genuine love or affection for someone and leaves to that person substantial assets, the influence may be strong but not "undue," that is, it arises from a regular life process. For an influence to be "undue" the influencer must employ a degree of manipulation or deception in engaging the affections of the testator and swaying him consciously or unconsciously to alter the will in his or her favor.

When family members left out of a will feel slighted, they might interpret the supposed interloper's influence as undue when it in fact stemmed from a healthy and nurturing relationship. A common scenario for a lawsuit based on undue influence is an affluent older person married to one much younger bequeathing to the young spouse all or a major portion of his assets at the expense of other family members. Such a circumstance existed after the deaths of the Johnson & Johnson billionaire John Seward Johnson, Charlie Chaplin, and the novelist Taylor Caldwell. In artist Georgia O'Keefe's case, the beneficiary was not a spouse, but a companion, heightening the vulnerability of the bequest. Other family members brought suit alleging undue influence of the beneficiary on each of these renowned persons. Of course, final disposition of the cases differed according to other circumstances.

Encompassing the concept of "undue influence" is the broader philosophy of "free and voluntary acts." Those who challenge a will in a court of law first usually try to prove that the will was not a voluntary act, with the testator's original intentions in effect being usurped by the beneficiary, and the beneficiary in turn must submit evidence that the will was voluntary. For instance, in *Rose v Dunn*,[13] a divided Arkansas Supreme Court affirmed a lower court's decision that an 89-year-old testator was competent to execute his will, a deed, and two trusts, and that these executions were free and voluntary acts. The testator's lawyer testified that the testator knew what he wanted when he failed to leave his property to the family members who contested the will. In this case the beneficiary drove the testator to an attorney and participated in the initial discussions concerning the will. The attorney, who suspected that some undue influence was being exerted, asked the beneficiary to leave the room in order to satisfy himself that the testator's decision was not the product of said influence. The attorney was satisfied and drew the will, and vast wealth was left to the beneficiary, a person whom the testator knew only for a short time. During the trial a physician testified that although the testator had a small stroke he was alert and competent. A banker also testified that the testator always handled his own affairs and had a mind of his own.

A dissenting judge in *Rose* held that the documents were procured by undue influence because the testator had known the defendant for a short time only, and had nevertheless deeded over a 160-acre farm for one dollar.

Mental competency and undue influence are two separate and distinct issues. A person may be mentally competent and a transaction performed by him can still be invalidated as the result of undue influence. Instead of questioning basic mental capacity, the concept of undue influence takes into account the emotional vacillations and vulnerabilities that can lead a normal person to make a legally binding commitment during a moment of weakness that almost certainly would be regretted and negated by the person when they regained objectivity and stability or gained knowledge.

In *Roybal v Morris*,[14] we see the difference between mental incapacity and undue influence illuminated. The court noted that the father was mentally competent at the time he executed a deed, but evidence showed that he was in poor health, physically feeble, and readily susceptible to influence. His daughter took advantage and managed to encourage the testator to eliminate his son's name from the will. The daughter argued that the father had sufficient mental capacity at the time to understand the nature of the transaction. The court agreed but reiterated that the issue before it was not competency; it was "undue influence." The court found that the testator was unduly influenced by his daughter.

To be deemed undue influence, the influence must be dominating and controlling in nature, not merely suspicious. For instance, a suggestion to a testator by a potential beneficiary is not undue; a testator being led into a decision based on manipulation that the testator could not have escaped, or misinformation that the testator could not have learned the truth of, is undue. The court requires evidence that the testator was under the control of the beneficiary, not that the beneficiary helped the testator to draw a will. Based on this conception, a Minnesota court of appeals affirmed a county court's decision refusing to invalidate a will on the grounds of lack of testamentary capacity and undue influence. A brother and a sister of the decedent were challenging a will which left everything to another sister and her six children because the contents were a handwritten document made by the benefiting sister. The court found that although the beneficiary helped the testator, and handwrote the document used by the attorney to execute the will, the decedent knew what he was doing in the attorney's office when he executed the will.[15]

As in other cases where the mental capability of a person is called into question under the law, the concept of undue influence gives the benefit of the doubt to the testator or testatrix, assuming his or her act to be voluntary unless proved otherwise under specific guidelines.

REFERENCES

1. *Dexter v Hall* 1872; 15 Wall (US) 9.
2. *Beaver v Weatherly* 1983; 299 SE2d 730 (Ga Sup Ct).
3. *Apfelblat v National Bank Wyandotte Taylor* 1987; 404 NW2d 725 (Mich Sup Ct).
4. *Harris v Steel* 1987; 506 So2d 542 (La Ct App).
5. *Zobel ex Rel Hancox v Fenendael* 1985; 379 NW2d 887 (Wis Ct App).
6. Redmond F: Testamentary capacity. *Bull Am Acad Psychiatry Law* 1987;15:247–256.
7. *In re Estate of Kern* 1986; 716 P2d 528 (Kan Sup Ct).
8. *In re Estate of Sarras* 1986; 384 NW2d 119 (Mich Ct App).
9. *Succession of Riggio* 1985; 468 So2d 1279 (La Ct App).
10. *Park v George* 1984; 667 SW2d 644 (Ark Sup Ct).
11. *Farner v Farner* 1985; 480 NE2d 251 (Ind Ct App).
12. *In re Will of Slade* 1984; 483 NYS2d 513 (NY App Div).
13. *Rose v Dunn* 1984; 670 SW2d 180 (Ark Sup Ct).
14. *Roybal v Morris* 1983; 669 P2d 1100 (NM Ct App).
15. *In re Estate of Prigge* 1984; 352 NW2d 443 (Minn Ct App).

7

Civil Commitment

Civil commitment entails depriving a person of liberties against his or her will, and confining him or her involuntarily to an institution for the purpose of psychiatric treatment. Civil commitment is a last resort, since such deprivation of liberty goes against the grain of the country's philosophical and legal foundations and also against the public's fairly consistent priority of personal autonomy. Accordingly, strict guidelines have been formulated to ensure that commitment be used only when no other option is viable. Usually, the procedure is undertaken on evidence that a disturbed person presents an imminent physical danger either to himself or to others; or if a person is so mentally incapacitated that he or she is unable to function in the community.

HOW A PERSON BECOMES A SUBJECT
FOR CIVIL COMMITMENT

Several situations make a person a possible candidate for civil commitment: being apprehended by police; being brought to a hospital by relatives or friends; being converted from voluntary to involuntary patient status; or being taken into custody as a result of a legal petition submitted to and validated by a court.

Patients brought into a mental health institution through the involuntary civil commitment process should be screened as early as possible in order to avoid any unnecessary infringement of liberty, to ensure that they are guided quickly and effectively toward the placement and treatment indicated by their presenting problems, and to minimize waste of limited resources. Thus, adherence to the philosophical ideal of safeguarding patients' rights can achieve the practical benefits of efficiency and economy.

Once the psychiatrist or other qualified mental health professional decides that the patient meets the statutory commitment criteria, the mental health facility should activate its resources on the patient's behalf, providing treatment and arranging for patient care. Most state statutes empower mental health facilities to assume a fiduciary role for legal and medical necessities. This would include providing the requisite psychiatric and social services, and safeguarding the legal interests of the patient. All treatment and care should be undertaken with the patient's consent, unless an emergency situation requires forced treatment in accordance with current legal standards.

It is important for patients who are involuntarily committed to be advised of their rights and told as much as possible about the treatment plan. Conscientiousness in this regard serves not only to satisfy legal requirements, but to encourage a general constructive atmosphere of trust and cooperation between patients and staff. Some states insist that patients be given their rights in written form, or a copy of the commitment papers with the telephone number of their attorney.

Persons subject to civil commitment are usually appointed legal counsel by the state. The primary role of a respondent's counsel is to represent the respondent not from the perspective of psychiatric or legal authority but from the perspective of the respondent, to serve as a vigorous advocate for the respondent's wishes. The role of such counsel is emphatically not to take a caretaker stance and determine what is in the patient's best interest, which is presumedly being done by the psychiatric staff along with either family, friends, or law enforcement personnel, but to serve the patient's stated wishes. Keeping the respondent well-informed about all available options, and the legal consequences of those options, is part of the appointed counsel's job.

While treatment of mental illness is entrusted to mental health professionals, the decision to force an individual into a mental hospital or to receive specific treatment is the province of the judicial system, commentators have observed. It is a clear distinction on which the validity of the civil commitment procedure rests. The patient's attorney and the mental health professional each present their case to the court, and the judge acts as a neutral decision maker in accordance with the prevailing law. In any involuntary civil commitment, the patient has an interest in his or her liberty, in being left alone, and in being treated fairly. The state has an interest under its police power to protect its citizens from dangerously mentally ill persons and also under parens patriae to care for its sick and helpless individuals. Therefore, in any commitment hearing two counsel need to be present, one to articulate the patient's interest and one to articulate the state's interest.

The attorney representing the state should assist the state's representatives in defining their objectives by advising them of the options available for compulsory treatment and care, the consequences of each, and the probability of successfully pursuing such options. The counsel should recommend a course of action. The state's attorney must clarify to the state representatives so they in turn can fulfill the burden of proof borne by the state.

Once it has been determined that a court hearing on commitment will take place, it is imperative that the hearing be scheduled, and notice issued and delivered promptly to all interested parties so they can prepare their arguments. Hearings are usually conducted in a courtroom, or in a designated area within the institution setting which has the dignity of a courtroom setting, to give a proper solemn ambience and to aid objectivity. Seen in a hospital setting, the subjects of hearings may already seem like patients to the judge and even to themselves, presenting the judge with a *fait accompli*. Psychological nuances related to the burden of proof can influence the results of a hospital hearing, for the subjects must in effect prove that they do not belong where they are, although on paper it is the state which must prove that they do belong there. The fact of their already being in the institution could prejudice the neutrality of all but the most dispassionate judges.

In a typical hearing, a psychiatrist or qualified mental health professional presents his or her findings to the court. The patient's attorney cross-examines the presenter. The attorney for the institution also direct-examines the state's presenter. Then, after having heard all parties, the judge usually questions the respondent and makes a decision. Patients themselves may appeal to the judge for a chance to discuss with the judge their arguments and evidence supporting their release.

In most states the rules of civil procedure apply to the commitment process, but considerable variation exists regarding the extent to which hearsay evidence is admissible at such hearings. Hospital records are generally admitted under an exception to the hearsay rule that permits introduction of official records kept in the normal course of business. Expert testimony is admissible on behalf of either the respondent or the institution, and it is not unusual for the patient's attorney to ask an independent expert to appear to rebut the institution's expert. All expert witnesses should have personally examined the respondent and must be prepared to offer opinions regarding the presence or absence of mental illness, the respondent's current condition, and alternative treatment plans.[1]

CLINICAL FINDINGS

In a survey interview of 58 lawyers and 43 judges who participated in more than a thousand civil commitment cases, it was found that most lawyers and judges tended to view psychiatrists in favorable terms, respected psychiatrists as professionals in the mental health field, and regarded them as possessing valid tools and remedies for aiding the mentally ill.[2] However, the attitude of the attorneys and judges toward psychiatric hospitals was less favorable, as they saw the hospital as a last-resort alternative for helping the mentally ill, after other remedies have been exhausted. They also perceived mental illness as a medical problem and accepted the role of mental hospitalization in the treatment of mental illness. These findings match those from other studies.[3] Legislatures have long been concerned with the legal status of the psychiatric patient. Their presumption is that voluntary hospitalization is suitable for those who do not present a danger to themselves or others, and whose judgments are not grossly impaired. Involuntarily hospitalization is suitable, on the other hand, for those who are dangerous or unable to care for themselves.

Clinical data, however, suggest that there are no significant differences between these two groups. For instance, a study by Okin[4] of 198 patients admitted over a 2-week period to seven different state hospitals in Massachusetts shows that involuntary patients do not have a significantly greater prevalence of psychosis; further, involuntary patients were not more chronically ill than voluntary patients, if the number of prior hospitalizations is taken as one measure of chronicity. In fact, voluntary patients appeared to have more prior hospitalizations than involuntary patients, perhaps because they were more accepting of hospitalization in general. The overall conclusion is that the legal status of the patient seems to be unrelated to the severity and chronicity of the patient's mental condition. A radically different, paternalistic approach is presented by some, including Lamb and Mills,[5] who argue that involuntary treatment via commitment is actually the legal right of the mentally ill. They see withholding this option as inhumane.

Mental health professionals are concerned with the welfare of patients who are released instead of committed. In a study by Shore et al[6] of 189 patients who entered the commitment process in Oregon, the patients were assessed for commitment status, morbidity, and mortality at 6 and 19 months. Twenty-nine percent were formally committed. This group consisted largely of violence-prone psychotic patients plus a small number of elderly, demented patients with serious medical illness. A mortality of 10% included the elderly who died of natural causes and young adult patients who committed suicide. In the view of these investigators, the courts were utilizing the option of psychiatric commitment primarily to implement social policy for control of violent behavior in the community. The state ignored the consequences of morbidity and mortality for the other patients who were at least as gravely ill as the violence-prone patients but whose illnesses were interpreted as not threatening enough to warrant involuntary commitment by current laissez-faire legal standards.[6]

Nicholson studied patients who were initially admitted to a state hospital under an emergency commitment procedure.[7] The purpose of the study was to identify the variables associated with the patients' change of status: shifting to voluntary hospitalization, being released from the hospital, or becoming subject to judicial commitment. It was found that the released patients were younger, better educated, more likely to be employed at the time of admission, and less likely to have serious organic or psychotic disorders, or to receive government assistance. The voluntary patients were hospitalized twice as long as committed patients and were less frequently considered to have received the maximal benefits from hospitalization. In Nicholson's view, the lengthy hospital stay of many of the patients who changed to voluntary status warrants a provision to safeguard their constitutional rights. Periodic judicial review of the patients could be guaranteed by requiring the observation of hearings mandated under a patient's original involuntary confinement, even if the patient changes to voluntary status. Alternatively, periodic review of such patients by an independent panel of physicians could serve the purpose of safeguarding their rights.[7]

THE AMERICAN PSYCHIATRIC ASSOCIATION'S POSITION ON CIVIL COMMITMENT

To move beyond the narrow debate between lawyers and psychiatrists was the motive of Stromberg and Stone in designing a "model law" for the American Psychiatric Association (APA) for enactment of civil commitment procedures.[8] According to this model law, the patient's interest has priority over all other interests. This means that the presence of dangerousness should not be the sole reason for civil commitment. However, those individuals who are likely to suffer substantial mental or physical deterioration and are unable to care for their needs because of mental illness should be committed for care and treatment under the concept of parens patriae.

This model law also recommends that a state's police power may be utilized to commit those who present clear and convincing proof of likely dangerous conduct related to their mental disorder. Emergency psychiatric intervention may be undertaken in order to assess whether violent persons suffer from general mental illness or not. If violent persons are not severely mentally ill or if treatment will not help them, they should be dealt with by the criminal justice system or by other social service institutions.

Arguments have arisen as to how long involuntary commitment should be prescribed for. Although opinion among scholars differs, in general it seems that the problems which actuate the commitment process can be resolved within 30 to 90 days of inpatient hospitalization. Empirical studies have shown that more than 60% of committed patients have been discharged within 90 days.[9]

Initial commitment may last from 48 hours to 2 weeks and then may be renewed periodically as long as patients are seriously mentally ill and are unable to take care of themselves or present a serious danger to others. Most commentators informed on the subject believe that there is no justification to keep a patient involuntarily in a hospital setting indefinitely, and most legal scholars argue for the release of those patients, but mental health professionals generally believe that it is the ethical responsibility of the healing profession to give maximal care to needy people as long as it is necessary. Furthermore, to stabilize a person only temporarily but not have time to let a genuine recovery process take hold is a waste of resources if the patient's condition deteriorates back to incapacity again.

The liberty interest is certainly the fundamental right of an individual in this society, but that liberty can become meaningless for those suffering severe, disabling physical or mental illnesses. The question always lingers of what a mentally ill person would have wished if he or she were free of the mental disorder. One can raise the hypothetical situation, then, that if a person were to foresee the possibility of incapacitating mental illness while he was still stable, would he be more likely to stipulate that the state commit him by force for treatment, or would he more likely wish to be left alone? Especially if there were real chances for recovery with the commitment, on an emotional level probably most people would opt for the treatment. The noble concepts of fundamental rights and liberty interest resonate from a lofty realm and have indeed inspired many, but there is also a beauty, perhaps less poetic, in a person shifting from a nonfunctioning to a functioning state and reassuming his or her place in society, a person who can once again meaningfully exercise his or her liberty and fundamental rights precisely because they were temporarily withheld. Our clinical experience shows that the majority of those patients once committed have been grateful at the time of their discharge from the hospital for the care that the hospital initially enforced against their wishes.

STANDARDS OF PROOF

The heart of the issue of civil commitment is the question: What is the standard of proof required to commit an individual to a mental hospital? This question was addressed by the US Supreme Court in the landmark case, *Addington v Texas*.[10]

Addington, who had a long history of psychiatric disorder, was arrested on charges of "assault by threat" against his mother. His mother filed a petition with the State Court of Texas for indefinite commitment of her son in compliance with Texas law. Addington retained counsel and a trial was held before a jury in accord with the statute to determine:

1. Whether the proposed patient is mentally ill, and if so,
2. Whether he requires hospitalization in a mental hospital for his own welfare and the protection of others, and if so,
3. Whether he is mentally incompetent

The trial covering these issues took six days.During the trial, the state presented evidence that appellant Addington suffered from delusions and had threatened to injure others. Furthermore, he had caused substantial property damage both in his own apartment and his parents' home. Expert psychiatrists testified that Addington was afflicted with psychotic schizophrenia and paranoid tendencies, and that he was probably dangerous to himself and others. Addington did not contest the facts. Indeed, he conceded that he suffered from mental illness. He objected to being labeled dangerous, however. The trial judge submitted the case to the jury with instructions in the form of two questions:

1. Based on clear, unequivocal, and convincing evidence, is Frank O'Neal Addington mentally ill?
2. Based on clear, unequivocal, and convincing evidence, does Frank O'Neal Addington require hospitalization in a mental hospital for his own welfare and the protection of others?

The jury found that Addington was mentally ill and that he required hospitalization for his own and others' welfare. The trial court then entered an order committing appellant as a patient to Austin State Hospital for an indefinite period.

Addington appealed, arguing among other things that the standards for commitment violated his substantive due process rights and that any standard of proof for commitment less than that required for criminal conviction, that is, "beyond a reasonable doubt," violated his procedural due process rights. The case passed through several appeals stages and wound up in the Supreme Court. The issue before the court was what standard of proof is required to commit a person to a state mental hospital.

The Supreme Court recognized that civil commitment for any purpose constitutes a serious deprivation of liberty and requires due process protection. Meanwhile, the state has a legitimate interest under its parens patriae powers in providing care to its citizens who are unable because of emotional disorder to care for themselves. The state also retains authority under its police power to protect the community from the dangerous tendencies of some citizens who are mentally ill. In conclusion, the court felt that an individual's interest in the outcome of a civil commitment proceeding is of such weight and gravity that due process requires the state to justify confinement by proof more substantial than a mere preponderance of the evidence. By the same token, the court held that the standard of proof "beyond a reasonable doubt" has been reserved for criminal cases. The court noted that the extremity of the standard applied to criminal defendants manifests society's concern that the risk of error to the individual must be minimized even at the risk that some who are guilty might go free, but that the full power of that standard does not apply to a civil commitment.

The court therefore settled on a middle level of burden of proof that strikes a fair balance between the rights of the individual and the legitimate concerns of the state. This judicious standard holds that "clear and convincing" evidence is necessary in civil commitment, stopping short of "beyond a reasonable doubt."

DURATION OF COMMITMENT

Civil commitment, unlike imprisonment for criminal conviction, specifies no definite duration of hospitalization. Instead, the length of hospitalization is

related to the patient's mental condition. Patients may request hearings periodically to consider their release by a preponderance of evidence that they
no longer are mentally ill or dangerous. If the state disagrees with a patient's
contention in the hearing, it must prove by clear and convincing evidence
that the patient remains in need of treatment. Thus, although the state theoretically has a blank check for the duration of commitment, patients have an
opportunity to plead their cause, and procedures to ensure that the proper
authorities are aware of their plight, if they feel that their release is warranted.

A US Supreme Court ruling in *Jones v US*[11] tackled the issue of duration.
Petitioner Michael Jones was arrested for attempting to steal a jacket from a
department store. He was arraigned in the District of Columbia Superior Court
on a charge of attempted petit larceny, a misdemeanor punishable by a maximum prison sentence of 1 year. The court ordered the petitioner committed
to St Elizabeth's psychiatric hospital for a determination of his competency
to stand trial. Jones subsequently decided to plead not guilty by reason of
insanity. The government did not contest the plea, but entered into a stipulation
of facts with the petitioner, and he was committed to St Elizabeth's. If Jones
had not taken the insanity plea and been found guilty, a year's imprisonment
would have been the maximum term. After a year of hospitalization, therefore,
Jones requested release, arguing that he had served his 1 year.

The Supreme Court finally received this case. In this Court's view, when
criminal defendants establish by a preponderance of the evidence that they
are not guilty of a crime by reason of insanity, the Constitution permits the
government, on the basis of the insanity judgment, to confine such patients
to a mental institution until they have regained their sanity or are no longer
a danger to themselves or society. Further, insanity acquittees are not entitled
to release merely because they have been hospitalized for a period longer than
they would have been incarcerated if convicted. The length of a sentence for
a particular criminal offense is based on a variety of considerations, including
retribution, deterrence, and rehabilitation.

However, because insanity acquittees were not convicted, they may not
be punished. The purpose of their commitment is to treat their mental illness
and protect them and society from their potential dangerousness. There simply
is no correlation between the length of acquittees' hypothetical criminal sentence and the length of time necessary for their recovery. Furthermore,
defendants take the insanity plea voluntarily, in effect requesting treatment
instead of punishment. They cannot then expect the legal establishment to
consider that treatment to be a form of punishment when they wish to terminate it.

The dissenting justices in the *Jones* case expressed the opinion that in
many respects, confinement in a mental institution is more intrusive than
incarceration in a prison. Inmates of mental institutions, like prisoners, are
deprived of unrestricted association with friends, family, and community; they

must contend with locks, guards, and detailed regulation of their daily activities, and therefore the confinement must be for a limited period only, not indefinitely.

As we have argued that the liberty interest can lose its value if a person is too incapacitated to exercise it, we can similarly counteract the dissenting justices' argument as well, since how worthwhile is the abstract ability to associates with friends and family, if one is too ill to interact meaningfully with them? Often, lack of treatment of mentally ill persons actually damages their personal relationships, whereas treatment restoring them to stability would enable them to fill familial and social roles. It can be argued that indeed people have a right to associate with family and friends, and sometimes temporary institutionalization is required to enable them to exercise that right.

Prior to the *Jones* case, the US Supreme Court ruled that a person at the end of a penal sentence may not be committed to a mental hospital without the judicial proceedings available to all other persons. This issue was pursued in *Baxstrom v Herold, State Hospital Director*.[12] While serving a prison sentence of 2½ to 3 years for conviction of second-degree assault, Johnnie K. Baxstrom was found to be suffering from mental illness, and was transferred from his New York prison to Dannemora State Hospital, an institution under the jurisdiction and control of the New York Department of Corrections, and used for the purpose of confining and caring for male prisoners declared mentally ill during their incarceration.

Just prior to termination of Baxstrom's prison term, the director of Dannemora filed a petition in the county court and requested that Baxstrom be civilly committed. The court agreed but the Department of Mental Hygiene of New York, which has jurisdiction over civil hospitals, determined ex parte that Baxstrom was not suitable for care in a civil hospital. Thus, on the date when Baxstrom's penal sentence expired, custody over him shifted from the Department of Corrections to the Department of Mental Hygiene, yet he was detained at Dannemora.

Thereafter, Baxstrom sought a writ of habeas corpus in a state court. The writ was dismissed. After passing through the New York Court of Appeals, the case eventually arrived at the US Supreme Court. The issue before the Court was: May a person be civilly committed at the end of a penal sentence without the judicial proceedings available to all other persons civilly committed?

The Court's ruling was strongly critical of the procedural laxity in this case, holding that Baxstrom was denied the equal protection of the law which should be maintained by following the statutory procedure for civil commitment in New York. Further, he was denied the equal protection of the law by his civil commitment to an institution overseen by the Department of Corrections beyond the expiration of his prison term without a judicial determination that he was dangerously mentally ill, such as is afforded to all so committed, except those like Baxstrom nearing the end of a penal sentence. In the view of the Supreme Court, mental patients nearing the end of their penal sentence cannot be statutorily classified as insane, but are entitled to equal protection under the law governing civil commitment.

DUE PROCESS OF THE LAW

The question of whether a mentally ill prisoner could be transferred from a state prison to a state mental hospital without a due process hearing was tested in the US Supreme Court case of *Vitek v Jones*.[13] In the ruling, various procedures were established to ensure that sometimes delicately balanced rights are not transgressed.

Defendant Jones started this legal scuffle when he set his mattress on fire in his cell while serving a robbery sentence. He was severely burned. Following a medical hospitalization, a physician certified that Jones was mentally ill and could not receive adequate treatment in the penal facility and so he was transferred to the security unit of a Nebraska state mental hospital. Jones then joined another prisoner in a suit challenging the constitutionality of the statute under which the transfer had been effected. Finally the case went to the Supreme Court for ruling.

The Court found that Nebraska prisoners had an enforceable liberty interest generated by the expectation that they would not be transferred to a mental hospital unless found mentally ill. The Court upheld the lower court's decision that transfer from a prison to a mental hospital requires adequate notice to the prisoner, an adversary hearing before an independent decision maker, the availability of appointed counsel, and a written explanation of the basis for the decision. The absence of these protections violated the prisoner's right to due process of law.

In an article on the Court's approach to psychiatry, Appelbaum[14] has noted that the majority of justices unfavorably compared mental hospitals with prisons, and that the justices believed that such a transfer is an "adverse action." In the view of Appelbaum's commentary, the Court's decision in *Vitek* is consistent with an underlying suspicion of psychiatry, and particularly of state hospitals.[14] This of course reflects the feelings of the general public.

Basically, a person committed to a mental institution retains numerous rights for the duration of the commitment. The courts are concerned therefore that the state must exercise the same due process safeguards against unjustified deprivation of liberty when dealing with civil commitment as the law accords those accused of a crime. The scope of the court's concerns in this regard is demonstrated in *Lessard v Schmidt*.[15] This case begins with Alberta Lessard being picked up by two police officers in front of her residence in West Allis, Wisconsin. She was taken to the Mental Health Center, North Division, Milwaukee, and then she was detained on an emergency basis because of mental illness. Through an ex parte proceeding, the judge issued an order permitting the confinement of Lessard for ten days. The results of subsequent psychiatric examinations by two physicians prompted the court to keep extending the detention for ten-day periods. Neither Lessard nor anyone who might act on her behalf was informed of these proceedings. After several more such proceedings, a class action suit was brought alleging that the Wisconsin procedure for involuntary civil commitment defeated the due process of law. A three-judge court reviewed the allegation on constitutional grounds and decided that:

1. The power of the state to deprive persons of the fundamental liberty to go unimpeded about their affairs must rest on society's having a compelling interest in such deprivation.

2. Requirements of due process are not static but vary depending on the importance of interests involved and the nature of subsequent proceedings.

3. Unless procedural due process requirements for involuntary commitment are met, no person should be subjected to "treatment" against his or her will.

4. No significant deprivation of liberty can be justified without a prior hearing on the necessity of detention.

5. The state may sometimes have a compelling interest in emergency detention of prisoners who threaten violence to themselves or others, for the purpose of protecting society and individuals, but such emergency measures can be justified only for the length of time necessary to arrange for a hearing before a neutral judge at which probable cause for detention must be established. The individual detained and members of his or her family must be given notice of the hearing, and attendance by the detained party cannot be waived.

6. Due process requires that the maximum period of detention without a preliminary hearing on probable cause of persons who allegedly threaten violence to themselves or others cannot exceed 48 hours.

7. Due process is not satisfied by an ex parte hearing in which a person detained because of his or her person has no meaningful opportunity to be heard either due to incapacity caused by medication or lack of counsel.

8. Notice of a full hearing with respect to civil commitment of a detained person, to comply with due process requirements, must be given sufficiently in advance of scheduled court proceedings so that a reasonable opportunity to prepare will be afforded, and the basis for detention must be set forth with particularity.

9. The state cannot be consistent with the basic concept of due process if it commits individuals on the basis of their statements to psychiatrists without showing that the statements were made with the knowledge that the individual was not obliged to speak.

10. If individuals detained for civil commitment proceedings do not, because of mental illness, have knowledge of the use that may be made of their statements after their rights have been explained to them, subsequent findings of mental illness or mental incapacity on the basis of such statements

do not violate due process, but the state remains obliged to prove that the persons are dangerous and sustain a recommendation for commitment.

In light of the above, it seems that the Lessard court has confused civil commitment and criminal proceedings. The court posits the mental health professional as an adversary to the patient, and somehow has managed to perceive healers as prosecutors. In the ruling, the court covered one aspect of the issue quite thoroughly: protecting the liberty interest of patients; but virtually ignored the other crucial aspect: restoring mentally ill persons to a stable condition so that they can function in a meaningful manner and can contain their suffering if not alleviate it. One would wish that courts would recognize the necessity of creating the balance whereby these two seemingly contradictory needs can be met.

OUTPATIENT COMMITMENT

Outpatient civil commitment is capturing the attention of the psychiatric community. Task forces have been established by the American Psychiatric Association and the National Institute of Mental Health to study the different approaches to outpatient commitment. Most states have by now enacted into law statutory provisions that permit outpatient commitment.[16]

Mandatory posthospital outpatient treatment starts at the time of discharge from the hospital and may be renewed periodically, at times when the patient is no longer acutely ill. Induction into posthospital mandatory outpatient treatment requires a less severe degree of mental illness at the time of legal determination and less imminence of anticipated dangerousness than civil commitment, but it does require a past history of repeated serious incidents associated with acute mental illness, and a history of nonadherence to follow-up treatment plans.

The purpose of outpatient commitment mainly is to reduce the frequency of inpatient commitment and to provide the least restrictive alternative for patients. However, Tennessee data failed to suggest any relationship between the outpatient commitment law and the number of admissions to psychiatric inpatient hospitals[17].

Outpatient commitment is not necessarily a panacea. The use of coercive psychotherapy is a controversial issue among mental health professionals, specifically, the management and handling of transference and countertransference phenomena.[18] Also, the coercive nature of the treatment raises questions about psychiatrists' possible violation of patients' rights, and transgression of ethical standards.[19] Whether the problems with outpatient commitment can ever be successfully resolved will depend on the attitude of lawyers who specialize in mental health issues.[16] Collaboration between mental health professionals and legal activists is essential, along with a shift in emphasis from liberty interests to quality of care.[20]

One form of outpatient commitment is known as preventive commitment and its purpose is to prevent the predictable deterioration of a person's mental condition which would eventually lead to inpatient commitment. According to Stefan,[21] preventive commitment is characterized by a lower commitment standard than that for institutionalization, and often is accompanied by fewer procedural protections. Justification for preventive commitment includes concern about the "revolving door" patient, the prospect of lower costs associated with community services as compared to inpatient care, the increasing number of treatment-resistant chronically mentally ill people who refuse to seek treatment voluntarily in the community, and the concept of the least restrictive alternative.

The criteria for preventive commitment, according to existing statutes, are mental illness where with the lack of treatment the individual would soon meet standards for institutionalization, and mental illness that prevents voluntary treatment. Further, a suitable person for this kind of treatment must be capable of surviving safely in the community with the help of others.

In spite of the popularity of outpatient commitment, it was found that most people placed under such commitment were inappropriate candidates. Rehospitalization rates were not too different from those of the hospital outpatient population, and sometimes patients in outpatient commitment remained in the committed status indefinitely, which raises the question of whether such commitment is constitutionally sound or not.

CIVIL COMMITMENT OF HOMELESS PERSONS

People who do not have customary and regular access to a conventional dwelling or residence are considered homeless people. Between half a million and 3 million Americans are estimated to be homeless. The prevalence of psychiatric disorders among this population, according to various literature and the methodologies used, varies from 20% to nearly 90%. In a study of 722 homeless persons in Chicago, Rossi et al[22] found that three out of four (76%) of homeless people are male, sharply contrasting the Chicago adult population, which is 46% male. The average age of the homeless person is 40 years and a typical homeless person is a highschool graduate in his mid-thirties.

Homeless people have the most extreme level of poverty, and suffer from many disabling conditions that would ordinarily make it difficult or impossible for a person to do the things necessary for a normal life such as obtain employment, participate socially, and maintain relationships with others. Almost one in four (23%) of the Chicago sample reported having been in a mental hospital, with some having multiple hospitalizations. On psychiatric examination, Rossi et al found in their Chicago sample that 47% of homeless persons registered symptoms of depression, and one in four showed two or more signs of disturbed cognitive process.[22]

Homeless people often have a history of institutional separation from the family during childhood, or of delinquency and/or running away from home.[23] In a study on a community-based survey of 529 homeless adults, Gelberg et al[24] analyzed factors associated with their use of mental health services. Those homeless persons who had had a previous psychiatric hospitalization were the least likely to sleep in an emergency shelter; they had been homeless nearly twice as long as the rest of the sample; they had the worst mental health status; they used alcohol and drugs the most; and they were the most involved in criminal activities.

Whether a typical homeless person suffers from mental illness or not, municipal governments have shown interest in helping them by a diversity of means, including civil commitment to mental institutions. Court rulings suggest that when a municipal government takes a homeless person into custody for psychiatric hospitalization, the government bears the burden of showing that there is an immediate threat more substantial than an allegation that the proposed patient is acting bizarrely on the street.

Under certain circumstances the court may uphold the constitutionality of the protective placement of incompetent homeless persons, but the same reasoning does not extend to ordering psychotropic medication. Criteria for protective placement are (1) imcompetency; (2) a need for residential care; (3) incapability to take care of oneself to the extent of creating a substantial risk of serious harm to oneself or others; and (4) a disability that is likely to be permanent. These criteria must be proved by clear and convincing evidence by the municipal government.[25]

The state has a compelling interest in placing homeless people if they suffer from mental illness and are dangerous to themselves and others. But if the existence of mental illness is questionable and a person does not present any danger, then the court may order the state not to admit such a person to a mental institution. These issues became the focus of intense media and public attention with the appearance of the Billie Boggs case.

According to the record, Joyce Brown, also known as Billie Boggs, worked nearly 10 years as a secretary before she became homeless. While on the street she made money by panhandling, bought one meal a day, and kept herself warm by lying next to a vent that released hot air. She used the streets of New York City as her bathroom. She also was found burning money, and chasing and cursing at people, particularly black males. In October of 1987, team members of Project Help, an emergency program for homeless persons, forcibly removed her from the street and admitted her to Bellevue Psychiatric Hospital. Joyce Brown filed a petition for release and the American Civil Liberties Union (ACLU) assumed responsibility for Joyce Brown's defense.[26]

Bellevue psychiatrists testified that Joyce Brown suffered from schizophrenia, paranoid type. She was viewed by them as delusional, suicidal, incapable of insight, and incompetent to make decisions. She was deemed in need of hospitalization for psychiatric treatment. In addition, although she was not overtly suicidal, Brown's hostility toward others suggested that she might provoke others to harm her, claimed the psychiatrist. The psychiatrists for the ACLU testified that Brown was coherent, logical, had a good memory, and that there was no evidence of suicidal or homicidal ideation. They concluded that overall she was not psychotic or dangerous to herself or others.

The court was perplexed by the contrasting testimony and decided therefore to place great weight on the demeanor, behavior, and testimony of Joyce Brown herself. On the stand, Brown explained that she survived by collecting $8 to $10 a day panhandling. She refused money offered in a way she did not like. Since there were no public toilets conveniently located, she used the street, but covered herself when she did so. She told the court that Project Help and the police were intrusive. During the court procedures, Brown was alert, listened carefully, and fully cooperated with her attorneys.

After hearing the contradicting evidence, the court, unable to find clear and convincing proof of mental illness and dangerousness, ordered Brown's release. In the view of the presiding judge, "freedom constitutionally guaranteed is the right of all, no less of those who are mentally ill. Whether Joyce Brown is or is not mentally ill, it is my finding that she is not unable to care for her essential needs. I am aware her mode of existence," the court continued, "does not conform to conventional standards, that it is an offense to aesthetic senses. It is my hope that the plight she represents will also offend moral conscience and arouse it to action. There must be some civilized alternatives other than involuntary hospitalization or the street."

New York City appealed the court's decision. After reviewing pertinent literature, the appellate court gave more weight to the testimony of hospital physicians who believed Ms Boggs was mentally ill, rather than Boggs's experts, who presented evidence that she was not ill. In the view of the appellate court, the hearing court had erred in its determination in the matter. The city of New York had met the standard and presented clear and convincing proof that Ms Boggs should be involuntarily retained in a mental hospital for treatment since she suffered from a mental illness which, if untreated, was likely to result in serious harm to herself. The appellate court found that the hearing court had erred also in placing great weight on the demeanor, behavior, and testimony of Ms Boggs when she appeared before it. Her demeanor at that time only remotely resembled the one she exhibited when she lived on the street.[27]

The problems of Billie Boggs were not resolved by court decisions. Boggs refused to take medication. On de novo hearing, the court refused to order Boggs to be medicated against her will and the hospital eventually discharged the patient to the custody of the ACLU. Because of the case's notoriety, Boggs became an instant celebrity, appearing on a television talk show and lecturing at Harvard Law School. These moments of acclaim made all the more poignant the latest chapter of her drama. After a few weeks she was noticed once again begging in the streets of New York.

WRONGFUL COMMITMENT

Psychiatrists have an obligation to personally examine a patient before preparing commitment papers. Failing to do so renders them vulnerable to a lawsuit. This issue is examined in *Lanier v Sallas*,[28] wherein a patient's mother applied to a county court to have the patient (later the plaintiff) committed to a mental hospital for observation and treatment, as she suspected that her daughter had a mental illness. The court appointed two psychiatrists to examine the plaintiff, and the psychiatrists executed a certificate of mental examination saying that the plaintiff was mentally ill, without having examined her. After a court hearing the plaintiff was committed. Later the plaintiff brought suit and proved that she had never been examined by the psychiatrists. She won a $100,000 jury verdict on the medical malpractice issue and accepted a reduced award of $50,000.

During the trial the doctors argued that the plaintiff's claim against them was an action for misdiagnosis, not for medical malpractice. The court ruled, however, that the physicians failed to conform to the required standard of care. Further, they had made a diagnosis of schizophrenia without performing a proper mental examination.

On appeal, the psychiatrists took a different position. They argued that it was up to the plaintiff to prove that she is not schizophrenic! The court understandably rejected that argument and ruled that the psychiatrists bore the burden of establishing the defense that she was ill and required hospitalization.

Broad, consistent measures supporting patients' rights have been maintained by the courts: for instance, making the state bear the burden of proof for civil commitment, and in the incessant focus on due process. Generally, the recent court rulings have followed the liberty-interest trend which holds preeminent the right to be left alone, while the more paternalistic concept which views treatment and hospitalization as an equally fundamental right has fallen into disfavor. Rigorous standards and procedures are the means by which the courts have limited civil commitment. However, in this trend, mental health professionals feel that emphasis has turned too radically on rights that sound awesome on paper but do not amount to much when a person is too mentally ill to exercise or appreciate them, and they would like to see a more balanced perspective putting greater focus on healing.

REFERENCES

1. American Bar Association's Commission on the Mentally Disabled: National Task Force Guidelines on Involuntary Civil Commitment. *Men & Phys Dis Law Reporter* 1986;10:409–514.
2. Hiday VA: Are lawyers enemies of psychiatrists? A survey of civil commitment counsel and judges. *Am J Psychiatry* 1983;140:343–326.
3. Iowa Law Rev 1979;64:1284–1458.
4. Okin RL: The relationship between legal status and patient characteristics in state hospitals. *Am J Psychiatry* 1986;143:1233–1237.

5. Lamb, HR, Mills MJ: Needed changes in law and procedure for the chronically mentally ill. *Hosp Community Psychiatry* 1986;37:475–480.

6. Shore, JM, et al: Morbidity and mortality in the commitment process. *Arch Gen Psychiatry* 1981;38:930–934.

7. Nicholson, RA: Characteristics associated with change in the legal status of involuntary psychiatric patients. *Hosp Community Psychiatry* 1988;39:424–429.

8. Stromberg CD, and Stone AA: Statute—a model state law on civil commitment of the mentally ill in issues in forensic psychiatry, in *Issues in Forensic Psychiatry*. Washington, DC, American Psychiatric Press, 1984, pp. 57–180.

9. Tomellieri CJ, et al. Who are the committed? *J Nerv Ment Dis* 1977;165:288–291.

10. *Addington v Texas* 1979; 441 US 418.

11. *Jones v US* 1983; 463 US.

12. *Baxstrom v Herold, State Hospital Director* 1966; 383 US 107, 86 S Ct.

13. *Vitek v Jones* 1980; 445 US 480.

14. Appelbaum PS: The Supreme Court looks at psychiatry. *Am J Psychiatry* 1984; 141:827–835.

15. *Lessard v Schmidt* 1972; 349 FSupp 1078.

16. Appelbaum PS: Outpatient commitment, editorial. *Am J Psychiatry* 1986;143:1270–1272.

17. Bursten B: Posthospital mandatory outpatient treatment. *Am J Psychiatry* 1986; 143:1255–1258.

18. Schneider BK: Civil commitment to outpatient psychotherapy: a case study. *Bull Am Acad Psychiatry Law* 1986;14:273–279.

19. Geller JL: Rights, wrong and the dilemma of coerced community treatment. *Am J Psychiatry* 1986;143:1259–1264.

20. Rubenstein LS: Treatment of the mentally ill: legal and advocacy enters the second generation. *Am J Psychiatry* 1986;143:1264–1269.

21. Stefan S: Preventive commitment: the concept and its pitfall. *Ment Phys Disability Law Reporter* 1987; 11:288–297.

22. Rossi PH, et al: The urban homeless: estimating composition and size. *Science* 1987;235:1336–1341.

23. Susser E, et al: Childhood experiences of homeless men. *Am J Psychiatry* 1987;144:1599–1601.

24. Gelberg L, et al: Mental health, alcohol and drug use, and criminal history among homeless adults. *Am J Psychiatry* 1988;145:191–196.

25. *In re Guardianship of K.N.K.* 1987; 407 NW2d 282 (Wis Ct App).

26. *In re Boggs* 1987; No. 95656/87 (NY Sup Ct) (Nov 12).

27. *In the Matter of the Application of Billie Boggs* 1987; (NY Sup Ct) App Div 31519.

28. *Lanier v Sallas* 1985; 777 F2d 321 (5th Cir).

8

Competency to Stand Trial

The doctrine that a defendant who is mentally incompetent should not be made to stand trial has roots in the common law of mid-seventeenth century England. Blackstone, in his early commentaries on the common law, noted that a man should neither plead nor be tried if he is mentally defective. According to Blackstone, "if a man in his sound memory commits a capital offense and before arraignment for it, he becomes mad, he ought not to be arraigned; because he is not able to plead to it with that advice and caution that he ought . . . "[1] The British common law rules preventing the trial of mentally incompetent persons were transposed to US jurisprudence. In early cases such as *Youstsey v US*[2] and *US v Lawrence*,[3] the courts indicated that due process of law is not maintained when an insane person is subject to trial on an indictment involving liberty or life.

Through the first half of the twentieth century, most jurisdictions gradually modified and refined the common law doctrine on competency, ultimately affirming the need to inquire into defendants' understanding of the trial process and their ability to assist in their defense. As the disciplines of psychiatry and psychology first gained broad acceptance and then were applied in numerous aspects of the judicial process, they made a tremendous impact on the doctrine of competency.

THE SUPREME COURT ON INCOMPETENCY (DUSKY TEST)

In 1960 when it made its landmark decision in *Dusky v US*, the Supreme Court established what has become the procedural and philosophical foundation for the process of determining competency to stand trial.[4] The test it devised to serve that purpose has two basic psychological elements: (1) the cognitive element, which addresses the ability of defendants to understand the proceedings that are taking place against them; and (2) the verbal communication element, which addresses the ability of defendants to consult with their attorney.

The case arose when Dusky, the defendant, kidnapped and unlawfully transported a minor girl across interstate lines between Kansas and Missouri. At the trial, Dusky's attorney offered evidence that Dusky was both insane at the time of the alleged crime and currently mentally incompetent to stand trial. The trial court convicted him nevertheless. Dusky appealed. The appeal was based on the fact that the trial judge had failed to direct the jury to consider evidence that Dusky was, from the start, mentally incompetent to stand trial. The trial judge had allowed the jury to decide the issue of the defendant's sanity at the time of the crime without first adequately weighing his competency to stand trial. The US Court of Appeals, Eighth Circuit, affirmed the conviction and eventually the case arrived at the US Supreme Court, which reversed the decision and remanded the case.

Whether or not the trial judge had erred in failing to instruct the jury to consider evidence relevant to the defendant's competency to stand trial was the issue confronting the Supreme Court. The Court concluded that the defendant had the right to be determined mentally competent to stand trial prior to any trial. It is not sufficient for the trial judge to find that a defendant is oriented to time and place and has some recollection of events. The test for competency must be "whether the defendant has sufficient present ability to consult with his attorney with a reasonable degree of rational understanding and whether he has a rational as well as factual understanding of the proceeding against him."

The American Bar Association (ABA) has pointed out that a careful reading of the language in the Dusky standard reveals three separate requirements for finding defendants competent to stand trial: (1) defendants must have the ability to consult with their defense attorney; (2) they must be able to otherwise assist with their defense; and (3) they must have both a rational and a factual understanding of the proceedings against them.

Some jurisdictions have extended the Dusky standard to include other specific criteria: (1) that defendants have the mental capacity to appreciate their presence in relation to time, place and things; and (2) that their elementary mental processes are such that they comprehend *(a)* that they are in a court of justice charged with a criminal offense; *(b)* that there is a judge on the bench; *(c)* that there is a prosecutor present who will try to convict them of criminal charges; *(d)* that they have a lawyer who will undertake to defend them against those charges; *(e)* that they will be expected to report to the best of their mental ability the circumstances at the time and place of the alleged offense, if they choose to testify and that they understand that they have the right not to testify; *(f)* that there is or may be a jury present to pass upon evidence pertain-ing to their guilt or innocence with respect to such charges, or that if they should choose to enter into plea negotiations or to plead guilty, they comprehend the consequences of a guilty plea, and that they are able knowingly, intelligently, and voluntarily to waive those rights which are waived on such entry of a guilty plea; and *(g)* that they have the ability to participate in an adequate presentation of their defense.[5]

The Dusky formulation is thus a minimum standard. Judges are at liberty to assess cases by weighing an individual defendant's level of functioning against the complexity of the case. The ABA has taken the position that a finding of incompetence is not dependent on a determination of mental illness per se. Competency and incompetency specify degrees of functioning, not degrees of mental health. Courts and mental health professionals must remember to view competency in a functional context.

THE SUPREME COURT ON
COMPETENCY AFTER DUSKY

The *Dusky* case was only the beginning of a long involvement by the Supreme Court with the competency issue. By its unwillingness to compromise the respondent's Fourteenth Amendment rights, the Court in *Dusky* adhered to the judicial philosophy placing the integrity of due process before other more diffuse societal rights. The *Dusky* decision came at the dawn of an era when the highest court reflected a general civil libertarian drift, and elevated the rights of individuals, including criminal defendants. In decisions subsequent to *Dusky*, the Court has further clarified the roles of the courts, the prosecution, and mental health professionals in determining a defendant's competency to stand trial.

Six years after *Dusky*, the highest court ruled in *Pate v Robinson*[6] that the conviction of an incompetent defendant violates due process of law. The circumstances leading to this determination began with respondent Robinson's conviction of the murder of his common-law wife, Flossie May Ward. As an indigent he had been defended by court-appointed counsel. He was sentenced to life imprisonment. At the trial, his attorney conceded that Robinson had indeed shot and killed his common-law wife, but claimed that Robinson was both insane at the time of the incident and currently incompetent to stand trial. On a writ of error to the Supreme Court of Illinois, it was asserted that the trial court's rejection of these claims deprived Robinson of due process of law under the Fourteenth Amendment to the Constitution.

The Supreme Court of Illinois affirmed the conviction, however, on the grounds that no hearing on the defendant's mental capacity to stand trial had been requested by the defense and that the evidence was insufficient to require the trial court to conduct a sanity hearing on a sua sponte basis, or to raise a reasonable doubt as to respondent's sanity at the time of the homicide. The state of Illinois had introduced a stipulation by a psychiatrist, Dr Hains, that

Robinson knew the nature of the charges against him and was able to cooperate with his counsel. Robinson, on the other hand, presented four lay witnesses at trial who testified that he was insane, had a long history of disturbed behavior, had committed irrational acts of violence, and attempted suicide. After passing through the appropriate channels, the *Robinson* case arrived at the US Supreme Court and certiorari was granted. The Court ruled:

1. Evidence raised enough doubt regarding respondent's competence to stand trial that respondent was deprived of due process of law under the Fourteenth Amendment by the trial court's failure to afford him a hearing on that issue. The Court confirmed that *(a)* the conviction of a legally incompetent defendant violates due process; *(b)* the record in this case showed that the respondent did not waive the option of questioning his competence to stand trial; and *(c)* since the evidence did in fact raise doubts about Robinson's competence, the court was required to empanel a jury and conduct a sanity hearing, and could not rely in lieu thereof on the respondent's demeanor at trial or on the stipulated medical testimony.

2. The court further ruled that in view of the difficulty of retrospectively determining the issue of an accused's competence to stand trial, particularly where the time lapse is over 6 years as in this case, a hearing limited to that issue will not suffice, and the respondent must therefore be discharged unless the state conducts a new trial within a reasonable time.

Twelve years after *Dusky* and 6 years after *Pate,* in 1972 the US Supreme Court issued a new decision involving competency in the landmark case of *Jackson v Indiana,*[7] ruling that lengthy commitment of an incompetent who had little if any chance of recovery deprived that individual of the right to a speedy trial.

> Theon Jackson was a mentally defective, deaf mute with a mental age of a preschool child. He could not read, write, or otherwise communicate except through limited sign language. At the age of 27 he was charged in criminal court in Indiana with two separate robberies of women. The first robbery involved property—a purse and its contents of $4—, and in the second robbery $5 was stolen. The trial court put in motion the Indiana procedure for determining Jackson's competency to stand trial. The examining psychiatrists' reports showed that Jackson's complete lack of communications skills together with his lack of hearing and his mental deficiency left him unable to understand the nature of the charges against him or to participate in his defense. The psychiatrist testified that it was unlikely that Jackson could ever learn to read or write, even through sign language. Other witnesses also testified that Indiana had no facility that could help someone as badly off as Jackson to attain minimal communication skills.
>
> The trial court found that Jackson "lacked comprehension sufficient to make his defense" and ordered him committed to the Indiana Department of Mental Health "until such time as that Department should certify to the court that the defendant is sane." Jackson's counsel then filed a motion for a new trial, contending that there was no evidence that Jackson was "insane" or that he would ever attain a status which the court might regard as "sane" in the sense of competency to stand trial. Counsel also argued that Jackson's com-

mitment under those circumstances amounted to a life sentence without his ever having been convicted of a crime and that the commitment therefore deprived Jackson of his Fourteenth Amendment rights to due process and equal protection, constituting cruel and unusual punishment under the Eighth Amendment made applicable to the state through the Fourteenth. The trial court denied the motion and the case proceeded to the US Supreme Court. The highest court reversed and remanded to determine the defendant's criminal responsibility at the time of the alleged offense.

The Court ruled that the defendant Jackson had been subject to more lenient commitment standards and more stringent release standards than are normally applied to other persons not charged with offenses. By effectively condemning the petitioner to permanent institutionalization without requiring that he meet the standard for commitment, or giving him the opportunity for release afforded in ordinary civil commitment procedures, Indiana deprived the petitioner of equal protection.

The Court further stressed that Indiana's indefinite commitment of a criminal defendant solely on account of his incapacity to stand trial violated due process. Such a defendant cannot be held more than the reasonable period of time necessary to determine whether or not a substantial probability exists that he will attain competency in the foreseeable future. If it is determined that he will not, the state must either institute civil proceedings applicable to indefinite commitment of those not charged with a crime, or release the defendant. To virtually punish a defendant for being unable to stand trial is impermissible. Furthermore, the court ruled, since the issue of the petitioner's criminal responsibility at the time of the alleged offenses as distinguished from the issue of his competency to stand trial had not yet been determined, and other matters pertaining to petitioner's defense remained unresolved, the court felt it would be premature to dismiss the charges against the petitioner.

The US Supreme Court looked once again at the issue of competency in the landmark case *Drope v Missouri*.[8] Here, certiorari was granted by the Court to Drope, the petitioner, who claimed that he had been deprived of due process of law by the failure of the trial court to order a psychiatric examination with respect to his competence to stand trial and by conducting a portion of his trial on an indictment charging a capital offense without him being present.

Drope was indicted with two others for the rape of petitioner's wife. Following severance of petitioner's case he filed a motion for continuance so that he might be further examined and receive psychiatric treatment, attaching thereto a report of a psychiatrist who had examined him at his counsel's request and had suggested such treatment. The motion was denied and the case proceeded to trial. Petitioner's wife testified, repeating and confirming information concerning petitioner's "strange behavior," which was contained in the report and stating that she had changed her mind about not wanting to prosecute, petitioner because he had tried to kill her on the Sunday prior to trial. On the second day of the trial, petitioner shot himself in a suicide attempt and was hospitalized. In spite of his absence, the trial court denied a motion for a mistrial on the ground that his absence was voluntary. The trial continued. The jury returned a guilty verdict and Drope was sentenced to life imprisonment.

The *Drope* case passed through the court system and arrived at the US Supreme Court. Drope alleged inter alia that his constitutional right had been violated by the failure to order a pretrial psychiatric examination and by completing the trial without him. The Supreme Court ruled as follows:

1. The Mississippi courts failed to accord proper weight to the evidence suggesting petitioner's incompetence. When taken along with the information available prior to trial and the testimony of petitioner's wife at the trial, knowledge of petitioner's suicide attempt created a sufficient doubt of his competency to stand trial to warrant further inquiry.

2. Whatever the relationship between mental illness and incompetence to stand trial, in this specific case the bearing of the former on the latter was sufficiently likely that, in light of the evidence of petitioner's behavior including the suicide attempt and the court's lack of opportunity in his absence to evaluate that bearing in fact, the court's proper course would have been to suspend the trial until such an evaluation could be made.

3. Assuming that petitioner's right to be present at trial was a right that could be waived, there was insufficient inquiry to afford a basis for deciding the issue of waiver.

4. Petitioner's due process right could not be adequately protected by remanding the case for a psychiatric examination to determine whether he was in fact competent to stand trial back in 1969. But the state is free to retry him, assuming that at the time of the new trial he is competent to be tried.

The essence of the above three landmark Supreme Court decisions following in the wake of *Dusky* is that the law accepts the doctrine that trial of persons incompetent to stand trial violates the due process clause of the Constitution. A hearing is necessary whenever the evidence raises a bona fide doubt as to the defendant's competence to stand trial, and the duty of the trial court is to resolve the competence issue and to be alert before and during the course of the trial to any evidence signaling possible incompetence of a defendant.[6,8]

Determination of competence is and always will be an inexact science, and errors will be made regardless of how earnestly the doctrine is applied; however, if courts follow the spirit of the doctrine and the Supreme Court rulings, they will resolve most questions of competency correctly. In these rulings, the Court displayed the strength of the doctrine by requiring the state to be reticent and disciplined with its power over individuals. These same qualities must be applied when the issue is raised of commitment pending a defendant's likely recovery of competence to stand trial. Regarding commitment of an incompetent defendant, equal protection and due process require that a defendant be held for the briefest time necessary to restore competence, and only when there is a good likelihood of that occurring in the foreseeable future. If there is not, any institutionalization of the defendant would have to be guided by the same standards and principles as for civil commitment.[7]

CLINICAL CRITERIA FOR COMPETENCY ASSESSMENT

Courts and attorneys frequently request psychiatrists or other mental health professionals to evaluate a person's competence to stand trial. Several guidelines have been developed by the investigators with the goal of discerning clinical criteria for competency to stand trial.

McGarry and his colleagues at the Harvard Laboratory of Community Psychiatry devised two tests: (1) the Competency Screening Test (CST)[9]; and (2) the Competency Assessment Instrument (CAI).[10] These tests were designed with the aim of creating instruments which would be sufficiently comprehensible to both law and psychiatry professionals that productive communication would be effected, and competence accurately assessed.

The CST test is used as an initial screening tool. It consists of 22 sentences which the defendant completes using pencil and paper. The sentences are paraphrased as follows: (1) The lawyer told me that . . . (2) When I go to court the lawyer will . . . (3) Jack felt that the judge . . . (4) When Phil was accused of the crime, he . . . (5) When I prepare to go to court with my lawyer . . . (6) If the jury finds me guilty, I . . . (7) The way a court trial is decided . . . (8) When the evidence in George's case was presented to the jury . . . (9) When the lawyer questioned his client in court, the client said . . . (10) If Jack had to try his own case, he . . . (11) Each time the D.A. asked me a question, I . . . (12) While listening to the witnesses testify against me, I . . . (13) When the witness testifying against Harry gave incorrect evidence, he . . . (14) When Bobo disagreed with his lawyer on his defense, he . . . (15) When I was formally accused of the crime, I thought to myself . . . (16) If Ed's lawyer suggests that he plead guilty, he . . . (17) What concerned Fred most about his lawyer . . . (18) When they say a man is innocent until proven guilty . . . (19) When I think of being sent to prison, I . . . (20) When Phil thinks of what he is accused of, he . . . (21) When the jury hears my case, they will . . . (22) If I had a chance to speak to the judge, I . . .[9]

The CST scoring manual gives examples of interpretations and scores. A score of 2 indicates no impairment on an item; 1, possible impairment; and 0, serious impairment. A total score below 20 is considered a basis for further investigation to rule out incompetency by employing the CAI.

The CAI consists of 13 topics as follows: (1) Appraisal of available legal defenses; (2) unmanageable behavior; (3) quality of relating to one's attorney; (4) planning of legal strategy, such as a guilty plea to lesser charges; (5) appraisal of the role of courtroom personnel such as defense counsel, prosecutors, judge, jury, defendant, and witnesses; (6) understanding of court procedure; (7) appreciation of the charges; (8) appreciation of the range and nature of possible penalties; (9) appraisal of likely outcome; (10) capacity to disclose to attorney pertinent facts surrounding the offense; (11) capacity to realistically challenge prosecution witnesses; (12) capacity to testify relevantly; (13) self-defeating versus self-serving motivation in a legal sense.[10]

Apart from item (2), "unmanageable behavior," all these topics are legally oriented. They focus on specifics of the judicial procedure as it applies to the defendant's immediate legal situation. The interviewer is expected to elicit responses from the defendant touching on each of these topics and to indicate the degree of impairment on a scale basis as follows: 1 = total, 2 = severe, 3 = moderate, 4 = mild, 5 = none. Low scores indicate degrees of severity of incompetency, while a high score is seen as an indication of competency.

Praise and criticism both have greeted the competency assessment instrument. The praisers have used this test to design a treatment plan to reduce or eliminate those symptoms that interfere with competence to stand trial. The goal of this treatment plan usually is to orient patients to the nature of the proceedings against them and to build relationship skills essential to cooperating with defense counsel.[11] Schreiber et al[12] have found that the CAI goes too far in its emphasis on legal issues to the virtual exclusion of mental status questions that may bear on a defendant's ability to participate in the legal process. In the opinion of these investigators, it would be more appropriate to develop a balanced perspective, taking both legal and psychological issues into account.

Another test, known as the Interdisciplinary Fitness Interview (IFI), has been invented which, in the opinion of its creators, differs from the CAI. It consists of four major sections: (1) legal issues; (2) psychopathological issues; (3) overall assessment of competency; and (4) a section for two examiners to reconcile their findings.

Legal Items

(1) capacity to appreciate the nature of the alleged crime and to disclose pertinent facts, events and motives; (2) quality of relationship with one's current attorneys; (3) quality of relationship with attorneys in general; (4) anticipated courtroom demeanor and trial conduct; (5) appreciation of the consequences of various legal options.

Psychopathological Items

(1) primary disturbance of thought; (2) primary disturbance of communication; (3) secondary disturbance of communication; (4) delusional processes; (5) hallucinations; (6) unmanageable or disturbing behavior; (7) affective disturbances; (8) disturbances of consciousness/orientation; (9) disturbances of memory/amnesia; (10) severe mental retardation; (11) general impairment of judgment/insight.

Overall Evaluation

(1) overall fitness judgment; (2) rating of confidence in judgment; (3)

comment on basis for decision about defendant; (4) other factors which the evaluator feels should be taken into account in reaching the decision.

Consensual Judgment

(1) fitness judgment after conferring with partner; (2) changes in rating of individual items after conferring; (3) reason for changes.[12]

The instrument asks evaluators to indicate a defendant's status on five legal issues, using a three-point scale ranging from no or minimal incapacity to substantial incapacity. For the mental status items the instrument provides a simple yes/no checklist. However, evaluators must indicate the importance of both the legal and the mental status items in their overall judgment on an adjacent three-point scale, ranging from no bearing to substantial bearing on the competency decision.[12]

In clinical evaluations of competency to stand trial, most authors have concluded that the *Dusky* formula is insufficient. An example of an alternative is the "fourfold analysis" model which has been introduced to incorporate the issue of causality and address the problems generated by the looseness of the *Dusky* formula. This fourfold analysis involves (1) determination of the particular legal issue; (2) the specific legal criteria that are required to resolve the legal issue; (3) the collection of data through the clinical examination of the defendant; and (4) the application of the clinical data to the legal criteria.

Drob et al[13] have noticed that once the particular legal issue has been determined, such as competency to stand trial, the three remaining components of this analysis are (1) the clinical examination, and (2) its application to (3) the legal criteria. In the fourfold analysis model the patient's psychiatric status and the causal relationship between this psychiatric status and the patient's functional capacity will be assessed.

The ABA has settled on five basic criteria to aid fair and accurate competency determinations: (1) understanding of the nature of the trial process, without undue perceptual disorder; (2) capacity to maintain the attorney-client relationship; (3) ability to recall and relate factual information; (4) capacity to testify relevantly; and (5) the above abilities in light of the particular charge, extent of defendant's participation, and complexity of the case. If a defendant shows deficiency in one or more of these areas, then further clinical examination is necessary for the purpose of treatment and assessing the likelihood of regaining competency.[1]

In spite of this reliable testing system, nothing can substitute for a good clinical interview in competency assessment. Schreiber and the other inventors of the IFI evaluated the major three instruments, CST, CAI, and IFI, in 120 defendants against one-time interviews by well-trained persons, and they concluded that the one-time interview by a qualified clinician can lead to accurate competency decisions in a majority of cases.[12]

Instrumental testing and clinical interviews can fail to detect malingering from real competency. Mutism, for example, is one of the problems that makes competency evaluation difficult for the clinician. Genuine mutism may occur in a variety of organic and functional mental conditions, ranging from brain damage to catatonic stupor. The critical issue for a clinician is to discern whether the mutism is due to genuine neuropsychiatric disorder, or is faked to try to escape trial and punishment. Daniel and Resnick[14] recommend a comprehensive evaluation including neurologic workup, repeat interviews, observation of the defendant at unsuspected times for communicative speech with other inmates, study of handwriting samples, collateral nursing documentation, and thiopental sodium (Pentothal) interviews to establish the authenticity of the mutism.

Although some authors have contended that hospitalization for competency assessment is rarely necessary,[12] one cannot ignore the role of multi-interdisciplinary treatment in the overall assessment and detection of mental illnesses. The observations by hospital staff and psychiatric teams of a defendant's behavior during participation in therapeutic activities, and a defendant's interaction with other patients and staff, are a valuable tool whose effectiveness cannot be ignored or eliminated, and which cannot be replaced by a one-time interview. While the assessment instruments and interviews have their merits, nothing can substitute for the scope and duration of hospitalization to achieve thoroughness. Whereas the instruments and interviews rate, assess, and hypothesize, hospitalization actually exhibits and displays a defendant's functional mental and interpersonal processes; after a given time of observing, the observer can say unequivocally: "He reacts thus to X stimulus; I've seen it 5 times," at this date and time, etc. Not only is a determination of competency under such circumstances more accurate, but it will hold up under critical scrutiny better than other methods because it is based on more substantive data, that is, extensive observation, compared to conclusions drawn. Successful malingering can also be reduced with this method, since it would be hard to maintain the act steadily.

Finally, as Appelbaum and Roth have recommended,[15] psychiatrists evaluating competency must continue to think clinically about the issues before them. A finding of probable incompetency on an initial assessment requires further workup and a differential diagnostic approach. Mental health professionals must be clinically and medically oriented to the competency evaluation. Their task and service are to provide facts for the court to use as a basis for its eventual legal determination.

COMPETENCY TO STAND TRIAL WHILE A DEFENDANT IS ON MEDICATION

Soon after the introduction of effective psychotropic medication as a valid and generally accepted treatment method, courts were faced with a new dilemma in dealing with the medicated defendant. If competency was a tough issue before, this added dizzying dimensions. In a survey, it was found that

13 states applied "automatic bar rule," that is, the court automatically prohibited the trial of any defendant taking "psychoactive drugs." Some courts have taken a contrary view, however. They consider that defendants may be able to proceed with trial, or to have their convictions or pleas upheld, despite treatment with neuroleptics.[16] Some courts remain concerned that the medications might induce a state of "synthetic sanity" or that jurors might become confused when confronted with defendants who have a history of bizarre behavior but whose psychiatric symptoms are controlled by medication.[17] The landmark case *Commonwealth v Louraine*[18] provides a relevant decision showing the court's concern over a patient's demeanor at the time of trial.

> The defendant, Peter Louraine, allegedly stabbed a man 21 times and killed him. Louraine was indicted for murder in the first degree. He was tried by jury and sentenced to life imprisonment. Louraine appealed his case to the Massachusetts Supreme Court on several grounds including that he was deprived by a judge's ruling of an opportunity to present his demeanor in an unmedicated condition to the jury. He objected as well to the administration of drugs which affected his demeanor and mental process at trial.
>
> Louraine's psychiatric history shows that he had several hospitalizations. He was admitted twice to state hospitals in the past. He suffered from flashbacks attributed to mescaline. He was also diagnosed "schizophrenic." Among his symptoms were a delusion that he was a prophet of God and had to defend himself against demons.
>
> At the time of the crime, Louraine was not taking any medication. After his arrest, Louraine spent a major portion of his time in Massachusetts Maximum Security State Hospital, where he was treated with neuroleptics and antidepressants. In a pretrial motion the defendant requested that any competency evaluation be done while he was unmedicated and that if found competent, he be able to attend the trial unmedicated. The rationale behind this motion was that if a defendant raises the insanity defense, he should be able to demonstrate his demeanor to the court in an unmedicated state. The motion was denied, with the judge ruling that Louraine could support his insanity defense by using expert testimony to show the jury how the medication was affecting his demeanor in the courtroom.

The *Louraine* case was appealed to the Massachusetts Supreme Court. This court reversed the decision of the lower court and ruled that defendants at a murder trial who had raised an insanity defense were entitled to have the jury view their demeanor in an unmedicated condition. The Massachusetts Supreme Court said further that permitting the Commonwealth, over defendants' objection, to administer antipsychotic medication to them that visibly affected their demeanor and mental processes at trial was a denial of their right to a fair trial as guaranteed by the Sixth and Fourteenth Amendments to the Constitution. The court also noted that the ability to present expert testimony accurately describing the effects of medication on a defendant was not an adequate substitute, and could not compensate for the positive value to a defendant's case of his or her own demeanor in an unmedicated state.

Commentators have raised questions as to whether it is really necessary for a jury to see defendants in an unmedicated state to appreciate what their mental status might have been at the time of the alleged event. Along that line, if a patient's mental status at the time of an alleged crime was affected by the ingestion of medication or other substances, does the court need to provide the defendant with the resources to obtain, and the opportunity to ingest, these substances or medications at trial, so the jury can see what he or she is like while on them? Since people inevitably change over time anyway, defendants in an incompetent unmedicated state at trial do not necessarily have the same demeanor that they would have had in an incompetent unmedicated state a month or year prior, at the time of the alleged crime. To believe that one can duplicate a prior demeanor is a fallacious assumption, medication or no. Regarding competency to stand trial, do we actually protect defendants' rights by allowing them to demonstrate their demeanor at the cost of their competency? From a clinical perspective it is sound to assume that the defendant on medication is somewhat altered, or has synthetic sanity, whereas the unmedicated defendant represents the real person. However, if a defendant becomes able through medication to understand something, it is the actual defendant that is doing the understanding, after all, not the drug.

On the issue of medication and competency, the author believes it is unfair to defendants to leave them unmedicated and untreated for the sole purpose of displaying their unadulterated self to the jury and judge. There is an unsavory, lurid element about that which resembles a circus side show or freak show. Fundamentally, it is inhumane to put a suffering, incapacitated individual center-stage, no matter how doing so is rationalized. It also says little for the jury system if jury members are denigrated by being considered incapable of understanding clear and succinct descriptions of a defendant's mental incapacities, whatever they might be, supported by documentation and expert testimony.

It is always the role of physicians to treat their patients to the best of their ability. That guiding principle must be adhered to regardless of legal ramifications. Physicians cannot let their patients degenerate, if they can avoid it, merely to help the patients appear more credible as incompetents in the legal arena. Treating physicians do have a duty to the court, however: to guide the jury, judge, and other involved parties to understand the effects of medication on a defendant's behavior and thought processes. Testimony and documents should suffice in this regard. The court is also rightly concerned with whether the side effects of medication may have changed a defendant's demeanor, and if so, exactly how. Medicating patients and restoring them to a normal demeanor carries the peril of lawsuits. A defendant has the right to avoid antipsychotic medication, and if one administers antipsychotic medication against a defendant's wishes, a lawsuit may be the result. According to the record, this is what occurred in *Bee v Greaves*.[19]

> After Bee was put in the county jail, he developed hallucinations and other symptoms of psychiatric disorder. The jail's officials requested a psychiatric evaluation and the psychiatrist placed Bee on chlorpramazine (Thorazine). Bee

initially accepted chlorpramazine voluntarily, but then he refused to continue with the medication. The psychiatrist ordered that the drug be forced on him by injection. Bee sued the psychiatrist. At the trial, Bee cited the side effects of antipsychotic drugs and violation of his rights. The psychiatrist's counsel argued that pretrial detainees have no constitutional right to refuse medical treatment while they are incarcerated. The counsel further argued that even assuming such a right did exist in some circumstances, the defendant's action in medicating Bee was based on legitimate governmental concern that outweighed any constitutional right that Bee might have.

The three judges of the court disagreed with the defense's arguments and concluded that the state's interest in maintaining Bee's competent condition to stand trial by giving him medication against his will is an inappropriate reason for the use of antipsychotic drugs. The court added that a decision to administer antipsychotic drugs should be based on the legitimate treatment needs of the individual. Specifically, the needs of the individual, and not the needs of the prosecutor, must be paramount when the use of antipsychotic drugs is being considered.

A pretrial detainee retains certain constitutional rights, including freedom of speech and religion under the First and Fourth Amendments, protection against racial discrimination under the equal protection clause of the Fourteenth Amendment, and prevention of further deprivation of life and liberty or property without due process of law.[20] This concept of law has frequently been used by some defendants in order to avoid antipsychotic medication. The legal presumption holds that where the state interest conflicts with fundamental personal liberties, the means by which the state interest is promoted must be carefully selected so as to cause the minimum possible infringement on protected rights.

Patients may be found incompetent to stand trial but at the same time competent to make their own medical decisions. This includes the right to refuse antipsychotic medication, according to the Fourth Circuit court, in *United States v Charters*.[21] The defendant Charters was charged with threatening the president of the United States. Soon thereafter, Charters was found incompetent to stand trial and was confined to a federal correction facility. The government received a court order to medicate Charters against his will on the principle that the government's duty to treat the medical needs of a pretrial detainee overrided the defendant's liberty and due process interests. Furthermore, the government equated legal incompetency to stand trial with medical incompetency to make a personal health care decision.

The decision was appealed, and the Fourth Circuit court proceeded to balance the individual's interest in resisting forced medication against the government's interest in administering forced medication, and found that the right to be free from unwanted physical invasions was an integral part of an individual's constitutional freedom. The threat to individual rights is exacerbated when it involves a potential intrusion into the mind, or has the capacity to undermine the foundation of personality.

Commentators have noted that the decision in *Charters* is important in that it applies the corpus of the right to refuse medication to the circumstances of a criminal pretrial detainee, and to the context of a criminal prosecution.[22]

THE RESPONSIBILITY OF COURTS
AND ATTORNEYS TO RAISE
THE ISSUE OF COMPETENCE

Primary responsibility lies with the trial court to ensure that the proceeding against a defendant is both valid and fair. The court therefore has the obligation to raise and resolve the issue at any time if a good faith doubt of competency arises. This obligation was affirmed by the US Supreme Court in *Pate v Robinson* and *Drope v Missouri*. In each of those cases, a judgment of guilt was reversed because of the failure of the trial court to order an evaluation of the defendant's competency to stand trial (see above).

The ABA has recommended that if a court has a good faith doubt of competency, whether that doubt arises from the motion of the parties or from any other sources, the court must order a psychiatric evaluation and render a decision on the issue of competence before the trial. Prosecutors also have the responsibility to disclose information indicating incompetence, not only to the court but to the defense attorney as well. This requirement comes from the doctrine that the obligation of the prosecutor is to seek justice rather than to merely seek conviction. The US Supreme Court, in a series of cases beginning with *Brady v Maryland*[23] and *Giles v Maryland*,[24] has required that the prosecutors furnish the defense counsel with material that might be an exculpatory factor in sentencing a defendant. The author believes that this requirement for revelation of exculpatory materials stems not from the court of law, but from an even more enduring source. It is the very foundation of a civilized society's ethic to distinguish between what we call justice and what we call revenge.

Sometimes, unfortunately, defense attorneys weigh whether it is in their client's best interest to proceed to trial and receive a short-term imprisonment for their client, or to declare incompetency for their client which would result in a lengthy civil commitment to a mental hospital. This tactic is contrary to professional ethics. It is not uncommon that a defendant who suffers from mental illness after release from prison commits another crime. The second crime is often more serious than the first one. The incompetency procedure exists in the law for the benefit of a defendant who suffers from mental illness, and for the benefit of society. It would be improper to ignore the fundamental right of a defendant, which is restoration of competency through adequate treatment. The attorney's duty, according to the ABA, is to maintain the integrity of the judicial procedure. Therefore defense attorneys are required to advise the court if they suspect that their client may be incompetent. Attorneys should not take a merely tactical approach, weighing whether short-term imprisonment is more appealing to their client than a long-term psychiatric hospitalization.

Another point of view argues that in any trial, defendants retain their sole right to make certain personal choices, that is, to waive or to demand trial by jury, andto decide whether or not to testify in their own behalf, and to decide what plea to enter. Obviously those decisions could not be made by an incompetent defendant, and they may not be made by the attorney. The crux of this aspect of the competency question is found in the simple principle that defense attorneys have an obligation to the judiciary and to their client to inform the court if they suspect that their client is incompetent to stand trial. This infers a higher goal that corresponds to a prosecutor's duty to seek justice instead of merely conviction.

In addition, defense counsel has another responsibility. The American Psychiatric Association and the ABA in their policy statements specify that defendants be represented by counsel before being required to submit to an evaluation for competency. The US Supreme Court in *Coleman v Alabama*[25] established the principle that counsel is required at any critical stage of the proceedings where important rights of the defendant might be affected. The competency evaluation is obviously of critical importance. Therefore, the advice of counsel is required in order to protect the defendant against self-incrimination or revealing unnecessary matters to an examining psychiatrist.

Competency to stand trial does not mean that defendants are competent to make critical decisions in all aspects of a trial such as waiving the right to counsel and representing themselves in defense procedures. It is the reponsibility of the trial judge to ponder and then determine whether an accused has appropriate intelligence and knowledge and whether he or she is or is not competent to waive the right to counsel. This issue was raised by the US Supreme Court in *Westbrook v Arizona*,[26] a case in which the defendant was convicted of murder. He waived his right to attorney after being found competent to stand trial. On appeal, he argued that although he was competent to stand trial, he had been incompetent to represent himself. The Supreme Court concluded that the constitutional right of an accused to be represented by counsel invoked, of itself, the protection of a trial court. Further, this protecting duty imposes the weighty responsibility on the trial judge of determining whether there is an intelligent and competent waiver by the accused. Therefore, in the event that a defendant who is suspected of being incompetent wants to proceed with a pro se representation, the trial judge may deny that person's request and appoint counsel for the accused.

COMPETENCY REFERRALS

Several problems plague the interaction between judges and psychiatrists. It is commonly felt in the psychiatric community that judges are imprecise or unclear in what they expect from psychiatrists or other qualified mental health professionals. Psychiatrists and psychologists in turn do not know what they should provide for the courts. The court offers no checklist for psychiatrists to fill out. And often, judges fail to inform psychiatrists of just what they wish to know about an accused defendant.[27] Further muddling the situation, psychiatrists often send judges narrowly focused reports that make a diagnosis but do not mention criteria of competency. Sometimes also, it is not clear why the court has ordered a competency examination.[28]

Another problem is that the courts as well as psychiatrists sometimes confuse the concept of competency and the concept of criminal responsibility.[29] Owens et al studied this issue.[30] They sent a brief questionnaire to 52 supreme court judges of the state of New York. The judges were asked about their reasons for ordering competency examinations, about the information they would want in a psychiatric report, and several questions about the adequacy of the reports they receive. Twenty-two (42%) judges answered the investigators (16 orally and six by returning the questionnaire). The result was that the judges gave two primary reasons to order the examination: (1) request of a defense attorney; (2) the judge's own observation of the defendant's demeanor and behavior in the courtroom. The majority of the judges were interested to know whether the defendant understood the charges and court procedures as well as their desire for complete information, particularly asking for psychiatric assistance in making a decision on sentencing and disposition with a view to obtaining a treatment plan for the disturbed defendant.[30]

In spite of the above findings and the US Supreme Court's rulings on the importance of incompetency, sometimes the judges and the attorneys do not have scholarly information regarding the significance of incompetency. The more abstract and arcane elements of the issue sometimes escape less intellectually sophisticated courts and judges. For instance, the author once witnessed an accused brought into the courtroom for allegedly assaulting a police officer, violation of probation, and resisting arrest. The defendant refused to be represented by counsel and undertook his own defense. His behavior appeared to be bizarre and his verbalization was irrelevant. He asserted that the court had no jurisdiction to put him on trial. He stated that he received messages from a foreign embassy. He claimed that there was a conspiracy against him by his political enemies. The list dragged on. It was clear, even to a lay person, that the defendant was psychotic and delusional. Nevertheless he was found guilty and sentenced to prison. Such scenes might be taking place every day in obscure courtrooms in this country, with no one knowing what injustices are occurring, not from maliciousness, but more tragically, from ignorance.

Unfortunately, in spite of the Westbrook principle the lower courts sometimes will uphold the conviction of a defendant with a prior history of psychiatric disorders if he waives the right to counsel and does not raise the competency issue. A trial court need only determine if the defendant has the mental capacity to understand the probable risks and consequences of waiving the right to counsel. No determination of the defendant's capacity to conduct a defense in a rational manner is required. In *California v Clark*,[31] the California appeals court upheld the conviction of an ex-felon, Clark, with a prior history of a psychiatric condition, who waived the right to counsel and represented himself. Despite Clark's abusive manner and failure to understand and follow procedural rules at trial, he was permitted to represent himself. He participated in jury selection, made an opening statement, cross-examined witnesses, and presented a closing argument. A posttrial probation report revealed that Clark suffered from paranoid disorder.

The differences between legal and clinical competency are made clear in the *Clark* case. To mental health professionals, Clark was suffering from grandiose delusion, paranoid thought, and therefore he could not possibly be able, rationally, to defend himself. To legal authorities, Clark understood the consequences of his decision regarding waiving the right to counsel and other procedures; therefore, he was found competent to stand trial.

A defendant's mental status is not the only reason for making a competency referral. There are usually a variety of strategies behind the competency referral. Besides being a delaying tactic, invoking the competency procedure is a sure way of obtaining a psychiatric examination. Such an evaluation may help the defense or prosecutor to find alternatives to trial on the charges available. One investigator has noted that the competency procedure is frequently initiated if the type of crime is especially serious, violent, or atrocious. In these circumstances, a determination of incompetency removes public pressure for severe punishment from the prosecutor. Also, for both the prosecutor and defense attorney, a trial by jury on the responsibility issue is avoided. Conversely, a competency referral can also be seen from the defense's point of view as groundwork for a not guilty by reason of insanity plea in serious crimes.[32]

Massachusetts data indicate that most referrals fall into burglary, larceny and theft categories.[28] Florida data resemble Massachusetts data. In Pennsylvania, Temple University studies showed assault as the main reason for referring for competency evaluations.[33] Cook et al[34] studied 329 records of persons who were seen for competency evaluation. They found that the main reason for referral was based on some strategy rather than on a legitimate concern over mental status.

All the above findings indicate that in reality, competency evaluation requests are not related, in most cases, to the seriousness of mental illness. This tactical maneuvering diminishes the integrity of the judicial system and of those law professionals willing to take advantage of a process based on the assumption of good faith. The waste to the mental health profession and society at large is obvious. The former is forced to squander its resource of skilled professionals' time and energy; the latter, money on unnecessary tests. But the most poignant victims of this practice are the genuine incompetents, who acquire the stigma of manipulative opportunists through the abuses of others. Perhaps in the future a method will be devised to separate the truly valid referral requests from the merely tactical ones.

It is important, once again, to stress that a finding of incompetency to stand trial does not constitute a finding of insanity, although the former is sometimes used as part of the support for an insanity plea. While the extension of the *Dusky* doctrine into a more refined and thorough set of criteria has been valuable, improvement can still be made in some areas of incompetency determination. Specifically, allowing clinicians the prerogative of hospitalizing a defendant for observation would give their final determination better substantiation. Also, elimination of the abuse of competency procedures for exclusively tactical moves is imperative to protect the integrity of those determination procedures, and the morale of those whose jobs are to make them work. Commendable progress has been made in creating a system for determining competency to stand trial that is worthy of the Constitution, but there is still much more that can be accomplished to that end.

REFERENCES

1. American Bar Association Standing Committee on Association Standards for Criminal Justice: *Proposed Criminal Justice Mental Health Standards*. Presented at Annual Meeting, Chicago, Aug 7–8, 1984.
2. *Youtsey v US* 1899; 97 F 937 (6th Cir).
3. *United States v Lawrence* 1935; F Cas No. 15, 577.
4. *Dusky v US* 1960; 362 US 402.
5. *Wieter v Settle* 1961; 193 FSupp 318 (WD MD).
6. *Pate v Robinson* 1966; 383 US 375.
7. *Jackson v Indiana* 1972; 406 US 715.
8. *Drope v Missouri* 1975; 420 US 162.
9. Lipsett PD, Lelos D, McGarry AL: Competency for trial: a screening instrument. *Am J Psychiatry* 1971;128:105–109.
10. McGarry AL, et al: *Competency to Stand Trial and Mental Illness*. US Dept of Health, Education and Welfare publication No. (HSM) 73-9105. National Institute of Mental Health, 1973.
11. Pendleton L: Treatment of persons found incompetent to stand trial. *Am J Psychiatry* 1980;137:1098–1100.
12. Schreiber J, et al: An evaluation of procedures for assessing competency to stand trial. *Bull Am Acad Psychiatry Law* 1987; 15:187–203.
13. Drob SL, et al: Competency to stand trial: a conceptual model for its proper assessment. *Bull Am Acad Psychiatry Law* 1987;15:85–94.
14. Daniel AE, Resnick PJ: Mutism, malingering and competency to stand trial. *Bull Am Acad Psychiatry Law* 1987;15:301–308.
15. Appelbaum PS, Roth LH: Clinical issues in the assessment of competency. *Am J Psychiatry* 1981;138:1462–1467.
16. Geller JL, Appelbaum PS: Competency to stand trial, neuroleptic medication and demenaor in court. *Hosp Community Psychiatry* 1985;36:6–7.
17. Gutheil TG, Appelbaum PS: Mind control synthetic sanity—artificial competence and genuine confusion. *Hofstra Law Rev* 1983;12:77–120.
18. *Commonwealth v Louraine* 1983; 390 Mass 28.
19. *Bee v Greaves* 1984; 744 F2d 1387.

20. *Bell v Wolfish* 1979; 441 US 520.
21. *United States v Charters* 1987; 829 F2d (4th Cir).
22. Perlin ML: *United States v Charters:* Right of pretrial detainees to refuse medication. *Am Acad Psychiatry Law Newsletter* 1988;13:4–7.
23. *Brady v Maryland* 1963; 373 US 83.
24. *Giles v Maryland* 1967; 386 US 66.
25. *Coleman v Alabama* 1970; 399 US 1.
26. *Westbrook v Arizona* 1966; 384 US 150.
27. Robey A: Criteria for competency to stand trial. A checklist for psychiatrists. *Am J Psychiatry* 1965;122:616–622.
28. Balconoff EJ, McGarry AL: Amicus curiae, the role of the psychiatrist in pretrial examination. *Am J Psychiatry* 1969;126:342–347.
29. Group for Advancement of Psychiatry: *Misuse of Psychiatry in the Criminal Courts: Competency to Stand Trial Report* No. 8, 1974, pp 859–919.
30. Owens H, et al: The judges' view of competency evaluation. *Bull Am Acad Psychiatry Law* 1985;13:389–397.
31. *California v Clark* 1985; 213 Cal Rptr 837.
32. Matthews AR: *Mental Disability and the Criminal Law: A Field Study*. Chicago, American Bar Foundation, 1970.
33. Jacon NC, et al: A unique forensic diagnostic hospital. *Am J Psychiatry* 1970; 126:139–143.
34. Cook G, et al: Factors affecting referral to determination of competency to stand trial. *Am J Psychiatry* 1973;130:870–875.

9

The Insanity Defense

As early as the sixth century BC, commentary on Hebrew scriptures distinguished between harmful acts traceable to fundamental wrongfulness of judgment or action, and harmful acts occurring out of fundamental innocence. To the ancient scholars, the paradigm of the latter type of act was one committed by a child, who was seen as incapable of weighing the moral implications of behavior. The retarded and the insane were considered to share with children this fundamental state of innocence. This distinction between the culpable and nonculpable was thought by the Greek philosophers, as far back as 500 BC, to be among the "unwritten laws of nature supported by the universal moral sense of mankind." The teachings of Christianity and Islam have also stated that the insane are not responsible for their behavior. Ancient Islamic literature places the lunatic at the mercy of God.

Interaction between Christian theology and Anglo-Saxon law gave rise to the idea that a madman can be pardoned for criminal behavior. At least as early as 1300, documents show that English kings were pardoning murderers because their crimes were committed while they suffered from madness. The first record of jury acquittal by reason of insanity can be traced back to the 1500s. Sir Matthew Hale, a seventeenth century jurist, in his commentary wrote that "the consent of the will is that which renders human action either commandable or culpable . . . where there is a total defect of the understanding there is no free-act of the will. . . ."[1]

Another jurist of the seventeenth century formulated views quite similar to Sir Matthew Hale's. Sir Edward Cook held that most idiots and madmen who lose their memory and understanding should be found nonresponsible. Justice Tracey in 1723 instructed a jury that in order to be found nonresponsible, a man must be totally deprived of his understanding and memory, "so

152

as not to know what he is doing, no more than an infant brute, or a wild beast."[2] It is not surprising that these legal clarifications occurred in the eighteenth century, during the Enlightenment, the era containing the birth of the philosophical concept of the "social contract."

M'NAGHTEN DOCTRINE AND ITS DERIVATIVES

The modern formulation of the insanity defense derives from rules defined by the House of Lords in the Daniel M'Naghten case in 1843.[3] M'Naghten was indicted for having shot Edward Drummond, secretary to the Prime Minister of England, Robert Peel. Medical testimony indicated that M'Naghten was suffering from the delusion of persecution, and the jury in the case returned a verdict of not guilty by reason of insanity. This verdict became a subject of controversy of particular concern to Queen Victoria, and in *The Queen v M'Naghten*,[4] the conflicts inherent in the issue were condensed to their essence: "To the eye of reason, every murderer may seem a madman, but in the eye of the law he is still responsible." As a result, the House of Lords asked the judges of that body to provide an advisory opinion answering the five questions the law delineated for governing such cases. The combined answer to two of those questions has come to be known as the M'Naghten rule: "To establish defense on the grounds of insanity, it must be clearly proved that, at the time of the committing of the act the party accused was labouring under such a defect of reason from disease of mind as not to know the nature and quality of the act he was doing; or if he did know it, that he did not know he was doing wrong."

In the 1870s, the New Hampshire Supreme Court, apparently influenced by Isaac Ray, adopted a rule commonly known as the "product test," which elaborated on the fundamental concept of the M'Naghten rule. As the court puts it, "No man shall be held accountable, criminally, for an act which was the offspring and product of mental disease . . . no argument is needed to show that to hold a man may be punished for what is the offspring of disease would be to hold that he may be punished for the disease. Any rule which makes that possible cannot be law. . . ."[5] The creation of the causative link whereby "being punished for what is the offspring of disease" becomes "[being] punished for the disease" was to have a profound impact a century later, when US courts struggled with interpretations of alcoholism and drug addiction and the criminal acts perpetrated by the victims of those afflictions.

Toward the end of the nineteenth century, several courts found that the insanity defense in the M'Naghten rule was too narrow and generally inadequate. They supplemented the M'Naghten rule with a rule focusing on the volition impairment of the defendant. Known as the "irresistible impulse doctrine," this rule posited that a person who could not control his or her actions shall not be held criminally responsible for them.

In 1886, the first American court case on this issue to be resolved unequivocally clarified that defendants are not legally liable if two conditions occur: (1) if under the duress caused by such mental disease, they have lost the power to choose between right and wrong and thus lost their ability to exercise free will, their act could not have been avoided by the determination of their free will; and (2) if concurrently the alleged crime was so connected with the mental disease by causation as actually to be the product of it.[6]

DURHAM DOCTRINE

Dissatisfied with the scope of the M'Naghten rule and the irresistible impulse doctrine, the court adopted a more comprehensive view in the opinion drawn in the landmark 1954 case, *Durham v United States*.[7] The essence of the Durham doctrine is that, first, "an accused is not criminally responsible if his unlawful act was a product of mental disease or mental defect," and more striking, second, when lack of mental capacity and claim to mental disorder is introduced, sanity must be proved (by the prosecutor) beyond a reasonable doubt. Thus, procedure was inextricably entwined with the issue, determination of sanity or insanity. The defense need not prove insanity to be given the benefit of the doubt, but only to provide evidence of it. If such evidence is produced, the final burden of proof lies with the prosecution, to prove sanity. This concept is in accordance with a liberal interpretation of the "rights of the accused," in which a defendant's rights are paramount when conflict between the defendant's rights and the state's rights arises.

The chain of events leading to this ground-breaking ruling began when Durham, who had a long history of psychiatric hospitalization and imprisonment, was discharged from the Navy at age 17 after a psychiatric examination showed that he suffered from personality disorder and was thus unfit for the Navy. When he was 19, Durham pleaded guilty to violating the National Motor Theft Act and was placed on probation for 3 years. He attempted suicide and as a result was hospitalized in St Elizabeth's Hospital in Washington, DC for 2 months.

In January of 1948, he was charged with passing bad checks and as a result, his probation was revoked and he was sent to jail. His conduct in the first few days of imprisonment led to a lunacy inquiry in the municipal court where the jury found him to be of unsound mind. Again he was committed to St Elizabeth's, where he remained for 15 months under a diagnosis of "psychosis with psychopathic personality." He was discharged from the hospital in July of 1949 as "recovered" and was returned to jail to serve the balance of his sentence. In June of 1950, he was conditionally released from jail, and he violated the condition by leaving the District of Columbia. When he learned of the warrant for his arrest as a parolee violator, he fled south, obtaining money by passing several bad checks. After he was located and returned to the District of Columbia, the parole board referred him to the district court for a lunacy inquisition, wherein a grand jury found him to be of unsound mind. He was readmitted to St Elizabeth's in February of 1951. This time a diagnosis was made of "without mental disorder, psychopathic personality." He was discharged, for the third time, in May of 1951. The crime of breaking into a house that gave rise to the Durham doctrine took place a mere 2 months later, on July 13, 1951.

Because he was found to be of unsound mind, in October of 1951, Durham was deemed incapable of going through court proceedings. He was readmitted to St Elizabeth's again and this time was treated with insulin therapy. Durham was released in February of 1953 and was certified competent to stand trial. Eventually, after passing through technical proceedings, he was brought before the court for retrial.

After reviewing the history of criminal responsibility, Judge Bazelon ruled on the right-wrong test which had been approved in the District of Columbia jurisdiction in 1882 and was applied exclusively in the district until 1929, when it was supplemented by the test of irresistible impulse in *Smith v U.S.*[8] Judge Bazelon concluded that the right-wrong test and the irresistible impulse test are both misleading and inadequate, since they had no scientific basis. He determined that a broader test should therefore be adopted. The judge further stated that any test for criminal responsibility should reflect whether an unlawful act committed by an accused person was the product of a mental disease or defect. This use of the word "disease" means a condition which is considered capable of improvement or deterioration. "Defect," on the other hand, means an inherent flaw, which may be congenital or the result of injury or the residual effect of physical or mental disease, and capable neither of improvement nor deterioration.

The *Durham* case, therefore, achieves its historical importance in two distinct areas: its application of borderline medical and psychiatric criteria to the process of determining insanity, and its clarification of the procedure for that determination, which places the final burden of proof on the prosecution after introduction of evidence of unsound mind by the defense.

THE McDONALD DOCTRINE:
INSTRUCTING A JURY

Another crucial procedural element of the insanity defense was defined and elucidated in *McDonald v US*[9] As a direct result of the ruling in this case, whenever the issue of the insanity defense is brought into the proceedings, a judge must explain to the jury that a defendant may be found not guilty by reason of insanity and if the jury makes such a determination the defendant will receive treatment in an institution.

Motivated by the chain of events in the *McDonald* case, the American Bar Association (ABA) has recommended that acquittees who at trial have been found beyond a reasonable doubt to have committed a felony involving serious bodily harm be confined for evaluation for up to 30 days or longer if good cause is shown. Acquittees may be committed for a term not to exceed the maximum prison term designated for their offense, subject to periodic review.

In order to commit defendants and to continue their confinement on review, the court must find by clear and convincing evidence that the acquittees (1) are mentally ill or mentally retarded; (2) pose a substantial threat of serious bodily harm to others; and (3) do not meet these criteria solely because they are undergoing treatment or habilitation which is unlikely to continue unless they remain confined in a secure facility. The ABA has proposed further that a trial jury be told of these dispositional consequences, at least in general terms, before it retires to deliberate on the verdict.

The events which led to the creation of these guidelines for advising juries began with the manslaughter conviction of Ernest McDonald, who received a 5- to 15-year prison sentence. He had been charged with second-degree murder for aiding and abetting his employer. After the conviction, the defendant appealed on the basis of expert testimony on his behalf indicating that at the time of the crime he suffered from a mental defect, specifically a state of mental development below the level of average intelligence, leaving him incapable of evaluating the situation he was in or the consequences of his actions. When instructing the jury, the judge offered it five possible verdicts to choose from, none of which was "not guilty by reason of insanity." McDonald felt that this exclusion was an error.

The court of appeals supported McDonald's appeal in forma pauperis, and a rehearing en banc was ordered on sua sponte. The US Court of Appeals, District of Columbia Circuit, noted that first, the lower court failed to state that if appellant were acquitted by reason of insanity, appellant would be confined to a mental hospital until he was determined to be no longer dangerous to himself or others; and second, the lower court twice enumerated the alternative verdicts available to the jury but failed to include "not guilty by reason of insanity." The five verdicts offered by the lower court to the jury were:

1. Guilty of second degree murder
2. Guilty of manslaughter
3. Guilty of assault with a dangerous weapon
4. Guilty of assault
5. Not guilty

The lower court later gave additional advice to the jury on the criminal responsibility issue, saying, "If you are not satisfied beyond reasonable doubt that the act was not a product of mental defect, then your verdict must be not guilty because of insanity."

The US Court of Appeals ruled that there was some evidence supporting the defendant's claim of mental disability and an expert testified to the fact that at the time of the crime the defendant suffered from a mental defect (McDonald's IQ was below average). Therefore, McDonald was entitled to have the instruction given to the jury on the issue of a "not guilty by reason of insanity" verdict in which case treatment would be provided. Once the defendant produced expert testimony showing he was suffering from a mental defect at the time of the crime, stated the appeals court, the judge should have explained that if he was found guilty by reason of insanity he would receive treatment in an institution. The judge erred in twice giving the jury only five possible verdicts to consider.

The timing and content of instruction to the jury of the availability of the verdict, and the institutionalization and treatment that would take place if the verdict is rendered were thus codified in *McDonald v US* And again, the ruling demonstrated a conscientious protectiveness toward the rights of the accused.

STATES' DIFFERENCES IN DISPOSITION INSTRUCTION TO JURIES

Twenty-one states and several federal circuits have ruled that it is not an error to refuse a dispositional instruction, while several other states have prohibited such instruction altogether (eg, Kansas, South Carolina, and Vermont). Two states allow the court to give an instruction sua sponte (Massachusetts and Wisconsin). Other states only allow the court to give the instruction on the defendant's request (Colorado, Florida, and Hawaii). Only ten states hold that the defendant is entitled to have the jury know the consequences of the nonresponsibility verdict (eg, Kansas, New Hampshire, and North Carolina).

Arguments have been offered for and against jury instruction regarding the disposition of those found not guilty by reason of insanity. The jurors who are not informed of possible sentencing alternatives might base their decisions on irrelevant considerations, one side contends. For instance, they might sentence someone whom they consider insane to prison if they believe the only alternative is allowing him or her to walk the streets. In this case, they would be trapped in a "which is the least unfair" decision, that is, whom will they elect to victimize, the defendant or the potential innocent victims. Instruction of disposition could eliminate this predicament. Conversely, jurors should not be told that a person acquitted by reason of insanity will be confined to a hospital, another argument goes, otherwise they may be more willing to find a defendant insane as a compromise between prison and the street. The comfort of this alternative could cloud their focus on the actual fact of whether or not the defendant was insane. Without dispositional knowledge, the jury would be more likely to base its decision solely on the evidence adduced during the trial.

PROHIBITION OF LABELS AND
CONCLUSIONS

Psychiatrists and other mental health professionals were forbidden by the Court in *Washington v United States*[10] to testify using diagnostic terms or other labels which could have varied or indistinct meanings to the members of the jury. The case is significant because it is the first case under the *Durham* precedent that limits the testimony of psychiatrists in the courtroom. In *Washington*, the defendant was convicted in the US district court of rape, robbery, and assault with a deadly weapon. His principal defense was not guilty by reason of insanity. The court found that the defendant was not insane at the time of the crime. Further, Chief Justice Bazelon ruled that in any insanity case trial, the court should restrict psychiatrists' use of medical labels such as "schizophrenia" or "neurosis".

In his concluding comments, Judge Bazelon ruled that classification of mental illness has evolved for purposes such as treatment and communication, but was not appropriate for assessing responsibility in criminal cases. The judge intended to ensure that the views of the experts would not bind the fact-finders. Thus it was decided, Judge Bazelon added, to give mental illness a broad definition independent of its medical meaning, and that unexplained medical labels such as schizophrenia, paranoia, psychosis, neurosis, psychopathic, etc, were insufficient and too misleading to appear in testimony. While medical terms were out, however, medical substance could be included in the guise of descriptions and explanations of the origin, development, and manifestations of the alleged diseases. Providing such substantive information was indeed the chief function of the expert witness.

The main value of expert testimony in this field, as in all fields, rests with the material from which the opinion is fashioned, and the reasoning by which the expert progresses from the material to his or her conclusion, that is, in the explanation of the disease or defect and its dynamics, and how it occurred, developed, and affected the mental and emotional capacities of the defendant. Judge Bazelon stated, in essence, that the *Durham* ruling had been intended to restrict to its proper medical function the part played by the medical expert.

AMERICAN LAW INSTITUTE TEST

The court and more specifically Judge Bazelon himself eventually grew dissatisfied with the *Durham* formulation of criminal responsibility. Different criteria were used in the landmark case *United States v Brawner*,[11] with the court holding that *Durham* was not after all a satisfactory test, and borrowing with some modifications a doctrine from the American Law Institute (ALI) to replace the determining role of the *Durham* ruling. This newer ruling, in force since 1972 and adopted by other federal circuit courts of appeal, states: "A person is not responsible for criminal conduct if at the time of such conduct as a result of mental disease or defect, he lacks substantial capacity either to appreciate the criminality (wrongfulness) of his conduct or to conform his conduct to the requirements of law."

The circumstances leading to the implementation of this new definition arose during a party in September of 1967 attended by Archy W. Brawner, Jr and his uncle Aaron Ross. During the evening several fights broke out. In one of them, Brawner's jaw was injured when he was struck and pushed to the ground. This took place about 10:30 PM. After the fight, Brawner left the party, telling Mr Ross that some boys had jumped him. Later in court, Ross testified that Brawner looked like he was out of his mind. Other witnesses who saw him after the fight testified that Brawner's mouth was bleeding and that his speech was unclear. Angry and staggering, Brawner returned to the party at 11:00 PM and fired five shots. Two shots struck and killed Billy Ford.

At trial, all expert witnesses, both those for the defendant and those for the prosecution, concurred that Brawner was suffering from an abnormality of a psychiatric or neurologic nature. The medical labels were various: epileptic personality, brain syndrome, etc.

The defendant was convicted of second-degree murder by a jury. During appeal, the US Court of Appeals for the District of Columbia set forth the new ALI standard for insanity, quoted above, which weighs the defendant's capacity for comprehension and judgment at the time of the crime, and abandoned the Durham doctrine. Further, it declared that the new standard would be adopted as the criterion "for insanity for all trials beginning after today." The same court ruled that in addition to the ALI test, (1) the McDonald definition of mental disease or defect is retained; (2) past criminal and antisocial actions introduced to substantiate an insanity plea will not be considered evidence of mental disease unless accompanied by expert testimony that is further supported by a responsible segment of professional opinion to the effect that these actions constitute convincing evidence of an underlying mental disease; and (3) the court maintains its approach of permitting a broad presentation to the jury concerning the condition of the defendant's mind and the consequences of that condition.

The ALI test became popular and was accepted by the court in Brawner's case although it had been in existence since 1952. The ALI test differs from M'Naghten's in three crucial respects: (1) ALI substitutes the concept of "appreciation" for that of cognitive understanding in the definition of insanity, thus apparently introducing an affective, more emotional, more subjective, personalized approach for evaluating the nature of a defendant's knowledge or comprehension; (2) the ALI definition for insanity does not require a defendant's lack of appreciation or knowledge of the nature of his conduct to be total, but only that he or she "lacks substantial capacity"; and (3) the

ALI test, like the irresistible impulse test, incorporates a so-called volitional approach to insanity, thus adding as an independent criterion for insanity the defendant's ability (or inability) to control his actions.[3]

It takes only an instant to grasp the tremendous impact that the broader, looser ALI standard has on trial proceedings where the insanity plea is operative, compared to the stricter, more rigid M'Naghten rule. Juries are charged with judging a more subjective state, and must in turn employ a more subjective method as well, since understanding of the term "appreciation" surely varies from person to person more than does understanding of cognitive process.

CRIME AND MENTAL ILLNESS

A question currently arousing controversy is whether mentally ill persons commit more crimes than ordinary citizens. Since it became fashionable to discharge mentally ill patients from state facilities into communities in the late 1960s and early 1970s, when budget-cutters joined forces with the more radical of the civil rights advocates in an unusual alliance, a number of investigators have tried to learn whether there is any correlation between the rate of arrests and related crime to the number of mentally ill persons in the community.

Among the first to make a serious effort to determine the nature of such a relationship were Zitrin et al.[12] Zitrin and his associates, studying the earlier literature, noticed that research done from 1920 to 1940 indicated that the arrest rate for patients discharged from psychiatric hospitals was lower than for the general population. A massive study by Brill and Malzberg[13] of a population of 10,247 male patients who were released from New York state hospitals between 1946 and 1948 found that the overall arrest rate for the ex-patients was 122 per 10,000 while the rate for the general population was 491 per 10,000.

The consistency of these findings ended in the 1960s. Studies performed after 1965 show ex-mental patients having a significantly higher rate of arrest than the general population for serious crimes such as assault, homicide and robbery. Zitrin et al studied the arrest records of 867 patients discharged from the Bellevue Psychiatric Hospital, New York City's catchment area.[12] Their study revealed that the arrest record of those former psychiatric patients for criminal behavior, including violent offenses, was higher than the corresponding rates in the general community. The studies of Zitrin et al indicated that of 867 mental patients, 202 (23.3%) had been arrested at least once during the 2 years before and 2 years after the study. Of those 202 patients, 117 (13.5%) had been charged with a nonviolent offense only, and 85 patients (9.8%) had been charged with a violent offense.

Further studies by Sosowsky[14] of 301 mental patients in the cohort found that 142 (47.2%) had been arrested at least once during the 3½ years before and 4½ years after the "liberalization of California's involuntary commitment procedure." Of those 301 patients, 71 (23.6%) had been charged with non-violent offenses and 71 (23.6%) with violent offenses, rates much higher than for the general population. Sosowsky noted that the arrest rate for violent offenses occurred in relation to the implementation of California's legal reforms. This investigator concluded that the mentally ill, who are traditionally treated in state hospitals, are more prone to criminal activity than individuals in the public at large.

In a study by Holcomb and Ahr[15] of a statewide (Missouri) random sample comprising 611 young adult patients who received public inpatient, outpatient, and community residential care, 38% were found to have been arrested at least once in their adult lifetimes, with 35% arrested on felony charges and 18.9% for violent crimes. Patients with a primary diagnosis of drug or alcohol abuse had the greatest overall frequency of arrests and also the greatest frequency of arrests for burglary, offenses against public order such as disturbing the peace or loitering, and probation and parole violations. No significant differences between diagnostic groups were found for arrests for violent crimes. In the investigators' view, the results of the study suggest that since past research on the arrest records of psychiatric patients was based on samples of former state hospital patients, the prevalence of arrest records among psychiatric patients has been exaggerated. However, in this study the arrest rate for young psychiatric patients with severe diagnoses a year after admission to public mental health services is still 17 times greater than the arrest rate for the same-age general population (in Missouri).[15]

Rabkin made a critical appraisal of all available evidence in the literature up to 1978, including a review of an epidemiologic prospective study of arrests and convictions among discharged mental patients in comparison to arrests and convictions of the general public, and their changes over time.[16] She discovered that discharged mental patients as a group are not significantly less likely than others to exhibit dangerous or criminal behavior. In this investigator's opinion, there is no evidence of causation whereby the patient's mental status raises the arrest risk, but rather that antisocial behavior and the behavior characteristic of mental illness apparently coexist, particularly among young, unmarried, unskilled, poor males, and especially those belonging to ethnic minorities.

Rabkin concluded that under the limited evidence available, patients discharged from mental hospitals are not, by virtue of their psychiatric disorder or hospital experience, more prone to engage in criminal activity than are people demographically similar to them who do not have a history of mental illness. Since arrest and conviction rates vary so widely in the general population according to age, socioeconomic status, family history, and ethnicity, the incidence of these factors in the discharged mental patients sample would have to be duplicated almost identically in the "general population" sample for the comparisons to be considered definitive. And although patients as a group do have a higher arrest rate than nonpatients as a group, this could be attributed to inappropriate use of mental hospitals as an alternative to the criminal justice system.[16]

In a British study,[17] 203 psychotic and nonpsychotic males from the Brixton remand prison in London were examined to determine the relationship between mental state and offense. The findings showed that only nine of 121 men who were diagnosed as having some form of psychosis were symptom-free at the time of the offense and have remained so after remand. Even though a higher rate of positive symptoms of psychosis existed within the sample, only 23 (19%) of the actively psychotic men were directly driven to crime by their psychotic symptoms, and further, 26% probably were so driven. For 29 men, a delusional motive was considered probable cause. If indirect consequences of psychosis are also taken into account, 82% of their offenses were probably due to illness. Nonpsychotic men never claimed psychotic justification for their offenses, but half of the psychotic men claimed ordinary nonpsychotic motives for their offending acts. This investigation concluded that a delusional subgroup of psychotic offenders was much more likely to commit offenses with serious consequences than other psychotics, and that the importance of delusional drive in relation to serious violent crimes may be greater than previously thought.[17]

Phillips et al[18] linked data from police records, court reports, and clinical files for 2735 psychiatric referrals from the criminal justice system of Alaska from 1977 through 1981. They found that only 0.2% to 2.0% of all schizophrenic persons in the community had been arrested for violent crimes each year, accounting for 1.1% to 2.3% of all arrests for violent crimes; that psychiatrists agreed about competency and responsibility in 79% of the cases evaluated by more than one clinician; and that a successful insanity defense occurred in 0.1% or less of all criminal cases.

In spite of the foregoing data, mental illness may remain unrecognized in some offenders. In this regard, an interesting study was done by Lewis et al.[19] These investigators gave clinical examinations to 15 death row inmates (13 men and two women) who were chosen for examination because of the imminence of their executions and not for evidence of neuropsychopathologic disorders. They learned that all the subjects had a history of head injury which could be corroborated. In total, five subjects had major neurologic impairments, including seizure, paralysis, and cortical atrophy, and seven others had a history of blackout, dizziness, a variety of psychomotor epileptic symptoms, and numerous minor neurologic signs. There was a suspicion of brain dysfunction in five subjects. Psychological testing suggested that ten inmates had cognitive dysfunction. All but one of the subjects tested were of normal intelligence. Nine subjects suffered psychiatric symptoms during childhood that were severe enough to warrant consultation and/or preclude attendance in a normal classroom. Three of these subjects had attempted suicide during childhood and one had tried to kill himself during adolescence. Six subjects were found to be chronically psychotic and their history indicated that their psychoses antedated incarceration. The staggering list continues: one subject had a loose illogical thought process, suffered from delusions and hallucinations, and often behaved in bizarre and sometimes sadistic ways; three subjects were episodically psychotic, and two were manic-depressive.

Lewis et al extended their study to include juveniles who were condemned to death in the United States.[20] They found that all 14 juveniles, incarcerated in four states, suffered severe psychopathologic disorders. Nine had major neurologic impairment, seven suffered psychotic disorders antedating incarceration, seven evidenced significant organic dysfunction on neuropsychological testing, and only two had full-scale IQ scores above 90. Twelve had been brutally physically abused and five had been sodomized by relatives. Lewis noticed that for a variety of reasons the subjects' vulnerabilities were not recognized at the time of trial or sentencing.

The authors of these studies concluded that many condemned persons probably suffer a multiplicity of severe but undetected psychiatric and neurologic disorders that are highly relevant to consideration of mitigation in clemency appeals. Most likely, the main reason why these vulnerabilities were never identified is simply that nobody suspected their existence, and hence nobody looked for them. The findings of this study strongly contradict the popular notion that murderers are just sociopaths feigning mental illness to get off the hook. To the contrary, a majority of these subjects did not consider themselves sick or impaired and did not request a specialized evaluation. They did not know enough to do so. The inertia of the system carried them toward executions they probably could not comprehend the purpose or consequences of. Since few of these subjects were flamboyantly psychotic enough to command attention, their neuropsychiatric conditions escaped the notice even of their own attorneys.

Indeed, the reality may be the complete reverse of the common cynical perception of supposedly sane criminals who "use" the insanity defense. Instead, the insanity defense may illuminate only the surface of a deep and broad population of criminally insane, who suffer unbeknownst not only to others but to themselves.

RIGHT TO PSYCHIATRIC ASSISTANCE IN THE INSANITY DEFENSE

The right of defendants to obtain psychiatric assistance in preparing an insanity defense or argument to mitigate capital punishment was first set forth in 1985 in *Ake v Oklahoma*.[21] In *Ake*, the US Supreme Court ruled that (1) an indigent defendant in a criminal proceeding has a constitutional right to psychiatric evaluation and assistance when his or her mental state at the time of the offense is a pivotal issue; and (2) the defendant also has a right to such assistance at the capital sentencing proceeding when the prosecution introduces psychiatric evidence of the defendant's future dangerousness.

A review of the history of this case shows that the defendant's mental condition was in question right from the beginning of court proceedings.

Glen Ake was charged with first-degree murder of a minister and his wife and shooting their two children with intent to kill in 1979 in Oklahoma. At Ake's arraignment, the trial court found his behavior bizarre and thus a psychiatric examination was ordered to determine the defendant's fitness. Based on the testimony of psychiatrists, Ake was delusional and probably paranoid schizophrenic, certainly in need of prolonged psychiatric care. Ake was found incompetent to stand trial, and was committed to a state hospital. Six weeks later, the hospital reported that Ake's competency was restored and the court therefore scheduled him for trial.

At a pretrial conference, Ake's attorney informed the court that an insanity defense would be used, and requested a psychiatric evaluation at the state's expense, because the defendant was indigent. The trial court denied the defendant's motion. Although there was testimony by the state psychiatrist that the defendant was dangerous, there was no expert evidence assessing the defendant's sanity at the time he committed the crimes. The jury convicted Ake of two counts of first-degree murder and two counts of shooting with intent to kill.

The state sought the death penalty. At sentencing, a state psychiatrist testified regarding the likelihood of the defendant's potential for dangerous behavior in the future. Ake presented no expert witness to rebut the state's expert, or to provide evidence to mitigate the sentence. The judge sentenced Ake to death for each murder count, and 500 years imprisonment on the two-count shooting with intent to kill verdict. On an appeal to the Oklahoma Court of Criminal Appeals, the verdicts and sentences were affirmed. The appeals court rejected the defendant's constitutional argument defending his right to have a psychiatric expert at state expense. The only path left for Ake was to request review by the US Supreme Court.

The issues the case placed before the Supreme Court were: (1) whether the Constitution required that an indigent defendant be provided access to a psychiatric examination when the defendant's sanity at the time of the offense has become a determining issue; and (2) whether the defendant facing the death penalty was entitled to psychiatric assistance in rebutting evidence of dangerousness adduced by the prosecution. After reviewing previous cases, the Court noted that "a criminal trial is fundamentally unfair if the state proceeds against an indigent defendant without making certain that he has access to the raw materials integral to the building of an effective defense." The Court continued that to determine whether competent psychiatric assistance is constitutionally required, three factors must be weighed: (1) the private interest affected by the state action; (2) the governmental interest affected if the safeguard is provided; and (3) the probable value of the additional or substituted procedural safeguards that are sought and the risk of an erroneous deprivation of the affected interest if those safeguards are not provided.

The Court recognized that "the private interest in the accuracy of a criminal proceeding that places an individual's life or liberty at risk is almost uniquely compelling . . . and weighs heavily in our analysis." The Court rejected the state's assertion that an extraordinary burden would be placed on the state if it had to provide Ake with the requested psychiatric assistance. In respect to the second factor, a state may not legitimately assert an interest in maintenance of strategic advantages over the defense, if the result of that advantage is to cast a pall on the accuracy of the verdict obtained. And in respect to the third factor, the Court found that psychiatry has come to play a vital role in criminal proceedings. Psychiatrists, unlike lay witnesses, can do more than describe symptoms. They can identify the often obscure symptoms of insanity and they can translate a medical diagnosis into language that will assist the trier of fact.

In this ruling, the Supreme Court made it clear that psychiatric assistance must be limited to those instances "when the defendant is able to make an ex-parte threshold showing to the trial court that his sanity is likely to be a significant factor in his defense." The psychiatrist must be competent to assist in the evaluation, preparation, and presentation of the defense, but there is nothing in the opinion which suggests that there is a constitutional right to choose a particular psychiatrist.

In an analysis of the *Ake* case, Petrila and Fitch[22] have noted that the Supreme Court based its ruling on the same principle underlying its decision in *Gideon v Wainwright*,[23] the case that created the right to counsel, in emphasizing that a defendant must be given access to the tools necessary to participate fully and fairly in trial. In *Ake*, the Court also appeared to direct that equally qualified experts for both the prosecution and the defense be presented in proceedings, rather than one single examiner whose report is submitted to both the prosecution and defense. As a footnote, the Supreme Court sat out from its own research and found that 40 states provided psychiatric assistance to defendants in criminal trials prior to the *Ake* ruling.[24]

In the light of *Ake v Oklahoma*, some defendants have tried to obtain psychiatric assistance for purposes unrelated to the insanity defense. The courts so far have rejected these requests. Some examples, however, are noteworthy: In *Martin v Wainwright*,[25] the defendant Nollie Martin was convicted in Florida of first-degree murder, kidnapping, armed robbery, and forcible sexual battery. He was given the death sentence, and challenged the decision by filing a writ of habeas corpus, arguing that his right to psychiatric assistance had been violated and that his confession had been involuntary because of his mental incompetency. The defendant then claimed that he needed a neuropsychologist to examine him for organic brain damage, an examination the defendant was prevented from ordering because of indigence. The court disagreed, finding that the *Ake* case guaranteed access to a competent psychiatrist, which he had received. In this case, seven mental health experts were appointed by the court with the approval of the defense counsel, or by the defense counsel himself. Two of those experts assisted with the insanity defense. The fact that only one of those experts examined the defendant for organicity and came to the conclusion that the defendant's condition was not organic did not necessitate the appointment by the trial court of another expert to perform the same examination to verify the first opinion, or as the defendant hoped, to contradict it. Under a system which endeavors to give a defendant every opportunity to construct and present a thorough defense, there are still limits, and the court time and again must draw the line between ample fairness and indulgence: "The defendant is not constitutionally entitled to the appointment of an expert who would agree to testify in accordance with his wishes."

It seems that after the initial *Ake* ruling giving defendants expert psychiatric assistance in limited and specific situations, every remote possibility provides defendants with an inspiration to try and have that ruling applied to their case. In *Liles v Oklahoma*,[26] the court found that being prescribed and taking psychotropic drugs does not entitle a defendant to psychiatric assistance under the Ake doctrine. In this instance, Mark Liles was convicted of first-degree murder and given the death penalty. The court had early on ordered an evaluation of the defendant's sanity, and psychiatrists had concluded that the defendant was not mentally ill and did not require psychiatric treatment. The defendant waited 2 months before asking for psychiatric assistance to prepare his insanity defense and argument regarding mitigating circumstances. One basis of his appeal was the obligation of the state to provide an indigent defendant with access to competent psychiatric assistance in the preparation of an insanity defense. However, that obligation only existed if the defendant's sanity was viewed as a significant factor in the trial. If the defendant exhibited no other reason to doubt his sanity, being placed on psychotropic drugs at a state mental hospital did not conform to the requirement that insanity would be a key issue at the trial. Furthermore, in *Liles*, the state did not present psychiatric evidence of its own, as it did in *Ake*, thus obviating application of that section of the ruling allowing a defendant to rebut state expert testimony. The Supreme Court in the landmark *Ake* case clarified two specific circumstances when defendants could justifiably request expert psychiatric assistance, at the state's expense if they were indigent, and strict guidelines were delineated to limit the application of those rulings to when a defendant's sanity at the time of the offense was in question, and to rebut the state's expert witnesses.

As the insanity defense develops a substantial body of prior rulings, and as courts, in ruling on new aspects, have access to more and more documentation and actual history to inform their considerations, the rulings seem to become increasingly sophisticated and detailed. Courts have learned from experience how incomplete, loosely argued rulings produce unsatisfactory results.

CONCEPT OF GUILTY BUT MENTALL ILL

As an alternative to the insanity defense, the guilty but mentally ill verdict (GBMI) has attracted attention. Michigan was the first state to adopt this verdict, in 1975. The history of the concept of GBMI, as reported by Petrella et al,[27] began when Michigan handed down the decision in *People v Mc-*

Quillan[28] in 1974. This decision was based on the principles of due process and equal protection. Sixty days of mandatory commitment for diagnosis and observation were imposed on those found not guilty by reason of insanity. After that commitment period, two options remained: the recipients of that verdict would (1) have to meet civil commitment criteria which indicate that a person must be mentally ill and by reason of that mental illness dangerous to himself or others, or unable to meet his basic needs; or (2) be released.

In the *McQuillan* decision, the court ordered that all previously committed insanity acquittees be evaluated and then released if they failed to meet the criteria for civil commitment. Within a year, 270 patients previously found not guilty by reason of insanity, and indefinitely committed, were evaluated by the clinical staff at the Center for Forensic Psychiatry and subjected to judicial review. After probate court hearing, 64 of them were released because they did not meet the criteria for civil commitment.

Less than a year after the *McQuillan* decision, two persons who had been released from custody committed heinous crimes, including rape and murder. Pressured by public criticism, the Michigan legislatures passed the statute of "guilty but mentally ill," in order to protect society by allowing for incarceration of defendants who might otherwise be found not guilty by reason of insanity and subsequently released for not meeting civil commitment criteria. The legislators anticipated that this statute would reduce the number of insanity acquittals, and solve the problems of disposition and jury deliberation. The intention of the legislature was an assurance that mentally ill offenders would not be released back into the community before a definitive sentence had been served. As the statute in Michigan is written, the insanity defense has not been abolished, but the alternative option has been created for juries to select, in appropriate circumstances, an option which in effect would close the procedural gap between the verdict of not guilty by reason of insanity and meeting civil commitment criteria, since the former in no way presupposed the latter.

Michigan, a pioneer in applying this GBMI verdict, has continued its use. In numerous cases, for instance *Michigan v Baily* and *Michigan v Walker*,[30] the Michigan Court of Appeals found that the defendant's right to due process of law is not violated by this verdict. This verdict option is not intended as a compromise verdict, but rather as one choice among many, giving jurors a fuller range of criminal responsibility to consider. Any negative effect was deemed minimal, and therefore constitutionally permissible.

Alaska, Illinois, Georgia, Indiana, and Kentucky have adopted some version of GBMI. Those states and a few others, in spite of severe opposition from professional societies such as the American Bar Association, the American Psychological Association, and the American Psychiatric Association, continue to offer the concept of GBMI in their panoply of verdicts.

The court in the Alaska case *Hart v Alaska*[31] explained that only those who fit the first criteria of the ALI test, that is, "those unable to appreciate the nature and quality of their conduct due to mental illness or defect," are exempt from criminal responsibility. The rest may be found guilty but mentally ill. The court went on to say that concepts such as mental illness, insanity, and criminal responsibility are legal and ethical rather than medical terms. Further, the law presumed that men and women are moral agents with the power to choose between good and evil and therefore may be held accountable for their acts. The determination therefore of at what point a person's mental condition justifies exculpation is an ethical question for legislatures and jurors. The panel in Hart's case also concluded that this decision does not mean that any offense caused in part by mental illness is necessarily mitigated under Alaska law. A mitigating factor is "some degree of duress, coercion, or compulsion insufficient to constitute a complete defense, but which significantly affected the defendant's conduct."

Illinois also upheld the constitutionality of the GBMI verdict. However, in *Illinois v Carter*[32] and *Illinois v Smith*,[33] the court rejected the premise that all defendants found guilty but mentally ill are entitled to receive treatment. The Supreme Court of Illinois interpreted the Illinois legislature's law to mean that all defendants found guilty but mentally ill do not necessarily receive treatment automatically. There was, however, no intention to create two arbitrary classes of defendants found guilty but mentally ill, that is, one group put on probation, and another imprisoned without treatment. Rather, discrepancies in treatment are based on the legitimate state interest in recognizing differences in rehabilitation potential, and treatment is accordingly undertaken during incarceration. Discretionally, treatment was deemed to be a rational means of furthering this legislative purpose. In the Georgia cases *Nelson v Georgia*[34] and *Awtrey v Georgia*,[35] the Indiana case *Truman v Indiana*[36] and the Kentucky case *Wellman v Kentucky*,[37] the GBMI verdict was addressed on various points, including the constitutional questions of sufficiency of evidence and due process implications, which appear to be contrary to the concept of psychiatric and mental illness.

An empirical study in Michigan shows that annual numbers of insanity acquittals before and after implementation of the GBMI verdict did not significantly change. Furthermore, it was found that GBMI defendants were more like the guilty defendants than like the insanity acquittals on a number of demographic variables including drug and alcohol use, previous psychiatric treatment, and criminal charges. The same investigator concluded that the GBMI verdict has failed to reduce the number of insanity acquittals.[38]

The creation of this GBMI verdict stemmed from the commendable motive of protecting innocent people from violent, mentally ill criminals in Michigan, and effecting due process and equal protection. It may be recalled that those found guilty by reason of insanity in Michigan did not necessarily meet the criteria for civil commitment, and thus through a procedural loophole were released. The new verdict of GBMI was installed as an alternative verdict recognizing mental incapacity but allowing incarceration. Coming from worthy motives, this verdict nevetheless seems to have grown into a muddle. The clear, unimpeded view of the qualifications for "not guilty by reason of insanity" is blurred as jurors weigh this partial answer alongside it. The original "not guilty" verdict never negated the existence of degrees of mental illness, but helped to distinguish the fine line past which liability vanishes. Further, GBMI is an inherently vague concept, so the procedural rules based on it are weak, easy to challenge, and undermine the authority of the reason of the law. The verdict seems to confuse philosophy with procedure. Perhaps, to solve its procedural dilemma, Michigan would have been better advised to undertake systematic modifications to ensure that legally insane criminals were contained in institutions rather than freed into the community. An additional statute overruling the civil commitment qualifications for such cases is an example of a possible solution.

NO DEFENSE FOR THE INSANITY DEFENSE

Advocacy for the abolition of the insanity defense was not the impetus of lawmakers or practitioners. Psychiatrists were the first to argue that mental illness is a myth and that anyone who commits a crime should be punished regardless of his or her mental condition.[39] When the new concept of the insanity defense was introduced by the lawmakers into the justice system, some psychiatrists and mental health professionals argued for and some argued against that doctrine.

Publicity about heinous crimes in general, and Hinkley's trial and acquittal by reason of insanity in particular, caused lawmakers to question the current trend of strong reliance on expert psychiatric testimony and weigh instead the advisability of limiting the power of psychiatry in the courtroom. Lawmakers ignored the fact that those who enter a plea of incompetent and then stand trial under that plea make up only 10% of all felony trial proceedings. Over 90% of those examined are found to be competent, and over 90% of those evaluated for criminal responsibility are found to be responsible. Therefore, successful insanity acquittal constitutes a very small portion of acquittals. Those few who are so acquitted must enter mental hospitals for long periods. In spite of these facts, publicity spotlights the occasional sensational exceptions, and the public in turn increases pressure on psychiatrists and mental health workers.

Montana has pioneered in abolishing the insanity defense. The constitutionality of the Montana statute has been tested in *Montana v Korell*,[40] with the Montana Supreme Court concluding that a statute abolishing the state insanity defense did not violate the Constitution's due process clause. Montana rejected the notion that insanity has been recognized since the earliest period of the common law. Instead, Montana's position is that "one who lacks the requisite criminal state of mind may not be convicted or punished." This is consistent with US Supreme Court rulings in *Leland v Oregon*[41] and *In re*

Winship.[42] In essence, Montana denies the causative leap which occurs in saying that convicting a mentally ill person subjects that person to an unconstitutional burden. A person with a proven criminal state of mind is accountable for his acts regardless of mental condition or motivation. The judge must only consider the defendant's mental illness in making a disposition or determining sentence. The facts of *Montana v Korell*, and the Montana Supreme Court's opinion which more or less reflects the opinion of others who are against the insanity defense, are as follows:

> Jerry Korell, a Vietnam veteran who experienced several traumatic episodes during his tour of duty, was admitted to a Veterans Administration hospital twice for psychiatric problems and treated with antipsychotic drugs. In 1976 he was jailed briefly for harassing a US Senator. Four years later, Korell entered a community college in his junior year, and was sent to a hospital for a clinical internship in echocardiology. During his internship, he had a bitter dispute with his supervisor and the supervisor placed him on probation. Around the same time, Korell was under extreme pressure from graduation requirements, financial problems, and a recent divorce. He set two fires, was arrested and released on bail. Shortly thereafter, Korell attempted to kill his former supervisor and was charged with attempted homicide and aggravated assault. At the trial, he gave notice of his intention to show that on the night of the alleged crime, he was suffering from a mental disease or defect. The court denied his request and instructed the jury that under current state law, it would consider mental disease or defect only insofar as such negated the defendant's requisite state of mind. The jury found him guilty of both charges.

The Montana Supreme Court reviewed the case and came to the conclusion that no fundamental right to an insanity defense exists in "our system of justice." In so doing, the court referred to the cases of *Powell v Texas* and *Robinson v California* (these two landmark US Supreme Court decisions are discussed in chap. 2) and found that the Supreme Court indicated that the nature of the defense should be left to the state. States therefore retain strong interpretive powers regarding the insanity defense, especially in light of the Supreme Court's laissez-faire approach in *Montana v Korrel*.

SILENCE IS NOT EVIDENCE OF SANITY

The idea of silence being evidence of sanity (or a reason for suspiciousness arising from paranoia and insanity) has aroused debate in courts of law. Some courts hold that keeping silent after a Miranda warning is an indication that the accused has understood the charges and was well aware of his or her guilt or innocence. Other courts have considered it an error to allow a prosecutor to impeach a criminal defendant's insanity plea by using as evidence the defendant's silence after receiving the Miranda warning.

The justices of the US Supreme Court struggled with this issue in *Wainright v Greenfield*[43] and agreed that to promise suspects that their silence would not be used against them, as the Miranda warning states, and then for the government to turn around and use that silence as evidence at trial was fundamentally unfair. It is equally unfair to breach the same promise and use a defendant's silence to overcome an insanity plea. The justices rejected, as well, that a suspect's silence after the Miranda warning should be understood as comprehension of the warning, and that comprehension was far more indicative of sanity than of understanding the offense and its ramifications.

In *Wainwright v Greenfield*, the defendant David Greenfield was charged with forcible sexual battery in 1975. He based his defense on a not guilty by reason of insanity plea. Two of the defendant's witnesses, both psychiatrists, testified that Greenfield was a paranoid schizophrenic and did not know the difference between right and wrong. In his summation to the jury, the prosecutor maintained that the defendant's silence after being arrested, and his request for an attorney, demonstrated the defendant's capacity to understand the consequences of his actions, and therefore he was sane at the time of the crime. After being found guilty in a state court, the petitioner sought either a new trial or an acquittal notwithstanding the verdict, because of the prosecutor's summation. His conviction was affirmed. The *Greenfield* case eventually was decided first in the Eleventh Circuit, and then the US Supreme Court granted certiorari.

In a landmark decision in 1986, the Supreme Court determined that the prosecution had violated due process when it used the defendant's deliberate silence on receiving the Miranda warning as evidence to rebut his insanity plea. The justices based their decision on a previous Supreme Court case, *Doyle v Ohio*,[44] and noted that a state's legitimate interest in providing that the defendant's behavior appeared to be rational at the time of his arrest could have been served by carefully framed questions which would avoid mention of the defendant's exercise of his constitutional right to remain silent and consult counsel. "What is permissible is the evidentiary use of an individual's exercise of his constitutional rights after the state's assurance that the invocation of those rights will not be penalized." Based on the *Doyle* holding, the Court again concluded that it was fundamentally unfair for the prosecutor to breach the implied Miranda assurance by using Greenfield's silence in the same context as evidence of his sanity.

Those who work in the mental health professions are well aware that a patient may remain silent in response to a question for a variety of reasons. For example, a suspicious patient motivated by inner fantasies and delusional thought might avoid answering any question in a psychiatric examination. It is quite clear that in general, silence in response to inquiry does not at all imply that a person is of sound mental health and only maliciously refuses to answer. From the clinical perspective, silence may well indicate a mental disorder rather than willful maliciousness. Compared to many other aspects of the insanity defense, that of interpreting silence is relatively clear-cut, since permitting silence as evidence of sanity by the prosecution is a direct and unquestionable contradiction of the content and spirit of the Miranda warning.

SPONTANEOUS CONFESSION

While using a defendant's silence as evidence of sanity has been disallowed, the opposite phenomenon of spontaneous confession by a mentally ill person becomes a related judicial issue. Can such a confession, in light of the Miranda warning, be presented in a trial as evidence?

A divided Supreme Court found that a defendant's mental condition alone does not determine whether a confession is considered coerced or a waiver of rights under the Miranda ruling. The decisive factor, according to the US Supreme Court justices, is the existence of an essential link between coercive activity by the state and the resulting confession by the defendant. Coercive police activity is a necessary predicate to finding that a confession is not "voluntary" within the meaning of the due process clause. This narrow application of "coercion" rules out a defendant's being coerced by his own delusions or hallucinations. Further, the question of the voluntariness of the confession in regard to the defendant's mental state at the time of confessing was not deemed important. The following involved and notorious case displays how this limited interpretation was arrived at.[45]

On August 18, 1983, Officer Patrick Anderson of the Denver Police Department was in uniform, working in an off-duty capacity in downtown Denver. Francis Connelly approached the officer, and without any prompting stated that he had murdered someone and wanted to talk about it. The officer immediately advised Connelly that he had the right to remain silent, that anything he said could be used against him in a court of law, and that he had the right to an attorney prior to any police questioning. Connelly indicated that he understood all those rights; further, he denied that he had been drinking or taking drugs, but stated that he had been a patient in several mental hospitals in the past, and would like to confess to murder because his conscience was bothering him. Shortly thereafter, another detective again advised Connelly of his rights. Connelly responded that he had come all the way from Boston to confess to the murder of Mary Ann Junta, a young girl whom he had killed in Denver in November of 1982. Using the defendant's information, the body of a girl was found and Connelly was charged with murder.

The next day during the interrogation in the presence of a public defender, Connelly became disoriented. He began giving confused answers to the questions, and stated that voices had told him to come to Denver and that he had followed the directions of these voices (auditory hallucinations) during his confession. Connelly was initially found incompetent to stand trial. He was committed to a state hospital to restore his competency through psychiatric treatment. By March 1984, his competency was restored and the trial proceeded.

At the trial, Dr Metzner, a psychiatrist, testified that respondent Connelly was suffering from chronic schizophrenia and was in a psychotic state before and during his confession. The psychiatrist further revealed that Connelly had auditory hallucinations, hearing a voice of God telling him to withdraw money from the bank, to buy an airplane ticket, to go to Denver and confess to the killing, or to commit suicide. According to the testimony of the expert psychiatrist, this command hallucination prevented him from making a free and rational decision and his volitional ability was grossly impaired. The psychiatrist further testified that Connelly's illness did not significantly impair his cognitive abilities. Thus, the respondent Connelly understood the rights he had when Officer Anderson and the other detective advised him that he need not speak. Under cross-examination, Metzner admitted that the "voices" could in reality be Connelly's interpretation of his own guilt, but explained that in his opinion, Connelly's psychosis motivated his confession.

The trial court suppressed the defendant's statements as involuntary, and concluded that the confession could be admissible only if it was a product of the defendant's rational intellect and free will, even though the police had been guilty of no wrongdoing. The Colorado Supreme Court affirmed, and added that the proper test for admissibility was whether the statements were a product of a rational intellect and a free will, and that a valid waiver of the Miranda rights must be based on clear and convincing evidence, which this particular situation did not supply.

This case created a public uproar, and finally arrived at the US Supreme Court for final ruling. A majority of justices found that the Colorado court failed to recognize what it considered the necessary connection between coercive state activity and the defendant's confession. Being wholly unable to choose rationally whether or not to confess apparently did not impress these justices as justification for voiding the validity of the confession. According to them, the flaw in the defendant-respondent's constitutional argument was that it would expand the meaning of "voluntariness" into a far-ranging requirement whereby the courts must divine defendants' motivation for speaking or acting as they did even though there exists no claim that government conduct coerced their decision. They obviously felt that making such a determination of motivation was beyond the scope of the state's responsibility, even when the life and liberty of a defendant were at stake.

The Supreme Court continued that suppressing Connelly's statement would serve absolutely no purpose in enforcing constitutional guarantees. The purpose of excluding evidence seized in violation of the Constitution is to substantially and specifically deter future violations of the Constitution. Thus, the Court determined that the forceful police activity was a necessary element in declaring a confession involuntary. This decision reversed the direction of the case's likely outcome, since the admission of the defendant-respondent's confession was held not to violate the due process clause. While the defendant's mental condition may be a significant factor in the voluntariness calculus, it is not necessarily to be concluded that his mental condition, separate from its relation to official coercion, should ever require inquiry into constitutional "voluntariness."

The court added that whenever the state bears the burden of proof in a motion to suppress a statement allegedly obtained in violation of the Miranda doctrine, the state needs only a preponderance of evidence to prove the right was acceptably waived. The Colorado Supreme Court thus erred in applying a "clear and convincing evidence" standard to Connelly's confession. Furthermore, notions of "free will" have no place in this area of constitutional law, and respondent's perception of coercion flowing from "the voice of God" is a matter to which the federal Constitution does not attend.

Commentators have noticed that the majority of opinions in this case were focused on the issue of voluntariness in analyzing issues related to the defendant's confession and waiver of his Miranda rights. The Supreme Court made no reference to the amicus brief submitted by the American Psychological Association in support of the petitioner, which focused on issues related to behavioral science, volition and determinism.[46]

Finally, dissenters to the Supreme Court's findings waged a vigorous protest by saying that on the day of its final ruling, the Court denied Connelly his fundamental right to make a vital choice with a sane mind, making way for a determination that could allow the state to deprive him of liberty and even life. The dissenters believe that this holding is unprecedented: in this stage of our civilization, a most basic sense of justice is affronted by the spectacle of incarcerating a human being on the basis of a statement he made while insane, and that the use of a mentally ill person's involuntary confession is antithetical to the notion of fundamental fairness embodied in the due process clause.

THE AMERICAN PSYCHIATRIC ASSOCIATION POSITION ON THE INSANITY DEFENSE

The insanity defense, according to the American Psychiatric Association (APA), helps maintain one of the fundamental premises of the criminal law, namely that punishment for wrongful deeds should be predicated upon moral culpability. This renders the retention of the insanity defense essential to the moral integrity of criminal law and the criminal justice system. Therefore, the APA officially stands behind the belief that the insanity defense should be retained in some form.

The APA is extremely skeptical regarding the concept of the guilty but mentally ill verdict, or any similar indeterminate verdicts. Presented by judges as an alternative to the traditional insanity verdict, GBMI usually ends up being a compromise verdict instead, which the jury can grasp when the going gets tough. Not to doubt the intentions of juries who choose this middle-ground verdict, still, GBMI lessens the pressure on the jurors, offering them an "easy out," and makes it unnecessary for them to undergo the emotional and intellectual strain of choosing among the definitive verdicts of not guilty, not guilty by reason of insanity, or guilty.

Rigorous and difficult deliberations by jurors in deciding cases are a vital aspect of this system of democracy. Nowhere was it written that such deliberations would or should be easy. They set a high standard, and give meaning to society's ideas about responsibility and morality. The willingness of citizens to face and grapple with the ultimate decisions they confront during jury duty is a profound symbol of acceptance of the responsibility required for a participatory democracy. This symbolic role is demeaned and diminished by the use of the GBMI verdict, which functions mainly to lighten the load of thought, decision, and responsibility.

The APA is not opposed to state legislatures or Congress making statutory changes in the language of the traditional insanity verdicts. The verdicts are never "finished," and fine-tuning can always make them clearer and stronger. The APA suggests, however, that all revisions of the insanity defense standard indicate that any mental disorder potentially leading to exculpation must be acute. Such disorder should usually be of a severity, if not quality, of condition which justifies a psychiatric diagnosis as psychosis.

Bonnie's proposal[47] on relevant psychiatric testimony in the insanity defense has been adopted by the APA: "A person charged with a criminal offense should be found not guilty by reason of insanity if it is shown that as a result of mental disease or mental retardation, he was unable to appreciate the wrongfulness of his conduct at the time of the offense." The terms "mental disease" and "mental retardation" include only those severely abnormal mental conditions that grossly and demonstrably impair a person's perception or understanding of reality and that are not attributable primarily to the voluntary ingestion of alcohol or other psychoactive substances. The APA is exceedingly reluctant to take a position on assigning the burden of proof to either the defendant or the prosecution in insanity cases, believing that this matter is clearly in the legislative domain.

As to limiting the content of expert testimony psychiatrists may give, the APA feels that the law can indeed prevent psychiatrists from testifying in a conclusive fashion as to whether defendants lack substantial capacity to conform their behavior to the requirement of the law, or lack a substantial capacity to appreciate the criminality of their act, or were unable to distinguish right from wrong at the time of the act. On the other hand, the APA maintains that psychiatric testimony in insanity defense trials should provide an explanation in medical and psychological terms of how the offending act was affected and influenced by a defendant's mental illness.

The distinction between these two types of testimony illustrates the concern of the APA to keep a firm line between the disciplines of law and medicine. In describing a defendant's "capacity to appreciate criminality," for instance, a psychiatrist would have to be an expert on criminality as well as psychiatry for his testimony to be truly "expert." In keeping strict compliance to the area of behavior and illness, the testifying psychiatrist's credibility remains sound, and his testimony all the more valuable to the defense. Thus, the APA does not oppose restricting psychiatric testimony on the aforementioned issues where psychiatry intersects with law.

It is important, however, for psychiatrists, if they are to testify, to be able to do so fully about the defendant's psychiatric diagnosis, mental state, and motivation at the time of the alleged act. This permits the jury or judge to reach an ultimate decision about issues which psychiatrists and not themselves are the experts. Determining whether a criminal defendant was legally insane is a job for the legal fact-finders, not for experts. Regarding the disposition of the violent insanity acquittees, the APA presents these guidelines:

1. A special piece of legislation should be designed for those persons charged with violent offenses who have been found not guilty by reason of insanity.

2. Confinement and release decisions should be made by a board chosen to include psychiatrists and other professionals representing the criminal justice system, akin to a parole board.

3. Release should be conditional upon having a treatment supervision plan in place with the necessary resources available to implement it.

4. The board having jurisdiction over the release of insanity acquittees should also have clear authority to reconfine.

5. When psychiatric treatment within a hospital setting has reached the maximum treatment benefits possible and the board believes that if for some reason confinement is still mandated, the insanity acquittee should be transferred to the appropriate nonhospital facility.[3]

In general, the APA favors legislation to identify insanity acquittees who have committed violent acts as a unique group of persons who, because of the important societal interest involved, should be handled under different criteria and procedures than persons civilly committed.

The APA opinion is confirmed in a study by Lamb et al done on 79 persons found not guilty by reason of insanity who were referred to and accepted for court-mandated community outpatient treatment.[48] They found that during the 5-year follow-up period 25 persons in the sample (32%) were rearrested, 18 (72%) for crimes of violence; 37 (47%) were hospitalized; and 38 (48%) had their conditional releases revoked. In the view of these investigators, persons who have been found not guilty of a crime by reason of insanity are difficult to treat in the community. They need social controls and treatment for long periods of time if they are to adjust well in the community and also for the protection of society. Creating these suggested items of legislation would have the further benefit of lessening the number and cost of court proceedings while increasing efficiency and fairness to society at large and mentally ill defendants.

THE AMERICAN MEDICAL ASSOCIATION'S POSITION ON THE INSANITY DEFENSE

On December 6, 1983, the House of Delegates of the American Medical Association (AMA) supported the abolition of the special defense of insanity. The AMA voted to support in principle "the abolition of the special defense of insanity in criminal trials and its replacement by a statute providing for acquittal when the defendant as a result of mental disease lacked the state of mind (*mens rea*) required as an element of the offense charged." This extreme position stirred controversy and debate among the members of the AMA, and received staunch opposition by the American Psychiatric Association (APA) and the American Bar Association. After a few years of debate, the APA and AMA agreed to a joint policy. Eventually a joint statement was prepared and approved by the boards of trustees of the APA and AMA in 1985.

In the joint statement, the organizations politely criticize each other, while exchanging compliments, and resolving that they share a concern over the role of medical testimony in the legal system. The highlights of the APA-AMA statement are as follows: ". . . both associations agree that mental impairment should exonerate criminal behavior only in a narrow class and that the defendants so exculpated should not suffer punishment or hardship as a result." Beyond that paramount general concern, there are two other matters directly affected by the insanity defense that are of special importance to the medical profession: (1) assurance of proper medical and psychiatric treatment to disorder-suffering criminal offenders; and (2) establishment of appropriate roles for physicians who testify in legal proceedings. The AMA and the APA in their joint statement conveyed the belief that while there is no established correlation between mental illness and crime, the persistence of mental illness in a convicted offender can only impede the effective reduction of future criminal behavior by that offender.[49]

In reading the statement carefully, one can find in addition to an exchange of complimentary words between the two associations, the conviction that they both hold as inviolable the protection of the public against violent acts, the right of mentally ill offenders to adequate and humane treatment, and the protection of the system of justice itself.[50]

The joint statement failed to reach a definite formulation or guidelines for the legislatures and courts. The basic differences between the two groups—the APA policy was to retain the insanity defense while restricting it significantly by emphasizing cognitive as opposed to volitional disturbances and further by limiting it to psychotic-level disorders, as opposed to the AMA's policy of calling for abolition of the insanity defense by adopting a position of mens rea—remain unchanged.

THE AMERICAN BAR ASSOCIATION'S POSITION ON THE INSANITY DEFENSE

A resolution was passed by the American Bar Association's House of Delegates in February of 1983 which states: "The ABA approves, in principle, a defense of non-responsibility for crime which focuses solely on whether the defendant as a result of mental disease or defect was unable to appreciate the wrongfulness of his or her conduct at the time of the offense charged."[2]

The resolution rejected the volitional prong of the American Law Institute's nonresponsibility test. Historically, the ABA noted, insanity was related to the concept of mens rea as a generalized requirement of the moral blame worthiness required for criminal liability. In the twentieth century, mens rea terminology has evolved to refer to the specific state of mind needed for conviction for particular criminal offenses. Today, in the absence of an independent nonresponsibility defense, persons can be convicted of a crime as long as they knew what they were doing at the time they committed the offense and possessed the intent to do it, even if they were under the power of a mentally disabling condition such as delusion. A conviction in such a case would meet the letter but not the spirit of the law.

The ABA has pointed out that the issue of criminal blameworthiness should receive deeper inquiry. Implicit in this concept is a certain, almost indefinable, quality of knowledge and intent, going beyond a minimal awareness and purposefulness. Without searching inquiry, for instance, a defendant who knowingly and intentionally kills his son under the psychotic delusion that he is the Biblical Abraham and his son the Biblical Isaac could be held criminally responsible. The mens rea limitation forces judges and jurors confronted with defendants who are unquestionably psychotic either to return conviction, which would be morally obtuse, or to acquit in outright defiance of the law. Neither alternative is conscionable.

The abolitionist approach, the ABA continued, as embodied within the mens rea limitation, would inhibit if not prevent the exercise of human judgment, and it is this exercise of human judgment which has distinguished our criminal law heritage. For this reason the ABA has rejected the mens rea approach. The ABA, along with the APA, disapproves of any type of guilty but mentally ill (GBMI) verdict. Furthermore, the ABA believes that those GBMI statutes which make the concept into a verdict option, rather than a substitute for a nonresponsibility verdict, are untenable on functional and theoretical grounds.

This new verdict fails on its own terms, and if the confusion it engenders ended there, it would be bad enough. Unfortunately, it introduces conceptually alien elements into the criminal justice system as well, undermining the consistency of moral foundations necessary for the public's faith in the criminal justice system to endure.

BURDEN OF PROOF

The burden of producing evidence differs from the burden of persuasion and proof. Evidence is substantial enough to warrant serious consideration of something—for instance, that a criminal defendant was severely mentally disturbed during the commission of a crime. Persuasion and proof contain more thorough and incontrovertible substance, enough to create a certainty, as our legal system explains, beyond a reasonable doubt. If any doubt is to be raised about the defendant's criminal responsibility, the burden of providing evidence to support nonculpability is borne by the defendant. Generally, the criminal defendant is presumed responsible from the opening of trial.

From the 47 states which retained the insanity defense, certain states and the District of Columbia, in nonfederal cases, placed the burden of proof in the insanity defense on the defendant by only a preponderance of evidence standard. One state, Arizona, places the burden of proof on the defendant to produce clear and convincing evidence. In contrast, 16 states require the prosecution to prove that the defendant is responsible beyond reasonable doubt. In federal courts, the burden of proof is borne by the prosecution as ruled by the Supreme Court at the turn of the century in *Davis v US*[51] and later settled in *In re Winship*.[42] Idaho,[52] Montana[53] and Utah[54] permit evidence of a mental illness on the requisite that the mental condition somehow influenced the crime, but eliminated the insanity defense as an independent issue.

The ABA, unlike the APA, takes a position on which side has ultimate responsibility in the persuasion issue. According to the ABA's suggestion, in states using the M'Naghten doctrine the burden of proof must be borne by the prosecutor to prove that a defendant is not insane; and for those states utilizing the ALI test, the burden of proof must be borne by the defendant to prove that the defendant is insane.

THE AMERICAN CIVIL LIBERTY UNION'S POSITION ON THE INSANITY DEFENSE

Criminal defendants have a right to put before the trial evidence of their mental state at the time the alleged crime was committed, according to the American Civil Liberties Union (ACLU). If they are determined legally insane, the ACLU continues, they should be found not guilty of the crime. The ACLU does not define "legally insane," however.

The organization's reasoning is straightforward: criminal conviction, like any other restriction of civil liberties, must be justified, and criminal conviction of the insane is not justified because the consequence of conviction, punishment, is not justifiable under the circumstance. Retribution, or vengeance, is inappropriate because insane persons lack the qualities that must be present for blameworthiness. According to the ACLU perspective, the purpose of the insanity defense is to distinguish those cases in which a punitive-correctional disposition is appropriate, from those in which a medical-custodial position is the only one the law should allow.

The role of a defendant's mental state in determining guilt as interpreted by the ACLU is that no person may be convicted of a crime unless the prosecution has proved beyond a reasonable doubt that the defendant has the requisite mental state as pertains to each element of the crime. In determining whether the prosecution has met this burden, the jury or the trier of fact must be permitted to consider evidence relevant to the defendant's mental state at the time the crime was committed. So far, the ACLU position regarding the burden of proof for mental condition is the most liberal, implying that even when no question of culpability has been raised, the prosecution must still prove sanity.

The ACLU also has unique ideas on the consequences of a verdict of not guilty by reason of insanity. In the ACLU's view, a person found not guilty by reason of insanity is literally not guilty of the crime specified. Consequently, such a person may be involuntarily confined in a mental hospital only after being found to be subject to civil commitment in accordance with constitutionally adequate civil commitment standards and procedures. A defendant found not guilty by reason of insanity may not be involuntarily confined immediately following the verdict unless the crime charged is a violent crime, and then only for the minimal period necessary to determine the appropriateness of instituting civil commitment procedures against the person.

As regards the right to representation, the ACLU contends that a person who pleads not guilty by reason of insanity has the constitutional right to adequate assistance by a suitable professional to prepare and present the insanity defense. Such professionals should be fairly compensated by the state if the defendant is unable to afford such compensation.[55]

Some of the ACLU's positions may seem extreme, especially in a practical framework, but they are nonetheless highly valuable to the ongoing debate over the insanity defense, in that they provide focus at one end, permitting the final statutes and judicial decisions to fall in a generally moderate range. The relentless vigilance this organization undertakes toward patients' rights, while creating occasional headaches for the practitioners of mental health and law, is a vital element in the system of participatory democracy. Without such a group balance would be lost, and in a drift to the other extreme moderates would lose credibility and authority.

THE POSITION OF CONGRESS ON THE INSANITY DEFENSE

In October of 1984 the 98th Congress of the United States passed a law eliminating the volitional prong of the ALI test for the insanity defense, permitting use of the defense only in instances where "the defendant suffered from a mental disease or defect that grossly and demonstrably impaired the defendant's perception and understanding of reality, and as a result of that impairment, the defendant could not appreciate the wrongfulness of that conduct." Now the defendant has the burden of proof to produce clear and convincing evidence. This legislation also excludes expert testimony on the issue of a defendant's particular mental state, and establishes procedures for federal civil commitment.[56]

After years of liberalization, this new law parallels the latest trend toward stricter treatment of criminal defendants. Longer prison sentences, higher bail, and mandatory sentences are other features of this conservative drift. That Congress enacts a more stringent insanity law under the circumstances is par for the course.

NEUROSIS IN SERVICE OF
THE INSANITY DEFENSE

Freud suggested that guilt feelings originate from repressed antisocial cravings, primarily oedipal tendencies, and that these cravings and feelings are often the chief determinants of criminal acts. His article, "Criminality From a Sense of Guilt" has influenced the thinking of those psychoanalysts who have investigated criminal behavior.[56] Franz Alexander, the first to challenge from a psychoanalytic perspective existing legal methods of dealing with offenders, contended in a link to the Freudian theory that the neurotic character who expresses his neurosis in criminal acts is beset with unconscious guilt resulting from forbidden unconscious wishes.

Alexander first studied psychoanalytic unconscious motivation for criminal acts when he was called in by a German court for expert testimony in the case of a young female kleptomaniac who had been under his psychoanalytic treatment shortly before she had committed several thefts. The presiding judge had been puzzled when he learned that the girl had stolen worthless objects, and thrown those objects of some value into the river. Her preference was for cheap reproductions of paintings of the Madonna with the child. Alexander told the court that the girl was a deprived orphan who had decided to become an actress. While studying for the stage she became the girlfriend of a carefree bachelor who had made it clear to her that he would never marry her. She wanted desperately to have a child, but prudence prevented her from renouncing her control. This conflict drove her to gratify her desire symbolically and to identify with the Virgin Mary, who could have a child by virgin birth. During the treatment, the girl became aware of the connection between her longing for motherhood and her stealing, and succeeded in controlling the kleptomania. The judge, convinced by this argument, gave the girl a suspended sentence, with the stipulation that she continue her psychoanalysis.

Impressed by the willingness of usually conservative judges to take psychiatric factors into consideration, Alexander and a Berlin lawyer, Hugo Staub, studied a series of cases in which they suspected unconscious motivation as the predominant factor. In 1929 they published a book in which they discussed only offenders who were neurotic criminals. Neurotic symptoms may seem to be a person's private affair. But in reality, these private symptoms have a tremendous impact on the general environment and the general population, as the above example of the kleptomaniac illustrates.[56]

What was designated as neurosis by Freud, in modern psychiatry has been broken down into a series of disorders basically known as anxiety disorders. One of the features of the anxiety disorder known as posttraumatic stress disorder is commonly utilized in our modern criminal justice system as a factor in an insanity defense. According to the *Diagnostic and Statistical Manual of Mental Disorders* (DSM-III-R), posttraumatic stress disorder is characterized by:

A. Existence of a stressor that is outside the range of usual human experience and that would produce stress in almost anyone;

B. Reexperiencing of the trauma in one or more of the the following ways:
   (1) recurrent and intrusive recollections of the event;
   (2) recurrent dreams of the event;
   (3) a sudden sense of reliving the event though actions or feelings;
   (4) intense distress at exposure to events that symbolize or resemble an aspect of the traumatic event;

C. Avoidance of stimuli associated with the trauma, or numbing of general responsiveness, as indicated by a least three of the following:
   (1) avoidance of thoughts or feelings associated with the trauma;
   (2) avoidance of activities or situations arousing recollections of the trauma;
   (3) inability to recall important aspects of the trauma;
   (4) markedly diminished interest in significant activities;
   (5) feeling of detachment or estrangment from others;
   (6) restricted range of affect;
   (7) sense of foreshortened future;

D. Symptoms of increased arousal, as indicated by at least two of the following:
   (1) difficulty falling or staying asleep;
   (2) irratibility or angry outbursts;
   (3) difficulty concentrating;
   (4) hypervigilance;
   (5) exaggerated startle response;
   (6) physilogic reactivity upon exposure to events that symbolize or resemble an aspect of the traumatic event;

E. Symptoms in B, C, and D above lasts at least one month.

Establishing a valid link between posttraumatic stress disorder and criminal behavior is an imposing task, as was noted by Sparr and Atkinson.[58] In order to prove cause and effect, one must investigate (1) the causal connection between the traumatic stressor and the psychiatric syndrome; and (2) a causal connection between the psychiatric syndrome and the criminal act.[59] It is interesting to note that in this three-level chain, the connecting link—the psychiatric syndrome—is also the least concrete.

Although some courts have accepted posttraumatic stress disorder as a type of disorder constituting a valid defense for not guilty by reason of insanity, other courts have rejected it. The psychiatric community overall believes that only in rare instances do dissociative episodes related to posttraumatic stress disorder directly lead to unpremeditated criminal activity, making an appropriate defense. Sparr and Atkinson have suggested that posttraumatic stress disorder itself is a difficult diagnosis to confirm. An individual may display certain symptoms suggesting posttraumatic stress disorder, yet not actually have the disorder because many of the symptoms are nonspecific and can reflect the existence of other psychiatric illnesses; or the symptoms can be easily fabricated and escape the scrutiny of examining psychiatrists.[58]

In *Arizona v Jensen*,[60] the defendant Jensen, who had been convicted on two counts of first-degree murder in a lower court, petitioned for a new trial because he claimed that at the time of the commission of the crime, he had been suffering from mental illness, specifically, posttraumatic stress disorder. He argued in his petition that his disorder was not officially recognized at the time of the trial, and therefore it affected the outcome of his trial.

Jensen aroused suspicion. His claims regarding military service in Vietnam could not be reasonably verified. Discrepancies existed between his version of the facts and that noted in government documents. The defendant claimed that he had been engaged in combat activities. The government showed proof that Jensen spent most of his time in sick bay or light duty activity.

The government attempted to discredit the defendant's contention that the murders of two teenagers for which he was charged were the results of combat flashbacks. The defendant claimed that after he heard an airplane overhead, he became convinced that the two teenagers were North Vietnamese army soldiers and therefore he captured and executed them. The government introduced testimony that the execution of North Vietnamese prisoners in the field was not a policy, and as a matter of fact, the prisoners were valuable as sources of information. As the case progressed, it became more clear that the defendant was fabricating the symptoms of posttraumatic stress disorder. The Superior Court of Arizona eventually found the defendant guilty on two counts of first-degree murder.

Wilson and Zigelbaum have proposed a link between posttraumatic stress disorder and criminal behavior in which (1) the crime must present actual or symbolic repetition of war experience; (2) the crime is an expression of conflict about the war experience; and (3) the crime is an attempt at the retrieval of experiences that have been intensely repressed with the unconscious goal of getting killed, venting rage, or getting caught in order to receive aid.[61]

One instance where the defendant was found not guilty due to posttraumatic stress disorder is the case *Pard v US*,[62] which is interesting for several reasons. The defendant Pard was initially charged with three counts of attempted murder for which he entered the plea of not guilty by reason of insanity. In his criminal trial, the jury reached a verdict of not guilty by reason of mental disease or defect due to posttraumatic stress disorder.

Pard subsequently brought a lawsuit against the United States. In the new proceeding the insanity defense was no longer the issue. The allegation by Pard shows that the Veterans Administration had failed to diagnose and treat Pard for part of the posttraumatic stress disorder and because of the failure on the part of the VA, his mental state had deteriorated steadily, resulting in an attempt to kill his ex-wife. A shootout occurred with police

184

officers in which the veteran was wounded in the leg, head, and hand. Pard made claims against the United States totaling $9.5 million. The claim sought compensation for the injuries and loss of consortium with his wife.

The government now, in lawsuit, presented evidence that Pard did not suffer from posttraumatic stress disorder. Pard took the position that during the 4½ months in Vietnam, he had survived several close brushes with death. He claimed that he had witnessed the death of four fellow crewmen in a helicopter gunship. Thus he had to shoot three children at close range in selfdefense. The government then introduced testimony which the plaintiff claimed were all distorted facts. After hearing all testimony from all parties, the District Court of Oregon concluded that the plaintiff did not suffer from posttraumatic stress disorder and that the VA was not guilty of any of the negligent acts charged by the plaintiff.

The interesting and ironic point about Pard's legal situation, and a revealing point regarding the vicissitudes of human perception even under standardized guidelines, is that the defendant was found not guilty on criminal charges due to posttraumatic stress disorder, and the same defendant as a plaintiff in a civil suit was found not to be suffering from mental illness due to posttraumatic stress disorder. This conflict appears to be related to the economic and financial situation between the parties, however, rather than the existence or nonexistence of mental illness.

HEAT OF PASSION VERSUS CRIMINAL INTENT

Criminal intent (murder) and killing in the heat of passion or on sudden provocation (manslaughter) have been distinguished as distinct crimes by law, and punishment differs for these two crimes. Persons acting under criminal intent have a psychopathic personality and will conceal their act and rarely confess their crime. On the other hand, people who commit manslaughter often feel guilt and remorse after committing the aggressive act. They are the ones who are likely to go to the police and confess, or even to commit suicide. From the psychiatric point of view, heat of passion describes to those people who under frustration and stress are unable to control their aggression and therefore discharge this aggressive desire in a destructive fashion without having any conscious intent.

In psychiatric language, heat of passion is a borderline phenomenon corresponding to brief reactive psychosis and phobic disorder, in which a person acts irrationally under psychological stressors. Perplexity, rapid shifts of mood, aggressiveness, suicidal behavior, loss of control, and a feeling of impending doom are all common in heat of passion, as the judicial system calls it, or brief reactive psychosis–phobic disorder, as mental health professionals label it.

The question of whether the defendant or the prosecutor should have the burden of proof to show that the act of killing arose from actual criminal intent or simply occurred in the heat of passion has received the attention of the US Supreme Court in *Mulaney v Wilbur, Jr.*[63] This case moved the Court to set forth the rule "under the due process clause of the Fourteenth Amendment, that the prosecution prove beyond a reasonable doubt every fact necessary to constitute the crime charged and [second] to satisfy due process, the prosecution must prove beyond a reasonable doubt the absence of heat of passion or sudden provocation when the issue is properly presented in a homicide case." This is the only sensible conclusion, since the state defines and specifies the crimes charged in the first place. The responsibility differs little from that which the state bears in other crimes, for example, if the state charges an individual with possession of illegal substance, the state must prove that possession. So, if the state charges homicide, it must be able to prove homicide, in which intent is inherent.

The following details show the choices at work. In June of 1966, respondent Stillman E. Wilbur, Jr fatally assaulted Claude Herbert in a hotel room. Wilbur, Jr claimed that he had attacked Herbert in a frenzy, provoked by Herbert's homosexual advance. The defense offered no evidence, but argued that homicide was not applicable since the respondent lacked criminal intent. As an alternative, Wilbur, Jr's counsel asserted that at most, the homicide was a manslaughter, since it occurred in the heat of passion provoked by homosexual assault. The Supreme Court, after analyzing the case and reviewing the history of homicide in the context of law, established two important points:

1. The presence or absence of the heat of passion on sudden provocation has been, almost from the inception of common law of homicide, the single most important factor in determining the degree of culpability attached to an unlawful homicide.

2. The clear trend has been toward requiring the prosecution to bear the ultimate burden of proving this fact.

Since criminal intent is essential to the definition of homicide, and lack of it is essential to the definition of manslaughter, to leave the prosecution free of this particular burden of proof would be in effect permitting the prosecution arbitrarily to charge crimes while retaining no responsibility for proving the allegations. Common sense has been upheld, and the criminal justice system strengthened, with this ruling.

THE INSANITY DEFENSE IN PATHOLOGIC GAMBLING

According to DSM-III-R,[57] a gambler is a person who is chronically and progressively unable to resist the impulse to gamble. Chronic gambling has the effect of compromising, disrupting, or damaging family, personal, and

186

vocational pursuits, and is indicated by the occurrence of at least four of the following:

1. preoccupation with gambling or with obtaining money to gamble;
2. frequent gambling of more money or for longer periods than intended;
3. a need to increase the size or frequency of bets to achieve the desired excitement;
4. restlessness or irritability if unable to gamble;
5. repeated loss of money when gambling and returning to win back losses;
6. repeated efforts to stop or reduce gambling;
7. frequent gambling when expected to meet obligations;
8. sacrifice of some important activity in order to gamble;
9. continuing to gamble despite mounting debts, or despite other significant problems that the person knows to be exacerbated by gambling.

According to DSM-III-R, chronic gambling is not due to antisocial personality disorders, as it may at first seem.

Social gamblers differ from pathologic gamblers in the sense that they can quit gambling anytime, whether they are winning or losing. This ability seems to derive from three factors:

1. No self-value is tied to winning or losing.
2. Other aspects of life are more important and rewarding.
3. A "big win" is rarely experienced.[64]

Pathologic gamblers possess the opposite characteristics. In persons susceptible to compulsive gambling, stress leads to an intensification of the gambling behavior. So right from the start, these people experience gambling not as entertainment, but as a tool or self-medication to relieve stress; they "use" gambling. Gambling can make such people feel important, powerful, influential, and respected. Losing can make them feel inadequate and unimportant with a loss of self-esteem and control.

This cycle mirrors that experienced by alcoholics or chemically dependent people, where feelings of inflated power and control while under the influence sink to remorse and self-contempt at the low point. Gambling can also induce the tranquilizing, pain-relieving response often sought by substance abusers. Often, a gambler will report all of the positive sensations of the "up" part of the cycle occurring simultaneously. Pathologic gambling has been called a "drugless" impulse disorder.[64]

Some investigators have suggested that pathologic gamblers may have functional disturbances in the noradrenergic system in their brain. This system, it has been postulated, underlies sensation-seeking behaviors, aspects of which are thought to be abnormal among pathologic gamblers.[65] If this hypothesis is correct, then gamblers could indeed be considered as having a type of brain dysfunction.

The description above of pathologic gambling places pathologic gamblers in the realm of psychiatric disorder. Nevertheless, the courts consider gamblers as having a personality disorder and therefore unentitled to the insanity defense if they raise such a claim. The court believes that pathologic gambling cannot be introduced in support of an insanity defense. Examples of the court's reasoning are as follows. In *United States v Torniero*,[66] the defendant was charged with ten counts of interstate transportation of stolen goods. He filed notice of his intent to rely on the insanity defense and to introduce expert testimony showing that his pathologic gambling disorder led to an accumulation of debts which, in turn, compelled him to steal. The government's motion to "exclude any expert testimony regarding the defendant's alleged mental disorder, compulsive gambling" was granted by the Second Circuit district court.

Another perspective is demonstrated in *United States v Lewellyn*.[67] The defendant in this case was a stockbroker charged with embezzling more than $17 million from two Iowa banks. At a pretrial hearing, Lewellyn introduced the DSM-III criteria together with expert testimony that some persons suffering from pathologic gambling disorder are unable to resist engaging in criminal activity to support their gambling compulsion. The district court ruled that the evidence was inadmissible and the defendant was subsequently convicted in a bench trial. The trial judge's ruling and the conviction were affirmed later by the Court of Appeals for the Eighth Circuit.

Bonnie has observed that although the opinion for the district court in *Torniero* and the Eighth Circuit court in *Lewellyn* reached the same result, they did so by different rulings.[68] Relying on the Frye test concerning admissibility of so-called scientific evidence, the Eighth Circuit court concluded that Lewellyn had failed to show that the opinion espoused by his expert witnesses possessed their requisite indication of scientific reliability. The court explained that in order to make the necessary minimal showing of insanity, Lewellyn was required to demonstrate that there is general acceptance in the fields of psychiatry and psychology of the principle that some pathologic gamblers lack a substantial capacity to conform their conduct to the requirement of the law. There is no evidence in the record, however, either in DSM-III or in expert testimony, that this principle is generally accepted in the mental health profession. Indeed, the records show that the pathologic gambling disorder itself has only recently been recognized in DSM-III, and that there is scant experience and limited knowledge concerning this condition.

The district court in *Torniero* reached its ruling by a different path. The court concluded that a compulsion to gamble, even if it does exist, does not have sufficient direct bearing on the criminal act charged (interstate transportation of stolen goods) to establish the legal predicate for exculpation on the grounds of insanity. As the court eventually stated, "unless the defendant could show that his insanity had a direct bearing on his commission of the acts with which he is charged, any psychiatric evidence he might seek to

188

reduce would have to be excluded as irrelevant. The defendant has not offered to introduce expert testimony on compulsive gambling for the purpose of showing such a direct connection."

The Fourth Circuit court in *United States v Gould*,[69] like the Second and Eighth Circuit courts before, concluded that the insanity defense was unavailable to a man who claimed that pathologic gambling made him commit robbery with intent to commit larceny. The court rejected compulsive gambling as the basis for an insanity defense to criminal offenses collateral to gambling. Relevancy was the guiding factor: whether a causal relationship between a specific disorder and a specific conduct has substantial acceptance in a specific community. Relativity characterizes this aspect of the issue. Because there was no substantial evidence in the field of psychiatry that pathologic gambling may deprive persons of their capacity to conform their conduct to the requirement of the law as required under the ALI test of insanity, the test of relevancy was not met. Since relevancy was not established, evidence of insanity through pathologic gambling could not be considered by the jury.

In another case, *United States v Gillis*,[70] the Fourth Circuit court upheld the exclusion of expert testimony regarding pathologic gambling because the relevance of this affliction to the charge of fraud for which the defendant sought the insanity defense had not been properly demonstrated. In *Gillis*, an expert psychiatrist for the defense testified that Gillis suffered from the mental disorder or defect of pathologic gambling. The court instructed the jury, mentioning that such a disorder, by itself, did not meet the ALI test for insanity.

The Seventh Circuit court joined the other federal courts in *United States v Davis*[71] by ruling that expert testimony supporting a claim of insanity based on compulsive gambling was correctly barred as irrelevant and as not sufficiently probative to outweigh possible jury confusion. Davis, the defendant, claimed insanity to charges of fraud and forgery in converting the government's check payable to his deceased relative. The government objected to the compulsive gambling defense because the expert report failed to show that the defendant's gambling rendered him incapable of appreciating the wrongfulness of his conduct or of conforming to legal requirements when he forged and converted the checks.

It seems that the federal courts have established that compulsive gambling, although listed under mental illness in DSM-III, is a misleading issue, confuses the jury, and does not have any support in the court of law give substance to an insanity defense. Indeed, the courts have been almost unanimous in their decisions on this issue, although reaching their conclusions by a diversity of approaches. The fact that so many roads lead to nearly the same conclusion strengthen its authority, especially since the various reasonings followed have not been far-fetched. Furthermore, the medical and psychiatric communities in general concur with this elimination of compulsive gambling as a basis for an insanity defense.

As compulsive gambling has been compared to substance abuse and addiction in its physical and emotional effects on its victims, it also resembles these afflictions in a legal framework. For while compulsive gambling may be a contributing factor in the commission of criminal acts, those suffering from it retain criminal liability for the offenses they commit.

THE INSANITY DEFENSE IN CIVIL ISSUES

In the foregoing sections the doctrine of insanity in criminal issues was discussed. However, the insanity defense has also been utilized in civil cases. Perr has noted that the civil liability of the mentally ill may become a more frequently appearing legal issue in the future because of (1) the increased number of mentally ill in the community due to deinstitutionalization; (2) the increased financial resources of psychiatric patients due to disability and pension systems as well as money in trusts or money earned; (3) the increase in litigation generally; and (4) the trend even in mental hospitals to hold patients accountable for their behavior.[72]

Perr also noted that under the doctrine of a respondeat superior, if a mentally ill person commits a crime, his or her insurance company can be held liable and thus responsible for indemnification.[72] In the case of *Ruvolo v. American Gas Company*,[72] a psychotic physician shot and killed his associate in their medical practice. On pretrial examination, he was found incompetent to stand trial. Psychiatrists proffered opinions to the effect that the defendant was not criminally responsible due to mental illness. The wife of the deceased sued the defendant and his insurer for wrongful death. The court sided with the wife and kept the insurance company liable. According to the court, when the death or loss was the product of an "insane act," recovery is not barred. If the person doing the act did not have the mental capacity to do it intentionally, nevertheless, the insurance company, the policy reads, "would pay for all damages including the death of any person resulting from the insured's ac-tivities . . .."

One can conclude that the law might not keep mentally ill persons responsible for criminal activity, but may yet keep them liable for compensation in civil lawsuits. The issue could evolve into a clash between victims' rights and the general good, considering the detrimental effects of increased liability costs to the medical profession directly and to the public indirectly. On the other hand, victims' losses are compounded if they cannot receive any compensation for their suffering merely because the criminal was mentally ill. The victim in a sense would be paying for the defendant's incapacity, and thus paying double.

Further, the insanity defense is not a defense to civil liability, ruled a Kentucky appeals court in *Goff v Taylor*.[73] After a jury returned a $703,510 verdict to the estate of a shooting victim who was killed by a person suffering a brain disease, the court rejected the defendant's claim that liability should be measured by a *subjective standard*. Such a standard would assess whether the person possessed the ability to distinguish right from wrong, and could conform his conduct to the law, and whether it was fair to hold a person responsible for a wrong he could not avoid. In *Goff*, the court refused to relieve a person of liability for his actions on the basis of mental disability. As the court puts it, "it does not penalize the mentally incompetent, it merely places them on a par with the rest of society in terms of responsibility for their wrongful acts." The above judgment appears to be a standard decision in the majority of jurisdictions.

MULTIPLE PERSONALITY AND THE INSANITY DEFENSE

Public interest in such celebrated cases as "Sybil" and the dramatization of multiple personality cases in media have attracted the attention of mental health professionals as well as legal authorities. While the condition is considered to be rare and psychiatrists may therefore have a low expectation that the person they are examining suffers from it, multiple personality may exist more widely than is presently supposed. Although the cause of multiple personality is not clear, it has been shown that a high incidence of patients with multiple personality disorder were victims of child abuse. Early sexual molestation, dissociation phenomena, and identification with an aggressor all play important roles in the development of multiple personality.[74]

Multiple personality is a condition characterized by two distinct elements: (1) the existence within the person of two or three distinct personalities or personality states (each with its own relatively enduring pattern of perceiving, relating to, and thinking about the environment and self); and (2) at least two of these personalities or personality states recurrently take full control of the person's behavior.[57]

In the majority of cases, patients with this disorder try to hide, deny, or dissimulate their condition rather than dramatize or exploit it. However, there are times when one personality remains dormant and the second one begins to act in a dramatic manner, and engage in criminal activities, which would give rise to legal complications. It may be argued that the mental state essential for criminal responsibility is diminished in persons who are not aware of what they were doing while "in" the second personality, and therefore such persons were not consciously aware of their criminal act; or in legal terms, their capacity with respect to malice aforethought was diminished. Such persons indeed may not be aware that they have committed a crime. They may vigorously and sincerely deny that they have any responsibilities for their act. In addition, people suffering multiple personality disorder may not show any sign of remorse, and may accuse another person as the culprit.

Howe[75] has pointed out that identification of offenders with double personality and dissociative state is a complicated matter, because these conditions can be suggested, mimicked, or successfully faked. Moreover, assessing the degree to which these persons "lack appreciation and control" is most difficult. Every single case is unique, requiring lengthy and thorough study. Although from a clinical point of view it is possible that a person commits a crime in a dissociative state, it is unlikely that one could use this condition in a successful insanity defense. It would not be surprising if a judge were to say that the second personality is guilty, and sentence it to jail![75, 76]

Almost no issue where the legal and psychiatric fields intersect is more complex or has such a rich and diverse history as the insanity defense. It reaches from the broadest philosophical issues, to the minutiae of diagnoses, procedures, and standards. It contains sweeping concepts, such as the fundamental innocence of the insane, unchanged since antiquity; and other elements that change year to year, for instance, the particulars of mental illness detection and treatment, or the development of improved diagnostic methods.

REFERENCES

1. Hale M: *The History of Pleas of the Crown* [ed 1, 1736]. Philadelphia, 1847.
2. American Bar Association Standing Committee: *Association Standard for Criminal Justice Mental Health Standard.* Presented at Annual Meeting. Chicago, August 7–8, 1984.
3. American Psychiatric Association: *Statement on the Insanity Defense in Issues on Forensic Psychiatry,* 1982.
4. *The Queen v M'Naghten* 1843; 10CL & Fin 200, 8 Eng Rep 718.
5. *State v Jones* 1871;50 NH 369.
6. *Parsons v State* 1986; 81 Ala 577, 596 250 854.
7. *Durham v United States* 1954; 214 F2d 862.
8. *Smith v US* 1929; 59 AppDC 144 36 F2d 548, 70 ALR 654.
9. *McDonald v US* 1962; 312 F2d 847.
10. *Washington v United States* 1967; 390 F2d 444.
11. *United States v Brawner* 1972; 471 F2d 969.
12. Zitrin A, Hardestry N, et al: Crime and violence among mental patients. *Am J Psychiatry* 1976;133:142–149.
13. Brill H, Malzberg B: Statistical report based on the arrest records of 5,354 male ex-patients released from N.Y.S. hospital during 1946–1948. *Mental Hospital Supplement 153,* Washington, DC.
14. Sosowsky L: Crime and violence among mental patients reconsidered in view of the new legal relationship between the state and the mentally ill. *Am J Psychiatry* 1978;135:32–42.
15. Holcomb WR, Ahr PR: Arrest rates among young adult psychiatric patients treated in inpatient and outpatient settings. *Hosp Community Psychiatry* 1988;39:52–57.
16. Rabkin JG: Criminal behavior of discharged mental patients: a critical appraisal of the research. *Psychol Bull* 1979;86:1–25.
17. Taylor PJ: Motives for offending among violent and psychotic men. *Br J Psychiatry* 1985;147:491–498.
18. Phillips MR, et al: Psychiatry and the criminal system: testing the myths. *Am J Psychiatry* 1988;145:605–610.

192

19. Lewis DO, et al: Psychiatric, neurological, and psychoeducational characteristics of 15 death row inmates in the United States. *Am J Psychiatry* 1986;143:838–845.
20. Lewis DO, et al: Neuropsychiatric, psychoeducationsl, and family characteristics of 14 juveniles condemned to death in the United States. *Am J Psychiatry* 1988;145:584–589.
21. *Ake v Oklahoma* 1985; 105 S Ct 1087.
22. Petrila J, Fitch WL: *Ake v Oklahoma* (analysis). *Newsletter Am Acad Psychiatry Law* 1985;10:8–9.
23. *Gideon v Wainwright* 1963; 372 US 335.
24. *Ment Phys Disability Law Reporter* 1985; 9:83.
25. *Martin v Wainwright* 1985; 770 F2d 918 (11th Cir).
26. *Liles v Oklahoma* 1985; 702 P2d 1025 (Okla Crim App).
27. Petrella RC, et al: Examining the application of the guilty but mentally ill verdict in Michigan. *Hosp Community Psychiatry* 1985;36:254–259.
28. *People v McQuillan* 1974; 392 Mich 511, 221 (NW2d 569).
29. *Michigan v Bailey* 1985; 370 NW2d 628 (Mich Ct App).
30. *Michigan v Walker* 1985; 370 NW2d 394 (Mich Ct App).
31. *Hart v Alaska* 1985; 702 P2d 651 (Alaska Ct App).
32. *Illinois v Carter* 1985; No. 84-579 (Ill Sup Ct July 25, 1985).
33. *Illinois v Smith* 1984; 465 NE2d 101 (Ill Sup Ct).
34. *Nelson v Georgia* 1985; 331 SE2d 544 (Ga Sup Ct).
35. *Awtrey v Georgia* 1985; 332 SE2d 896 (Ga Ct App).
36. *Truman v Indiana* 1985; 481 NE2d 1089 (Ind Sup Ct).
37. *Wellman v Kentucky* 1985; 694 SW2d 696 (Ky Sup Ct).
38. Smith GA, Hall JA: Evaluating Michigan's guilty but mentally ill verdict: an empirical study. *Univ Mich J Law Reform* 1982;16:77–144.
39. Szasz TS: *The Second Sin*. London. Routledge & Kegan Paul, 1974.
40. *Montana v Korell* 1984; 690 P2d 992 (Mont Sup Ct).
41. *Leland v Oregon* 1952; 343 US 790.
42. *In re Winship* 1970; 397 US 358.
43. *Wainwright v Greenfield* 1986; No. 84-1480 (US Sup Ct).
44. *Doyle v Ohio* 1976; 462 US 610.
45. *Colorado v Connelly* 1986; No. 85-660 (US Sup Ct).
46. Metzner J: *Colorado v Connelly:* confessions of the mentally ill. *Am Acad Psychiatry Law Newsletter* 1987;12:4–7.
47. Bonnie RJ: The moral basis of the insanity defense. *Am Bar Assoc J* 1983;69:194–197.
48. Lamb HR, et al: Court mandated community outpatient treatment for persons found not guilty by reason of insanity: a five-year follow up. *Am J Psychiatry* 1988;145:450–456.
49. Joint statement of the AMA and the APA regarding the insanity defense. *Am J Psychiatry* 1985;142:1135–1136.
50. McGrath JJ: Editorial: toward unity. The joint statement on the AMA and the APA regarding the insanity defense. *Am J Psychiatry* 1985;142:1058–1059.
51. *Davis v US* 1895; 160 US 469.
52. *Idaho Code* 1982; Sec 18-207.
53. *Montana Laws* 1979; Sec 713.
54. *Utah Code* 1983; Sec 76-2-305 (1).
55. American Civil Liberties Union: *Board Meeting Minutes*. April 16–17, 1983.
56. Alexander F, Selesnick S: *The History of Psychiatry*. New York, Harper & Row, 1966, pp 351–353.
57. American Psychiatric Association: *Diagnostic and Statistical Manual of Mental Disorders*, ed 3, revised [DSM-111-R].

58. Sparr LF, Atkinson RM: Posttraumatic stress disorder as an insanity defense. *Am J Psychiatry* 1986;143:608–613.
59. Apostle DT: The unconscious defense as applied to posttraumautic stress disorder in Vietnam veterans. *Bull Am Acad Psychiatry Law* 1980;8:426–430.
60. *Arizona v Jensen* 1985; CR 75687 (Super Ct Ariz, Maricopa County).
61. Wilson JP, Zigelbaum SD: The Vietnam veteran on trial: the relation of post-traumatic stress disorder and criminal behavior. *Behav Sci Law* 1983;1:69–83.
62. *Pard v US* 1984; 589 FSupp 518 (D Or).
63. *Mulaney v Wilbur, Jr* 1979; 421 US 684.
64. Custer RL: Profile of the pathological gambler. *J Clin Psychiatry* 1984;45(Sec 2)35–48.
65. Roy A, et al: Pathological gambling: a psychobiological study. *Arch Gen Psychiatry* 1988;45:369–373.
66. *United States v Torniero* 1984; 735 F2d 725 (2nd Cir).
67. *United States v Lewellyn* 1983; 723 F2d 615 (8th Cir).
68. Bonnie RJ: Compulsive gambling and the insanity defense. *Am Acad Psychiatry Law Newsletter* 1984;9:5–7.
69. *United States v Gould* 1984; 741 F2d 45 (4th Cir).
70. *United States v Gillis* 1985; 773 F2d 549 (4th Cir).
71. *United States v Davis* 1985; 772 F2d 1339 (7th Cir).
72. Perr IN: Liability of the mentally ill and their insurers in negligence and other civil actions. *Am J Psychiatry* 1985;142:1414–1418.
73. *Goff v Taylor* 1986; 708 SW2d 113 (Ky Ct App).
74. Kluft RP: An update on multiple personality disorder. *Hosp Community Psychiatry* 1987;38:363–373.
75. Howe EG: Psychiatric evaluation of offenders who commit crimes while experiencing dissociative states. *Law Hum Behav* 1984;8:253–282.
76. French AP, Schechmeister BR : The multiple personality syndrome and criminal defense. *Bull Am Acad Psychiatry Law* 1983;11:17–25.

10

Psychiatry in the Sentencing Process and the Death Penalty

When the possibility of the death penalty looms, the ethics and impact of psychiatrists testifying in sentencing procedures arouses heated debate. At the center of this controversy is Dr James Grigson, a psychiatrist whose testimony was considered pivotal in the imposition of a death sentence in Texas. First, Grigson examined the defendant Smith for 90 minutes and found him competent to stand trial. A jury trial followed and Smith was convicted of murder. Then in a separate sentencing proceeding before the same jury, Grigson testified about the defendant's character, his probable future dangerousness, and potential for rehabilitation. Based partly on Grigson's assertions, the jury voted for execution. Ernest Benjamin Smith had been indicted for murder in his participation in an armed robbery of a grocery store in Dallas. During the course of the robbery, Smith's accomplice fatally shot the store clerk. The prosecution, complying with the Texas penal code on murders resulting from a felony committed with malice aforethought, announced its intention to seek the death penalty for Smith.

Grigson's presence affected all phases of the trial process. He was the physician examining the defendant for competency to stand trial at first. Then at the end, during sentencing, his perceptions as voiced to the jury painted the picture of a man it could hardly resist killing. The nature of his testimony in the sentencing process represented virtual advocacy of capital punishment by a psychiatrist against an individual defendant. A review of the testimony reveals its unscientific and nonmedical content. Grigson starts by claiming, "[H]e will continue his previous behavior—that which he has done in the past. He will do it in the future." According to this psychiatrist, Smith would "only get worse." He was a "very severe sociopath," having "complete disregard for another human being's life." Could he change, be helped, recover?

"We don't have anything in medicine or psychiatry that in any way at all modifies or changes this behavior. . . . Nothing that's going to change this behavior." Grigson concluded that "certainly" Smith would commit similar criminal acts in the future.

Grigson is by no means the only psychiatrist willing to testify in capital cases, but his extreme style has made him the focal point of a complex disagreement. He has been described as wearing the compassionate demeanor of a Marcus Welby stereotype over a "hangman" mentality lacking all empathy and concern. To some, his testimony is frightening. It is also, according to Tybor,[1] incomprehensible to a profession which regards its obligation at the very least to refrain from inflicting harm.

Grigson's personal manner is unique but his testimony in capital cases complies with a trend in which courts and juries rely increasingly on psychiatrists' opinions in determining whether individual defendants will live or die. There are so-called hanging psychiatrists such as Grigson, and there are others who invariably testify for the defense. Yet the unanswered question lingers: does this sort of psychiatric testimony belong in the courtroom at all?

Opponents of psychiatric testimony in death penalty proceedings see such testimony as analogous to a physician's direct participation in an execution through the prescription or injection of lethal doses of barbiturates and other drugs. While several states (Idaho, New Mexico, Oklahoma, and Texas) have laws permitting execution by lethal drugs, and physicians can and do participate in the executions by prescribing drugs, supervising others, monitoring the prison during lethal injections, and pronouncing the prisoner dead, many physicians believe such participation is in violation of the Hippocratic oath. In particular, a majority of psychiatrists are opposed to physicians actively participating in state executions. Only 28% of 5600 psychiatrists surveyed by HoffmanLa Roche Inc in 1981 condoned it,[2] and many have argued that testimony such as Grigson's is tantamount to active participation. Considering their general sentiment opposing physician participation in executions, it is interesting that 63.5% of psychiatrists believe that capital punishment is a deterrent to crime, a majority of those feeling that it should be reserved for individuals with a history of violence who are a proven menace to society.[2] Implicit in the pro-capital punishment leanings among psychiatrists is an ideologic basis for the view that psychiatric testimony in capital cases can serve the interests of justice.

Those favoring psychiatric testimony in such circumstances argue that a physician's participation does not constitute active participation in an execution, or that even if it did, it still does not violate the physician's role as healer and his oath to "do no harm." It is further argued that without psychiatric testimony in capital cases the juries would be left to find answers on their own, without the aid of the latest advances in psychiatric knowledge, to scientific questions such as future dangerousness, potential for rehabilitation, and the structure of a defendant's character. A ban on psychiatric testimony such as Grigson's, it is argued, would also bring a halt to testimony on behalf of capital defendants, and ultimately create a less compassionate system of justice with an increase in the number of executions.

Several US Supreme Court decisions on this issue have greatly affected the role and impact of psychiatric testimony in capital cases. The battle lines delineated above do not remain static, but shift in response to new court decisions.

CONSTITUTIONALITY OF THE DEATH PENALTY

Psychiatrists joined many others in the late 1950s and early 1960s in efforts to abolish the death penalty in the United States. This trend lasted several years. Those opposing capital punishment argued that the death penalty contravened the "evolving standards of decency which mark the progress of a maturing society"[3] and therefore constituted "cruel and unusual punishment" violating the Eighth Amendment of the Constitution[4] Then in 1972, granting certiorari in *Furman v Georgia*,[5] the US Supreme Court agreed to consider the constitutionality of the death penalty. By a majority of seven to two, the court confirmed that for certain murder crimes, under specified conditions, the death penalty was not unconstitutional. Since *Furman*, the court has heard a variety of capital punishment cases in which psychiatrists participated as experts or have filed amicus briefs presumedly reflecting the views of the psychiatric profession on capital punishment as it is applied in specific cases.

Opponents of the death penalty have focused on the issue of racism, claiming that the death sentences imposed on certain inmates may be the result of race discrimination, and therefore unconstitutional. Their clarification of the racial element in capital sentencing was based on a statistical analysis by Baldus et al.[6] Use of the racism issue has been one of the most common and effective weapons in the hands of death sentence opponents. Baldus et al examined more than 2000 Georgia murders that occurred from 1973 to 1979. Their study revealed that defendants charged with killing whites were sentenced to death in 11% of the cases, whereas those charged with killing blacks were condemned in just 1% of the cases. It could only be concluded that the race of both the defendant and the victim strongly influenced the sentencing. The odds of a death sentence for those charged with killing whites were 4.3 times higher than the odds for defendants who killed blacks.[6]

The Supreme Court has been unimpressed with the statistical demonstration of racial disparities in the imposition of the death sentence, however, and in *McCleskey v Kemp*[7] the Court ruled in favor of Georgia.

Warren McCleskey, a black man, was condemned for murdering a white police officer during a store robbery. On postconviction litigation, the attorney for McCleskey argued that the Georgia death penalty statute had been imposed in a racially discriminatory fashion in violation of the Eighth and Fourteenth

Amendments, and presented the Baldus et al findings as evidence. The majority of justices (five to four) did not challenge the validity of the Baldus et al findings nor did they deny that the data proved purposeful racial discrimination. The Supreme Court expressed the view that McCleskey needed instead to prove that the decision makers in his case acted with discriminatory purpose or intent. The revelations of the Baldus statistics were insufficient to infer that purposeful discrimination had been an element in McCleskey's capital sentence. The Baldus et al study also failed to demonstrate that the Georgia legislature passed or maintained its death penalty statute with the purpose of making it racially discriminatory.

The dissenters contended that the demonstration of a significant risk of discrimination, rather than definitive proof of its existence, is enough to present a constitutional violation. Further, the dissenting justices argued that Mc-Cleskey's inability to prove racial bias in his individual case was irrelevant when arbitrary and capricious bias was clearly demonstrated. The Baldus et al study showed that the risk of discrimination is as significant a factor in who is sentenced to death as the defendant's having a prior murder conviction. Six out of every 11 defendants on Georgia's death row convicted of killing a white would not have been condemned if their victims had been black, and among defendants with aggravating and mitigating factors similar to Mc-Cleskey's, 20 out of 34 would not have been sentenced to death had their victims been black.

The Court's failure to clearly define the pivotal but vague phrase "for the purpose of racial discrimination" and what type of evidence is required to prove its existence in its *McCleskey* ruling began a slow and steady acceleration of death sentences. Psychiatrists would be expected and asked to be the determining element in whether or not individual inmates are mentally competent to be executed.[8] As such, it seems that the psychiatrists inherit the role of opening and closing the door to the electric chair.

MENTAL HEALTH PROFESSIONAL AS PREDICTOR

The path was paved for mental health professionals to contribute their wisdom to the determination of future dangerousness in *Jurek v Texas*.[9] In this decision the court noted that "prediction of dangerousness" already occurred in almost every phase of the trial process, from bail setting to sentencing to the parole system. The circumstances of *Jurek* begin brutally. Twenty-two-year old Jerry Lane Jurek was convicted of the rape, strangling, and drowning death of a 10-year-old girl. In cases where a defendant stands convicted of a capital offense, Texas law requires the trial court to conduct a separate proceeding to determine sentence before the same jury that tried the guilt finding. Arguments are heard from the prosecution and defense for and against imposition of the death penalty. The jury is then presented with two or three questions, which if answered in certain ways will bestow a death sentence.

Those statutory questions in *Jurek* were (1) whether the evidence established beyond a reasonable doubt that the murder of the deceased was committed deliberately and with the reasonable expectation that the death of the deceased or another would result; and (2) whether the evidence established beyond a reasonable doubt that there was a probability the defendant would commit criminal acts of violence that would constitute a continuing threat to society. The jury unanimously answered yes to both questions and the defendant, Jurek, was sentenced to death.

The Supreme Court granted certiorari to consider whether imposing the death penalty violated the Eighth and Fourteenth Amendments to the Constitution. Jurek's attorneys contended that question (2) above was an improper one for the trial court to place to the jury, regarding the probability of defendant-petitioner's committing future criminal acts. The attorneys explained that the question was so vague as to be virtually meaningless because, they argued, future behavior is essentially impossible to predict. The court rejected the petitioner's arguments, stating in a majority opinion that prediction of future dangerousness may be difficult, but that does not mean it has no constructive value or should not be undertaken.

Since the issue of future dangerousness was first allowed to be raised at sentencing in capital cases, the door has opened for mental health professionals to testify regarding the application of the death penalty. Predicting future behavior is without question primarily the territory of the mental health field, and psychiatrists quickly accepted the new opportunity to apply their knowledge. This new participation was a logical next step in the evolution of capital court procedures, for if a jury of laymen is considered able to predict the future conduct of an individual and is indirectly asked to do so all the time, why not bring in experts such as psychiatrists to contribute their expertise?

PSYCHIATRISTS' TESTIMONY IN CAPITAL PROCEEDINGS

Several decisions following *Jurek* held implications for the role of psychiatric testimony in capital offenses. In *Lockett v Ohio*[10] the court ruled that in every capital sentencing procedure the prosecution and the defense must be permitted to introduce aggravating and mitigating evidence and testimony. In *Gardner v Florida*,[11] the court maintained that the Eighth Amendment prohibited a sentencing judge from considering information in a report which had not been disclosed to defense counsel and thereby opened to the scrutiny of the adversarial process.

In the case bringing fame to Dr Grigson, *Estelle v Smith*,[12] the Supreme Court considered the question of whether the Fifth Amendment right against self-incrimination extended to information provided to a prosecution psychiatrist which would later be used in a capital proceeding. As noted earlier,

Smith was indicted for murder in connection with an armed robbery in Dallas. The defense counsel had not raised the issue of Smith's competency or sanity at the time of the offense, yet the trial judge informally ordered the prosecution to arrange a psychiatric examination of Smith to determine his competency to stand trial. Grigson was the examining psychiatrist who found Smith competent, and after a trial ending in the defendant's conviction for murder, Grigson was called to testify on the question of whether Smith should receive the death penalty. Defense counsel objected to Grigson's testifying on the grounds that he was not on the state's list of witnesses. The trial court denied the motion, Grigson testified on the penalty proceeding, and Smith was given a death sentence.

Smith's attorneys contended that the Fifth and Sixth Amendments would preclude Texas from using evidence based on a psychiatric examination of a defendant unless that defendant were (1) warned before the examination that he or she had a right to remain silent; and (2) given the opportunity to consult with counsel in deciding whether or not to submit to the examination. The Supreme Court granted certiorari to consider the matter.

Texas argued that Smith was unentitled to Fifth Amendment protection because the psychiatric testimony was used only to determine punishment after conviction in that case, not to establish guilt. "Incrimination is complete once guilt has been adjudicated," according to the state, and therefore the Fifth Amendment right against self-incrimination had no relevance to the penalty phase of a capital trial. The court sided with Smith, however, concluding that "any effort by the state to compel a defendant to testify against himself at a sentencing proceeding would clearly contravene the Fifth Amendment." The court found that the state's attempt to predict respondent's future dangerousness by relying on statements he made to Grigson infringed on his Fifth Amendment rights.

The court sought an example in *Miranda v Arizona*,[13] in which the prosecution was prevented from using statements stemming from custodial interrogation of a defendant unless it could demonstrate the use of procedural safeguards effective to secure the privilege against self-incrimination. The court held that the Miranda rule encompassed a pretrial psychiatric examination. Criminal defendants who neither initiate a psychiatric evaluation nor attempt to introduce any psychiatric evidence may not be compelled to respond to a psychiatrist if their statements might later be used against them in a capital sentence proceeding. The court further noted that the defendant's Sixth Amendment right to the assistance of counsel is abridged when the defendant is not offered a chance to consult with counsel on an upcoming psychiatric examination prior to submitting to it.

PSYCHIATRIST AS RETRIBUTOR

The assumption that psychiatric testimony can be used in a capital sentencing proceeding was not fundamentally challenged by *Estelle v Smith*. The case instead placed important limits on the manner in which the state can elicit information needed in testimony. The court did later consider a direct challenge to incriminating psychiatric testimony in *Barefoot v Estelle*,[14] however.

Thomas A. Barefoot, petitioner, was convicted of capital murder after a jury trial in a Texas state court. A separate sentencing hearing followed before the same jury to weigh the imposition of the death penalty. One of the questions submitted to the Texas jury, as per Texas statute, was whether there was a probability that the petitioner would commit further criminal acts of violence and constitute a continuing threat to society. At this crucial juncture the state called two psychiatrists who in response to hypothetical questions testified that there was such a probability. The jury sentenced the petitioner to death.

To hear arguments concerning the role of psychiatrists in capital punishment cases, certiorari was granted by the US Supreme Court. Barefoot's attorneys attempted to prove that psychiatrists, individually and as a group, are incompetent to predict with an acceptable degree of reliability that a particular criminal will commit future crimes and thus constitute a danger to the community. They argued further that in any event psychiatrists should not be permitted to testify about future dangerousness in response to hypothetical questions and without having examined the defendant personally. They concluded that the testimony of the psychiatrists in this case was so unreliable that the sentence should be set aside.

The Supreme Court rejected each of the petitioner's arguments, stating: "The suggestion that no psychiatrist's testimony may be presented with respect to a defendant's future dangerousness is somewhat like asking [us] to disinvent the wheel." While the court agreed that it is difficult to predict future behavior, it concluded that doing so was neither impossible nor unnecessary. The court rejected the amicus brief of the American Psychiatric Association (APA) siding with the petitioners, which argued that psychiatrists cannot predict future dangerousness. The justices noted that the APA amicus brief did not claim to represent views universally held among members of the association or the psychiatric profession. There are indeed qualified psychiatrists who disagree with the APA opinion and are willing to testify at the sentencing hearings. While such testimony may increase the likelihood of a defendant being sentenced to death, this does not make the testimony inadmissable any more than it would other relevant evidence against a defendant in a criminal case.

The three-justice dissent in *Barefoot* relied on the APA's amicus contention that the established unreliability of psychiatric predictions concerning long-term future dangerousness should preclude the profession from testifying in such cases. The dissenters argued that unlike other situations in which unreliable testimony can be rebutted through the adversarial process, psychiatric predictions rest on intuitive clinical categories which are not readily susceptible to cross-examination or rebuttal. The Constitution mandates reliability in all issues concerning life and death, and therefore psychiatric testimony should be excluded in capital sentencing proceedings.

The Supreme Court decision in *Barefoot* was truly a watershed, bringing the psychiatric profession into the judicial process with a new level of participation and giving it a new level of power.

MITIGATING EVIDENCE

Much of the legal debate in capital cases stems from what kind of evidence and testimony is permissible or should be permissible, as with *Estelle v Barefoot*. Another aspect of the issue addressed by the US Supreme Court is mitigating evidence. In *Eddings v Oklahoma*,[15,16] the Court underlined the constitutional requirement first articulated in *Lockett v Ohio,* that in capital cases a court must consider all evidence a defendant introduces to mitigate the death sentence.

In *Eddings* a 16-year-old boy was convicted and sentenced to death for killing a police officer. The defense presented substantial evidence in mitigation of the death sentence, focusing on the troubled background of the defendant. Defense experts testified that he was emotionally disturbed at the time of the crime and that his mental development lagged several years behind his chronologic age. A psychologist testifying for the prosecution stated that Eddings had a sociopathic or antisocial personality. Attorneys for the petitioner argued that in sentencing Eddings to death the trial court had not sufficiently considered the mitigating evidence that had been presented. The Supreme Court agreed, reversing the decision and remanding the case back to the sentencing judge for a fuller consideration of the mitigating evidence.

What emerges clearly in *Barefoot* and in *Eddings* is that the Supreme Court has found it advisable to allow and actually encourage psychiatric testimony from both sides in a capital sentencing proceeding. Do not psychiatrists relish this power? On the contrary. As will be shown, the psychiatric profession is actually uneasy about its new judicial role.

ROLES OF THE MENTAL HEALTH
PROFESSIONAL IN CAPITAL PUNISHMENT

Mental health professionals remain at odds regarding their function in death sentence cases. Some believe that the participation of psychiatrists in capital cases undermines the values cherished by the medical community. Their opponents argue that it is the responsibility of psychiatrists or psychologists to contribute their expertise. In many instances, only expert psychological testimony can provide the mitigating evidence needed to save defendants from execution.

The APA has outlined a series of ethical principles for psychiatrists who participate in the sentencing process.[3] The APA acknowledges that when psychiatrists conduct examinations for the purpose of sentencing they act primarily as agents for society. In practical terms, this will require the psychiatrist to obtain the maximum amount of information from the individual being examined. This obligation of the psychiatrist is derivative of the court's obligation to promote justice and protect society.

The APA's position echoes that of the noted forensic psychiatrist Seymour Pollack, who has argued that the application of psychiatry in legal settings is always for legal ends and legal purposes and that professionals who have been hired by the prosecution are only obliged to serve their client, the prosecutor, and have essentially no special obligation to the defendant under examination.[17] The Ethics Committee of the APA departs from this radical view in its insistence that a physician always be dedicated to providing competent medical service with compassion and respect for human dignity.[18,19] In this ethical framework the committee contends that psychiatrists should not participate in a legally authorized execution, even if their participation, for example, by giving the injection of a sedative, superficially makes the execution more compassionate and dignified. The committee insists, in short, that the physician-psychiatrist be a healer, not part of a team of killers, even if the team be the state and no matter how well-justified the killing may be. These APA guidelines, however, would not prohibit a psychiatrist from testifying in a death penalty proceeding. There is a world of difference between being party to an execution and presenting professional analysis during sentencing procedures.

An opposing viewpoint sees the participation of psychiatrists in death penalty proceedings as reflecting the erosion of the profession's obligation to help "bring people back, rather than push them over the brink." Robitscher has enunciated this opinion.[20] He compares psychiatrists' "prediction of future dangerousness" with a "vote for death" and argues that such testimony is out of harmony with medical ethics. Other opinions on psychiatrists' participation in sentencing proceedings agree with Robitscher, interpreting the principle that "physicians shall be dedicated to providing competent medical service with compassion and respect for human dignity" as a bar to their participation in death penalty cases.[21] Those psychiatrists who would prohibit on humanitarian grounds expert testimony for the prosecution in capital proceedings have not made it clear whether they believe the defense should be barred from presenting such expert testimony as well.

An argument supporting psychiatric testimony for the prosecution in capital cases holds that if psychiatrists firmly believe certain defendants will pose a continuing threat to society if free, and to the prison population and personnel if incarcerated, their duty as healers would be to prevent future harm to society and the unknown persons whom they sincerely believe will be the defendants' victims. This would require them to warn the public if the opportunity arises in a trial. It is evasive to imply that psychiatrists "only" testify in capital sentencing proceedings and thereby avoid direct participation because they will surely be aware of the consequences. But it is rarely mentioned that the meaning of "responsibility to heal" in this issue is open to interpretation. In a sentencing proceeding where a defendant is considered dangerous, the responsibility of a psychiatrist could be to refrain from testifying to prevent possible harm to a defendant, or it could be to go ahead and testify to prevent possible harm to a defendant's potential victims.

The quality and accessibility of expert psychiatric testimony for typical defendants charged in a capital case become important factors in determining how the law is applied. Often introducing expert psychiatric testimony declaring them psychologically abnormal is the only hope such defendants will have to mitigate their sentence. Psychologic testimony thus tends to occupy a central role in any effort by such defendants to be spared the death sentence. Quality expert testimony is costly, however, and would be available only for wealthier defendants, raising the dangers of justice for sale and life for sale. These issues were before the US Supreme Court when it considered the right of criminal defendants to expert psychiatric testimony. The decision in *Ake v Oklahoma*[22] held that an indigent defendant in a criminal proceeding has a constitutional right to psychiatric evaluation and assistance when his or her mental status at the time of the offense is seriously questioned.

An argument opposing psychiatric testimony in capital cases asserts that the psychiatrists testifying might lend false medical credibility and "pseudoscientific" trappings to essentially moral opinion.[20] When sentencing a defendant to death, according to this view, the judge or the jury is giving expression to the community's moral outrage regarding a defendant and the crime he or she has committed. By permitting such judgments to be based, even in part, on a supposedly scientific prediction of dangerousness, a judge or jury can be deluded into believing that the imposition of the death penalty is a straightforward application of the law to a given set of "facts."[23] Considerations such as these led so astute a commentator on the criminal mind as Karl Menninger to argue that "what all courts should do, what society should do, is to exclude all psychiatrists from the courtroom,"[24] and former Chief Justice Warren Burger to comment that "medical experts and psychiatric techniques can do more for society in hospitals, clinics and penitentiaries than in courtrooms."[25]

There are also psychiatrists such as Pollack[23] who contend, contrary to the above opinion, that psychiatrists who testify can present valuable data to the judge and jury which they could not receive any other way, and should therefore be allowed and encouraged to do so. While the precise relevance of findings about schizophrenia, anxiety states, depressions, phobias, etc, can be debated and will vary from one case to another, there can be little doubt that such findings are indeed relevant in certain cases and the only access to them is through experts who are willing to testify.

Forensic psychiatry has been construed by the American Academy of Psychiatry and the Law (AAPL) as applying combined scientific and legal expertise to legal issues in legal contexts. This function must always be performed in accordance with the ethical principles understood and expected by the profession of psychiatry. The most urgent question confronting the forensic specialty is whether its essential ethical principles do, or should, prohibit psychiatrists from testifying in capital cases.

The development of a body of knowledge to be utilized in the prevention of violent and aggressive crime is a primary aim of forensic psychiatry, contends Bromberg.[26] Bromberg claims that the psychiatric study of criminals has "the same heuristic value as measuring earthquakes with seismographs, estimating pollution standards in the air or studying disease with the aim of future control." He concludes that forensic psychiatry, with appropriate caveats regarding its reliability, can and should be presented before juries in the sentencing process.

If psychiatry and especially forensic psychiatry are seen as devoid of scientific content, and if they are relegated to the realm of philosophy, psychiatrists would not belong in the courtroom at all. But if psychiatry is deemed a science, then its findings and discoveries are significant resources for the triers of fact to have at their disposal. If the data are at times unreliable or colored more than occasionally by a personal ethical or evaluative component, the adversarial process should be used to separate the wheat from the chaff, rather than discarding the whole harvest.

The interpretation of psychiatric testimony in a forensic context is often an extremely difficult task. Even where psychiatric experts agree on a given defendant's diagnosis and psychodynamics, they are apt to disagree on the implications of their findings for a patient's culpability. If a patient is found to have severe character pathology, for example, should this be viewed as a psychiatric illness which mitigates a defendant's responsibility for his or her crime, or does it simply confirm that the defendant is indeed a bad character who should be punished to the full extent of the law? Or, for instance, if an individual is found to be acting out unconscious hostilities in committing a crime, does this fact mitigate or exacerbate the severity of the crime? Should individuals be held responsible for their own unconscious, repressed motives? These and many other philosophical issues are apt to be raised by psychiatric experts testifying in capital sentencing proceedings. They are difficult and complex issues, and some argue that because of their difficulty, juries should not be troubled with psychiatric testimony at all. The author's view is that such philosophical questions are already at the heart of each and every capital sentencing proceeding. That the issues are difficult, perhaps impossible, for juries to analyze objectively might serve as an argument against capital punishment. It should not serve as an argument to sweep away the questions. In short, while the proper interpretation of psychiatric data is almost always a formidable task, the perils of failing to use this resource are greater than the perils of ignoring its value.

A GENERAL GUIDELINE

The opportunity to present mitigating psychiatric testimony in capital proceedings, an act which complies with the aim of the Hippocratic oath, must be contingent on the alternate possibility of exacerbating testimony being presented by the prosecution. Mental health professionals who testify for the prosecution in such cases are thus providing a service that is consistent with the notion of "saving lives" in the long run. However, several safeguards should be instituted to help assure that such testimony is properly understood by juries and the judiciary. These safeguards are summarized below:

1. Psychiatrists or qualified mental health professionals should be permitted to testify with "medical possibility" or "probability" but not with so-called reasonable medical certainty. Given the current state of knowledge, juries should perhaps be reminded of the tentative and controversial nature of psychiatric testimony, particularly in capital cases.

2. Psychiatrists or qualified mental health professionals should never be permitted to address the ultimate legal questions while on the witness stand. For example, they should not veil their testimony in the rhetoric of responsibility, culpability, etc, but should rather present their findings in the very terms in which they are regarded to be expert: psychodynamic explanations of criminal behavior, prognosis, diagnosis, and treatment recommendations.

3. Lawyers should be permitted and in fact encouraged to present juries with alternative interpretations of psychiatric findings. This reinforces the fundamental aim of simply providing finders of fact with as much relevant data as possible, instead of influencing them on their decisions. There are complicated philosophical issues involved in interpreting psychodynamic hypotheses in terms of legal categories such as responsibility. For example, as mentioned, there is no unanimous opinion on whether the existence of an unconscious motive mitigates or exacerbates a crime. Juries should be apprised of these difficulties and lawyers should be permitted to introduce separate expert testimony addressing them. Such testimony should be distinguished from testimony of a purely psychiatric nature.

4. State legislatures should be discouraged from constructing their death penalty statutes out of language which precludes alternative interpretations of psychiatric testimony. For example, the Texas statute under which defendants Jurek and Smith were sentenced to death requires the jury to consider two statutory questions. The second of these is whether the evidence established beyond a reasonable doubt that there was a probability that the defendant would commit future criminal acts of violence which would constitute a continuing threat to society. Grigson's controversial testimony in the Smith case focused on this question and the psychiatrist's belief was that there was no medical or psychiatric treatment that could or would change the defendant's pattern of behavior. While Grigson's testimony was clearly intended to be aggravating with respect to the defendant's

sentence, we can readily imagine similar testimony that would be interpreted as mitigating his responsibility for a criminal act. The Texas statute, however, by defining future dangerousness as aggravating, precludes an alternative interpretation and thus basically answers a series of important questions that should be left to the judge and jury to answer in particular cases.

Effective use of psychiatric or psychological testimony in any criminal proceeding rests with an understanding that such testimony, as with any and all evidence, is always, theoretically, amenable to a variety of interpretations. While the interpretation of psychiatric testimony is a complicated task which can be above the heads of typical jurors without proper instruction, this difficulty should not be permitted to undermine its potential value. Juries are asked to perform a fundamentally philosophical task in deciding whether to sentence prisoners to die. If they cannot perform this task properly with all the evidence before them, this certainly does not justify eliminating vital evidence because it is difficult to master and incorporate into the entirety of evidence at their disposal. Doing so would set a disturbing precedent, because one of the earliest arguments against a democracy based on voting and jury systems was that "regular citizens" were not in possession of sufficient intelligence to understand or decide such complex issues.

COMPETENCE AND CAPITAL PUNISHMENT

Convicts who have been sentenced to death should not be executed if they are currently mentally incompetent. This is not only a generally accepted ethic, but it is the express belief of all involved organizations including the American Bar Association (ABA).[27] If a condemned convict is determined to be currently mentally incompetent, execution should be stayed. The ABA position further states that convicts are incompetent to be executed if, as a result of mental illness or mental retardation, they cannot understand the nature of the pending proceedings, what they were tried for, the reason for the punishment, or the nature of the punishment. Convicts are also incompetent if, as a result of mental illness or mental retardation, they lack sufficient capacity to recognize or understand why their criminal acts were unjust or unlawful, or lack the ability to convey such information to counsel or to the court.

According to the court, however, low intelligence level is not grounds to escape punishment, even an execution. If a defendant was found competent to stand trial and then was found guilty for a capital offense, which means criminally responsible, then he or she is competent to receive a death sentence, and that punishment is deemed not to be cruel or unusual.[28]

The ABA recommends that following the hearing, if the court finds that a convict is currently incompetent, it should stay the order of execution for the duration of the convict's incompetence. The court's finding on the issue of incompetence should be considered a final, appealable order. In addition, when the appropriate state official has reason to believe that a condemned convict who has been found incompetent is restored to competence, the official may petition the court for an order recognizing the restoration to competence and lifting the stay of execution. On receipt of such a petition, the court should order the convict's current mental condition reevaluated. Counsel for the defendant should be notified that such an evaluation will be conducted. Following the reevaluation, the court should hold a hearing on the convict's current mental condition. The convict should be represented by counsel at the hearing. Following the hearing, the court should lift the stay of execution if it finds, by a preponderance of the evidence, that the convict is no longer incompetent. The court's finding on the issue of competence should be considered a final, appealable order.

A case that addressed the competency issue directly was *Ford v Wainwright*,[29] in which Alvin Bernard Ford was convicted of murder and sentenced to death. There was no suggestion that he was incompetent at the time of his offense, trial, or sentencing. While incarcerated, Ford began manifesting behavior change. It started as an occasional peculiar idea or confused perception and grew more serious over time. Ford became obsessed with the Ku Klux Klan, believing that he had become the target of a complex conspiracy involving the Klan and assorted others, designed to force him to commit suicide. He believed that the prison guards were part of the conspiracy and that they had been killing people and putting the bodies in the concrete enclosures used for beds. His delusion gradually broadened to include every aspect of his life. He believed, for example, that his female relatives were being tortured and sexually abused somewhere in the prison, and he claimed that the people who were tormenting him in prison had taken members of his family hostage. The list of hostages expanded to senators and other national leaders. His delusions became grandiose and he began referring to himself as "Pope John Paul III" and claimed that he had appointed nine new justices to the Florida Supreme Court.

Counsel for Ford asked Dr Jamal Amin, who had examined the prisoner earlier, to continue seeing him and to recommend appropriate treatment. Dr Amin concluded that Ford suffered from a severe uncontrollable mental disease which closely resembled paranoid schizophrenia with suicide potential. A second psychiatrist, Dr Harold Kaufman, also examined the patient and concluded that Ford had no understanding of why he was being executed, made no connection between the homicide of which he had been convicted and the death penalty, and indeed believed that he would not be executed because he owned the prison and could control the governor through mind waves. Eventually Ford regressed further and further, becoming nearly incomprehensible and speaking only in his own symbolic code language.

Following the statutory procedure in force in the state of Florida, the governor appointed three psychiatrists who together interviewed Ford for the purpose of determining his competency to be executed. Each psychiatrist filed a separate report with the governor's office. The reports reached conflicting diagnoses but were in accord in declaring Ford incompetent. The governor nevertheless eventually signed a death warrant. The case arrived at the US Supreme Court after passing through appropriate channels, and a writ of certiorari was granted. The Supreme Court decided that the Eighth Amendment prohibits the state from inflicting the death penalty on a prisoner who is insane. The court concluded that

> . . . the reasons at common law for not condoning the execution of the insane—that such an execution has questionable retributive value, presents no example to others and thus has no deterrence value, and simply offends humanity—have no less logical, moral and practical force at present. Whether the aim is to protect the condemned from fear and pain without comfort or understanding or to protect the dignity of society itself from the barbarity of exacting mindless vengeance, the restriction finds enforcement in the Eighth Amendment.

The majority also delivered the opinion that the petitioner Ford is entitled to a de novo evidentiary hearing in the district court on the question of his competence to be executed.

The dissent in *Ford* agreed that the Eighth Amendment does prohibit a state from carrying out a lawfully imposed execution on a person who is currently insane. However, they held that it is an equally important and unchallenged precedent in common law that it is the *executive* and not the judiciary that passes on the insanity of the condemned. The dissent argued, "So, when the court today creates a constitutional right to a determination of sanity outside of the executive branch, it does so not in keeping with but at the expense of our common-law heritage." The dissenting justices referred to the prior case *Solesbee v Balkcom*[30] in which a man was condemned to death and the governor, with the help of experts, found him to be sane to be executed. To summarize, the dissent in *Ford* argued that the final determination of postsentencing competency is the function of the executive, or of the prisoner's custodian.

Appelbaum has forecast that with the increasing number of executions, psychiatrists will have to confront the difficult and somewhat ironic ethical dilemma of treating death row prisoners and restoring them to competency so they can be executed.[31] Psychiatrists may feel that treating a death row inmate under these circumstances would violate the same medical ethics that many feel prohibit physicians from participating in executions. Once the AAPL posed this question to three well-known forensic psychiatrists.[32] One, Harry, avowed that while certain intellectual gymnastics might permit some clinicians to treat an incompetent condemned inmate, he would not do such treatment unless it were specified in advance that the inmate's sentence would be commuted to life imprisonment. On the other hand, Goldstein, herself personally opposed to the death penalty, would offer psychiatric treatment on a voluntary basis even though that treatment might restore an inmate to competency and lead to his execution. She would treat a patient involuntarily only if the inmate were a danger to himself or others. Maier sees the lack of consensus on this issue as stemming from a conflict among three essentially valid ethical principles: (1) that physicians have a duty to relieve suffering; (2) that patients have a right to refuse treatment; and (3) that physicians should "at least do no harm." Each of these principles leads to a different conclusion regarding the treatment of death row prisoners, the first to the view that it is justified, the second that it should be done only when the patient requests it, and the third that it should not be undertaken at all.

Some opponents of the participation of psychiatrists have gone so far as to compare the psychiatrist working with and treating the death row inmate to Dr Josef Mengele, a Nazi physician who earned the sobriquet "angel of death." Sargent believes that psychiatrists are actually being asked to remove a condition that is the only thing standing between the patient and death; that failing to warn the patient the therapist is colluding with the state in removing the last barrier to execution is dishonest; and that therapy not inherently grounded in the patient's welfare is dishonest.[33] Behind the acknowledged realities of death row therapy, prisoners harbor unarticulated, trustful expectations that the encounter with the physician will prove beneficial. That trust is betrayed when psychiatrists treat patients so that the patients may be executed. To many physicians, this may seem like treating the patient to death. The patient ought to be reminded at every stage that execution will follow recovery. But how many therapists can bring to death row this macabre frankness?[33]

Obviously, a consensus has yet to emerge on this perplexing issue. Appelbaum[31] is critical of the Supreme Court for not addressing it. However, it is not clear that the dilemma should necessarily be addressed by the legal community or in a legal forum. While it is understandable that some psychiatrists may feel that working therapeutically with death row prisoners violates their Hippocratic oath to at least do no harm, others would see such work as exemplifying their commitment to restore persons to a state of rational autonomy. Indeed, a number of commentators regard restoration to rational autonomy as the supreme if not the only function of the psychiatric profession.[34,35] Such rational autonomy, it could be argued, would be necessary in order for a sentenced prisoner to evaluate and proffer any further appeals for clemency, and would also be a condition for his facing the consequences of his acts with human dignity as well as a spirit of genuine repentance.

Physicians with worthy motives and ideals can easily arrive at opposing conclusions with respect to these issues. For the present, therefore, this ethical knot belongs to the class of moral problems on which reasonable minds disagree.

REFERENCES

1. Tybor JR: Dallas' doctor of doom. *Law J*, Nov 24, 1980.
2. Hoffman-LaRoche, Inc: *Psychiatric Viewpoints Report, Violence and the Contemporary Psychiatrist*. Nutley, NJ, Hoffman-LaRoche, 1981.
3. American Psychiatric Association: *A Report of the Task Force on the Role of Psychiatry in the Sentencing Process*. Washington, DC, American Psychiatric Press, 1984.
4. *Trop v Dulles* 1958; 356 US 86, 101.
5. *Furman v Georgia* 1972; 408 US 238.
6. Baldus DC, et al: Arbitrariness and discrimination in the administration of the death penalty. *Stetson Law Rev* 1986;15:133–261.
7. *McCleskey v Kemp* 1987; 107 SCt 1756.
8. Radelet ML: McCleskey: racial disparities and the death penalty. *Am Acad Psychiatry Law Newsletter* 1987;12:13–15.
9. *Jurek v Texas* 1976; 428 US 262.
10. *Lockett v Ohio* 1978; 438 US 586.
11. *Gardner v Florida* 1977; 430 US 349.
12. *Estelle v Smith* 1980; 451 US 454.
13. *Miranda v Arizona* 1966; 384 US 436, 467.
14. *Barefoot v Estelle* 1983; 82-6080 US.
15. *Eddings v Oklahoma* 1981; 455 US 104.
16. Koson D: Synopsis on *Eddings v Oklahoma*. *Am Acad Psychiatry Law* 1983; 8:21.
17. Pollack S: Forensic psychiatry: a specialty. *Psychiatry Law* 1974;2:1–6.
18. American Psychiatric Association: *The Principles of Medical Ethics with Annotations, Especially Applicable to Psychiatry*. Washington, DC, American Psychiatric Press, 1981.
19. American Psychiatric Association: *Opinions of the Ethics Committee on the Principles of Medical Ethics with Annotations, Especially Applicable to Psychiatry*. Washington, DC, American Psychiatric Press, 1985.
20. Robitscher J: *Newsletter Am Acad Psychiatry Law* 1981;6:2–3.
21. Bonnie R: Psychiatry and the death penalty: emerging problems in Virginia. *Va Law Rev* 1980;66:167–189.
22. *Ake v Oklahoma* 1985; 105 Sup Ct 1087.
23. American Academy of Psychiatry and Law: Meeting in Chicago, 1980. *Newsletter Am Acad Psychiatry Law* 1981; 6.
24. Menninger K: *The Crime of Punishment*. New York, Viking Press, 1966.
25. Burger W: Psychiatrists, lawyers and the courts. *Fed Probation 28* (June):1964.
26. Bromberg W: *Psychiatric News* May 21, 1982.
27. American Bar Association: *Criminal Justice Mental Health Standards*. Chap. 7, Addition, Aug 1987.
28. *Brogdon v Butler* 1987; 824 F2d 338 (5th Cir)
29. *Ford v Wainwright* 1986; US 82-5542.
30. *Solesbee v Balkcom* 1950; 339 US 9.
31. Appelbaum P: Treating death row prisoners—an ethical dilemma. *Clin Psychiatric News* Aug 1986.
32. *Newsletter Am Acad Psychiatry Law* 1987;12:11-12.
33. Sargent DA: Treating the condemned to death. *Hastings Cent Rep* 1986;16:5–6.
34. Moore M: *Law and Psychiatry: Rethinking the Relationship*. Cambridge, Cambridge University Press, 1984.
35. Edwards R (ed): *Psychiatry and Ethics: Insanity, Rational Autonomy and Mental Health Care*. Buffalo, Prometheus Books, 1982.

11

The Rights of Children under the Constitution

FREEDOM OF EXPRESSION AND RIGHTS UNDER THE FIRST AMENDMENT

Conflicts involving the First Amendment have made headlines since the amendment was first implemented, and have been among the most pivotal issues in US history. While the First Amendment has become a symbol of American freedom, its specific guarantees of freedom of speech, freedom of the press, and right to peaceable assembly are actually often in the process of being challenged by special interests or groups with opposing needs and functions. The First Amendment is thus usually embroiled in controversy. Frequently the challenge comes from the government itself, since the government is prohibited from interfering with or abridging the rights safeguarded by the First Amendment. As citizens, children are also entitled to exercise their First Amendment rights. However, their First Amendment rights are often circumscribed by the rights and responsibilities of various persons and institutions having legal authority over them.

The right to express ideas on political topics is guaranteed by the Constitution, and as the US Supreme Court stated in *Tinker v Desmoines,* "Students do not shed their constitutional rights to freedom of speech or expression at the school house gates."[1] The *Tinker* case arrived at the Supreme Court after school authorities prohibited a student from wearing a black armband in protest of the Vietnam War. Constitutionally, students cannot be punished simply for expressing their personal views on the school premises, whether in the cafeteria, on the playing field, or on the campus during school hours. The students' expression may be limited by the authorities only if they deem such expression to interfere substantially with school functioning or to impinge on the rights of other students.

The broad freedom of expression upheld in *Tinker* was characteristic of a year and an era in which "protest," "rebellion," and "freedom of speech" seemed synonymous, and socioeconomic groups clashed deeply over how much was permissible. *Tinker* is a perfect example of such a confrontation. On the surface it seems that the liberals won in *Tinker* because the armband was a protest against the Vietnam War. However, conservatives can also claim a victory since lack of government interference has always been a classic conservative ideology, and in *Tinker* the government was prevented from interfering with a student's freedom of expression. The general assessment of *Tinker* remains that it is a liberal victory, however. Today, the national mood has changed drastically, swinging to a conservatism characterized not by concern for individual freedom but for order and authority. The Supreme Court reflects the general population in this change. Fifteen years later, a case with some similarities to *Tinker* resulted in the narrowing of children's rights under the First Amendment to the degree that speech or expression by a student need not be tolerated if it is found by school authorities to be unsuitable for the school environment as they define it. This case, *Bethel School v Fraser*,[2] aroused much public interest, as First Amendment conflicts often do, and recalled confrontations of an earlier era.

The case arose when Fraser, a student in Bethel School District No. 403, delivered a speech nominating a fellow student for a student elective office at a voluntary assembly that was held during school hours as part of a school-sponsored educational program in self-government. It was attended by about 600 students. During his speech, Fraser referred to his candidate using an elaborate graphic sexual metaphor. In his endorsement of a fellow student's candidacy for school office, Fraser described the candidate as "a man who is firm. He is firm in his pants. He is firm in his shirt. His character is firm," etc. Because of the sexual innuendo in his speech, Fraser was suspended for three days on charges of violation of the school's "disruptive conduct rule."

Fraser filed suit alleging that by punishing him for the content of his speech, the school violated his First Amendment right to freedom of speech. The lower court agreed and the decision was affirmed on appeals. Then on a writ of certiorari to the US Supreme Court, the lower court's decision was reversed.

The majority of justices, quoting the historians Charles and Mary Beard, stated that "public education must prepare pupils for citizenship in the republic. It must inculcate the habits and manners of civility as values in themselves conducive to happiness and as indispensible to the practice of self-government in the community and the nation." These justices continued to the effect that the determination of what manner of speech is inappropriate in the classroom or school assembly properly rests with the school board. The schools, as instruments of the state, may determine that the essential lessons of civil, mature conduct cannot be conveyed in a school that tolerates lewd, indecent, or offensive speech, or conduct such as that indulged in by this "confused boy." The justices found that the pervasive sexual innuendo in Fraser's speech was plainly offensive to teachers and students, indeed to any mature person. By glorifying male sexuality, the speech was also acutely insulting to the female students. In drawing their conclusion the justices referred to previous Supreme Court decisions recognizing that school authorities should act in loco parentis in order to protect children from exposure to sexually explicit, indecent, or lewd speech.

Although the First Amendment right of free speech bars all government officials, including public school officials, from violating free speech rights, in the public schools the officials may restrict student speech more than government may restrict the speech of citizens generally. Schools have especially wide latitude to censor student speech in newspapers and other activities sponsored and financed by the school. A school and school authorities do not have to tolerate student speech that is inconsistent with its basic educational mission. A school has broad powers to refuse to lend its name and resources to the dissemination of student expression that it considers inappropriate. If the students were allowed to publish uncensored material, it would weaken and threaten the authority of the boards of education, and would interfere with the curricula.

The extent to which educators may exercise control over the contents of a school newspaper was analyzed by the US Supreme Court in *Hazelwood School District v Kuhlmeier.*[3] This ruling has been much publicized, with commentators noting how the authoritarianism of the decision represents the political climate.

The respondents, three former students of Hazelwood East, contended that the school officials violated their First Amendment rights by deleting two pages of articles from the May 13, 1983 issue of *Spectrum,* the school paper. Principal Robert Reynolds objected to two of the articles scheduled to appear in that edition. One of the stories described three Hazelwood East students' experiences with pregnancy, and the other discussed the impact of divorce on students at the school. Reynolds was concerned, among other things, that the articles' references to sexual activity and birth control were inappropriate for some of the younger students at the school. The respondents commenced actions seeking a declaration that their First Amendment rights under the US Constitution had been violated by deleting the two pages of the newspaper. After passing through lower courts, the case arrived before the Supreme Court.

In the view of the justices of the highest court of the land, the First Amendment rights of students in public school are not automatically coextensive with the rights of adults in other settings. Instead they must be applied in light of the special characteristics of the school environment. The majority referred to their own earlier case, *Fraser,* and reiterated once more that a student could be disciplined for having delivered a speech that was "sexually explicit" but not obscene in a legal definition, at an official school assembly, because the school was entitled to "disassociate itself" from the speech in a manner that would demonstrate to others that such vulgarity is wholly inconsistent with the fundamental values of public school education. The highest court pointed out also that, as decided in the *Fraser* case, the determination of what manner of speech in the classroom or school assembly is inappropriate properly rests with the school board. In the comparison of the *Hazelwood* and *Fraser* cases, the court chose not to address the issue of the offensive material. Fraser tried to use the First Amendment guarantees to protect what is essentially bad manners and the school authorities contended that it was part of their responsibility to disallow such bad manners because learning proper conduct was part of the educational process. It belittles student journalism to compare Fraser's self-indulgence to the endeavors of the young journalists in *Hazelwood,* who sought to use the First Amendment rights to address serious and timely issues. The Supreme Court view that the younger high school students lacked the maturity to handle sex-related issues in a school paper when they are confronted with them daily in every other medium in far less serious and concerned terms seems troubling. The Court could have upheld the editorial prerogatives of school authorities and yet made some guidelines for the fair application of that prerogative, that is, discriminating between the frivolous and the serious. To equate Fraser's sexual slur with the journalistic treatment of issues involving sexuality requires an immense imaginative leap.

The Supreme Court also compared the *Hazelwood* case to the *Tinker* case, and found that in *Tinker* the issue was whether the educators are able to silence a student's personal expression when it happens to occur on the school premises, whereas in *Hazelwood* the question was whether educators have authority over school-sponsored publications, theatrical productions, and other expressive activities that students, parents, and members of the public might reasonably perceive as bearing the imprimatur of the school. These kinds of activities are part of school curricula and therefore educators are entitled to exercise control over this form of expression to ensure that participants learn whatever lessons the activity is designed to teach, and that readers or listeners are not exposed to material that may be inappropriate for their level of maturity.

In summary, the majority justices hold that educators do not violate the First Amendment by exercising editorial control over the style and content of student speech in school-sponsored expressive activities so long as their actions are reasonably related to legitimate pedagogical concerns.

The dissenting justices, in voicing their opposition, showed concern over the constitutional rights of students in public schools. According to them, censorship would convert our public schools into enclaves of totalitarianism strangling free minds and neutralizing the First Amendment. They contend further that the First Amendment permits no such blanket censorship authority and that students in public school "do not shed their constitutional rights to freedom of speech or expression at the schoolhouse gate," as decided in *Tinker* 19 years earlier. Public educators, the dissenters feel, must accommodate some student expression even if it offends them or voices views or values that contradict those the school wishes to inculcate.

The message from the Supreme Court in its current guise is unmistakably clear. The First Amendment guarantees to children are limited. Schoolchildren can express views on politics, history, philosophy, society, and other such topics as long as doing so does not interfere with the educational function. They cannot, however, express their views on issues involving sexuality if a school authority considers the topic too inflammatory. Further, school officials have been given the authority to rule out lewd conversation when it may appear to be under the school's aegis or where it will offend listeners. Indeed, not only are school authorities permitted to outlaw vulgar language, the court has implied that it is part of the socializing function of education to set behavior limits mirroring society's. Teachers take on a parental role in the absence of the parents, and they have authority to decide what a student should write or read, and if in their judgment a book or other material is unsuitable or contains vulgar language, such material can even be removed from the bookshelves.[4] So from the heady days nearly two decades ago when almost anything was permissible—the days of black armbands and high-school students going on strike and dictating curricula—the pendulum has swung way back. It is again fine for schools to teach and expect students to demonstrate self-control in their personal expression; it is again the prerogative of school authorities to exercise their authority. Yet it is very much in keeping with the spirit of the First Amendment for feisty students to challenge that authority from time to time, whether their attempt is merely immature as in *Fraser,* or high-minded as in *Hazelwood.*

RIGHT TO PRIVACY WITH A VIEW TOWARD ADOLESCENT SEXUAL BEHAVIOR

The right to privacy is not explicitly written into the Constitution, and therefore remains a charged issue. However, this enigmatic right has long been debated among constitutional scholars. When the issue narrows to children and the right to privacy, it grows even tougher to define and analyze.

The consensus is that the right to privacy does exist in the penumbra of specific guarantees enumerated in the Bill of Rights. Several US Supreme Court rulings recognize an implicit right to privacy in the Constitution, a right with which the government cannot interfere unless there is some "compelling state interest." Children, like adults, may enjoy a right to privacy if the issue concerns their very private affairs. They do not retain an absolute, unsupervised right to total privacy.

The right to carry through a pregnancy and the right to have an abortion seem to be the only privacy rights children have been unconditionally guaranteed. The Supreme Court justices have been extremely concerned for and sensitive to the privacy of what they call a "mature minor" regarding the decision making in certain medical conditions involving the consensual invasion of bodily integrity. Abortion of course is the paramount issue along these lines, as is carrying a pregnancy to term without parental or judicial interference.

Constitutional law encompasses the opinion that a "mature minor" has the ability to make sound judgments for herself. This legal concept is in contrast to psychological views of child development. From the perspective of developmental psychology, children under 12 in general do not have the cognitive and judgmental ability to make major decisions. The ability of those between 12 and 18 years old also remains questionable, depending on a variety of factors such as intelligence, education, culture, and socioeconomic class. The crucial point is that children in this 12- to 18-year-old age group *may* be able to make sound decisions. Of necessity, however, the law has fixed a certain age as the boundary between major and minor. Below 18 or 21 years is a minor, and that age and above is a major, also called "full age." This dividing line contrasts the actual gradual pace of maturing.

Psychiatry and law have conflicting perceptions and opinions regarding the adolescent age group, roughly those between 13 and 18 years old. Psychiatry sees adolescence as the time when a person struggles toward independence yet remains dependent on adults for guidance in certain private matters. The law, on the other hand, emphasizes the privacy aspect, especially the privacy to make decisions regarding one's own body. The choice adolescents have regarding abortion and pregnancy, which has caused so much controversy in legal and psychological circles, shows how the Constitution does extend to adolescents the right of self-determination in certain circumstances involving the most private aspects of life.

This right to privacy was clarified by the US Supreme Court in *Planned Parenthood of Central Missouri v Danforth*,[5] in which a Missouri statute was challenged. Missouri requires that when an unmarried pregnant girl under the age of 18 seeks an abortion, her physician must obtain the written consent of her parents to perform the abortion. The Supreme Court ruled that this statute was unconstitutional. "Constitutional rights do not mature and come into being magically only when one attains the state defined age of majority," voiced the justices. The Court stipulated that an adolescent does not need her parents' approval to terminate her pregnancy. The same court maintained the view that if the girl is mature enough to become pregnant, she then has the right to privacy and to determine what to do with her own body, including the termination of a pregnancy. The justices, apparently confused between physiologic maturity and psychological maturity, prepared no guidelines as to who should decide whether the girl is mature enough or not, or for the girl to follow as conditions—prenatal care, for example—if she is given the right to a full-term pregnancy.

Three years after *Danforth*, the Court once more faced the issue of pregnancy in adolescents and the right to privacy in *Bellotti v Baird*.[6] And again, this court ruled that a Massachusetts statute similar to Missouri's regarding parental or state permission for abortion is unconstitutional. Massachusetts had required parental consent prior to an abortion being performed on a minor, and if the parents refused such permission then the minor could go to court and show good cause and the court could permit the abortion. The majority of justices found such a procedure unconstitutional. A minor female has a constitutionally protected right to be free from either parental or judicial veto as regards her childbearing decisions and actions.

The right to privacy and self-determination in this sensitive issue has been extended even to the degree that the physician should not notify the parents of a minor who seeks an abortion without the minor's consent. In *H.L. v Matheson*,[7] the Supreme Court struck down Utah's law requiring that a physician notify the parent of a young female who seeks an abortion.

The privacy right has been implicitly extended in some areas when issues related to sexuality are involved. For instance, adolescents have the right to purchase contraceptive material. In *Cary v Population Services International Inc*[8] a New York statute prohibiting the sale and distribution of contraceptives to minors was struck down.

Overall, the Supreme Court decisions upholding the privacy right of adolescents regarding pregnancy and termination of pregnancy offer virtually no psychosocial benefits for the teenage group they supposedly protect. Actually, young people are deprived by these rulings of the parental advice and guidance they may deeply need and desire, and deprived as well of the comfort of knowing the parents will and must share with them the anguish of the decision. To toss all responsibility and freedom into a teenager's hands when it comes to childbearing decisions seems on the surface perhaps brave, respectful of their autonomy and rights, and so forth. It may be cruel, however, to instill the illusion that physical maturity and emotional maturity march in step.

It is the responsibility of mature adults to aid and guide youth through troubling decisions and to help them face the consequences of their actions, and to turn one's back on a teenage girl when she most needs guidance and structure is an evasion of responsibility masquerading as high-minded respect for bodily integrity. Of course, it would be unfair to a teenager who wanted an abortion to let her parents prevent her on the basis of their personal religious and moral beliefs. But to cut them out so completely from their child's life at a crucial moment weakens the family as a unit and its role in society. To keep the parents involved does not have to mean letting them overrule their daughter's decision, but simply facilitating communication and sharing responsibility. A balance must be maintained recognizing the legitimate interests of all parties, which indeed is more difficult than handing over all the decisions to a youngster by saying "it's her body." That's the same as saying, in effect, "it's her problem."

Premarital adolescent sexual relations and pregnancy have always been important issues for that circle of concerned parties which includes mental health professionals, religious organizations, courts of law, and other groups with an interest in these phenomena. Lawsuits, for example, were brought by religious organizations claiming that taxpayer funds may not be used for certain purposes, including family planning services and counseling, or to promote abortion as an available option to teenagers. Liberals have argued that taxpayer money should not be provided to religious organizations that counsel teenage girls to abstain from sex and avoid abortion, as such funding appears to be contrary to the separation of church and state.

Those views were tested in the Supreme Court in the case known as the *Kendrick* case.[9] The majority of justices found that the *Adolescent Family Life Act* (AFLA),[10] which was passed by Congress in 1981 in response to the severe adverse health, social, and economic consequences that often follow pregnancy and childbirth among unmarried adolescents, is essentially a scheme for providing grants to public or nonprofit private organizations or agencies for services and research in the area of premarital adolescent sexual relations and pregnancy. These grants are intended to serve several purposes, including the promotion of self-discipline and other prudent approaches to the problem of adolescent premarital sexual relations. The AFLA also promoted adoption as an alternative for adolescent parents, the establishment of new approaches to the delivery or care services for pregnant adolescents, and the support of research and demonstration projects concerning the social causes and consequences of adolescent premarital sexual relations, contraceptive use, pregnancy, and child rearing. The AFLA was challenged by a group of federal taxpayers, clergymen, and the American Jewish Congress, who contended that the AFLA violates the religion clauses of the First Amendment. The district court agreed and held that the AFLA was invalid on a constitutional basis as it allows religiously affiliated organizations to participate as grantees or subgrantees in AFLA programs.

The case arrived at the US Supreme Court. The highest court struck down the lower court decision and upheld the federal AFLA law providing money to religious groups to counsel teenage girls to abstain from sexual relations and to avoid abortion. The majority of justices noted that the AFLA expressly mentions the role of religious organizations in four places. It states (1) that the problems of teenage sexuality are best approached through a variety of integrated and essential services provided to adolescents and their families by, among others, religious organizations; (2) that federally subsidized services should emphasize the provision of support by, among others, religious organizations; (3) that the AFLA program shall use such methods as will strengthen the capacity of families to make use of support systems such as religious organizations; and (4) that grant applicants shall describe how they will involve religious organizations, among other groups, in the provision of services under the act. In the view of the justices, when Congress passed the law, it recognized that prevention of adolescent sexual activity and adolescent pregnancy depends primarily on developing strong family values and close family ties. Accordingly, it seems quite sensible for Congress to recognize that religious organizations can influence values and have some influence on family life, including parents' relations with their adolescent children.

The essence of the *Kendrick* case, as this author understands it, is that religious organizations, just as secular ones, can be funded by the government, and that both types of organizations can give counseling on sex-related matters to adolescents, and further that doing so is quite in accord with constitutional law.

The four dissenting justices felt that the AFLA, without a doubt, endorses religion. Because of its expressed solicitude for the participation of religious organizations in all AFLA programs in one form or another, the statute creates a symbolic and real partnership between clergy and fisc in addressing a problem with substantial religious overtones.

The application of the *Kendrick* decision has created confusion and frustration for mental health professionals. For adolescents, it surely must create confusion as well. Instead of being the comfortable "home remedy" it may seem, it shows teenagers that there is indeed a profound lack of consensus about how to help them travel from childhood to adulthood with health and emotional stability. Depending on where an adolescent goes for counseling, he or she may receive quite contradictory advice. All the advice will be legally permissible to render, but unfortunately not all of it will be within the boundaries of knowledge applied by science and psychology. The adage that good intentions are not good enough is relevant, for if they were, perhaps the discipline of psychiatry would be needed far less than it is.

At any rate, the right of minors to bear a child or to terminate a pregnancy without parental, governmental, or judicial consent belongs to those adolescents who are competent to make what a court considers sound decisions. If an adolescent was found incompetent because of mental illness or retardation, the parents have the right to consent for abortion. Once the incapacity has been established, the doctor or the institution may rely on the consent of the relative to prescribe an abortion, and if the relative is unavailable the facility must obtain judicial approval for the medical procedure.[11]

Rights are always accompanied by responsibilities. Thus, if an adolescent becomes pregnant and gives birth to a baby, she would be held responsible for the well-being of the newborn. Should she abandon her baby she may face the legal consequences of abandonment.[12] The rules that govern her concerning child abuse and neglect are the same as those that govern an adult mother.

Children's right to privacy, like many other constitutional rights for children, has limits. It can be curtailed by the government or by those who have authority and responsibility for the well-being of a child. For example, the First Amendment entitles adults to see and read materials generally deemed obscene and offensive. Children are denied such a constitutional right. In *Ginsberg v New York,*[13] the Supreme Court sided with the state of New York and found that New York had every right to control the conduct of its children and to determine what material a child might read and see. The distribution and sale of pornographic material and smutty magazines to individuals who are under the state's full age can constitutionally be prohibited.

Denial of the privacy right to children has been extended to other areas. For instance, children were found not to be entitled to enjoy the protection guaranteed in the Fourth Amendment of the Constitution, which secures the right of people to their belongings against unreasonable searches and seizures. This amendment goes so far as to prohibit issuing warrants for search and seizure unless there is probable cause supported by oath or affirmation, particularly describing the place to be searched and the persons or things to be seized. In ruling on this issue in *New Jersey v T.L.O.,*[14] the Supreme Court justices determined that children must remain under the supervision and the authority of the school in the parents' absence.

As regards *T.L.O.*, school authorities searched a student purse for cigarettes and found the cigarettes plus marijuana. A delinquency proceeding was initiated against the student in a juvenile court. The attorney for the student argued against the admissibility of the marijuana as evidence because the search and seizure was done without warrant and therefore the school violated the right of a citizen to the Fourth Amendment protection. The New Jersey Supreme Court agreed with the student's arguments and found the search of her purse illegal, concluding that the evidence could not be used against the minor. The case was appealed and eventually arrived at the US Supreme Court for final ruling. The government on behalf of New Jersey argued that a constitutional narrowing is necessary to reduce crime and disorder in school. Further, the teachers have a responsibility similar to parents and must have the authority to supervise the children. The majority of the Supreme Court justices sided with New Jersey and concluded that school children are not entitled to the same Fourth Amendment protection as adults.

Inconsistency characterizes the court rulings applying the Fourth Amendment privacy right to children. When the focus is on teenage pregnancy, the Supreme Court has refrained from involving others in the fundamental decision to terminate or continue a pregnancy. No rules, conditions, or guidelines were set forth to ensure that the young mother-to-be understands her responsibilities and the ramifications of parenthood. For issues unrelated to bodily integrity, children's right to privacy is narrower than adults', specifically as concerns their right to see and read pornography, and to be free from search and seizure. Except perhaps where they are most needed, for pregnant teenagers, limits rightly and humanely abridge children's Fourth Amendment right to privacy.

It is recognized that children still need protection against their own youth, so to speak, because they are not yet able to know what is in their best interest. It is hoped that these limits will help ensure that when they do reach their majority and receive the full benefits of the guarantee, they will have acquired the maturity to use them wisely.

CHILDREN AND PSYCHIATRIC TREATMENT

The law's concept of "the family" rests on a presumption that parents possess what a child lacks in maturity, experience, and capacity for judgment required for making life's difficult decisions. Thus it has recognized that the natural bonds of affection inspire parents to act in the best interests of their children. Some parents may at times act against the interests of their children, creating a basis for caution, but that is hardly justification to discard wholesale those pages of human experience that teach that parents generally do act in the child's best interest.

Against this backdrop appears the issue of children and the right to psychiatric treatment. The law has proved sensitive to those children who need medical or psychiatric treatment and care. It has not usurped the role of parents, however, and parental decisions have a substantial role in providing the care and treatment deemed necessary. If there is a conflict between the parental opinion and the state interest regarding psychiatric treatment of children, the parental authority supersedes the governmental power.

In *Parham v J.R.*[15] a constitutional right is handed to parents in dealing with children when the physical or mental health of the child is jeopardized. When a parent's decision is disagreeable to the child or involves a risk, decision making is not automatically transferred to a state agency or officer. Only when the child has been placed in the care of the state as a neglected child does the state maintain the authority and control of a natural parent.

The infant J.R. was found to be neglected at the age of 3 months. Thereafter he was raised in various foster homes and eventually was transferred to a Georgia state mental hospital because of abnormal behavior and the inability of the foster parents to maintain care for him. Georgia statute provides for admission of a child on the application of a parent or guardian to a state mental facility if the superintendent of the hospital finds evidence of mental illness and the child is suitable for treatment. No specific procedures, such as hearing tests, are mandated.

Child rights advocates brought a class action suit against the Georgia statute on behalf of J.R. and other children similarly situated, claiming that children are entitled to the same due process of law as adults before being committed to psychiatric hospitals by their parents or guardians, and also that they should be placed in a less confining environment. The lower court ruled in favor of the advocates, maintaining that Georgia's statute is unconstitutional.

The appeal process led to the US Supreme Court and the Court reversed the decision, ruling that Georgia statutes for admitting children for treatment in a state mental hospital are reasonable and consistent with constitutional guarantees, and further that no formal adversarial hearing is necessary prior to a voluntary admission of a child by his parents to a mental hospital. Once a child is placed in an institution, however, there should be a "neutral factfinder" to determine whether the child is properly placed and whether there is a continuing need for commitment. This neutral fact-finder is presumed to be the medical-psychiatric team at the hospital.

The language in *Parham* indicates that the parents have the right to hospitalize their minor children for psychiatric treatment without judicial review and the child's liberty interest is protected by being subject to an independent medical review.

Once a child has been admitted to a psychiatric hospital, it is within the authority of the professional to decide which treatment course is most suitable for the child. Parents cannot dictate to the medical and psychiatric professionals the course and style of the treatment. Further, minors who are voluntarily committed by their parents to psychiatric facilities, unlike adults, have no constitutional right to the least restrictive environment. Neither the parents nor the child have a constitutional right to communicate with one another in contravention of a no-communication rule that was established for therapeutic and medically legitimate reasons in *Doe v Public Health Trust of Dade County*.[16]

The *Doe* decision is interesting in that it shows how the court relies on professional opinions and methods in treating children. John Doe voluntarily admitted his daughter Jane to an adolescent psychiatric ward for a 1-week evaluation. The treatment plan for Jane required, among other things, that she should earn all her privileges, including the right to communicate with her parents in person or in writing. After 1 month, Jane still had not earned any privileges. Her parents by this time were getting impatient. They tried to restore communication with Jane in spite of psychiatric staff advice. The hospital officials kept rebuffing the parents' efforts to visit with their child. The parents then brought a lawsuit alleging that they and their daughter were deprived of their constitutional rights by the hospital, due to the hospital's no-communication rule. The issues that the court had to decide were whether the child became de facto an involuntary patient after admission to a psychiatric hospital, and whether the no-communication rule was entirely nontherapeutic and therefore medically illegitimate.

In a per curiam opinion, the Federal Appeals Court for the Eleventh Circuit, after reviewing previous cases determined by the US Supreme Court such as *Donaldson v O'Connor* and *Parham v J.R.*, ruled that the least restrictive requirements would not apply when minors have been voluntarily committed by their parents. The court concluded, additionally, that the parents did not have a right to decide what medical care and treatment their child should receive without a compelling state interest. The no-communication rule for therapeutic purposes was deemed a valid therapeutic method as long as it does not depart from acceptable professional methods, as the Supreme Court noted and set standards for in *Youngberg v Romeo*.[17]

Children therefore retain a right equal to adults in having access to help from mental health institutions. This right is exercised only through their parents or another party, however, and once a child enters an institution his or her right to a certain degree of self-determination is far less than an adult's. A neutral fact-finder is expected to make decisions in the child's best interests. Furthermore, a child's parents have less right to oversee and accept or reject their child's treatment than an adult patient would exercise over his own.

THE RIGHT TO DUE PROCESS
AND EQUAL PROTECTION

No state shall "deprive any person of life, liberty, or property without due process of law; nor deny to any person within its jurisdiction the equal protection of the laws," declares the Fourteenth Amendment to the Constitution. Although the Fourteenth Amendment was passed in the years following the Civil War, over the decades it has been broadened by judicial interpretation to become an important instrument in the continuing defense of the civil rights and individual liberties of all Americans. Its due process clause is regarded as protecting from state invasion almost all rights guaranteed in the Bill of Rights. The equal protection clause has been invoked to integrate schools and outlaw a multitude of individual discriminatory acts.

As citizens of the United States, children are entitled to these protections, but in a limited degree. The differences and the similarities between children and adults in this context are strikingly portrayed in criminal proceedings. One of the earliest such cases was the landmark *Application of Paul L. Gault & Marjorie Gault*,[18] in which these issues were extensively explored and decided for the first time.

> Gerald Gault, who lived in an Arizona town, was 15 years old at the time of his arrest. Motivated by emerging sexual impulses, he made lewd telephone calls to a woman in the neighborhood. He was charged with breaking the law and appeared in court for what was supposed to be an evidentiary hearing. No witnesses appeared against him except the arresting police officer and a probation officer who gave the neighbor's version of the case. The probation officer's testimony was hearsay, which is not supposed to be admissible in courts of law in such situations. Moreover, no lawyer was present in the proceeding. The judge committed Gerald Gault as a juvenile delinquent to a state school until he reached the age of 21. The statute applicable to those proceedings did not permit an appeal. Gault's parents petitioned first the federal court and then the US Supreme Court for a writ of habeas corpus.

The Supreme Court decided that neither the Bill of Rights nor the Fourteenth Amendment was exclusively for adults. Those constitutional rights apply equally to juveniles in quasi-criminal proceedings wherein their freedom is at stake. In hearings, the juvenile court must meet the standards of essential due process and fair treatment. This means that every juvenile has the right to assistance of counsel, notice of hearing, right to confront witnesses, protection against the use of hearsay, right to refuse to testify against oneself, and the right to be questioned by police only after the notification of the child's parents and then only in a nonthreatening environment.

As the number of delinquency cases increased, however, the courts began to narrow the constitutional rights of delinquent children. Approximately 15 years after the *Gault* case, the Supreme Court wrestled to define and refine the rights of children in criminal proceedings against the right of the state in its duty to protect citizens in *Schall v Martin*.[19] The court decided that although due process is applicable in juvenile proceedings, there must be differences between how it is applied to children and to adults.

> Gregory Martin was arrested on December 13, 1977 and charged with first-degree robbery, second-degree assault, and criminal possession of a weapon based on an incident in which he, with two others, allegedly hit a youth on the head with a loaded gun and stole his jacket and sneakers. Martin was 14 years old at the time and therefore came within the jurisdiction of New York's family court. A petition of delinquency was filed. The family court judge held that Martin lacked supervision and ordered that he be detained. Under prevailing law at that time, a probable cause hearing was held five days later and eventually Martin was found guilty of the robbery and criminal possession charges. He was adjudicated a delinquent and placed on 2 years' probation. Martin was detained for a total of 15 days between the initial appearance and the completion of the fact-finding hearing.
>
> On Dec 21, 1977, still in preventive detention and pending his fact-finding hearing, Gregory Martin instituted a habeas corpus class action on behalf of those persons who were, or during the pendency of this action would be, preventively detained. As several constitutional issues were involved in this case, it eventually arrived at the US Supreme Court for final ruling.

The Supreme Court justices found that undoubtedly the due process clause is applicable in juvenile proceedings. However, the precise impact of the due process requirement on such proceedings should be ascertained. The majority noted that certain basic constitutional protections enjoyed by adults accused of crimes also apply to juveniles, such as notice of charges, right to counsel, privilege against self-incrimination, right to confront and cross-examine[18] the safeguard against double jeopardy,[20] and finally proof beyond a reasonable doubt.[21] At the same time, the Constitution does not mandate elimination of all differences in the treatment of juveniles; for example, lack of right to trial by jury in juvenile cases,[22] or the right of the state in preserving and promoting the welfare of the child.[23]

While the similarities are many, the two differences cited above are substantial enough to allow the assertion that a juvenile proceeding is fundamentally different from an adult criminal trial, and from a constitutional perspective there is no mandate to eliminate all such differences in the treatment of juveniles. Children, in the view of the Supreme Court justices, are assumed to be subject to control by their parents and if parental control falters, the state must play its parens patriae role.

Preventive detention is thus more widely accepted as used against juveniles. It is deemed, under statute, to serve the legitimate objective, held in common with every state, of protecting both the juvenile and society from the hazards of pretrial crime. This objective is compatible with the fundamental fairness demanded by the due process clause for juvenile proceedings. Pretrial detention need not be considered punishment merely because a juvenile is subsequently discharged subject to conditions or put on probation. Even when a case is terminated prior to fact-finding, it does not follow that the decision to detain the youth amounts to due process violation.

The three dissenting justices in *Schall* voiced the concern that pretrial detention of a juvenile inflicts injuries comparable to those associated with the imprisonment of an adult. In both situations, the detainees suffer stigmatization and severe limitation of their freedom of movement. Juveniles subjected to preventive detention may come to see society at large as an enemy, hostile and oppressive, and to regard themselves as irremediably delinquent, or conversely as outrageously victimized. In summary, preventive detention constitutes punishment before adjudication of guilt, a clear violation of the due process clause. When the *Gault* case was heard in 1967, a liberal atmosphere was assuming prominence in the nation and the Supreme Court reflected this trend. The rights of criminal defendants received much sympathetic attention. "Criminal defendant" had almost come to imply "victim of the system." Then as this overzealousness subsided, the stage was set for the return to a more moderate political dynamic. Criminals were once again seen as people who failed the system, and not vice versa. As the *Schall* case demonstrates, courts were less hesitant to limit the due process rights of juvenile defendants.

ON PUNISHMENT AND EIGHTH AMENDMENT RIGHTS

Punishment as a means of disciplining wrongdoers has accompanied every step of human development. To this day, corporal punishment in public schools is not uncommon. Indeed, the general opinion indicates that a majority of teachers and parents favor a moderate use of corporal punishment. The practice of corporal punishment still continues to play a role in the public education of schoolchildren in most parts of the United States, although a few states have prohibited corporal punishment through legislation. There is no trend toward its elimination in those states where legislatures have not acted against it, however, and state courts have uniformly preserved the common law rule permitting teachers to use reasonable force in disciplining children in their charge.

Whether or not corporal punishment actually violates the constitutional rights of children, the issue was once strongly debated by the US Supreme Court in *Ingraham v Wright*.[24] Petitioner Ingraham et al, pupils in a Dade County, Florida, junior high school, filed an action alleging that petitioners and other students had been subjected to disciplinary corporal punishment in violation of their constitutional rights. The Florida statute then in effect authorized corporal punishment after the teacher had consulted with the principal, but specified that the punishment was not to be degrading or unduly severe. A school board regulation, which contained specific directions and limitations, authorized corporal punishment administered to a recalcitrant student's buttocks with a wooden paddle. The petitioners presented evidence showing that the paddling of the pupils was excessively harsh. Initially, the case was dismissed in a lower court but eventually found its way to the Supreme Court on the constitutional issue of whether the cruel and unusual punishment clause of the Eighth Amendment applies to disciplinary corporal punishment in public school or not.

The Eighth Amendment specifies that "Excessive bail shall not be required, nor excessive fines imposed, nor cruel and unusual punishments inflicted." The Supreme Court found that these three issues—bail, fines, and punishment—traditionally have been associated with the criminal process, and that these do not apply to the paddling of children as a means of maintaining discipline in public schools. In the reasoning of the majority of justices, the schoolchildren have little need for the protection of the Eighth Amendment because the school is an open institution and the child is invariably free to return home and discuss the events of the school day frankly. The openness of the public school and its supervision by the community afford significant safeguards against the kinds of abuses from which the Eighth Amendment protects incarcerated criminals. Public school teachers and administrators are privileged under common law to inflict only such corporal punishment as is reasonably necessary for the proper education and discipline of the child. While schoolchildren do not need the protections of the Eighth Amendment to prevent excessive corporal punishment, according to the Constitution, the states may legislate their own rules if they choose to do so. Furthermore, it is clear that the Supreme Court gives to the teacher authority similar to parents in disciplining children, and that the same limits apply. For example, parents and school authorities are allowed to ground children and spank them.

The corporal punishment issues and the lack of rights under the Eighth Amendment divided the Supreme Court justices, and the four dissenting justices protested strongly. They stated that the Eighth Amendment places a flat prohibition against the infliction of "cruel and unusual punishment." That the framers of our Constitution did not choose to insert the word "criminal" into the language of the Eighth Amendment is strong evidence that the amendment was designed to prohibit all inhumane or barbaric punishment, no matter what the nature of the offense for which the punishment is imposed. The dissenters continued that if some punishments are so barbaric that they cannot be imposed for the commission of crimes designated by our social system, similar punishments may not be imposed on persons for less culpable acts, such as breaches of school discipline.

One of the most controversial issues now being debated involves a practice considered by some as below the standard of decency: the application of the death penalty to juveniles, and the related phenomenon of condemning to death on attainment of adulthood those who have committed heinous crimes while under the legal age. Lewis et al[25] have noted that the execution of juveniles in America dates back to the seventeenth century, when a child was executed for the crime of bestiality, and since then 272 juveniles have been executed. However, the last execution of a person for a crime committed while under the age of 16 was in January 1948, when Louisiana executed a juvenile named Mattio, who was 15 at the time of his crime. Not until 1988, when the Supreme Court struggled with the issue while deciding *Thompson v Oklahoma*,[26] were such executions prohibited. In a plurality of opinion, the Court barred execution of inmates who were under the age of 16 years. In *Thompson*, petitioner William Wayne Thompson was 15 years old when he actively participated in a brutal murder and killed his former brother-in-law, evidently because of physical abuse of his sister. As Thompson was a child, the district attorney filed a statutory petition seeking that he be tried as an adult, which the trial court granted. Thompson was then convicted and sentenced to death.

The US Supreme Court granted certiorari to the Court of Criminal Appeals of Oklahoma, and four justices concluded that the Eighth Amendment prohibits the execution of a person who was under 16 years of age at the time of his or her offense. And one justice (O'Connor) agreed that Thompson's death sentence must be set aside but on the ground that states may not execute persons for crimes committed at the age of 15 or younger under the authority of capital punishment statutes, such as the state of Oklahoma's, that specify no minimum age.

The majority of Supreme Court justices noted that the death penalty is said to serve two principal social purposes: retribution and deterrence of capital crimes by prospective offenders. Given the lesser culpability of juvenile offenders, teenagers' capacity for growth, and society's fiduciary obligations to its children, the retributive function is simply inapplicable to the execution of a 15-year-old offender. And for such a young offender, the deterrence rationale is equally unacceptable. The Supreme Court justices noted that about 98% of the arrests for willful homicide involved persons who were over 16 at the time of the offense. Excluding younger persons, therefore, from the class that is eligible for the death penalty will not diminish the deterrent value of capital punishment for the vast majority of potential offenders.

The Court further expounded on the potential deterrent value of the death sentence with respect to those under 16 years of age, stating that it is obviously insignificant for two reasons. First, the likelihood that a teenage offender has made the kind of cost-benefit analysis that attaches any weight to the possibility of execution is so remote as to be virtually nonexistent. Second, even if one posits such a cold-blooded calculation by a 15-year-old, it is fanciful to believe that the youth would be deterred by the knowledge that a small number of persons his age have been executed during the twentieth century. In short, the court was not persuaded that the imposition of the death penalty for offenses committed by persons under 16 years of age has made, or can be expected to make, any measurable contribution to the goals that capital punishment is intended to achieve. It is therefore nothing more than the purposeless and needless imposition of pain and suffering and thus an unconstitutional punishment.

The three dissenting justices noted that the statistics about executions demonstrate nothing except the fact that our society has always believed that executions of 15-year-old criminals should be rare. They contended that this general belief provides no rational basis for the supposition that no one so much as a day under 16 can ever be mature and morally responsible enough to deserve that penalty. The dissenters further held that there is no justification, except our own predilection, for converting a rare statistical occurrence into an absolute constitutional ban. In the view of the dissenters, the prohibition against cruel and unusual punishment was not originally intended to ban execution of juveniles and thereby limit the evolving standards of decency appropriate for our consideration to those entertained by the society rather than those dictated by our personal consciences.

The whole gamut of issues regarding children and the Constitution presents a mirror image of the uncertainties and identity confusion of society at large. In just two decades, vacillations from extreme liberalism to strong conservatism mean that children today grow up with quite different values and expectations than the former generation. It seems that the due process issue is still settling down, and it is hoped it will take a moderate form after recovering from the conservative reaction to the prior liberalism. A broad, general discomfort with issues related to sexuality continues to plague our society, and children certainly absorb this uneasiness. Behind a mask of solicitousness about bodily integrity, girls are denied social reinforcement of parental guidance regarding pregnancy, abortion, and contraception, even if they are just entering puberty, yet school papers may be restrained from printing articles earnestly addressing problems of teen sexuality.

Children and adults have different needs—emotional, physical, and constitutional. In allowing differences in constitutional interpretation for children, the Supreme Court simply addresses reality. Consistency has been found by psychologists and psychiatrists to be one of children's greatest emotional needs, and much has been said and written advising parents to be as consistent as possible. Perhaps society at large can serve the interests of its future generations by heeding that advice and creating greater consistency in its approach to children and their constitutional rights.

REFERENCES

1. *Tinker v Desmoines Independent School* 1969; 393 US 503.
2. *Bethel School District No. 403 v Matthew Fraser (a minor) and E. L. Fraser, guardian ad litem* 1986; No. 84-1667.
3. *Hazelwood School District v Kuhlmeier* 1988; No 86-836.
4. *Board of Education v Pico* 1982; 457 US 853, 871–872.
5. *Planned Parenthood of Central Missouri v Danforth* 1976; 428 US 52.
6. *Bellotti v Baird* 1979; 443 US 622.
7. *H.L. v Matheson* 1981; 450 US 398.
8. *Cary v Population Services International Inc* 1977; 431 US 678.
9. *Brown and Others v Chan Kendrick* 1988; No. 87-253 (decided June 29, 1988). *The United States Law Week* 1988:56 LW 4818.
10. *Adolescent Family Life Act* [AFLA] Pub L No. 97-35, 95 Stat 578.
11. *In re Barbara C.* 1984; 474 NYS2d 799.
12. Ratner R: A case of child abandonment; reflection on criminal responsibility in adolescence. *Bul Am Acad Psychiatry Law* 1985;13:291–301.
13. *Ginsberg v New York* 1968; 390 US 629.
14. *New Jersey v T.L.O.* 1985; 105 Sup Ct 733.
15. *Parham v J.R.* 1979; 422 US 584.
16. *Doe v Public Health Trust of Dade County* 1983; 696 F2d 901 (11th Cir).
17. *Youngberg v Romeo* 1982; 102 S Ct 2452.
18. *Application of Paul L. Gault & Majorie Gault* 1967; 387 US 1.
19. *Schall v Martin* 1984; 104 S Ct 2403.
20. *Breed v Jones* 1975; 421 US 519.
21. *In re Winship* 1970; 397 US 358.
22. *McKeiver v Pennsylvania* 1971; 403 US 528.
23. *Santosky v Kramer* 1982; 455 US 745.
24. *Ingraham v Wright* 1977; 430 US 651.
25. Lewis DO, et al: Neuropsychiatric, psychoeducational family characteristics of 14 juvenile offenders condemned to death in the U.S. *Am J Psychiatry* 1988; 145:584–589.
26. *Thompson v Oklahoma* 1988; No. 86-6169 (June 29, 1988).

12

The Rights of Handicapped Children

The concept of the rights of handicapped children is relatively new, having existed in American law for only the past ten to 15 years. Federal legislation providing funding for research in the area of education for handicapped persons was passed as early as the mid-1960s.[1] However, it was not until the Rehabilitation Act of 1973 (29 U.C.S.), which prohibits discrimination against otherwise qualified handicapped persons in programs conducted by or receiving funds from the federal government, that Congress addressed the substantive rights of handicapped children. Regulations issued under SECTION 504 of the Rehabilitation Act require schools receiving federal financial assistance to provide a "free appropriate public education" to each qualified handicapped person who is in the recipient's jurisdiction, regardless of the nature or severity of the person's handicap. Even so, however, it soon became clear that large numbers of handicapped children were still receiving either inadequate educational services or no educational services at all.

The Education for All Handicapped Children Act, which was passed by Congress in 1975, authorized "annual appropriate public education" to those children who suffer from mental retardation, learning disabilities, physical handicaps, or who are emotionally disturbed. The Education for All Handicapped Children Act (EAHCA) was designed to provide the funds allowing states to implement programs and services for the handicapped in fulfillment of the promise of equal educational opportunity.[2]

Although the scope of this legislation and the regulations promulgated under it were quite broad, litigation over substantive and procedural rights granted to handicapped children has been relatively contained.

RIGHT TO EDUCATION

The US Supreme Court has recognized and ruled that government at federal, state, and local levels should provide personalized instruction and adequate supportive services to ensure that handicapped children actually benefit from their education. Amy Rowley was a gifted but deaf student with minimal residual hearing and excellent lip reading skills. As required by EAHCA, an Individualized Educational Program (IEP) was designed for Amy to meet her unique needs, the preparation of which included special services and an instructor. The IEP also included a hearing amplifier, the services of a special tutor for one hour each day, and a speech therapist. Amy's parents demanded that a qualified sign language interpreter be added to her IEP. The school authorities refused to grant their demand. Amy's parents then filed a lawsuit in federal district court alleging the denial of a free appropriate education. Eventually, the case was heard by the New Jersey Supreme Court.[3] The court reviewed the EAHCA and noted that under the statutory scheme, "special education" and "related services" are essential to the education of handicapped children. "Special education" as defined in the EAHCA means "specially designed instruction, at no cost to parents . . . to meet the unique needs of a handicapped child, including classroom instruction, instruction in physical education, home instruction, and instruction in hospitals and institutions." "Related services" is defined as "transportation, and such developmental, corrective and other supportive services . . . as may be required to assist a handicapped child to benefit from special education."

The court held that Amy Rowley was not entitled to a sign language interpreter to help maximize her educational potential since she was already receiving a number of special services that allowed her to outperform the average child in her class. The court noted also that Congress intended to bring previously excluded handicapped children into the states' public education systems and to require the states to adopt procedures effecting individualized consideration of and instruction for each child. There was no language in the EAHCA creating a substantive standard prescribing the level of education to be accorded handicapped children, and most particularly, no language which required the local governments to maximize handicapped children's potential commensurate with the opportunity provided to other children.

RIGHT TO PSYCHOTHERAPY

Under the EAHCA, states are not required to provide medical services for purposes other than diagnosis or evaluation. Psychiatric treatment or psychotherapy, if performed by a psychiatrist, can be viewed as medical treatment, in which case the state would have no obligation to pay for such services. In the landmark case of *Piscataway v T.G.*,[4] a New Jersey school board argued that it need not pay for a student's psychotherapy because the therapy was administered by a social worker under a psychiatrist's supervision and was therefore a medical service.

The case was heard by the United States Court of Appeals for the Third Circuit. The court of appeals ruled that psychological counseling is included in the definition of "related services," provided such counseling is necessary for a child to benefit from his or her educational program and is not a purely "medical service." If the child would effectively be denied the opportunity to benefit from his education without the counseling, the mere fact that the service could in other contexts be classified as a medical service does not preclude its inclusion as a "related service" under the provisions of the EAHCA. The US Supreme Court refused to hear this case and review the decision of the court of appeals. The *T.G.* case indicated, however, that if the same kind of psychotherapy is provided by a child psychiatrist, the state could refuse to pay for the service from public funds.

RIGHT TO FACILITATE
THE LEARNING PROCESS

The US Supreme Court has established parameters within which different kinds of services should be evaluated (eg, health services provided by a nurse as distinguished from services provided by a physician). In the case of *Irving Independent School District v Tatro*,[5] the Supreme Court unanimously concluded that an 8-year-old child with spina bifida must be provided with intermittent catheterization services to enable her to empty her bladder during the school day. The Court noted that the procedure was simple and could be performed by a nurse rather than a physician, and therefore it fell under "related services" as provided in EAHCA. The Supreme Court noted further that if catheterization was not provided to the student, she could not attend school, thus denying her the benefits of a public education. The Court ruled that any service which enabled a handicapped child to remain at school during the day is an important means of providing the child with the meaningful access to education as intended by Congress.

In another recent case, the Court held that the transportation of a handicapped child to another facility with personnel better qualified to train the student is at the discretion not of the parents but of the school authorities. The United States Court of Appeals for the Ninth Circuit, in *Wilson v Marana Unified School District of Pima County*,[6] affirmed the lower court's decision. Jessica Wilson had cerebral palsy. She was of normal intelligence but had difficulty in learning. Due to the child's failure to improve after receiving remedial teaching, the school authorities elected to send her to a different school 30 minutes away, so she could benefit there from a special education teacher certified in physical disabilities. Jessica's parents objected to the plan, arguing that EAHCA did not require the state to provide handicapped children with the best possible education. As long as their daughter received adequate local education, the parents felt, her educational needs were satisfied.

The Court rejected the parents' contention. In the Court's view, "It may be true that the EAHCA does not require the state to provide handicapped children with the best education possible. This does not mean, however, that the states do not have the power to provide handicapped children with an education which they consider more appropriate than that proposed by the parents." The Court thus supported the school authorities and acknowledged that deference to their judgment may be advisable in connection with the question of what constitutes appropriate education for handicapped children.

EXPULSION FROM SCHOOL

School authorities face a dilemma when a handicapped child exhibits behavioral problems, especially aggressivity. Opting for expulsion is hardly the simple solution it might seem. In fact, most of the time it will be legally unacceptable. Expulsion, obviously, would entail a change of placement and therefore violate the provision of the EAHCA which bars state or local officials from unilaterally excluding handicapped children from the classroom for disruptive or dangerous conduct resulting from their disabilities. Handicapped children may be expelled, however, if their misbehavior is properly determined not to be a manifestation of their handicap. As the court has noted in *Doe v Maher*,[7] behavior problems are not a monopoly of the emotionally disturbed, and there is no justification for exempting handicapped children from expulsion if their misbehavior did not result from a handicapping condition.

In *Doe*, two emotionally disturbed children with aggressive tendencies had been suspended indefinitely for aggressivity and misbehavior. After 30 days, one plaintiff was returned to school and the other was provided with a half-day of home tutoring. Doe sued. The federal district court held that the plaintiffs' damage claims against the state under EAHCA were barred by the Eleventh Amendment to the Constitution. Damages could nevertheless be sought from the local school district. The plaintiffs Doe finally settled their damages claim against the school district for $1600 each. (Since then, the Rehabilitation Act Amendment of 1986 has altered the law, stating specifically that a state shall not be immune under the Eleventh Amendment from suit in federal court for a violation of Sec 504 of the Rehabilitation Act.[8])

The Ninth Circuit Court struck down the state law permitting a local school district to exclude from attendance any child whose physical or mental disability made him dangerous to other pupils. In the court's view, expulsion or exclusion from regular classes constitutes a change in placement, which in turn means that the procedural requirement and safeguards established under

EAHCA must be taken into consideration prior to any placement changes. Further, the court made it clear that the child must remain in his or her current educational placement during review proceedings. The court contended that school officials dealing with misbehaving handicapped children were free to use reasonable discipline that would not deprive the children of an appropriate education. These alternative disciplinary measures are the same ones that teachers and principals have traditionally used to maintain order in the classroom, including fixed and temporary periods of suspension of up to 30 days, but not indefinite expulsions or exclusions.

Finally *Doe* was heard by the US Supreme Court, which affirmed the Ninth Circuit's ruling. The highest court also refused to impose a "dangerousness" exception onto this provision because it found that Congress had deliberately omitted such an emergency exception. Under the EAHCA's implemention regulations, however, school officials are permitted to temporarily suspend a student who poses an immediate threat to the safety of others for up to ten school days.[9]

The essence of the court's ruling is that aggressive handicapped students should bear no extra stigma of dangerousness. Additionally, because of their disadvantaged condition, more precautions must be taken before imposing disciplinary action on them.

RIGHT TO LIVE IN THE COMMUNITY IN A GROUP HOME

Discrimination against handicapped children and especially against those with mental retardation is deeply rooted in this society. It was not uncommon for a community or even a state law to exclude retarded handicapped persons from public school, to permit their involuntary sterilization, and to deny them the right to marry. It has even been accepted and allowed to exclude such persons from living in communities near their families and friends.

Now this bastion of discrimination against retarded handicapped people has been eliminated by the US Supreme Court. No longer can affluent communities wave ordinance zoning laws to exclude a group home for the mentally retarded from an area zoned for apartment houses or other congregate living facilities. If an ordinance excludes retarded handicapped persons from group housing in their community, it simply violates the constitutional right of those who have been affected. In the view of the Supreme Court, retarded people retain substantive constitutional rights in addition to the right to be treated equally under the law. Retarded people cannot be excluded from a community based on fear, false stereotypes, and prejudice.

This decision was unanimously rendered by the Supreme Court justices in the *Cleburne Living Center* (CLC) case.[10] The center intended to lease a building in the city of Cleburne, Texas, to operate a group home for 13 mentally retarded people supervised by a staff. The city informed the center that it had to obtain a special permit under zoning regulations governing the construction of a special facility for feeble-minded persons. The permit was refused. In response, the CLC filed suit in federal court and the case proceeded to the US Supreme Court since there was a question of the constitutional status of laws that discriminated against mentally retarded persons, with the discrimination being highlighted by the fact that the city of Cleburne had earlier issued a permit for a nursing home without applying the ordinance regulation.

By a nine-to-zero vote, the justices concluded that the ordinance was unconstitutional because it required a group home to obtain a special use permit, while similar group living arrangements such as nursing homes or fraternity houses needed no such permit. The court held that the denial of the permit was based on irrational prejudice against mentally retarded people. The *Cleburne* decision thus involved two fundamental issues: (1) the ability of communities to exclude retarded people by means of discriminatory zoning laws; and (2) the level of protection the Constitution affords retarded people against discriminatory laws in general.

The highest court found that the requirement for the special permit violated the equal protection clause of the Fourteenth Amendment. The special use permit was found deficient because it required compliance by a group home for mentally retarded residents, but not by other communal living situations. The differences between mentally retarded people and people who would be found in other residential situations such as nursing homes or fraternal orders were irrelevant to any legitimate concerns the city claimed. The city of Cleburne, in this case, provided no rational basis to support the belief that the group home would pose a special threat to the city's legitimate interests. The justices dismissed the city's purported concern about such factors as the size and location of the group home, or the proximity of a junior high school, or about the legal responsibility for actions which the mentally retarded residents might take, as well as fire safety, congestion, and the serenity of the neighborhood. In each instance, the Court concluded that the city's purported concerns were a smoke screen for prejudice and unconstitutional discrimination. The court once more reiterated the opinion, articulated in other discrimination cases, that " . . . private biases may be outside the reach of the law, but the law cannot directly or indirectly give them effect."

Although all nine justices found that the city ordinance was unconstitutional, they split on the basis for unconstitutionality and the test for unconstitutionality of the issue in question. Six justices felt that the rational basis test can be adopted to rule on the *Cleburne* case, while the minority of three sided with the amicus brief that was presented to the court by various professional organizations. The brief stated that the case is entitled to the special constitutional protection, and "heightened scrutiny" must be used in the determination of issues related to discrimination against mentally retarded people.

ATTORNEYS' FEES IN
EAHCA ALLEGATIONS

The question of who should pay attorneys' fees in EAHCA cases has remained unresolved. The US Supreme Court in *Smith v Robinson*[11] denied a request that the attorney's fees be part of the settlement. In this case the parents of Tommy Smith, a child with cerebral palsy, were informed by the local school that the school would no longer fund Tommy's special education. The parents brought a lawsuit and won their case. The court also awarded attorney's fees to the parents. The US Court of Appeals for the First Circuit reversed the decision, holding that the EAHCA does not provide for the payment of legal fees to the prevailing plaintiff. Eventually the case was heard by the Supreme Court. The highest court concluded that the plaintiffs would not be entitled to attorney's fees because whether the right to a free appropriate public education is available to a handicapped child hinges on either the EAHCA or the equal protection clause of the Fourteenth Amendment. But as the exclusive avenue through which the child and the parents or guardian can pursue their claim, the EAHCA does not provide for attorneys' fees.

After the *Smith* case, in which the Supreme Court barred the award of attorneys' fees in litigation brought under the EAHCA, President Reagan signed into law on August 5, 1986 the Handicapped Children's Protective Act of 1985,[12] which provides courts with the discretion to award reasonable attorneys' fees to the parents or guardians of handicapped children who have prevailed in lawsuits under the EAHCA.

CRITICALLY ILL CHILDREN

The "Baby Doe" Cases

Congress passed the Child Abuse Amendment Law[13] to prevent the withholding of treatment from infants born with mental or physical impairments. In the first section of the statute, Congress prohibited any failure to report an infant's life-threatening condition caused or aggravated by the withholding of medically indicated treatment (including appropriate nutrition, hydration, and medication) which, in the treating physician's reasonable medical judgment, would be most likely to ameliorate or correct all such conditions.[14]

Exceptions were permitted to the foregoing prohibition, however. The following conditions, if found by the treating physician, could obviate treatment: (1) the infant is chronically and irreversibly comatose; (2) the treatment would merely prolong dying, would not correct all of the infant's life-threatening conditions, or would be futile in helping the infant survive; (3) the treatment would be futile in terms of the infant's survival and the treatment "itself under such circumstances would be inhumane."

Second, the new law required each state's child protective agency to develop a system to respond to reports of medical neglect of infants. Each must have a system in place to: (1) have appropriate health care facilities designate staff members to handle cases of suspected neglect and facilitate notification by those individuals; (2) coordinate and consult with those designated individuals within the appropriate health care facilities; and (3) authorize the state's child protective services agency to pursue legal remedies to prevent the withholding of treatment from disabled infants.

Finally, the law provides that the Secretary of Health and Human Services is authorized to make grants to states for the development and implementation of information and education and training programs to improve services to disabled infants with life-threatening conditions.

In accordance with the above doctrine, the Supreme Court, in the so-called Baby Doe case,[15] held that if the parents of the critically ill infant consent to the withholding of treatment, there is no violation of the statute. In *Bowen*, the parents of a congenitally defective child refused to give physicians their consent to operate on their infant. The applicable statutes and regulations, however, required the hospital not to withhold medical treatment for handicapped infants solely on the basis of their present or anticipated mental and physical impairments. When the American Hospital Association objected to the implementation of these regulations, its position was upheld in federal district court and the court of appeals. Next, the US Supreme Court agreed to hear and rule on the government's appeal. The Supreme Court decided that a hospital cannot be in violation of the statute or regulation for withholding treatment from an infant if it has parental consent. The Court held that indeed it would almost certainly be a tort as a matter of law to operate on an infant without parental consent.

Children Afflicted with AIDS

The Centers for Disease Control (CDC) defines pediatric acquired immunodeficiency syndrome (AIDS) as occurring in a child younger than 13 years[16] who has had (1) a history of risk factors associated with AIDS, (2) evidence of human immunodeficiency virus (HIV) infection (antibody or viral isolation), and (3) evidence of immunodeficiency (hypergammaglobulinemia or T cell immunodeficiency).[17] The number of children who fit these criteria continues to rise. Transmission of HIV to children occurs primarily via maternal transfer of the virus (approximately 80% of the cases), and transmission of the virus through blood products (approximately 15% of the cases). The remaining 5% of cases could occur as a result of vaginal secretions, sexual contact, and possibly breast-feeding.[18]

Children at risk fall into six basic categories: (1) infants of infected mothers, (2) recipients of blood transfusions prior to 1985, (3) hemophiliacs, (4) sexually abused children, (5) intravenous drug abusers, and (6) homosexuals.[19]

The incubation period for AIDS is from 6 to 12 weeks, but asymptomatic periods may last for 4 or more years. Clinical manifestations of AIDS in children include opportunistic infection, bacterial infection, failure to thrive, parotitis, lymphoid interstitial pneumonitis, central nervous system abnormalities, dysmorphic syndrome, and hypergammaglobulinemia plus abnormal T cell function.[20]

Under the law, children with AIDS are considered handicapped individuals. Thus they are protected by law against discrimination under the Rehabilitation Act.[21] Handicapped, in legal terms, means (1) those who have a physical or mental impairment which substantially limits one or more of such person's major life activities, (2) those who have a record of such an impairment, or (3) those who are regarded as having such an impairment.

Under this definition of handicapped, both AIDS carriers and those actually afflicted with AIDS are protected from discrimination. Handicapped children, including those having AIDS, must by law be educated alongside nonhandicapped students in a normal school setting. In an attempt to provide a normal educational experience for as many handicapped children as possible, the law goes further and requires that before removing any handicapped child from normal school classes, an opportunity must be given to contest suspension, expulsion, or protective isolation through specific due process standards, beginning at the administrative level and continuing, if necessary, in a court of law.[22]

Concerned parents of classmates of AIDS-afflicted children have argued that in a school setting, children with AIDS present a unique problem. For example, behavior that can result in the exchange of body fluids, such as fighting or sexual activity, is possible in the school environment and could create a contagious condition. Many states have therefore effected public health laws barring children with AIDS from school.

Generally, the courts have rejected the position of these parents. If a disease has not been proved contagious through proximity to the carrier of such disease, the carrier may not be excluded from his or her job in public places. As early as 1979, a court ruled that a child with hepatitis B could attend a New York public school, and that the school authorities could not separate that student from the others. Such a separation would be detrimental to the afflicted child's education and therefore illegal, affirmed the Second Circuit court.[23] Based on the policy provided in the Rehabilitation Act, removal of AIDS-afflicted children is not permitted. If the student is too ill to attend school, then the board of education must make available tutoring and other services in the home or hospital.

The first case regarding school children with AIDS was decided in New York City.[24] National attention focused on this test case, wherein New York City officials declared a policy of reviewing such students case by case to determine whether their health and development supported their attending school without restriction, rather than automatically excluding them from the public schools. The dispute arose originally when the health commissioner allowed a 7-year-old child with AIDS to go to school, and then kept the child's identity confidential.

The local community school board representing parents of other school-children filed a lawsuit to prevent the AIDS-afflicted child from attending the school, and to learn the child's identity. After hearing expert testimony, the court ruled that AIDS is a handicapped condition and that AIDS victims are protected under the law of the Rehabilitation Act, as Congress had not intended to exclude infection with contagious diseases as a handicap under the act.

In another well-publicized case,[25] the circuit court in Indiana lifted a restrictive order and allowed a child with AIDS to attend regular school classes. According to Indiana law, a student who has a contagious illness may be excluded from school until a physician certifies that the child poses no danger to other students. Ray White, the child in question, presented such a certi-fication. Thus the court ordered, over the objection of other parents, that the child should return to school and enjoy the same treatment as his classmates.

The psychosocial problems of children with AIDS, nevertheless, cannot be ultimately resolved by court order. In Ray White's case, for instance, townspeople slashed the tires of his family's car and pelted it with eggs. Schoolmates taunted him; someone fired a bullet through the living room window. Eventually the family left town and moved to Kokomo, Indiana.

The Justice Department considers AIDS victims to be handicapped peo-ple, making discrimination against them illegal in federal programs. The official statement of the Justice Department reads " . . . we have concluded that Section 504 of the Rehabilitation Act prohibits discrimination based on disability effects that AIDS and related conditions may have on prior victims . . . "[26]

It has become clear that the law prohibits school authorities from depriving a child of classroom education just because he or she has AIDS. Nevertheless, opponents to the presence of these children in classes have used the judicial system to thwart, if only temporarily, their attendance at school. For example, on the grounds of procedural due process, a child with AIDS can be kept out of school until authorities have had an opportunity to evaluate his or her condition. In the well-publicized New Jersey case, *Board of Education of the City of Planfield v Cooperman*,[27] two physicians specializing in AIDS certified that a 5-year-old child diagnosed as having AIDS was well enough to go to school. According to administration guidelines of the state of New Jersey, a student with AIDS or AIDS-related complex (ARC) should be permitted to attend regular school classes unless exceptional conditions exist (such as the child not being toilet-trained, or unable to control drooling, or violent). The opponents argued that a 30-day public notice and public hearing should be held in order to rule out the above conditions. The court conceded that such measures were appropriate. But eventually, after listening to witnesses, the court ruled that the child should be returned to school.

On appeal, the New Jersey Supreme Court approved regulations, submitted and promulgated by the state's commissioners of education and health, for determining the limited circumstances in which children with AIDS may be excluded from public school programs, and what due process procedures should be sustained during such determination. These regulations have had a national impact. They state that the board of education may exclude pupils in only very limited circumstances, and that the board bears the burden of proof therefor; that each party is entitled to submit evidence and the panel reviewing such evidence must render a written conclusion with supporting reasons and analysis included. Either party may then file an appeal with the commissioner based on written exception to issues of fact and law. The commissioner must then select one of three options: (1) have the pupil enrolled immediately, (2) confirm the board's decision to exclude the pupil from school, or (3) direct the case to the office of administrative law for further determination. The New Jersey Supreme Court concluded that this procedure satisfies constitutional due process concerns by creating the proper balance between the rights of the students with AIDS and the other students.[28]

The parents of a child with AIDS not only can sue and force the school to take the child back into regular classes, but also can claim financial compensation for legal and other costs.[29]

> A few days after Ryan Thomas, a child with AIDS, was placed in kindergarten, he got into a fight with another child and he bit the other child on the leg. This caused no laceration or bleeding, however. The "committee of health professionals" recommended psychological evaluation for Ryan in order to determine whether Ryan could endanger others or not. A psychologist who examined Ryan concluded that Ryan would behave aggressively in a kindergarten because his social and language skills and maturity level were below those of the other children. The committee then recommended that Ryan be kept out of class and given home tutoring for the rest of the academic year. Accepting this recommendation, the school board voted to exclude Ryan from the school.
>
> Ryan's parents sued the school under SECTION 504 of the Rehabilitation Act. After reviewing all allegations and the standard recommendations by the CDC regarding school attendance for children infected with the AIDS virus, the federal court found that the school district was a recipient of federal funds and under the language of SECTION 504, Ryan was a "handicapped person." Further, the court found no evidence of a significant risk of harm to his kindergarten classmates. The court ruled that the school violated federal law, and ordered Ryan to return to school. In addition, the school district had to pay over $42,000 in attorney's fees and other expenses to Ryan's parents.[29]

AIDS is an inflammatory topic in general, and no aspect of the AIDS crisis ignites emotions more swiftly or intensely than children afflicted with the disease. When the medical establishment has made an effort to reassure parents that children with AIDS pose no actual danger in the classroom, the public reaction has been mistrust of the medical profession rather than acceptance of its professional determination. The rationale behind this medical assertion is virtually meaningless to parents, because AIDS is a killing disorder and therefore creates a phobia in parents who in turn may transmit that fear to their children.

The ramifications are clear: a child afflicted with AIDS suffers not only the physical ailment but also emotional and social rejection by his or her peers and sometimes the general community. While a systematic psychiatric assessment remains to be undertaken of this specific effect of AIDS on its child victims, we can infer the consequences.

The media have helped us understand the images that torment and frighten parents. They envision a scenario of biting, bleeding, sexual activity, etc, taking place in school: an atmosphere wherein their child could contact AIDS. Helping relieve parents of these vivid scenarios is a formidable task for the clinicians called on for consultation. Child psychiatrists must broaden their focus and respond with sensitivity and understanding to both sides of this controversial issue.

In this writer's view, mental health professionals can best adhere to the responsibility of helping AIDS-afflicted youngsters by refraining from splitting into "camps," or aligning themselves with any one side. Further alienation of parents from the medical establishment on this issue will only be counterproductive to the aim of alleviating the suffering of children with AIDS. A group dynamics therapy in which parents of both sides participate is somewhat helpful in lessening the fear and anger often expressed by parents of normal children, and reducing the guilt and shame in parents of AIDS-afflicted children.

Those psychiatrists directly involved with AIDS cases must keep in mind the necessity of confidentiality.[16] No information regarding an AIDS-afflicted child's health may be disclosed to parents of normal children. Actually, the court in the New York City case mentioned earlier observed that the commissioner of education was in potential violation of the state's confidentiality statutes when he used New York City health records to identify the child in question for evaluation by the panel. The court, interestingly, rendered a scientific opinion by saying that the surveillance data of the health department is to be used for statistical purposes, or for research and study of the epidemiology of the disease, and not for use by panels charged with making recommendations and determinations of a child's fitness for attending school. If the commissioner did intend to take affirmative action based on the panel's recommendation, then he would indeed have violated the confidentiality statute.

The dilemma of AIDS-afflicted youngsters proves how insufficient legal rights can sometimes be if local communities lack a corresponding willingness to respect and uphold these rights. The unique situation of these children carves a new niche for mental health practitioners, who, in their commitment to healing, must extend their professional focus beyond individual victims of the disease to whole communities.

242

REFERENCES

1. Public Law No. 89-750 (1965).
2. Public Law No. 94-142 (1975).
3. *Board of Education of the Hendrick Hudson Central School District v Rowley* 1982; 50 USLW.
4. *Piscataway v T.G.* 1983; 576 FSupp 420, 423.
5. *Irving Independent School District v Tatro* 1984; 04 (S Ct 3371).
6. *Wilson v Marana Unified School District of Pima County* 1984; 735 F2d 1178 (9th Cir).
7. *Doe v Maher* 1986; 793 F2d 1470 (9th Cir).
8. Supreme Court limits exclusions of disabled students. *Ment Phys Disability Law Reporter* 1988; 12:9.
9. Doe v Maher. *Ment Phys Disability Law Reporter* 1986;10:560–562.
10. *City of Cleburne, Texas v Cleburne Living Center Inc* 1985; No. 84-468 (US Sup Ct) (July 1, 1985).
11. *Smith v Robinson* 1984; 104 S Ct 3457.
12. Public Law No. 99-372 (1986).
13. Public Law No. 98-457 (1984).
14. Position of Congress on "Baby Doe." *Ment Phys Disability Law Reporter* 1984; 8:560–561.
15. *Bowen v American Hospital Association* 1986; 84-1529 (US Sup Ct).
16. Centers for Disease Control: Classification system for human immunodeficiency virus (HIV) infection in children under 13 Years old. *MMWR* 1987;36:225–236.
17. Centers for Disease Control: Revision of the CDC surveillance case definition for acquired immunodeficiency syndrome. *MMWR* 1987;36 (Supp):105.
18. Centers for Disease Control: Public health service guideline for counseling and antibody testing to prevent HIV infection and AIDS. *MMWR* 1987;36:509–513.
19. Rubinstein A, Bernstein L: The epidemiology of pediatric acquired immunodeficiency syndrome. *Clin Immunol Immunopathol* 1986;40:115–121.
20. Ammans AJ: Pediatric Acquired Immunodeficiency Syndrome Information on AIDS for the Practicing Physician, in Information on AIDS for the Practicing Physician. Chicago, *American Medical Association,* 1987, vol 1, pp 17–23.
21. Parry J: AIDS as a handicapping condition—part II. *Ment Phys Disability Law Reporter* 1986;10:2–9.
22. *Shirley v Devine* 1982; 6670 F2d 1188, 1201 (DC Cir).
23. *New York State (A.R.C.) v Carey* 1979; 12 D 2nd 644 (2nd Cir).
24. *Application of District 27 Community School Board v Board of Education of New York City* 1986; No. 14940/85 (NY Sup Ct, Queens).
25. *Bogart v White* 1986; No. 86-144 (Ind Cir Ct Clinton City).
26. Justice Department's AIDS memo reviewed. *Ment Phys Disability Law Reporter* 1986;10:2–9.
27. *Board of Education v Cooperman* 1986; 507 A2-253 (NJ Super Ct App Div).
28. *Board of Education of the City of Plainfield v Cooperman* 1987; No. A 45/46 (NJ Sup Ct).
29. *Thomas v Atascadero Unified School District* 1986; 662 FSupp 376 (CD Cal).

13

Victimized Children

The victimization of children has cast its shadow over all of human history—all eras and all cultures and all races. The accumulated wisdom of religion, science, philosophy, and art has not freed people from their complicated and sometimes destructive urges and inadequacies, which cause them to torment those who are weaker.

In spite of this problem's seeming a tragically permanent part of the human condition, today's mental health professionals are addressing the issue directly. It is, in a sense, the "last frontier" of the mental health territory. Experts estimate that nationwide from 2000 to 5000 children die each year as a result of abuse. The reported number of abuse or neglect cases is about 2.2 million per year, and the number grows each year. Although many states have enacted stricter child welfare laws, there is at the same time a countertrend toward stronger legal rights for parents who are accused of abusing children.[1]

The medical community can be credited with drawing the attention of law enforcement agencies to the plight of abused children, and acting as a link between the victims and their protectors. Kempe et al, in their classic article, "The Battered-Child Syndrome," described the clinical condition in young children who receive serious physical abuse from parents or foster parents.[2]

Child abuse is such a tenacious problem because its roots grip the two basic units of human existence—family structure and social structure. Primary factors leading to child abuse are the cycle of violence engendered by inter-generational transmission of abuse, low socioeconomic status, and social isolation with weak community and family structures.[3] That a significant percentage of child abusers were themselves abused children is now a proven fact, illustrating the "cycle of violence" aspect of the syndrome. The statistics vary from report to report, ranging from 17% to 70% of abusers being former abusees.[3] In comparison, about 4% of the general population exhibits abusive behavior.

Although child abuse is found among all socioeconomic classes, the majority of cases take place in low-income families. The reasons for this disproportionate figure are many, but a notable factor is that lower economic groups are more vulnerable to being publicly recorded for abusive behavior. These people are less adept at hiding the symptoms of abuse, and less aware of the means at the disposal of the social service systems to uncover and remedy child abuse. However, actual causes for the abuse also exist in greater abundance in the lower economic groups, and include financial distress, unemployment, poor housing, larger families, social isolation, and inadequate education.

When treating physicians notice evidence of child abuse, the law requires that they report it to the authorities. Failure to report is a misdemeanor punishable by a fine and/or short-term imprisonment. In addition, the clinician can be subject to civil liabilities by concerned parties. The scope and magnitude of this problem are demonstrated in one of the earliest cases addressing it, the landmark *Landeros v Flood*.

> Dr Flood was a physician who examined an infant in an emergency room. The infant had a fracture of the tibia and fibula, apparently caused by a twisting force, plus bruises on her body. The mother had no explanation for these injuries. Flood did not report the suspected cause of the injuries. Two months later, the same infant was brought into a different hospital for treatment of new injuries, which included a bruise to the right eye, a puncture wound in the left leg and back, and bites on the face. The second hospital made a report to the police and the local child protection agency. Eventually, the child was placed for adoption. The new guardian of the infant, Gita Landeros, brought a lawsuit against the physician Flood, on the grounds that the physician's negligence in failing to inform the authorities of the abuse caused great pain and suffering to the infant. Flood was found guilty of a misdemeanor as well as negligent of malpractice.[4]

Similarly, cognizance of sexual abuse requires mental health professionals to report known incidences to higher authorities. Failure to do so could result in dismissal from their job and/or demotion based on the doctrine that the state's compelling interest in protecting abused children supersedes the mental health professional's right to confidentiality and possible constitutional right to privacy. This issue was explored in *Pesce v J. Sterling Morton High School District 201*.

> Pesce, a school psychologist, received a note from a male student expressing guilt and confusion about his sexual preferences. The note also indicated that a sexual encounter had occurred between the student and a male teacher. The psychologist called the student, assuring the student that their meeting would remain confidential. After their meeting, the psychologist honored his promise and did not notify school officials. One week later, the student gave the psychologist permission to reveal the information to school authorities. Accordingly,

the psychologist disclosed the information at this time. The school board criticized the psychologist for delaying the report, and the psychologist was suspended and demoted. The psychologist sued the school board alleging that it had violated his constitutional rights to due process and privacy.[5]

The federal court and court of appeals sided with the school board, finding that any threat to the safety and welfare of the students must be reported, and further that the therapist-patient privilege does not apply in such a situation. The courts suggested that the psychologist should not have waited until he received a minor's consent to reveal confidential material when sexual abuse is at issue. The court vigorously rejected the psychologist's argument that the school board violated his federal constitutional right of confidentiality that derived from the student's right to privacy. The court further noted that in light of the compelling state interest in protecting abused children, the psychologist and others in similar positions must promptly report child abuse to a state agency and that this state interest and requirement do not infringe on the professional constitutional right to confidentiality.

PHYSICAL ABUSE

Corporal punishment alone does not constitute physical abuse. Reasonable corporal punishment of a child by his parents or guardian or even school authorities is not against the law. Physical abuse is against the law, on the other hand, and must be reported by a treating physician when evidence of it exists. The law mandates that physicians and other professionals such as nurses and social workers report to law enforcement or other appropriate government agencies when they suspect that a child under their care or observation has been abused or neglected. The responsible agency then usually requires the reporter to provide all relevant information available in order to protect the child.

Reporting physicians should have a sound basis for the belief that a child has been abused or neglected before filling out the report with the authorities. It is not their job to substantiate a reasonable suspicion with absolute proof, however, and physicians should not wait until they feel they can prove abuse if sufficient evidence suggests it. The main role of physicians reporting abuse is to alert authorities to the likelihood of abuse. Their evidence simply begins the process, which then shifts to the legal establishment, of investigating the abuse and then taking action if necessary. The physician who provides the report has immunity from civil and criminal liability even if the report turns out to be false. The important issue is that the physician act in good faith.

False reports are fairly common. It is estimated that from the total suspicions of child abuse reported per year, 65% sound a false alarm. When the report is an emergency, the agency that receives the report can obtain a court order and remove the child from his or her guardian's home. The agency also has the option of proceeding with a court hearing. The court then decides either to leave the child with the parents, to place the child in foster care, or to terminate the parental rights on the basis of "clear and convincing evidence."

Certain information, although not mandatory to report, could be useful to the investigative agency. For example, a psychiatrist learns in the course of therapy that a patient is an addict and has frequent blackouts while caring for her young child, or that a patient is violent toward his children and uses physical discipline overstrenuously, although no evidence of physical harm to the children has surfaced. If physicians or psychotherapists report such occurrences, they most probably will be immune from a lawsuit. The courts have always maintained that "privileged communication" can be abrogated if the interest of a child is at stake, and specifically if the reporting physician is acting in good faith in reporting.

The prevailing legal opinion on breaching confidentiality in such a situation is illustrated in *Schaiffer v Spicer*.[6] The defendant psychiatrist revealed confidential information which he had obtained during the course of the plaintiff's therapy to the plaintiff's husband. The plaintiff and her husband had a legal dispute over custody of their child. The husband used the psychiatrist's information to support his claim that his wife was unsuited to have custody of the child, and the wife sued the psychiatrist for breach of confidentiality. The court ruled that the defendant psychiatrist is protected from liability toward his patient by the fact that he acted in what he thought was the best interest of the child. The same court recognized that the patient-physician privilege must yield to the paramount right of the infant, who obviously has no other means of defense.

SEXUAL ABUSE

A unique complication arises in the interface between child psychiatry and the law over children who have been victims of sexual assault, either by a stranger or from incest. Benedek and Schetky have noted that during the course of parental divorce, a variety of false accusations may be made by warring parents.[7] In the past, when the nuclear family was an accepted status quo and the morals sustaining it also sustained society (at least as an ideal), parents would accuse each other of neglecting the medical, educational, or social needs of a child in their attempt either to gain custody or change custodial arrangements. More hostile parents would sling charges of misdeeds such as adultery, which once signified immorality. In today's society, such accusations carry less weight, and the ultimate weapon is an accusation of child molestation.[7]

The number and scope of reported sexual abuse cases are growing, with an estimated 125,000 cases a year reported. Studies have found that 5% of adults now report some sexual abuse in their childhood. The figures for men and women differ. Russell's survey on 933 women in San Francisco showed that 38% had been sexually abused before the age of 18 and 16% of those had been abused by a family member.[8,9] A *Los Angeles Times* poll gives figures of 27% of the women and 16% of the men questioned as reporting childhood sexual abuse.[10] The types of sexual activity constituting the abuse break down as 16% to 29% involving intercourse or attempted intercourse; 3% to 11% involving oral or anal intercourse; and the rest involving manual touching of the genitals, and fondling.[11] Finkelhor[11] has reported five high-risk factors for child sexual abuse:

1. A child who is living without one of the biological parents
2. A child whose mother is unavailable as a result of employment, disability or illness
3. A child who reports that the parents' marriage is unhappy
4. A child who reports having a poor relationship with the parents or being subject to extremely punitive discipline or child abuse
5. A child who lives with a stepfather

The identification of these risk factors does not imply that any child whose environment contains one or more of these factors is at risk of sexual abuse. It simply indicates that, statistically, those children are at a higher risk than the normal population.

A profile of offenders has also been compiled by Finkelhor.[11] It has been found that:

The abusers tend to have unusual needs for power and domination which may be related to their offending behavior.

Most offenders show an unusual level of deviant sexual arousal from children.

Many offenders have histories of being victims themselves of sexual abuse.

Many offenders have conflicts over adult heterosexual relationships or are experiencing disruption in normal adult heterosexual partnership at the time of the offense.

Finally, alcohol has been shown to be connected to the commission of the acts in a large number of offenses.

Incest as a form of sexual abuse is not rare. It occurs with a relatively high frequency in families where a disturbed stepfather lives with his stepchildren. In a survey of 933 women, it was found that 17% of stepdaughters reported sexual contact with their stepfather as opposed to 2% of the biological daughters reporting sexual contact with their father.[8,9]

Other researchers have also discovered that incest is both more common and more severe in stepparent families. The reasons for this remain unclear. Erickson et al[12] studied and compared 59 incestuous stepfathers with 70 incestuous biological fathers and 198 offenders against unrelated children. There were few substantial differences in psychological characteristics between fathers and stepfathers, but their life histories and marital histories varied significantly. Stepfathers were far more likely to have prior convictions for sexual offenses and to have been sexually abused as children and to have juvenile criminal records. Stepfathers were also more likely to have histories of previous marital failure. All three groups displayed personality traits associated with serious difficulty in interpersonal relationships, and tendencies to act out their feelings destructively.[12]

Clinical Manifestations of
Childhood Sexual Abuse

The suffering that sexually abused children experience takes myriad forms which may appear immediately after the incidents of abuse or much later, and may continue and change over a long period. Children's initial reactions to sexual assault include acute anxiety, nightmares, and phobia. Personal guilt feelings, identity confusion, and depression are common symptoms. In adolescents, depression is more severe and the risk of suicide increases. With the case of incest, guilt feelings are more intense and dangerous. The child will often have anxiety dreams and respond to stress with a feeling of helplessness and disorganized thought. Older victims experience avoidance of certain places or people, maladjustment, and behavioral problems including delinquency, depression, and disturbances in object relationships.[13] Finally, the long-range danger of promiscuity is high for girls who have been victimized by incest.

The consequences of sexual abuse may continue on into adulthood. Clinical and research reports indicate that childhood physical and sexual abuse is more common among adults who develop major mental illness. Abuse may be a hidden feature in patients who are classified among the most difficult to diagnose and treat. Some studies have portrayed a direct connection between history of abuse in childhood and severity of psychiatric symptoms in adulthood.[14] In a study of 68 female psychiatric in-patients, Bryer et al[15] found that three fourths of them had been physically and/or sexually abused in their childhood. And the correlation of the severity of adult psychiatric symptoms with childhood physical and sexual abuse is the most valuable finding. The results suggest that the victims of childhood abuse continue to experience long-standing negative consequences of abuse. The adult psychiatric problems associated with childhood abuse appear to be more acute when the patient has experienced more than one type of abuse. Victims of both sexual and physical abuse often find it easier to describe details of the physical abuse than the sexual abuse. Therefore some of the patients reporting only physical abuse may also have been sexually abused. In addition, the researchers have found higher rates of suicidal symptoms in the sexually abused group.[15]

The psychological ravages of sexual abuse have concerned the earliest psychiatric innovators, who recognized it as a destructive element of disturbing frequency. The original hypotheses of Freud on the consequences of sexual abuse have been substantiated by modern researchers. In his studies of hysteria,[16] Freud formulated the idea that hysterical patients suffer from repressed memory of traumatic events of a sexual nature that are so distressing that the emotions they arouse cannot be faced at the time they surface. Hysterical symptoms, according to Freud, are the consequences of childhood sexual trauma.

In modern studies of psychiatric populations—suicidal persons, sex offenders, juvenile delinquents, and prostitutes—a link between childhood sexual abuse and internalized processes which result in abnormal personality have been demonstrated by many researchers. A study of 34 young people done 6 to 8 years after they had been sexually abused as children compared them to a control group of 34 subjects who had not been abused. A comparison was also made on subjects who had been abused for less than 1 year with those who had been abused for more than 1 year. The findings suggest that delinquency and criminal behaviors are associated with the previous trauma of childhood abuse.[17]

The literature shows that, in general, sexually abused children adapt by developing one of two contrasting styles. One group seeks active repetition of the trauma (ie, promiscuity) and the other group copes with the problem by avoiding relating to the opposite sex.[18]

Girls who have been sexually abused may develop psychosomatic disorders in adulthood, mainly in the form of chronic pelvic pain. A study was done by Walker et al[19] on 25 women with chronic pelvic pain and a comparison group of 30 women with specific gynecologic conditions. They found that the patients with chronic pelvic pain had a significant history of childhood sexual abuse. According to the hypothesis of Walker et al, which was drawn from their own data as well as data from other investigators, many patients with chronic pelvic pain come from multiproblem families in which they are not adequately protected and thus they become victims of childhood sexual abuse. As a result of the lack of care and protection and the childhood sexual abuse, women with chronic pelvic pain are likely to have sexual problems during adulthood, including decreased desire for intimacy and problems with orgasmic function. Chronic pelvic pain may be a metaphorical way of describing chronic psychological pain and may serve as a defense or coping mechanism to protect against painful, emotionally potent memories.[19] Clearly, what we designate as "sexual abuse of children" is in fact often a lifelong emotional crippler.

COURT HEARINGS

When allegations of sexual abuse arrive at the court of law and the parties involved seek the truth via the legal process, inevitably the child must take the stand. The allegations could have come from a variety of sources. In a custody dispute, parents may make such charges. The child, or a third party, may have made the allegations. The child's credibility will be tested by attorneys and/or by presenting the psychiatrist's or other mental health professionals' reports. Then the child will take the stand.

It is natural for a victimized child to be reluctant to report the details of sexual abuse, and often she will give an inconsistent and unclear story, which further complicates the legal developments. Child advocates have tried to convince the courts that a closed hearing rather than an open court should be utilized in all legal proceedings stemming from abuse. The constitutionality of closed hearings, however, has been questioned by the courts. The American Academy of Child Psychiatry (AACP) has urged legislators to adopt new judicial procedures for children testifying on sexual abuse.[20] According to the AACP, judicial procedures designed for adults are unsatisfactory for children testifying on sexual abuse. Such cases require special handling because direct public testimony can cause additional emotional stress for sexually abused children, who often see the atmosphere of the courtroom as threatening, confusing, and frightening. The AACP has recommended several modifications in legal proceedings for cases of child sexual abuse, including the following:

- Use of child psychiatrists or other qualified professionals to evaluate the competency of the child to testify, the credibility of the child's allegations, whether sexual abuse has caused the child emotional disturbance requiring treatment, and whether the child would be further psychologically damaged by giving testimony.
- Allow the child the option of not looking at the accused and allow the use of live, two-way closed circuit television for grand jury appearances and in certain cases during the actual trial.
- Have child psychiatrists or adequately trained professionals conduct the first interview, and record or video-tape this interview so that the child's initial statements are available regardless of when the case comes to trial.
- Give priority to child abuse cases in court schedules.
- Keep the testimony at a duration that is age-appropriate to the child and exclude spectators from the courtroom except as necessary to the trial

The above recommendations have not yet been adopted by more than a few state legislatures. And above all, they have no constitutional validity. There are several potential points of conflict between the rights of the child and the rights of a defendant, and where one or the other will have to be compromised.

The courts are anxious to receive psychiatric evaluations of victimized children prior to any proceeding. The role of the mental health professional, therefore, either as therapist or as an expert witness, is extremely important. Benedek and Schetky recommend, among other things, that the child should be interviewed alone.[7] The interviewer must establish rapport with the child.

The clinical playroom must be stocked with a variety of toys, dolls, puppets, and art materials, and the child must be allowed to explore the toys. After a period of free play, the examiner may briefly explain the reason for the interview and after following the stages of storytelling, "Simon says," etc, the child should eventually be asked if anyone has touched or tickled him in a scary way or in a private place. If the child responds affirmatively, the examiner might ask who the person was, who did the touching or hurting, and whether more than one person was involved. More details may be obtained in a nonthreatening fashion.

If the allegations of sexual abuse are being brought against a parent, it is helpful diagnostically to observe the child with that parent. Observing parent and child together reveals much about the parent-child relationship that might have been missed from obtaining a history alone at the conclusion of the evaluation. Benedek and Schetky recommend that the children be reassured that they have been believed and that they did the right thing in telling and sharing their stories.[7]

The expert psychiatrist or mental health professional should be aware that of all sex abuse allegations, it has been estimated that 36% to 55% could be false, specifically when custody of the child is an issue. The mental health professional should be aware that the child could have been brainwashed by a vindictive parent or influenced by a delusional mother who projects her own unconscious sexual fantasies of the spouse onto the child. Or, the child may make the sexual abuse allegations as an expression of child sexual fantasies rather than based on reality.[18] Revenge or retaliation toward the father could also be a motive for a child's allegations of incest if, in the mind of the child, the father is perceived as having abandoned the mother. The role of the mental health professional in the court proceeding must be confined to: (1) conveying the psychodynamics of sexual abuse and the impact of incest from the child's perspective to the attorney, jurors, and the court; (2) minimizing the child's further traumatization by the legal system; (3) recommending a patten of custody and visitation that would protect the child from possible molestation; and (4) assisting in drafting a realistic treatment plan and crisis intervention.[18]

Unexperienced psychiatrists are especially vulnerable to lawsuits by either the mother or the father if the therapist's clinical findings and reports were based only on psychodynamic conclusions rather than the presenting facts. In *Doe v Hennepin County Child Protection Unit*,[21] false allegations were filed by a neighbor and two young girls were removed from their parents without efforts being made to substantiate the charges of sexual abuse. The Does brought a lawsuit against Hennepin County and their psychotherapist, whose conclusion of sexual abuse was based exclusively on the psychodynamic of the defense mechanism of the child's "adamant denials" that her father molested her.

A psychiatrist's testimony can sometimes do more harm than good in a court proceeding. For instance, in *Wisconsin v Haseltine*,[22] a father's conviction for sexually abusing his daughter was reversed by a Wisconsin appeals court on the ground that the trial court had erred in permitting a psychiatrist to testify that "there was no doubt whatsoever" that the plaintiff was an incest victim. The appeals court felt that the psychiatrist's statement, "with its aura of scientific opinion," had too much influence on the jury.

In general, courts are more supportive of children and the therapists if there is solid evidence to suggest that child abuse probably did take place. In a case related to this aspect of the issue, *California v Younghaz*,[23] a father met a student counselor at a college community clinic and reported that he had been sexually involved with his deaf, borderline retarded-daughter. The father apparently was seeking help for himself there. The clinic informed the father that the law required all instances of child abuse to be reported to a child protection agency. Despite the warning, the father disclosed the details of his problem to the psychologist. The psychologist then filed a report of child abuse. Subsequently, charges were brought against the father.

At the hearing the father argued that, first, the psychologist's report of child abuse interfered with his privacy right to seek a cure for his illness. Second, the disclosure requirement was unconstitutional because it compelled him to incriminate himself. Third, since his deaf daughter would have to testify through sign language, his constitutional right to confront an opposing witness was denied. The court rejected all three arguments, noting that "the right to seek a particular form of medical treatment as a cure for one's illness has not been recognized as a fundamental right." The court also cited that the state interest in protecting children from abuse supersedes other issues. Further, the court noted that the father voluntarily, knowingly, and intelligently waived any right against self-incrimination when the clinic advised him that as a matter of law the incidents must be reported and he continued his revelations. Finally, the court found that there is nothing wrong in translating sign language, which he understood. The father's voluntary confession at the clinic is an example of the sound evidence that will encourage the courts to give the child's interest priority when there is a conflict between the rights of the defendant and the child in such cases. If the accusing evidence had been flimsy, the other arguments given by the defense may have appeared stronger and more worthy of consideration in contrast. So the inherent validity of the evidence can color the attitude of the court right from the start, and subsequent decisions are relative to the firmness of the basic evidence.

Clinicians should know that it is common to be invited for consultation in cases when sexual abuse is alleged. Mental health professionals must be very cautious in their testimony and in their conclusions, as Green has pointed out.[18] Even the best-trained expert in child sexual abuse will be unable to render a definitive opinion about whether or not a molestation has taken place. Some authors have applied public health models to treatment plans for sexual abuse cases. *Primary prevention* includes preventing sexual abuse through prohibitory legislation and through the education of the general public. *Sec-*

ondary prevention works through early detection and treatment of the victim, and *tertiary prevention* seeks to limit disabilities in victims.[24]

Mental health professionals who have responsibility for the well-being of a child may be charged with negligence if they fail to make appropriate recommendations to child protection agencies. In illustrating the scope of the problem, the case of *Bolton v Jones*[25] also shows how a professional can get into trouble unnecessarily. In this case, a Michigan appeals court reinstated a suit against a social worker and a psychiatrist for negligence in recommending that there was no need to supervise a family suspected of child abuse. A juvenile court determined that evidence suggested a child was being abused by her parents, but allowed the child to remain at home. A social worker was assigned to investigate the family; after 13 weekly visits to the home, interviews with the parents, and observation of interactions within the family, he recommended to a psychiatrist who also was assigned to the case that the family continue with counseling on its own and that the case be dismissed. Based on the social worker's report and one office interview, the psychiatrist concluded that there was no continuing need for supervision of the family. The court in turn dismissed the abuse petition. Three months later the child died after being beaten by her father. The court found that the defendants were not entitled to summary judgment on the basis of government immunity. Factual issues existed concerning the proper and adequate inspection, interviewing, and investigation of the parents' medical and psychiatric histories and records.

The pivotal point that mental health professionals must be aware of, as this case demonstrates, is that according to the court ruling the social worker and the psychiatrist owed a duty to the child to use reasonable care to keep her safe from harm by a third party. In other words, the court applied the Tarasoff doctrine (discussed at length in chap. 1) to child abuse cases, and in so doing effected a balance between the conflicting rights of the different parties involved. While extra responsibilities are placed on psychiatrists in this situation, those responsibilities are reasonably clear and comprehensible, and allow the practitioner to take precautions without violating professional confidentiality ethics.

THE RIGHTS OF DEFENDANTS ACCUSED BY CHILDREN

When the victim in a criminal case is a sexually abused child, the defendants retain their constitutional rights, a fact worth keeping in mind when automatic sympathy for a child plus the nature of the allegations can cause an assumption of guilt. To cross-examine a witness is a criminal defendant's constitutional right, and remains so in this type of case.

The issue grows more complex, however, when one asks whether defendants have the right to inspect the records of a child protective agency in order to safeguard their own constitutional rights, considering that those records will undoubtedly contain the name of the person reporting the abuse, witnesses' statements, notes made by mental health professionals, assessments, and other confidential information. The system created to protect children would likely collapse, and children go unprotected, if confidentiality could not be assured to persons reporting incidents. Does one jeopardize the system to protect individual children, or maintain the system at the possible expense of an individual child? Prosecutors have alternative forms of evidence available to them, but no such alternatives exist for the defendant comparable to child protective agencies. So a compromise must be made, and must be made in favor of the agencies. Absolute confidentiality is the only guarantee for the future cooperation of clinicians and others who make the effort to report abuse.

Defendants have the constitutional right to obtain exculpatory evidence; to sort out the unreliable evidence; and to arm themselves with those statements that could be used effectively in their defense during the cross-examination. These issues have been grappled with by the US Supreme Court. This Court has consistently held that to some degree, a criminal defendant's constitutional rights outweigh a state's interest in protecting the absolute confidentiality of child abuse records. If a trial court deems that the child protective agency records contain material vital to the defense, then those data alone are supplied to the defense. The Supreme Court rejected the notion that the defense has a right to unlimited access to a file.

Pertinent to discussion of these issues is the case of *Pennsylvania v Ritchie*,[26] in which Ritchie was charged with various sex offenses against his minor daughter. The matter was referred to the Children and Youth Services (CYS), a protective services agency established by Pennsylvania to investigate cases of suspected child mistreatment and neglect. During pretrial discovery, respondent Ritchie served CYS with a subpoena, seeking access to the records related to the immediate charges as well as certain other records compiled by the CYS investigators. CYS refused to comply with the subpoena, claiming that the records were privileged under a Pennsylvania statute which provides that all CYS records must be kept confidential, subject to specified exceptions. One of the exceptions is that the CYS may disclose reports to a court of competent jurisdiction pursuant to a court order. At an in-chambers hearing in the trial court, respondent argued that he was entitled to the information because the CYS file might contain the names of favorable witnesses as well as other unspecified exculpatory evidence. Although the trial judge did not examine the entire CYS file, he refused to order disclosure. At the trial, which resulted in respondent's conviction by a jury, the main witness against him was his daughter, who was cross-examined at length by defense counsel. A convoluted process began: on appeal, the Pennsylvania Superior Court held that the failure to disclose the daughter's statements contained in the CYS file violated the confrontation clause of the Sixth Amendment. Then, on the state's appeal, the Pennsylvania Supreme Court concurred, holding that, by denying access to the CYS file, the respondent's constitutional right under the Sixth Amendment had been violated. The Pennsylvania Supreme Court vacated the conviction and remanded the case to determine if a new trial was necessary. The court concluded that defense counsel was entitled to review the entire file for any useful evidence.

The case eventually arrived at the US Supreme Court for final disposition. The Court decided that the Pennsylvania Supreme Court erred in holding that defense counsel must be allowed to examine the confidential information. A defendant's right to obtain exculpatory evidence does not invite a free-for-all perusal of files, and it is inappropriate to give defense unsupervised authority to search files and to make determinations about what information is material to the case. Both the respondent's and the state's interests in ensuring a fair trial can be protected fully by requiring that the CYS files be submitted only to the trial court for in camera review. Further, to allow full disclosure to defense counsel in this type of case would sacrifice unnecessarily the state's compelling interest in safeguarding its child abuse information.

The dissenting justices voiced the opinion that the right of a defendant to confront an accuser is intended fundamentally to provide an opportunity to subject accusations to critical scrutiny. Essential to testing a witness's account of events is the ability to compare that version with other versions the witness may have recounted earlier. Denial of access to a witness's prior statements thus imposes a handicap that strikes at the heart of the cross-examination.

The Supreme Court's decision in *Ritchie* represents an effort to balance society's interest in protecting its children with its interest in preserving the rights of criminal defendants. The manner in which that balance was struck is consistent with long-standing principles regarding a defendant's right to exculpatory evidence. Vigilance in maintaining that balance is a necessity if fairness is to endure.

Most clinicians believe that it would have a traumatizing effect on a victimized child to go eyeball to eyeball with the person accused of the abuse during a trial proceeding. The views of clinicians in this regard have not impressed the legal decision makers, however. The most important issue to the courts is a defendant's right under the Sixth Amendment of the Constitution, that is, to be able to confront the witness alleging the crime. Therefore, any procedure designed to shield victims of child abuse and child sex abuse from having to face the accused abuser in the courtroom when they testify in criminal trials is unconstitutional. This is the finding of the US Supreme Court in *Coy v Iowa*.[27]

> The *Coy* case began when John Avery Coy was arrested in August 1985 and charged with sexually assaulting two 13-year-old girls earlier that month while they were camping out. According to the girls, the assailant entered their tent after they were asleep. Wearing a stocking over his head, he shined a

flashlight in their eyes and warned them not to look at him. Neither girl was able to describe his face. During the trial the state made a motion pursuant to a recently enacted statute[28] to allow the complaining witnesses to testify either via closed circuit television or behind a screen. The trial court approved the use of a large screen to be placed between the defendant and the child witnesses. During the testimony, the screen would enable the defendant to dimly perceive the witnesses, but the witnesses would not see him at all.

Coy, the defendant, strenuously objected to the use of the screen, basing his contention first on his right under the Sixth Amendment's confrontation clause, which gives criminal defendants the right to face-to-face confrontation. Second, Coy argued that his right to due process was violated, since the procedure would make him appear guilty and thus erode the presumption of innocence. The trial court rejected both constitutional claims, although it instructed the jury to draw no inference of guilt from the presence of the screen. After passing through state appeals phases, the case arrived at the US Supreme Court.

The majority of six justices noted and confirmed that the confrontation clause of the Sixth Amendment guarantees defendants a face-to-face meeting with witnesses appearing before the trier(s) of fact. The right of confrontation contributes to the establishment of a system of criminal justice in which the perception as well as the reality of fairness prevails. The justices acknowledged that face-to-face confrontation may, unfortunately, upset a genuine rape victim or abused child, but by the same token, it may confound and undo a false accuser, or reveal the child coached by a malevolent adult. This demonstrates the truism that constitutional protections have costs.

The Court asserted further that Iowa violated appellant Coy's right to face-to-face confrontation since the screen at issue enabled the complaining witnesses to avoid viewing appellant as they gave their testimony. The Court also stated that there was no merit to the state's assertion that its statute creates a presumption of trauma to victims of sexual abuse that outweighs appellant's right to confrontation. Even if an exception to this fundamental right can be made, it would have to be based on something more substantial than the type of generalized finding presented here, unless it were firmly rooted in jurisprudence.[27]

In the *Coy* case, the two conservative dissenting justices relied on available psychiatric literature and noted that maltreatment of children in the United States is rising. Moreover, the prosecution of these child sex abuse cases poses substantial difficulties because of the emotional trauma frequently suffered by child witnesses who must testify about the sexual assaults they have suffered. To a child who does not understand the reason for confrontation, the anticipation and experience of being in close proximity to the defendant can be overwhelming. The dissenting justices continued to present data from psychiatric literature in order to support their views, rather than from case law and statute.

In *Coy*, once again, the discipline of psychiatry has been of help in the formulation of opinions by Supreme Court justices. This time, unfortunately, the child-psychiatric data ended up in the opinions of the conservative dissenters, and were unable to influence the majority to strike a balance between defendants' rights and the special needs of child witnesses.

CHILDREN AS WITNESSES

No particular age has been designated as the standard legal age that a child must attain to be considered a competent witness. Instead, several criteria have been developed that the child must meet to be eligible to testify in court, which are summarized as follows:

1. The ability to understand the difference between truth and falsity
2. Memory sufficient to retain an independent recollection of the event
3. Ability to communicate and the capacity to understand simple questions

A child's failure to understand the meaning of an oath will not disqualify him or her as a witness, unlike a similar failure by an adult.[28] In the view of the court, to comprehend the duty to tell the truth and to comprehend the consequences of lying are the crucial issues.[29] The more abstract "code of honor" implicit in taking an oath is a not a normal or necessary part of childhood, and children should not lose credibility because they fail to grasp adult concepts. If their testimony is guided by the understanding of truthfulness and the value of telling the truth, it should hold up under scrutiny.

Witnesses were disqualified from testifying under early common law on several grounds. Simply being a child was one such ground. As our understanding of human development progressed, the courts came to realize that children's intelligence and perceptiveness allowed them to provide facts useful to the proceedings.[30] Indeed, to refuse access to this resource in the ascertainment of truth could shortchange the integrity of the legal process.

In *Wheeler v United States*,[31] the courts ruled on the age-limit issue, declaring that there is no one precise age at which competency begins. Competency depends instead on the maturity and intelligence of each child and his or her ability to discern truth from falsehood. The task of weighing the child's ability in this regard rests with the trial judge. The judge sees the proposed witness, and based on what he can learn about the child's manner and apparent possession or lack of intelligence, decides whether the child may testify.

A trend to put more children on the witness stand without considering the emotional consequences of the trial procedure on the child has been noted by law observers.[32,33] The credibility of a child can be attacked by an opposing attorney in an adversary proceeding. Furthermore, the jury can be easily dismissed if the opponent's lawyer argues about the psychodynamics of childhood fantasy and its effects on the child's perception of the reality.[34] Although current literature indicates that school-age children's ability to separate fantasy from factual memories almost matches that of adults,[35] the general idea of children's comprehension of reality lags behind the latest psychiatric discoveries. It is as if adults fantasize more about childhood than children do about reality. Juries thus may not be impressed with psychiatric literature. In any event, the judges are not interested in Piaget's theory of cognitive development or the Freudian hypothesis regarding childhood fantasies. What concerns the court is that a competent child is one who understands the meaning of truth. The age is not the determinant making the child a reliable witness. The ability to register, recall, and describe the event and to distinguish truth from falsehood and to appreciate his or her obligation to tell the truth to the court are the factors constituting credibility of a child witness.[36]

Mental health professionals should implement additional procedures in evaluating the credibility of a child to be a witness. Those procedures, according to Terr,[32,33] are (1) to corroborate psychiatric findings with the statements that were made either by the child or by others; (2) to refrain from suggesting anything to the child witness during the evaluation session and from proposing leading questions, and to keep the evaluation process separate from treatment; (3) to make word-for-word notes; and (4) to collect sufficient data before preparing a report.

To determine a child's competency to serve as witness, a judge will usually ask questions such as "What will happen to people who lie?" and if the child answers, "They will not go to heaven," the court requirement is being satisfied. In the view of mental health professionals, the competency and credibility of a child are interactive and relate to factors such as memory, suggestibility, confabulation, fabrication, and moral development.[29] Mental health professionals tend to be more sensitive and alert to the emotional consequences that are faced by the child who is put on the witness stand. The courts, on the other hand, appear to be somewhat insensitive to the psychological side effects of questioning a child or forcing a child to testify in the courtroom.[37]

With nonverbal children the court may allow qualified mental health professionals such as art therapists to give their interpretations of the child's artistic creations to the court. For example, a child victimized by a satanic ritual cult once was brought into the court and the child psychiatrist demonstrated how the infant was reenacting the traumatic events through play.

PLAY THERAPY

Play therapy is a technique whereby young children can express their emotions and feelings toward significant persons by engaging in play. This medium is intended to facilitate communication between the young patient and the therapist. During the play, toys and specifically dolls with full anatomical apparatus including genitalia, become the medium for the child's expression. This technique has become useful in eliciting evidence in sexually abused children.

Whether or not play with anatomically correct dolls should be used as the basis for expert testimony is an unresolved issue. Yates takes an affirmative stance.[38] She reviewed the work of White et al who compared 25 children aged 2 to 5½ years, suspected to be victims of sexual abuse, with 25 control subjects who were not suspected victims. The children suspected of having been abused demonstrated significantly more sexualized doll play and described significantly more sexual abuse situations than did the control group of children. In another study reviewed by Yates, Jampole and Weber compared ten children whose sexual abuse had been confirmed with a control group of ten nonabused children, and found that there were significant differences between the two groups in the occurrence of sexualized doll play.[38]

In Yates's view, sexually abused children probably are more likely than nonabused children to engage in sex play when exposed to the anatomically correct dolls. However, the results were not absolute: in the studies of both White and Jampole and Weber, there were children who had been abused or were suspected of being abused who did not engage in sex play; and children who had not been sexually abused but who did engage in sex play with the dolls. Thus, sex play with the dolls indicates that abuse may have occurred, but it is not actual proof that abuse did occur.[38]

In her opposing opinion, Terr has stressed that utilizing anatomically correct dolls for investigation, particularly in the hands of untrained investigators, is unreliable and may contain hazards.[39] Terr supports her view by referring to the work of Goodman[37] and Claman et al[40] in which a male member of their team talked and played for ten minutes with each of 31 normal 3-year-olds and 30 normal 5-year-olds. The children were then seen individually in a play session conducted a week later by a second investigator. The children were divided according to which, if any, dolls they were allowed to play with in the sessions: with no dolls, with ordinary dolls, and with sexually anatomically correct dolls. When leading questions were proposed to the children, the 3-year-olds gave a number of "false-positive" responses. The 5-year-olds tended to give correct answers in each of the three experimental situations. Even some of these older children gave false responses, however.

In Terr's view, the most traumatized children, infants and toddlers under 3 years old, appeared unable to articulate more than a few sketchy verbal recollections of documented episodes when asked months to years later. The sex abuse victim often habitually employs the defense of denial of external reality. Abused children may avoid, go mute, or otherwise hide from the world their impotent rage and sexual overstimulation. How then can one expect such victims to demonstrate accurately what they experienced by playing with sexually correct dolls? In fact, the abused child is the one who would be most inclined to drop the doll, discard it, or ignore it altogether.[39]

Courts may permit the experts to present their findings obtained through observation of a child's behavior with anatomically correct dolls, if this technique has been generally accepted as reliable in the relevant scientific community. This issue was explored and clarified in *In re Amber B.*

The Solano County Department of Social Services brought a petition alleging that a father had sexually molested his 3-year-old daughter and that his 1-year-old daughter was at risk of sexual abuse. The California court decided that the psychological technique of detecting child sexual abuse by observing the child's behavior during play with anatomically correct dolls, and then analyzing the child's reports of abuse, constitutes a new scientific method of proof and therefore is admissible as evidence in the court. The court gave much credence to the testimony of the child psychologist who observed that Amber placed her index finger in the vaginal and anal openings of the doll and pushed and twisted her finger vigorously. Based on the above finding and a few other minor reports, the court ruled that Amber had been molested while in the custody of her parents.[41]

The court's rationale for this order was grounded in the well-known Frye test, a US Supreme Court ruling of 1923 in which evidence based on a new scientific method of proof is admissible only on a showing that the procedure has been generally accepted as reliable in the scientific community in which it was developed. Also applied was the Kelly test, a California court decision in which an expert must demonstrate that correct scientific procedures were used in a particular case.[42]

On appeal, the higher court reversed its decision. The court of appeal in California found that the expert's general responses to a brief exploration of whether there was any disagreement among authorities upon which the expert relied, were insufficient to satisfy the Kelly and Frye tests. Failure to establish general acceptance of psychological technique in the relevant scientific community was a reversible error *In re Amber B*[41] and *In re Christine C. and Michael C.*[43]

As the situation stands, at least in California, the admissibility of evidence obtained through the use of anatomically correct dolls is barred until the procedure is accepted as reliable in the scientific community in which it was developed.

Today's children spend a great deal of time watching television. Very young children are fascinated with cartoons, and somewhat older ones enjoy adult programs. Implicit and explicit sexual interaction, especially in commercials, is commonplace on the screen. Even young infants memorize events and personally identify with characters. Children also wonder what would happen to them if they were one of those characters. Especially in commercials, the aim of being sexually attractive or active is glorified, and a youngster who is still oblivious of the facts of life will get that message clearly. The wish to be in the place of one of those characters who kisses on the lips or is kissed can be strong in a child. If the fantasy intensifies, the child may believe that it actually happened.

In playing with anatomically correct dolls in which the dolls' private parts are exposed, a child might match the genitals of the male doll to the genitals of the female doll out of simple curiosity. This could be a reflection of a fantasy or a replay of something seen on television. Furthermore, comparing similarities and differences between the dolls would be a most natural preoccupation for a bright youngster.

This author was once consulted to review the record of a child abuse case. A girl under 3 years old accused her father of putting ice cream on her genitals and then licking the ice cream. The infant apparently demonstrated the entire episode while playing with anatomical dolls. The untrained investigator alleged that the infant's play was related to the infant's experience with her own father. The author reexamined the child. The dolls were presented to the child as her mommy and daddy. On replay, the child made it clear that it was the daddy who ate the ice cream from the mommy's private parts!

In the opinion of this writer, sex play with dolls cannot be used as evidence to substantiate allegations. Sexual abuse of children is a felony crime. The triers of fact need strong evidence, that is, evidence beyond a reasonable doubt, in order to convict a person. Justice cannot be served through a playroom with anatomically correct dolls. The results and interpretations of "play therapy" can be presented to triers of fact as complementary evidence at best, but not as determining evidence. Children's imaginations and curiosities are powerful, and we do not honor them by misapplying them to incriminate adults.

PRESENCE OF THE DEFENDANT IN COMPETENCY HEARINGS

The confrontation clause of the Sixth Amendment to the Constitution guarantees a criminal defendant "the right . . . to be confronted with the witnesses against him," meaning that witnesses against the accused shall testify in his presence. This includes competency hearings at crucial phases of the trial.

The process of discovering the truth is enhanced by the physical presence of the defendant at such proceedings. For instance, in ascertaining witness competency, a trial judge must assess the witness's ability to recollect facts accurately and truthfully. To do this, the judge must make independent factual findings which serve as a measure of the witness's testimonial accuracy. These findings are critical to the judge's ability to determine witness competency to testify, but often the defendant is the only party capable of exposing inaccuracies in witness answers. A fair trial is obviously impossible without permitting the defendant this opportunity for self-defense.

The courts choose on occasion to disallow a defendant's presence at a competency hearing, however. If a minor is being examined to find out whether he will tell the truth, for instance, the issue is not the truth itself, which is material to the defense, but the child's intelligence or capacity, which are not directly material to the defense. Does refusing the defendant's presence in such a circumstance violate his rights under the confrontation clause? According to the US Supreme Court in *Kentucky v Stincer*,[44] it does not.

In *Stincer*, Sergio Stincer was indicted and charged with committing first-degree sodomy with T.G., an 8-year-old girl, N.G., a 7-year-old girl, and B.H., a 5-year-old boy (charges involving the boy were later dropped). After a jury was sworn, but before evidence was presented, the court conducted an in-chambers hearing to determine if the two young girls were competent to testify. Over the defense's objection, the defendant was excluded from the hearing, although his counsel was present.

The two girls were examined separately by the judge, the prosecutor, and the defense attorney. The questions, which were shaped to determine if the girls could remember basic facts and distinguish between telling the truth and telling a lie, consisted of subjects such as age, date of birth, the name of their school, and whether they could keep a promise to God to tell the truth. In open court, the girls on cross-examination testified about how the defendant had molested them, saying that he "put his d-i-c-k" in their mouth. The jury convicted the defendant of first-degree sodomy for engaging in deviate sexual intercourse, and gave him a 20-year prison sentence. Stincer appealed to the Supreme Court of Kentucky, arguing that his exclusion from the competency hearing of the two girls denied him due process and violated his Sixth Amendment right to confront the witnesses against him. The Kentucky Supreme Court agreed, and the case eventually arrived at the US Supreme Court.

The highest court held that Stincer's confrontation clause rights were not violated by his exclusion from the competency hearing. The majority contended that the function of the clause is to promote reliability in criminal trials by ensuring a defendant a chance to cross-examine. Stincer was present during the cross-examination, the justices noted, and he was available to assist his counsel. Moreover, the nature of the competency hearing militates against finding a confrontation clause violation, because questions at such hearings are usually limited to matters unrelated to basic trial issues.

The Court further found that Stincer's right under the due process clause of the Fourteenth Amendment was not violated by his exclusion from the hearing. This due process right requires that a defendant be present at critical stages of a criminal proceeding if his presence would contribute to the fairness of the procedure. It was deemed that his presence would have had no bearing on the outcome of the competency hearing, wherein questioning was limited to competency issues and substantive testimony was not discussed.

The three dissenting justices voiced the argument that more than reliability of competency determination was at stake in this issue. They maintained that the constitutional guarantee of the right of confrontation serves certain "symbolic goals" as well. The right to confront and cross-examine adverse witnesses contributes to the establishment of a system of criminal justice in which the perception as well as the reality of fairness prevails. It is implied that maintaining the perception of fairness will inspire a reality of fairness. To foster such a system, the Constitution provides certain safeguards to promote to the greatest possible extent society's interest in having the accused and accuser engage in an open and even contest in a public trial. The confrontation clause advances these goals by ensuring that convictions will not be based on the charges of unseen and unheard and unknown witnesses, an occurrence central to tyranny but antithetical to democracy. The dissenting justices noted that Stincer's right to be present at the competency hearing does not flow exclusively from the Sixth Amendment. Due process allows a defendant to attend any trial proceeding in which his presence is even indirectly related to his ability to carry out a thorough defense. The dissenters in *Stincer* believed that the competency hearing bore a substantial connection to the respondent's defense. Although questions of guilt or innocence are usually not asked at a competency hearing, the hearing retains a direct relationship with the trial because it determines whether a key witness will testify.

Given the sound and convincing arguments proffered by both the majority and the dissenting justices in *Stincer*, it is clear that a definitive ruling has yet to be formulated, and that the issue will undergo further argument and constitutional refinement. The continuing advances made by psychiatry in understanding the minds and capabilities of children will undoubtedly play a vital role in this process.

REFERENCES

1. *New York Times,* Jan 1, 1988.
2. Kempe CH, et al: The battered-child syndrome. *JAMA* 1962;181:17–24.
3. Gelles RJ: The family and its role inthe abuse of children. *Psychiatr Ann* 1987; 17:229–232.
4. *Landeros v Flood* 1976; 131 Cal 69.
5. *Pesce v J. Sterling Morton High School District 201* 1987; 830 F2d 789 (7th Cir).
6. *Schaiffer v Spicer* 1974; 215 NW 2d 135.
7. Benedek EP, Schetky DH: Problems in validating allegations of sexual abuse. Part 2, Clinical evaluation. *Monograph Am Acad Child Psychiatry* 1987;26:916–921.
8. Russell D: The incidence and prevalence of intrafamilial and extrafamilial sexual abuse of female children. *Child Abuse Neglect* 1982;7:133–146.
9. Russell D: *The Secret Trauma: Incest in the Lives of Girls and Women.* New York, Basic Books, 1986.
10. *Los Angeles Times,* Aug 25, 1985.
11. Finkelhor D: The sexual abuse of children: current research reviewed. *Psychiatr Ann* 1987;17:233–238.
12. Erickson WD: The life histories and psychological profiles of 59 incestuous stepfathers. *Bull Am Acad Psychiatry Law* 1987; 15:349–358.
13. Greenber N: The epidemiology of childhood sexual abuse. *Pediatr Ann* 1979; 8:16–28.
14. Carmen EH, et al: Victims of violence and psychiatric illness. *Am J Psychiatry* 1984;141:378–383.
15. Bryer JB, et al: Childhood sexual and physical abuse as factors in adult psychiatric illness. *Am J Psychiatry* 1987; 144:1426–1430.

16. Freud S: The etiology of hysteria, in *Collected Papers*. New York, Basic Books, 1959, vol 1.
17. Burgess AW: Abused to abuser: antecedents of socially deviant behaviors. *Am J Psychiatry* 1987;144:1431–1436.
18. Green HA: True and false allegations of sexual abuse in child custody disputes. *J Am Acad Child Psychiatry* 1986; 25:494–456.
19. Walker E, et al: Relationship of chronic pelvic pain to psychiatric diagnoses and childhood sexual abuse. *Am J Psychiatry* 1988;145:75–80.
20. American Academy of Child Psychiatry: Statement on protecting children undergoing abuse investigations and testimony. *J Am Acad Child Psychiatry* Feb. 8, 1986.
21. Schetky D: *Doe v Hennepin County Child Protection Unit,* reported in the *Newsletter Am Acad Psychiatry Law* 1985;10 (April).
22. *Wisconsin v Haseltine* 1984; 352 NW2d 673.
23. *California v Younghaz* 1984;202 Cal Rptr 907 (Cal Ct App).
24. Abright A R: Psychiatric aspects of sexual abuse. *Bull Am Acad Psychiatry Law* 1986;14:331–343.
25. *Bolton v Jones* 1987; 401 NW2d 894 (Mich Ct App).
26. *Penn v Ritchie:* Criminal defendents' right to child protective service records. *Am Acad Psychiatry Law Newsletter* 1987;12:15–17.
27. *Coy v Iowa* 1988; No 86-6757 (decided June 29, 1988).
28. Quinn KM: Competency to be a witness: a major child forensic issue. *Bull Am Acad Psychiatry Law* 1986;14:311–321.
28. *Iowa Code* 1987; Sec 910A.14.
29. Melton GB: Children's competency to testify. *Law Hum Behav* 1981;5:73–85.
30. *Jackson v Commonwealth* 1946; 301 Ky 562 SW2d 480.
31. *Wheeler v United States* 1985; 159 US 523.
32. Terr CL: The child as a witness, in Schetky D, Benedek P (eds): *Child Psychiatry and the Law*. New York, Brunner/Mazel, 1980.
33. Terr CL: The child psychiatrist and the child witness: traveling companions by necessity, if not by design. *J Am Acad Child Psychiatry* 1986;25:462–472.
34. Weiss HE, Berg R: Child victims of sexual assaults: impact of court procedures. *J Am Acad Child Psychiatry* 1982;21:513–518.
35. Johnson M, Foley MA: Differentiating fact from fantasy: the reliability of children's memory. *J Soc Issues* 1984;40:33–50.
36. Nurcombe B: The child as witness: competency and credibility. *J Am Acad Child Psychiatry* 1986;25:473–480.
37. Goodman G: The child witness: conclusion and further directions for research and legal practice. *J Soc Issues* 1984;40:163–175.
38. Yates A: Anatomically correct dolls: should they be used as the basis for expert testimony? (Affirmative) *J Am Acad Child Adolesc Psychiatry* 1988;27:254–257.
39. Terr C L: Anatomically correct dolls: should they be used as the basis for expert testimony? (Negative) *J Am Acad Child Adolesc Psychiatry* 1988;27:254–257.
40. Claman L, et al: The adolescent as a witness in a case of incest: assessment and outcome. *J Am Acad Child Psychiatry* 1986;25:457–461.
41. *In re Amber B.* 1987; 191 Cal App 3d 682.
42. *People v Kelly* 1976; 17 Cal 24.
43. *In re Christine C. and Michael C.* 1987; 191 Cal App 3d 691.
44. *Kentucky v Stincer* 1987; No. 86–572.

14

Child Custody

In the late 1950s and early 1960s a tremendous shift in social consciousness occurred. Although the divorce rate had been creeping upward, it surged at that time, for reasons both simple and complex, obvious and obscure. Divorce was no longer seen as an extreme solution to an extreme problem, but as a commonplace. When the nuclear family weakened as a social unit, its components weakened also, including the assumption of the mother as the natural guardian. The reassessment of parental roles may have its positive aspects, but the psychological impact of custody disputes on all involved is distressing, and remains so regardless of how ubiquitous such disputes have become. The legal ramifications are also compelling, to the extent that a whole new legal specialty has developed around custody, and legislatures and courts in defining rights must directly address the social transformations of the last several decades.

Historically, Roman law gave the father absolute control over his children, whom he could even sell or condemn to death with impunity. This concept of absolute paternal right carried over into English law and prevailed until the fourteenth century. Around the sixteenth century, children were given more focused interest as the Renaissance sensibility appreciated individuals as distinct from social groups and social functions. Soon thereafter, thinkers as different as Montesquieu and Locke addressed the issue of children and who was entitled to custody of them. The former writes: "Perhaps we are mistaken in conforming to this custom [of a long minority]. This might make it necessary for the father to continue in possession of his children's fortune during life. . . . But this is not agreeable to the spirit of monarchy."[1] Locke, whose influence on the founding fathers is well-known, writes: "But grant that both Parents made their Children. . . . This would give the *Father* but

265

a joynt Dominion with the Mother over them. For no body can deny but that the Woman hath an equal share, if not the greater . . ."[2]

Only in the twentieth century did the mother's right supersede the father's regarding child custody. In recent years state laws have tended to give equal weight to both parents in custody disputes in theory, yet in 90% of the cases the mother receives custody.[3]

The courts adopted the doctrine of "the best interest of the child" as early as 1925 in settling custody disputes and placing the child. That phrase was coined by Justice Benjamin Cardozo in his classic decision in *Finlay v Finlay*.[4] This doctrine, which still prevails, means simply that the judge determines with which parent the child would receive the best nurturing in each case, and then places the child in that home offering the maximum benefits.

Some mental health scholars were dissatisfied with this doctrine, finding it impractical and unrealistic. A half a century after the *Finlay* ruling, Goldstein et al[5] recommended that the "best interest" doctrine be replaced by a more realistic doctrine of "least detrimental alternative." Goldstein et al believed that . . .

> . . . the placement decision should safeguard the child's need for continuity of relationships. Once it is determined who will be the custodial parent, it is that parent, not the court, who must decide under what condition he or she wishes to raise the child. Thus the non-custodial parent should have no legally enforceable right to visit the child and the custodial parent should have the right to decide whether it is desirable for the child to have such visits.[5]

The same authors further recommended that the child in any contested placement should have full party status and the right to be represented by counsel.

The doctrine presented by Goldstein et al is subject to criticism on several accounts. Mental health professionals who work with parents in divorce and custody cases are well aware of the degree of vindictiveness the divorced parties may feel toward each other. It is common for a father to accuse his ex-wife of being unfit and the mother to bring false allegations of sexual abuse against her ex-husband for the purpose of revenge or other motivations with the goal of depriving him of custody and visitation. Custodial mothers are prone to use the child as a hostage in financial bargaining. Goldstein et al contend that their alternative is more realistic. Simplistic would be a more accurate description, however, because in placing continuity before all else, they overlook how complex continuity can actually be. Turning over all responsibility to one party does not ensure that that parent will consistently act in the child's best interest, especially as they experience the emotional vicissitudes and life style changes divorce often causes over a long period. Continuity may exist, but in a negative context, for instance, if the rejected parent becomes embittered and continually seeks access to his children in hostile ways, since the ruling ignores his parental feelings and he may not have the psychological wherewithal to deal with those feelings appropriately.

Continuity can mean also that children are continually deprived of the love and nurturing of the rejected parent if the triumphant parent revengefully denies any visitation. It seems much more realistic, after all, to produce custody laws that acknowledge the complexities of the situation but endeavor to meet the interests of all parties. The author believes that it is inhumane to give total decision making power to one parent and deprive the other's most basic paternal or maternal needs. Full authority in the hands of one parent has never been proved to be beneficial for the child and children continue to need two parents, even if the parents no longer need each other. Perhaps they need both parents more, with the family unit shattered. Furthermore, the parents are the first authorities the child learns to respect, and if a child witnesses a parent stripped of authority and thus humiliated, it can distort the child's future interpersonal and social relationships. Fortunately, the courts of law have been unimpressed with the thesis put forth Goldstein et al Instead, custody is usually given temporarily to one party and the other party retains the right to return to court and request modification if and when circumstances change.

In the view of the American Bar Association (ABA), litigation to modify custody arrangements must be prohibited for 2 years after the issuance of a custody decree in the absence of evidence of serious harm to the child. The ABA suggests that the court may appoint an attorney for the child, who has more prerogative than the guardian ad litem. The court may also order a custody investigation which may include professional consultation. The ABA further recommends that the courts take into consideration the following criteria to determine the best interest of the child: (1) the wishes of the child; (2) the interaction and interrelationship of the child with parents and siblings; (3) the child's adjustment to his or her home, school, and community; and (4) the mental and physical health of all involved persons. The ABA also recognizes that a child's psychological parent may not necessarily be the child's biological parent.[6]

From a psychological perspective, the author believes that the above approach is far superior to that of Goldstein et al. It is less detrimental to children's growth and development in a so-called broken home. It gives children a chance to carry a warm and positive image of their parents in their minds. By denying a parent any authority over his or her child, the court may claim to be upholding continuity, but the child, unable to take such abstractions to heart, will surely get the message that the parent was somehow so bad that the court prohibited visitation.

In assessing parents' suitability for custody, courts tend to impose the judge's personal moral values on the parents by guiding custody decisions on which parent best complies with their own system of values. For example, the Illinois Supreme Court decided that it would be immoral to give custody to a mother who was living with a man to whom she was not married. Sexual orientation of the parents has often been an issue in deciding custody cases, and homosexuality has usually been considered detrimental to the child's welfare. In *Irish v Irish*,[7] this issue so concerned the court that the court limited visitation because of it. A traditional bias against women may appear in custody disputes, contends Chesler, who authored a study showing that a double standard exists for fathers and mothers seeking custody.[8] Having an adulterous relationship or living with someone during separation was often viewed by the courts as more morally objectionable for women than for men, in whom the behavior seemed to be tolerated. This study suggests that a greater compliance with conventional morality is required of women seeking custody than of men seeking custody to be successful.

Judges apply another standard aside from morality in placing a child in custody disputes, and that is "tender age," meaning that a young child is generally better off placed with the mother.[9] This takes into account mother-infant bonding as a basis for healthy emotional development, and also the reality that women continue to be the primary caregivers in most families.

TERMINATION OF PARENTAL RIGHTS

The integrity of the child-parent bond has been given primacy by courts recurrently in cases involving the termination of parental rights. This tendency reflects the fundamental principle of governmental noninterference with personal and family matters except under the most dire or urgent circumstances. As such, children's rights are not seen to be in conflict with parental rights generally, since the interests of both parties are best served by keeping the bond intact, unless a child is in danger from neglect or abuse by his parents.

Termination proceedings are usually commenced by the state or a state agency in accordance with its parens patriae obligation, a doctrine giving the state the duty to protect those citizens who are unable to protect or care for themselves. When the state intervenes to remove a child from its home, the child's and the parents' legal rights diverge because while the state's parens patriae right is activated, the parents retain the constitutional right to raise the child as they see fit.

In such proceedings, the child's needs are given predominance. The question courts address when they rule on termination of parental rights and select the least detrimental alternative is whether the child's ongoing needs are being met by the parents. Factors such as parental substance abuse, emotional instability, or low IQ are relevant only insofar as they affect the parents' ability to provide the care their child requires. The guidelines for assessing the extent of such factors are (1) whether the parents' drug abuse, alcoholism, or retardation is severe enough to significantly undermine the ability "to be a parent"; (2) whether the parent emotionally endangers the child; (3) whether there is deprivation and neglect due to the erratic behavior of parents[10]; (4) whether the parents are unable to function as independent adults, and rely heavily on their families; and (5) whether environmental influences interfere to the degree that the child's normal functioning is adversely affected.[11]

The courts focus on whether such factors impair the parents' ability to provide adequate care. Degree of "parental quality" is immaterial; courts do not consider whether one parent is desirable compared with other parents. If a court terminates the parental right of a drug addict, that termination is based not on the fact of addiction but on the conclusion that the effects of addiction have rendered the parent incapable of meeting the child's needs. Or, a prostitute would retain parental rights unless the court saw sufficient evidence that such an environment adversely affected the child. Similarly, physical and mental disability are not grounds for termination of parental rights unless they impair one's parental capacity.[12] There is a clear correlation between this operative principle and the principle "innocent until proved guilty." Given the benefit of the doubt, parents are considered capable until proved otherwise.

When parents cannot properly care for their children, this failure is deemed neglect. Since neglect is the determining factor in termination decisions it does not matter if the neglect occurs innocently, without malice or intention to cause harm, as in the case of a parent's mental illness. Such a factor is given no more or less weight than would be given the conscious avoidance of parental responsibility. Only the result, the effect on the child, is judged.[13]

While state constitutions do permit a court to consider a parent's mental illness in making a determination of parental unfitness, the mental illness is only an issue for consideration, and not itself justification for termination. Parental rights cannot be terminated solely on the basis of the existence of mental illness. Statutes generally allow for termination only if the parents suffered from a condition that prevented them from providing sufficient parental care. Retardation or psychosis are not grounds for termination per se.

Failure to understand the special needs of a child is another important factor that courts consider in termination proceedings. For example, when a mother with a low IQ could not understand that her son needed to receive phenytoin (Dilantin) in order to prevent seizures, the court interceded and terminated her rights.[14]

To justify termination, a condition must not only interfere with parental functioning but must be unlikely to improve within a reasonable period of time. How these two criteria guide the progress and outcome of termination proceedings is demonstrated in the following cases. Although opposite conclusions were reached by two different state supreme courts, the courts used the criteria in interpreting the evidence and formulating decisions.

A mildly retarded mother with an IQ of 63 was hospitalized in a psychiatric hospital in Colorado when her baby was 8 months old. The father was discovered to have the borderline intelligence of a 71 IQ. Reports indicated that he had trouble coping with the baby. The mother was hospitalized in a psychiatric institution again when the baby was two years old. This time the father was also hospitalized, because of seizure disorder and psychosis. The state Supreme Court of Colorado noted that the treatment plans and all other modalities offered by the institution had not been successful. The parents were deemed unfit and the chronic and persistent nature of their mental illness was determined likely to continue beyond a reasonable time. The court assessed the detrimental effect of the parents' recurrent psychotic episodes on the child and found that the parents could not meet the ongoing needs of the child. Parental rights were terminated. When the parents contended that their rights were terminated because they were hospitalized for mental illness, the court explained that instead, the ruling was made after concluding that the child was traumatized by her parents' breakdowns.[15]

In the second example, the Supreme Court of South Dakota reversed the lower court decision and restored a mother's parental rights although the mother was diagnosed as alcoholic and schizophrenic. During her pregnancy she had been committed to a mental health program because of psychotic behavior. She was found to be dangerous to herself and others, and was so uncooperative and belligerent that she refused to attend the prenatal care program. In spite of the above, the court refused to terminate her parental rights because experts had testified that she was benefiting from antipsychotic medication and her condition was improving.[16] By logical extension, she may well be able to care for her child in a reasonable period of time, and must therefore be given the opportunity to do so.

These two cases show that the criteria most germane in judicial decisions of termination are (1) whether the child's needs are being adequately fulfilled, and (2) if not, whether the parental incapacity is temporary or long-term and ongoing. The first criterion exhibits the judiciary's reticence to impose rules for parental competence based on standardized parental behavior, and the second criterion reveals a deep reluctance to sever a parent-child relationship even when on its face the evidence might permit doing so.

The strength of the evidence required to substantiate charges of parental unfitness and remove a child from the parental home has been long debated. The lowest level, "preponderance of evidence," which stresses the quantitative and ignores the qualitative aspect of evidence, was rejected by the US Supreme Court as insufficient on which to base such a drastic measure as termination of parental rights. The highest level of evidence, "beyond a reasonable doubt," was considered too difficult to meet, in part because the fact-finders must evaluate medical and psychiatric data, which by its nature eludes absolute certainty. The middle level, "clear and convincing evidence," was found to satisfy the needs and protect the rights of all parties. "Clear and convincing" means evidence which is precise and explicit, and which will directly establish the point to which it is adduced.

The standard of proof issue was considered by the US Supreme Court in *Santosky v Kramer*.[17] In this case, the three children of John and Annie Santosky were removed from their home and the parental rights were terminated by a lower New York court based on a preponderance of evidence. The Santoskys challenged the standards of proof and eventually the case was heard by the Supreme Court. The Supreme Court justices were sharply divided, with the majority giving the parents broader rights, and the minority giving the children more substantial rights and the judgment of the state more credence.

In this case, the court focused on the rights of the natural parents in relation to the state, and found that until the state can actually prove unfitness, the child and the natural parents share a vital interest in preventing erroneous termination of the natural parents' relationship with their children. The interests of the child coincide with the interests of his parents in favoring procedures that reduce the chances of such error, and a stricter standard than preponderance would achieve that aim. The five-justice majority noted that the fundamental liberty interest of the natural parents in the care, custody, and management of their child does not disappear simply because they have not been model parents or have temporarily lost custody of their child to the state. Parents retain a vital interest in preventing the irretrievable destruction of their family life. When the state moves to destroy weakened family bonds, the Court continued, it must act against the parents with procedures that are fundamentally fair.

This decision of the Court to require a stricter standard of proof than preponderance was based on a prior ruling in *Mathews v Eldridge*,[18] which held that termination of parental rights should balance three factors: (1) private interests; (2) risk of error in the proceedings; and (3) countervailing governmental interests. The state has an interest in making an accurate decision in order to provide the child with a permanent home and protect the constitutional right of the parents. The highest court ruled, in conclusion, that a clear and convincing standard of proof must be met before a state may completely sever the rights of natural parents to their children.

On rare occasions, and under certain circumstances, a higher court might reverse a lower court decision and restore parental rights. If a parent proves that his or her mental condition has improved and experts testify to the fact that a formerly disabled person has become competent and able, the court will reconsider the case and may reverse previous decisions.[19] This has aroused controversy because it seems to flout the conventional and professional wisdom that children thrive best with consistency. Along those lines, Goldstein et al have urged that court termination decisions be permanent.[5] In rejecting their argument, courts do not deny the value of consistency and stability. Instead, they imply that if a choice must be made between consistency with no natural-parent relationship, and lack of consistency with a natural-parent relationship, the latter is preferable for both the child and the parent.

In all phases and aspects of termination proceedings, "the best interest of the child" remains the guiding principle. The idea behind termination of parental rights by a court coincides with the contention of Goldstein et al that if a child is being damaged by a lack of continuity in his or her parental home, that relationship may be subject to termination. However, if the level of adversity the child experiences is milder than actual damage, the court will sacrifice continuity to maintenance of the relationship between natural parent and child in the best interests of all parties.

Decisions by courts to terminate parental rights have implications for psychiatrists. The parents must be examined and investigated to determine whether they possess adequate judgment to understand what constitutes the well-being of a child. If they are found not to, the source of that failure must be sought. Is there a mental disorder? Substance abuse? Something else? After obtaining this information the psychiatrist makes recommendations to the court. The court will use this information to ascertain whether the problem interferes with the parents' ability to meet their child's needs. As noted earlier, however, a parent may be psychotic and still capable of taking care of her child, or may be sane but an unfit parent.

While consistency may seem to be swept aside in specific cases, a review of the macrocosm of parental-rights termination reveals a great uniformity of belief in the value of the bond between a child and his natural parents. There is irony in the fact that pervasive evidence of this profound belief in the parent-child relationship is found in the issues surrounding the termination of that special relationship.

BIOLOGICAL PARENTS VERSUS PSYCHOLOGICAL PARENTS

Disputes often arise between the natural parents and third parties such as relatives, foster, or adoptive parents, and other interested persons over who shall gain the custody of a child. When this occurs, the law in general presumes that the right of biological parents prevails. Courts generally award custody to the natural parents unless they find the parents grossly unfit, in which case it would be in the best interest of the child to be placed with a third party.

This issue has been explored in many cases. *Painter v Bannister*[20] illustrates that the court is willing to place a child with psychological parents to whom the child had maintained an affectionate relationship. In this case, the petitioner was a father who asked the court to return custody of his 7-year-old child from the child's 60-year-old maternal grandfather (the child's mother had been killed in an auto accident). The grandparents were stable, dependable, conventional middle-class people who had been providing a solid foundation and secure environment for the child. Although the father had remarried, he led a different life style, living in a poor business section of a California town. The court ruled that although there was a presumption of parental preference, the best interest of the child required that he be placed in a more stable situation with those having a secure life style rather than living in an undesirable place. The grandparents were awarded custody.

Conflicts can arise when a child is the product of an interracial marriage and the parents divorce. For example, is it in the best interest of a child to live with her white mother in a community that might show prejudice to blacks, or vice versa? If a community reacts with prejudice to a certain group of which the child is a member, does it constitute grounds to modify the custody or terminate parental rights? The US Supreme Court has struggled with this issue in *Palomare v Sidota*[21] and refused to accept a community standard as a reason to shift the custody from one parent to another.

The *Palomare* case received worldwide publicity and was the inspiration for dramatic movies. In *Palomare,* the state of Florida decided the fate of a child of a white woman who had divorced her white husband and married a black man. The Florida court decided that the child might become a subject of community prejudice and therefore the custody should be shifted from the mother to the father. Eventually this case reached the US Supreme Court for final ruling. The highest court struck down the Florida decision, with Chief Justice Burger concluding that there are private prejudices outside the reach of the law, but the law cannot directly or indirectly give in to them. In so stating, the Court acknowledged that difficulties, while being inevitable, should be neither run from nor acquiesced to. A crucial distinction was drawn between difficulty for a child and damage to a child.

VISITATION RIGHTS AND
CHILD SNATCHING

Visitation is defined as the right granted by a court to the parent or other relative who is deprived of the custody of a child to visit the child on a regular basis. Usually visitation is stressful for all involved parties: the custodial parent, the noncustodial parent, and the child. The parents often get into arguments during the visitation time regarding issues not directly related to the well-being of the child. Accusations fly and old conflicts surface. The noncustodial parent sometimes feels more isolated and cut off from his children during and after visitation, which can serve to remind him of what is missing as well as what is enduring in that abnormal parental relationship. The custodial parent, on the other hand, often experiences the visitation as an externally imposed disruption to the usual routines of the child and family, especially during holidays. The child will frequently feel anxious, worried, and torn, and may develop signs of regression manifested by clinging, provocativeness, aggressivity, and somatic complaints.[22]

There are as many reactions to visitation as there are families experiencing it. At best, it can be helpful and beneficial to the parents as a way of maintaining a meaningful relationship in spite of the divorce.[23] But it can also be painful, entailing serious negative consequences.[24] Mental health professionals must shoulder some of the burden of helping the family make visitation a fruitful and constructive time for all parties concerned. The clinical evaluation of a visitation problem, exploration of allegations, if any, clarification of complicated issues, handling regressive phenomena in the child, providing support for both parents, and explaining the goal and meaning of visitation to contested parties are a few of the mental health professional's tasks. Visitation requires ongoing cooperation, interaction, and planning, and thus emerges as a system difficult to maintain successfully. Interventions that emphasize and encourage parental planning, such as divorce mediation, may serve to alleviate some of the difficulty.[25]

Courts seldom terminate visitation rights. If there is a belief that visitation of the noncustodial parent may endanger the well-being of the child, the court might order visitation under supervision of certain authorities or under supervision of other family members. As defined by the law, removal of parental custody is an issue distinct from termination of visitation rights.

Battles for custody are battles for the one thing most cherished by each parent involved, and only one of them will win if joint custody is an impossibility. One parental party therefore will always leave the proceedings dissatisfied. This dissatisfaction is the root of multiple psychological and social problems with child snatching by the noncustodial parent as the most extreme. The act of child snatching is an indication of frustration and desperation in noncustodial parents. They are usually unaware of the psychological ramifications of their act, and do not foresee the personal and legal consequences of child snatching.

In order to prevent the removal of children by noncustodial parents to states with more favorable or lenient custody laws, Congress has passed a law, adopted by every state, prohibiting the modification of the original custody degree if the noncustodial parent takes the child to another state for a new hearing. This law[26] mandates that every state enforce and refuse to alter custody arrangements set forth earlier in other jurisdictions. In addition, some states have passed legislation making child snatching by a noncustodial parent or other family member a crime of either misdemeanor or felony severity. Even so, the emotional pull of parenthood lures many noncustodial parents into this desperate act.

HOMOSEXUALITY AND CHILD CUSTODY

About 1.5 million lesbian mothers are estimated to reside in the same household with their children. As opposed to the standards applied to mentally disturbed mothers, the law does not wait to discern whether a lesbian mother's sexual preference has a detrimental psychological effect on the children or prevents her from properly caring for them.[27] The justices feel that simply being a lesbian prevents a mother from being able to care for her children. According to the justices, the dangers of lesbians having custody include (1) an increased likelihood for the child to become homosexual; (2) a likelihood of social stigma or child peer rejection; (3) a likelihood for the homosexual mother to allow little time for ongoing mother-child interaction; and (4) the increased likelihood for child psychopathologic conditions.[28]

Two doctrines constitute the basis for the court's concern with the lesbian mother's family: psychoanalytic and social learning modeling in which a homosexual parent-child relationship would disrupt the oedipal process, resulting in aberrant gender identity and inappropriate sex-typed behavior. According to the social-learning theory, one's gender identity is based on significant same-sex models and differential reinforcement of appropriate sex role behaviors. The court believes that without a traditional sex role model within the home, the child will fail to develop appropriate sex role identity or behavior. The courts take it for granted that lesbians "hate men" and therefore will discourage any interaction between a child and a man.[29] That lesbians are no less desirous than heterosexual parents for their children to be happy and well-adjusted apparently has not occurred to the justices, whose opinions seem based on outmoded and defensive perceptions of homosexuals as neurotically obsessed with their sexual identity and automatically hostile to the opposite gender.

Investigators in the child development field disagree with the court's doctrine. They have noted that children spend a major portion of their time with peers in school, watch television, and have other interpersonal experiences with a wide range of adults. Therefore, the parental life style is not the most significant factor in determining a child's psychosexual development.[30] Indeed, a plethora of examples of heterosexual relationships worthy of emulation will be available to the child from the community, other family members, school, and entertainment media. Children of lesbians and single heterosexual mothers showed no significant differences in gender identity between the two groups. Lesbian parents have also been shown to be concerned and careful to provide male role models for their children. Important too is the fact that no difference in the occurrence of psychopathologic disorders between the two groups has been noted.[31]

The situation is somewhat different regarding homosexual fathers. A study of 18 homosexual fathers[32] indicated that these fathers must reconcile two identities: homosexuality at one extreme and social acceptance of fathers as custodial parents at the other extreme. As male homosexual relationships differ from lesbian relationships in longevity, with the male relationships being more transitory, children could be subject to stigma, particularly in male homosexual culture. As a loose rule, therefore, custody by a homosexual father is often inadvisable. Exceptions exist, however, and cases should be reviewed individually.

JOINT CUSTODY

After repeatedly witnessing the agony of custody battles, legal and mental health professionals began a search for a way to avoid it, and joint custody was devised. Today, more legislators and courts accept joint custody, and society perceives it as the least detrimental solution when it is a viable alternative. It is a new phenomenon sparking the interest of researchers. Benedeck and Benedeck have written extensively regarding the benefits and risks of joint custody.[33]

The benefits are many. Joint custody is likely to prevent the sense of loss by children whose parents divorce. The child receives adequate love, and exposure to the role models of both parents. The danger of divided loyalties and fantasies about the absent parent are reduced, and there is less chance that the child will "play" or "be played by" one parent against the other. Both parents participate meaningfully in the child's life and the winner-versus-loser aspect of custody disposition is eliminated.

There are also risks in joint custody. Joint custodial arrangements involve shuttling the child between different homes and life styles. The shared decision making process may expose the child to confusion and trauma, especially if the parents differ on how to raise the child. The tug of war over the child's affection can continue and parents can use this system to manipulate each other if they are too immature or resentful to be unable to share and compromise. Joint custody requires good faith on the part of the parents.

The emotional wreckage from custody disputes became so pervasive and distasteful that joint custody was acclaimed as an enlightened concept and treated with relief as a panacea when it was first developed. The increase in joint custody paralleled the rise of no-fault divorce, in which the parents want to end the marriage for reasons less catastrophic and dramatic than adultery, abuse, or desertion. Legislatures now favor joint custody and today more than half the states have laws providing for joint custody under certain circumstances. The majority of mental health professionals are in agreement that in joint custodies both parents must be committed to making it work by setting aside the differences that initially led them to the divorce.

In one study by Shiller[34] on families of boys aged 6 to 11 years in joint and maternal physical custody, a range of people were interviewed from 1 to 6 years following the paternal separation. According to the ratings made by parents and teachers, the boys in joint custody had fewer behavioral difficulties than their maternal custody counterparts. Joint custody parents also evidenced some strengths compared with parents with maternal custody, and Shiller concluded that joint custody is, at the least, a healthier arrangement than maternal custody for latency-age boys.[34]

For the parents who can separate their needs from their children's and retain fundamental respect for the former spouse's value as a parent, joint custody may indeed offer a feasible solution and avert the destructiveness of a custody dispute.

THE ROLE OF MENTAL HEALTH
PROFESSIONALS IN CUSTODY DISPUTES

Arguments have been made for and against the participation of psychiatrists and other qualified professionals in custody disputes. Those favoring participation believe that since the destruction of the family is surely the most stressful time of a child's life, help from able professionals is most appropriate in guiding the family and settling problems amenably. Psychiatrists can articulate the child's needs to the parents at a time when the parents may need to be reminded of them. They can, for instance, give guidance on how to exclude the child from their personal marital problems or how to avoid making their child feel guilty about the separation, to list two of the myriad ways a psychiatrist can reduce the pain of the separation process. Arguments have also gone against mental health professionals participating in custody disputes because psychiatrists and other clinicians have no way to infer the moral functioning of the persons involved if the court demands a report on the values and morality of the parties.[35]

Yet the involvement of psychiatrists and other qualified mental health workers in custody disputes is often unavoidable. If a therapist has already seen a contested child in a psychotherapeutic relationship, he or she should weigh carefully the advantage and possible risks of getting involved actively in a dispute by writing reports or testifying. The file of the therapist can always be subpoenaed by the court. According to Bernet[36] the therapist may choose to become involved indirectly by sharing information with the independent psychiatrist who is performing the custody evaluation rather than sending the report directly to the court. The therapist should also be alert to the possibility of a custody dispute when performing an evaluation on a new client whose parents have recently divorced. The best way to handle such a situation is for the therapist to clarify at the start that it usually is impractical for the same consultant to give treatment and recommendations to a court. If the therapist is invited by the court or other interested parties to make a recommendation, he or she may state that it is disadvantageous for the therapeutic process to take sides.[36]

It is also important for psychiatrists to be familiar with the privilege of communication if they have been subpoenaed by a court to testify in a child custody or child abuse case. This privilege specifies that the parents' right must yield to the best interest of the child. It does not matter who has requested the psychiatric evaluation—mother, father, or the court. This issue was clarified by the courts in *Nagle v Hook*.[37] Parents cannot claim privilege of communication or refrain from waiving such privileges in child custody hearings.

Another situation for psychiatrists and other qualified professionals to beware of is getting caught in between the disputing parties. This can engender a lawsuit against a therapist who has treated a child without the consent of the custodial parent. In *Dymek v Nyquist*,[38] a father brought suit against a psychiatrist who treated his son for 1 year by means of psychotherapy. The psychiatrist was aware that the mother did not have custody when he accepted her child as a patient for therapy. The lower court ruled that the psychiatrist had no authority to treat the child without the father's approval. Subsequently however, the appeals court held that the psychiatrist's conduct was not "so outrageous" and that the psychiatric treatment had done no damage to the child, and that therefore no malpractice claim could be brought against the psychiatrist.

Along similar lines, the court does not give absolute authority to the custodial parent to take the child for psychiatric treatment without some agreement or consent from the noncustodial parent, particularly if the psychiatrist prescribes "mind-altering medication." There are numerous cases (including one personally experienced by the author) where the noncustodial parent has gone to court and received a court order to terminate therapy, neuroleptic medication, or stimulants. Typically, the court first orders that all therapeutic procedures be halted. Then it appoints an independent psychiatrist to evaluate the situation and recommend to the court accordingly. Most likely the court will follow this recommendation rather than the wishes of either the custodial or noncustodial parent.

SURROGATE MOTHERS

The practice of an infertile woman's husband cohabiting with another woman so that she would conceive, bear, and then renounce her child to the husband and his wife, has been accepted and condemned, back and forth, since the beginning of Judeo-Christian culture: "And Sarah said unto Abraham, Behold now, the Lord hath restrained me from bearing; I pray thee, go in unto my maid; it may be that I may obtain children by her. And Abraham hearkened to the voice of Sarah." Abraham cohabited with the maid and Ishmael was born (Genesis 16:1–15). Those who view surrogacy as a modern evil or modern salvation each can find support for their positions in a long and tangled history. Yet after centuries of cultural evolution, all that is certain on the issue is that it is as perplexing and as unpredictable as it was in the first book of the Old Testament of the Bible.

The procedure has changed, and the troubling issue of cohabitation has been neutralized by scientific advance. Today a surrogate mother is impregnated by artificial insemination with the sperm of the father of the childless couple. This clinical method has not lessened the emotional response of those directly involved and society at large, however. The surrogate mother contracts with the couple to carry the child, and after delivery to relinquish the child, as well as all parental rights, to the biological father. Usually, the biological father is married to an infertile woman who hopes to adopt the child herself.[39] In research done on 125 women who applied to be surrogate mothers, Parker found that their mean age was 25 years (from a range of 18–38 years), 56% were married, 25% were divorced, and 24% had never been married. The motivations of these women were (1) desire and need for money; (2) the perceived degree of enjoyment and desire to be pregnant; (3) strong wishes to give the gift of a baby to a parent who needed a child; and (4) a need to master unresolved guilt stemming from a previous voluntary loss of fetus or baby through abortion or relinquishment.

The women who are willing to submit their bodies to surrogacy are found basically to be free of serious psychopathologic conditions. Tests such as the Minnesota Multiphasic Personality Inventory (MMPI) were administered to those women who applied for surrogate motherhood, and nine out of ten were found to have normal personality, and there was no evidence of psychosis or gross neurosis. In addition, individual profiles of the women showed high femininity and social extroversion scores.[40]

The right to procreate and bear a child is of fundamental magnitude as portrayed in a ruling by the US Supreme Court in *Carey v Population Services Int*[41] and even earlier in *Skinner v Oklahoma*.[42] But whether this right encompasses the surrogate mother arrangement and whether it is constitutionally protected remain to be determined. These issues, which are keeping the legal scholars busier than usual, were taken into consideration by the New Jersey Supreme Court in its final ruling on the much publicized *Baby M* case.[42,43]

The emotional courtroom and social battles for custody of babies born in surrogacy cast a sharp and disquieting light on the ethical and legal uncertainties surrounding the practice of surrogate motherhood. To some who have studied the surrogacy issue, the disturbing element lies in the overtone of class exploitation, harkening back to the Biblical prototypes with Abraham cohabiting with Hagar, Sarah's maid, offered by Sarah. The fact is that today, surrogate mothers tend to have less education and money than their clients. Religious leaders have bitterly opposed surrogate motherhood, claiming that it reduces a human baby to a commodity and makes the relationship between the mother and the biological father a form of adultery. Moreover, the long-term psychological effects of surrogate motherhood on everyone involved, particularly the offspring, are far from clear.

Few laws address the convoluted legal and ethical issues in surrogate motherhood. After the world-famous case of *Baby M,* however, states have begun to reexamine their adoption and artificial insemination laws in light of the growing public debate on surrogate motherhood. The recommendations so far run from prohibition of surrogate motherhood to denying the surrogate mother's right to change her mind and insisting that contracts must be enforced.

To review *Baby M*, surrogate mother Mary Beth Whitehead agreed to be inseminated with the sperm of William Stern. She was supposed to give the baby to Mr Stern and his wife when it was born, and they would then become the legal parents of the child. Whitehead changed her mind after her baby was born. Taking the baby, she fled from New Jersey to Florida. A lawsuit was filed and the Florida authorities returned the baby to the Sterns in New Jersey and a court action was instituted regarding the child's future custody and the rights of the biological mother and father. Evidence indicates that the Sterns were well qualified to be parents. The court found no serious physical or emotional problems with the Sterns except for Mrs Stern's mild multiple sclerosis, which certainly was no disability.

Whitehead's mental state complicated the philosophical issue tremendously, because she hardly painted the picture of the ideal mother which advocates of mothers' rights would have found most useful. Whitehead was known as an alcoholic with a history of alcohol-related traffic accidents. In addition, she seemed to have various emotional problems, mainly in the form of personality disorder, manipulative tendencies, and exhibitions of threatening behavior. For example, she told the Sterns that she would kill herself and the child if she could not keep the baby, and threatened to falsely accuse Stern of sexually molesting her 10-year-old daughter.

Several legal issues were before the court. First the court dismissed the allegation that Mary Beth Whitehead had not provided informed consent to the contractual arrangement. The court said informed consent should be applied in medical malpractice cases where the doctor and the patient are not on equal ground. Here, the parties were equal participants. Second, the court rejected the idea of joint custody. In the view of the court, the animosity between the parties made joint custody unrealistic and not in the best interest of the child. Third, the court decided to give minimal weight to any testimony regarding Whitehead's mental status, although experts had testified that she had personality and adjustment disorders with depression.

The court's decision was based on two findings: (1) there had been a contract between the parties, and (2) it was legally enforceable because its terms were consistent with the best interests of the child and New Jersey law. The court found that the Sterns would be better parents and awarded custody to them.

Interestingly, the one part of the contract deemed unconstitutional and unenforceable by this court was the clause prohibiting an abortion except as allowed by Mr Stern in case of a genetic abnormality discovered through amniocentesis. The court referred to the US Supreme Court case *Roe v Wade*[44] which stated that a woman has a constitutional right to decide what to do with her body, including abortion.[45]

In response to the concerns generated by the *Baby M* case and to the social and moral implications of contracts for surrogate motherhood, state legislatures have been preparing bills to regulate the practice of surrogacy. The bills vary from state to state, with some states banning the practice, and others allowing but regulating it. Some states, including Louisiana, have through their legislature declared that surrogacy contracts are unenforceable under state law. Although no penalties are imposed on the practice, surrogacy contracts are declared "null and void as contrary to public policy."[46]

Baby M continued to dominate the news media and attracted worldwide attention. The New Jersey court's ruling was the first time that a court held a surrogacy contract valid. That validity was soon to be tested in a higher court. Whitehead appealed her case to the New Jersey Supreme Court, declaring a surrogacy contract is against the law and cannot be enforced.

In a unanimous opinion, the New Jersey Supreme Court reversed and invalidated the surrogacy contract "because it conflicts with the law and public policy of this state." This court found that the payment of money to a surrogate mother was illegal, perhaps criminal, and potentially degrading to women. Although the New Jersey Supreme Court granted custody to the natural father it voided both the termination of the surrogate mother's parental rights and the adoption of the child by Stern's wife. The surrogate mother was thus restored to a position as the mother of the child. The fundamental concept of surrogacy remained intact, however. The court found no offense to present state laws if a woman voluntarily and without payment agrees to act as a surrogate mother provided that she is not subject to a binding agreement to surrender her child. The court noted that the money paid by Stern to Whitehead was to obtain an adoption, and not, as the Sterns argued, for the personal services of Mary Beth Whitehead. Payment for adoption is illegal and perhaps criminal. In this case, a termination of parental rights was obtained not through the proper course of providing the statutory prerequisites but by claiming the benefit of contractual provision.

The court took into serious consideration the role of money and noticed that this action is either the sale of a child or a mother's right to her child, the only mitigating factor being that one of the purchasers is the father. Almost every evil that prompted the prohibition of the payment of money in connection with adoption exists here. First, all parties concede that it is unlikely that surrogacy will survive without money, a fact supported by the research cited earlier showing that money was the primary reason the surrogate mother research subjects gave as a motive for their choice. Second, the use of money in conventional adoption does not produce the problem—conception occurs, and often the birth also, before illicit funds are offered. Third, in surrogacy, the highest bidders will presumedly become the adoptive parents regardless of suitability, so long as payment of money is permitted. Fourth, the mother's consent to surrender her child in adoptions is revocable, even after surrender of the child, unless it be to an approved agency.

The right to procreate very simply is the right to have natural children, whether through sexual intercourse or artificial insemination. It is no more than that. Mr Stern has not been deprived of that right. Through the artificial insemination of Mary Beth Whitehead, Baby M is his child. The custody, care, companionship, and nurturing that follow birth are not contained in the right to procreation; they are different rights which may also be constitutionally protected, but they are entirely separate issues from procreation.

On de novo trial, Mary Beth Whitehead, now known as Whitehead Gould, pregnant and with a new husband, was granted broad rights to see the daughter she bore to Stern 2 years earlier under the surrogacy contract. The superior court, presided over by a different judge, ordered that Mrs Whitehead Gould, effective immediately, will be allowed to have the girl Melissa at her home one day a week for up to six hours, and after 6 months the child can visit a second day every 2 weeks. A year after that, when Melissa is 3, the two-day visits can include an overnight stay. Eventually, the girl will be able to spend 2 weeks with her mother. With this ruling, the court has determined that Melissa's best interests would be served by unsupervised, uninterrupted liberal visitation with her mother. Further, the court found that no credible evidence or expert opinion showed that the girl would suffer psychological or emotional harm by continued and expanded visitation with her natural mother, who once had been merely a surrogate. In the view of the court, it no longer matters how Melissa was conceived. She and her mother have the right to develop their own special relationship. The court has urged Mrs Whitehead Gould to stop calling the child Sara and barred both sides from publicly discussing their relationship with Melissa or her personal activities and other private issues without prior approval from the court.

Although the New Jersey Supreme Court granted custody to the father, that decision was clearly based on "the best interests of the child," and not because of surrogacy arrangements or ideology. This court decision is not binding in other states, but it will influence decisions on surrogate motherhood in the states' courts and legislatures. This unanimous decision may be used as a guideline for future cases. Although 99% of surrogacy arrangements are carried out without conflict between the biological mother and the biological father, infertile couples might ponder more deeply the reasoning sustaining the New Jersey Supreme Court's ruling.

One can only wonder how the children born of surrogacy will view the circumstances of their birth 20 years or so hence, both those of amicable surrogacy arrangements and those of contentious ones. How will they view the money factor? How will they feel about their three parents?

REFERENCES

1. Montesquieu: Baron de La Brède: *The Spirit of the Laws*. New York, Hafner Press, 1949.

283

2. Locke J: *Two Treatises of Government.* New York, Cambridge University Press, 1960.
3. Derdeyn A: Child custody contests in historical perspective. *Am J Psychiatry* 1976;133:1369–1376.
4. *Finlay v Finlay* 1925; 148 NE 624 (NY).
5. Goldstein J, Freud A, Solnit AJ: *Beyond the Best Interest of the Child.* New York, Free Press, 1979.
6. Uniform marriage and Divorce Act 402, 9A UCA (1979).
7. *Irish v Irish* 1982; 102 Mich Ct App 75.
8. Chesler P: *Mothers on Trial: The Battle for Children and Custody.* New York, McGraw-Hill, 1986.
9. Weiner B: An overview of child custody laws. *Hosp Community Psychiatry* 1985;36:838–843.
10. *In re Welfare of M.M.D.* 1987; 410 NW2d 72 (Minn Ct App).
11. *E.L.B. v Texas Dept of Human Services* 1987; 732 SW2d 785 (Tex Ct App).
12. *In re Adoption of J.J.* 1986; 515 A2d 883 (Pa Sup Ct).
13. *In re J.S.* 1986; 397 NW2d 621 (Neb Sup Ct).
14. *In re Welfare of B.L.W.* 1986; 395 NW2d 426 (Minn Ct App).
15. *In re C.B.* 1987; 740 P2d 11 (Colo Sup Ct).
16. *In re J.Z.* 1987; 410 NW2d 572 (SD Sup Ct).
17. *Santosky v Kramer* 1982; 50 USLW 4333.
18. *Mathews v Eldridge* 1976; 424 US 319.
19. *In re Adoption of Ellingsen* 1985; 501 A2d 1123 (Pa Sup Ct).
20. *Painter v Bannister* 1966; 258 Iowa Sup Ct 1390.
21. *Palomare v Sidot* 1984; US Sup Ct No. 82-1734.
22. Barnum R: Understanding controversies in visitation. *J Am Acad Child Adolesc Psychiatry* 1987;26:788–792.
23. Blumenthal K, Weinberg A: Issues concerning parental visiting of children in foster care, *Foster Children in the Courts.* Boston, M Hardin, 1973.
24. Gean M, et al: Infants and toddlers in supervised custody. *J Am Acad Child Psychiatry* 1985;24:608–612.
25. Ash P, Guyer MJ: Relitigation after contested custody and visitation evaluations. *Bull Am Acad Psychiatry Law* 1986;14:323–330.
26. Public Law 96-611 (1980).
27. Kleber DJ: The impact of parental homosexuality in child custody cases: in view of the literature. *Bull Am Acad Psychiatry Law* 1986;14:81-87.
28. Lewin E: Lesbianism and motherhood: Implication for child custody. *Hum Organization* 1981;40:6-14.
29. Golombok S, et al: Children in lesbian and single parent households: a psychosexual and psychiatric appraisal. *J Child Psychol Psychiatry* 1983;24:551–572.
30. Green R: Sexual identity of 37 children raised by homosexual or transsexual parents. *Am J Psychiatry* 1938;135:692–697.
31. Kirkpatrick M, et al: Lesbian mothers and their children: a comparative survey. *Am J Orthopsychiatry* 1981;51:545–551.
32. Bozett FW: Gay father: evaluation of gay father identity. *Am J Orthopsychiatry* 1981;51:552–559.
33. Benedeck E, Benedeck R: Joint custody: solution of illusion? *Am J Psychiatry* 1979;136:1940–1944.
34. Shiller V: Joint versus maternal custody for families with latency age boys: parents' characteristics and child adjustment. *Am J Orthopsychiatry* 1986;56:486–489.
35. American Psychiatric Association: *Child Custody Consultation: A Report of the*

284

Task Force on Clinical Assessment in Child Custody. Washington DC, American Psychiatric Press, 1982.

36. Bernet W: The therapist's role in child custody disputes. *J Am Acad Child Psychiatry* 1983;22:180–183.

37. *Nagle v Hook* 1983; 460 A2d (Md Ct App).

38. *Dymek v Nyquist* 1984; 469 NE2d 659.

39. Parker PJ: Motivation of surrogate mothers: initial findings. *Am J Psychiatry* 1983;40:117–118.

40. Frank DD: Psychiatric evaluation of women in a surrogate mother program. *Am J Psychiatry* 1981;138:1378–1379.

41. *Carey v Population Services Int* 1977; 431 US 678.

42. *Skinner v Oklahoma* 1942; 316 US 535.

43. *In the Matter of Baby M* 1988; (A-39-37) NJ Sup Ct (Feb 3, 1988).

44. *Roe v Wade* 1973; 410 US 113.

45. *Ment Phys Disability Law Reporter* 1987; 11:176–177.

46. *New York Times,* Dec 13, 1987.

Glossary

Actus reus. (L) A wrongful deed which renders the actor criminally liable. The actus reus must be related to mens rea, a guilty mind, in order to constitute a crime.

Ad absurdum. (L) To the point of absurdity.

Ad hoc. (L) For this particular purpose.

Ad litem. (L) For the purposes of the suit being prosecuted.

Affect. The outward manifestation of a person's feelings, tone, or mood.

Aggravated assault. An assault where serious bodily injury is inflicted on the person assaulted.

Akinesia. A state of motor inhibition. A reduction of voluntary movement.

Amicus brief. A brief submitted by an amicus curiae.

Amicus curiae. (L) A person with strong interest in or views on the subject matter of an action may petition the court for permission to file a brief on behalf of a party, and suggest a rationale consistent with his own views.

Apnea. Temporary cessation of breathing.

Asbestos. A fibrous, incombustible, magnesium and calcium silicate used as thermal insulation. Its dust is believed to cause asbestosis and lung cancer.

Aseptic necrosis. Pathologic death of a portion of tissue occurring in the absence of infection.

Assault. An attempt or threat with unlawful force.

Battery. An unlawful touching, beating, or physical violence done to another without consent.

Bona fide. (L) In good faith; without fraud or deceit.

Bradycardia. Abnormal slowness of the heart rate and pulse.

Brief. A document prepared by counsel as a statement of the case, defining the issues, citing authorities, and presenting arguments.

Certiorari. (L) To review questions of law or procedure in the interest of justice by a higher court.

Clear and convincing. 1. A standard of proof. A quantum of evidence heavier than preponderance, but lighter than beyond a reasonable doubt. 2. Evidence which is positive, precise, and explicit, which tends directly to establish the point to which it is adduced and is sufficient to make out a prima facie case.

Compelling state interest. Term used to uphold state action in the face of attack grounded on equal protection or First Amendment rights because of serious need for such state action.

Compulsory process. 1. The right of a defendant to have the resources of the courts. For example, the right to subpoena to compel the appearance of witnesses before the court. 2. The Sixth Amendment provides that the accused shall have the right to have compulsory process for obtaining witnesses in his favor.

Conservator. One who is appointed by a court to manage the estate of a protected person.

Continuance. Postponement of an action or a session, hearing, trial, or other proceeding to a subsequent day or time.

Countertransference. The therapist's unconscious emotional feeling toward the patient, which originates in the therapist's early life experiences.

Delusion. A false belief firmly held despite incontrovertible and obvious proof or evidence to the contrary. The belief is not one ordinarily accepted by other members of the person's culture or subculture.

Denial. (a defense mechanism) Refusal to admit the reality of the truth.

De novo. (L) Once again. A second time. A de novo hearing means a new hearing.

Double jeopardy. The Fifth Amendment prohibits a second prosecution after a first trial for the same offense.

Due process of law. This phrase was made applicable to the states with the adoption of the Fourteenth Amendment which states that "nor shall any State deprive any person of life, liberty, or property, without due process of law." The phrase does not have a fixed meaning but expands with jurisprudential attitudes of fundamental fairness. The essential elements of due process of law are notice and opportunity to be heard and to defend in an orderly proceeding adapted to the nature of the case, and the guarantee of due process requires that every man have the protection of his day in court and the benefit of the general law.

Dysmorphic syndrome. A condition that creates different morphologic forms in cells and tissues.

En banc. (Fr) By the full court. Many appellate courts sit in parts or divisions of three or more judges from among a larger number constituting the full court. Sometimes, either on the court's motion or at the request of one of the litigants, the court will consider the matter by the full court rather than by only a part.

Et al. (L) Abbreviation of *et alii,* meaning "and others."

Ex parte. (L) Referring to an application made by one party to a proceeding in the absence of the other. Ex parte injunction is one having been granted without the adverse party having had notice of its application.

Ex rel. (L) The abbreviated form of *ex relatione,* which means by or on the relation or report (of).

Fait accompli. (Fr) A thing accomplished and presumedly irreversible.

Felony. A serious crime. A crime for which a person can be sentenced to death or long-term imprisonment.

Fixation (fixating). The arrest of psychological development in an individual.

Good faith. The concept has no statutory definition. It encompasses an honest belief, the absence of malice, and the absence of intent to defraud or to seek an unconscionable advantage.

Guardian. An officer or agent of the court who is appointed to protect the interests of minors or incompetent persons and to provide for their care, welfare, education, maintenance, and support.

Guardian ad litem. A person appointed by the court to protect the interests of a minor or legally incompetent person in a lawsuit.

Habeas corpus. (L) This term is used to bring the petitioner before the court to inquire into the legality of his confinement. The primary function of a habeas corpus writ is to release from unlawful imprisonment.

Hallucination. A sensory perception in the absence of an actual external stimulus.

Hearsay rule. A statement made out of the courtroom, without benefit of cross-examination, and without the witness's demeanor being subject to assessment by the triers of fact.

Heightened scrutiny. A higher standard of scrutiny; known also as strict scrutiny. A test to determine the constitutional validity of a statute that creates a classification of persons based on nationality, race, and other fundamental issues, and which affects the fundamental rights of persons.

Hindbrain. Called also rhombencephalon. The part of the brain developed from the posterior of the three primary brain vesicles of the embryonic neural tube.

Immunodeficiency. A condition resulting from a defective immunologic mechanism.

In camera. (L) In chambers. Refers to proceedings held in a judge's chambers or without the public present.

In forma pauperis. (L) Permission given to an indigent person to proceed without liability for the court's costs.

In loco parentis. (L) In the place of a parent; instead of a parent.

In re. (L) In the matter of.

Inter alia. (L) Among other things.

Laminectomy. Excision of a vertebral lamina.

Lymphoid. Resembling lymph or lymphatic tissue.

Malice aforethought. A predetermination to commit an act without legal justification or excuse. An intent, at the time of a killing, willfully to take the life of a human being, or an intent willfully to act in a callous and wanton disregard of the consequences to human life. Malice aforethought does not necessarily imply any ill will, spite, or hatred toward the individual killed.

Manic-depressive illness. Also known as bipolar disorder, a major affective disorder in which there are episodes of both mania and depression. *Manic*: characterized by excitement, euphoria, expansive, or irritable mood, hyperactivity, pressured speech, flight of ideas, decreased need for sleep, distractibility, and impaired judgment. *Depressive*: Characterized by lowered mood, slowed thinking, decreased movement or agitation, loss of interest, guilt, lowered self-esteem, sleep disturbance, and decreased appetite.

Manslaughter. Unlawful killing of another person without malice aforethought.

Material (materiality). Important, relevant evidence that can prove or disprove any ultimate issue.

Material evidence. That quality of evidence which tends to influence the trier of fact because of its logical connection with the issue.

Mens rea. A guilty mind; the mental state accompanying a forbidden act. For an act to constitute a criminal offense, the act must be illegal and accompanied by a requisite mental state (intent). Criminal offense is defined with reference to one of four recognized criminal states of mind that accompanies the actor's conduct: (1) intentionally, (2) knowingly, (3) recklessly, and (4) grossly (criminally) negligent. The mens rea may be *general* (a general intent to do the prohibited act) or *specific* (meaning that a special mental element is required for a particular offense), such as assault with intent to rape. In criminal prosecution, the state must prove beyond a reasonable doubt that the required mental state coexisted with the doing of the proscribed act. A defense of insanity may either nullify or mitigate the existence of a specific mens rea.

MMPI. Minnesota Multiphasic Personality Inventory: a psychological test which assesses personality structure and psychiatric diagnosis.

Miranda warning. The requirement that a person receive certain warnings relating to his privilege against self-incrimination (right to remain silent) and his right to the presence and advice of an attorney before any custodial interrogation by law enforcement authorities takes place.

Misdemeanor. An offense that is not a felony and that is punishable by a fine or a jail sentence of short duration.

Moot (case). A case is moot when a determination is sought on a matter which when rendered cannot have any practical effect on the existing controversy.

Murder. Unlawful killing of another human being with malice aforethought. This requires a premeditated intent to kill plus an element of hatred. *First-degree murder:* unlawful killing that is willful, deliberate, and premeditated. *Second-degree murder:* unlawful killing of another with malice aforethought but without deliberation and premeditation.

Myelogram. X-ray of the spinal cord.

Neuroleptic. Antipsychotic drug.

Neurosis. Emotional disturbances of all kinds other than psychosis. It implies subjective psychologic pain or discomfort beyond what is appropriate in the condition of one's life.

Non compos mentis. (L) This is a general term, embracing all varieties of mental derangement.

Oedipal process. Refers to the Oedipus complex. In psychoanalytic theory the child between the ages of 3 to 5 years develops attachment to the opposite sex accompanied by envious and aggressive feelings toward the parent of the same sex. These feelings eventually become repressed because of the fear of displeasure or punishment by the parent of the same sex.

Outrage. Abuse. Any species of serious wrong offered to the person, feelings, or rights of another.

Palsy. Paralysis or partial paralysis.

Paranoia. A psychological condition characterized by the gradual development of an intricate, complex, and elaborate system of thinking based on misinterpretation of an actual event. A person with paranoia often considers himself endowed with unique and superior ability.

Parens patriae. (L) The duty of the sovereign state to protect both the public interest and those with disabilities. It has been called into play when such persons could be a danger to themselves and to the public if not held under protective custody of the sovereign.

Per curiam (opinion). (L) An opinion by the court which expresses its decision in the case. This phrase is used to distinguish an opinion of the whole court from an opinion written by any one judge.

Police power. The limited constitutional power of the state to promote order, safety, health, morals, and the general welfare of its citizens. This authority is conferred in the Tenth Amendment on the individual states and is in turn delegated to local governments.

Preponderance of evidence. A standard of proof. The evidence presented to triers of fact appears more convincing than the opposing evidence. That is, evidence which as a whole shows that the fact sought to be proved is more probable than not.

Prima facie. (L) At first view. A fact presumed to be true unless disproved by some evidence to the contrary.

Prima facie case. A cased based on evidence which, if not explained or contradicted, is sufficient to determine an outcome adverse to the defendant.

Projection. (a defense mechanism) The process of thrusting on another the idea or impulses that belong to oneself.

Pro se. (L) Where one appears in a legal action on one's own behalf without the aid of counsel.

Psychosis. A major mental disorder of organic or emotional origin in which a person's ability to think, respond emotionally, remember, communicate, interpret reality, and behave appropriately is sufficiently impaired so as to interfere grossly with the capacity to meet the ordinary demands of life.

Quasi-criminal. Refers to noncriminal proceedings which nevertheless contain the possibility that sanctions be imposed on an individual or that the stigma that it might create is enough to warrant special safeguards for the procedure.

Rational basis test. The principle that the constitutionality of a statute will be upheld if any rational basis can be conceived to support it. The test is used when a general constitutional objection is raised to a law's reasonableness. This test does not apply if the statute or decision is unconstitutional.

Rationalization. (a defense mechanism) Justification of or making a thing appear reasonable, when otherwise its irrationality would be evident.

Reasonable doubt. 1. The proof must be so conclusive and complete that all reasonable doubts of the fact are removed from the mind of the ordinary person. 2. Reasonable doubt is such a doubt as would cause prudent men to hesitate before acting in matters of importance to themselves.

Respondeat superior. The superior reply. This doctrine stands for the proposition that when an employee is in fault, the employer and supervisor are held responsible.

Schizophrenia. A large group of disorders, usually of psychotic proportion, manifested by characteristic disturbances of language and communication, thought, perception, affect, and behavior which last longer than 6 months. Thought disturbances are marked by alterations of concept formation that may lead to a misinterpretation of reality, misperceptions, and sometimes, delusions and hallucinations. Mood changes include ambivalence, blunting, inappropriateness, and loss of empathy with others. Behavior may be withdrawn, regressive, and bizarre.

Severance. 1. The process by which the particular charge on which the defendant is currently to stand trial is chosen. 2. Separate trials of two or more defendants named in the same indictment who would normally be tried together.

Sinus tachycardia. Abnormally rapid heart rate.

Status epilepticus. Continuous epileptic seizures.

Stay. A judicial order whereby some action is forbidden or held in abeyance until some event occurs or the court lifts its order.

Stay of execution. Process whereby a judgment is precluded from being executed for a specific period of time.

Strict liability. In tort law, liability without fault or showing of negligence.

Sua sponte. (L) Through the court's own volition (on its own motion) without such a motion being made by either of the adverse parties.

Synaptic. Pertaining to or affecting a synapse.

Synapse. The site of functional apposition between neurons, at which an impulse is transmitted from one neuron to another by either electric or chemical means.

T cell. Lymphocyte cell, originated from thymus gland. Immunologically, this cell is very important.

Tardive dyskinesia. A variable complex of abnormal movements such as tongue writhing or protrusion, chewing, lip puckering, finger movements, toe and ankle movements, leg jiggling or movements of neck, trunk, and pelvis. These movements are involuntary, and may occur singly or in combination.

Testator (testatrix). One who makes and executes a testament or will. Testator applies to males and testatrix to females.

Transference. The unconscious assignment to others of feelings and attitudes that were originally associated with important figures (such as parents) in one's early life. The therapist utilizes this phenomenon as a therapeutic tool to help the patient understand emotional problems and their origins.

Unconscious. 1. That part of the mind or mental functioning of which the content is only rarely subject to awareness (*Psych*) 2. Not responding to sensory stimulation (*Med*)

Vacate. To render void. To annul.

Variable. Any characteristic in an experiment which may assume different values.

Void. Having no legal force. Unenforceable.

Ward. A person whom the law regards as incapable of managing his or her own affairs.

Writ. A written order issued by the court, requiring the performance of a specified act or giving authority to have it done.

Writ of error. A writ issued by a superior court to a lower court to obtain a trial record for the purpose of reviewing the judgment and examining the record with regard to alleged errors in law.

GENERAL REFERENCES

American Psychiatric Association: *Diagnostic and Statistical Manual of Mental Disorders,* ed 3 revised. Washington, DC, American Psychiatric Press, 1987 [DSM-III-R].

292

American Psychiatric Association: *Psychiatric Glossary*. Washington, DC, American Psychiatric Press, 1984.

Ballentine JA: *Ballentine Law Dictionary*, ed 3. Rochester, NY, Lawyers' Cooperative Publishing Co, 1969.

Black's Law Dictionary, ed 5. St Paul, Minn, West Publishing Co, 1979.

Dorland's Illustrated Medical Dictionary, ed 27. Philadelphia, WB Saunders, 1987.

Gifis SH: *Law Dictionary*. New York, Barron's Educational Series, 1984.

Hinse LE, Campbell RJ: *Psychiatric Dictionary*, ed 4. New York, Oxford University Press, 1970.

Kaplan HI, and Sadock BJ: *Comprehensive Textbook of Psychiatry IV*. Baltimore, Williams & Wilkins, 1985.

Stedman's Medical Dictionary (Illustrated), ed 4. Baltimore, Williams & Wilkins, 1982.

Webster's Third New International Dictionary. Springfield, Mass, Merriam-Webster, 1981.

INDEX